CURATIVE VIOLENCE

CURATIVE VIOLENCE

Rehabilitating Disability, Gender,

and Sexuality in Modern Korea

EUNJUNG KIM

DUKE UNIVERSITY PRESS

Durham and London

2017

Library of Congress Cataloging-in-Publication Data
Names: Kim, Eunjung, [date] author.
Title: Curative violence : rehabilitating disability, gender,
and sexuality in modern Korea / Eunjung Kim.
Description: Durham : Duke University Press, 2016. |
Includes bibliographical references and index.
Identifiers: LCCN 2016026987 (print)
LCCN 2016028135 (ebook)
ISBN 9780822362777 (hardcover : alk. paper)
ISBN 9780822362883 (pbk. : alk. paper)
ISBN 9780822373513 (e-book)
Subjects: LCSH: People with disabilities—Care—Korea
(South) | People with disabilities—Rehabilitation—Korea
(South) | Sociology of disability—Korea (South) | People
with disabilities in mass media.
Classification: LCC HV1559.K8 K54 2016 (print) |
LCC HV1559.K8 (ebook) | DDC 362.4095195—dc23
LC record available at https://lccn.loc.gov/2016026987

Cover art: Jiwon, *Daily Happenings* (details), 2005.
Acrylic on canvas. Courtesy of the artist.

ACKNOWLEDGMENTS

As I was finishing this book, I read in the newspaper about a young man with Tourette's syndrome who died of sepsis in Seoul. His body was found bruised, wounded, and emaciated, showing signs of repeated abuse and violence. His martial arts coach, to whom he had been entrusted by his family, had been keeping him in his custody and denied the family access, because he believed that the young man's disability could be cured by disciplining his body and mind. This belief led to constant corporal punishment and deadly abuse. I continue to come across accounts of people with disabilities being murdered by those who claimed that they could cure the disabilities. As I see it, these murders are not just individual crimes but instead reveal the persistent attempts to reject the presence of people with disabilities. This direct manifestation of violence in the name of cure indicates that today there remains much work to be done by scholars, activists, families, and people living with and without disabilities. It is my hope that this book serves as a modest offering to that collective endeavor to name, interrogate, and eliminate such violence.

I am deeply indebted to many disability activists in South Korea. Their calls for change and their everyday work of surviving have grounded my thinking and writing process. I am also indebted to those who spent hours and hours reading my drafts, listening to me, and sharing their thoughts, helping to make my writing clearer and my thinking deeper. I am still amazed by their generosity and commitment to scholarship. All those I list and those I cannot name here made me believe in what academic work could do in shaping and shifting ideas and affecting changes. These acknowledgments are not going to adequately express my gratitude and describe the time and energy offered to me by many people along the way.

During the early stage of research for this book, David Mitchell guided me with his great insights, humor, and support, and he helped me pursue my research in the humanities. I fondly remember the quotes from *Buffy the Vampire Slayer* that he sent to inspire my writing. His deep transdisciplinary understanding of disability and race has guided me. He saw my linguistic difference and my having to write in a second language not as a limitation but as an opportunity to write differently. He made me think about English as a tool for communicating my ideas to a broader audience rather than as an oppressive norm to which I have to conform. I thank him especially for teaching me this. I am grateful to Kyeong-Hee Choi for her passion for rigorous scholarship in Korean studies. When I first met her at a library café in Hyde Park more than a decade ago, she spent more than three hours listening to me and talking with me about disability within Korean literature. Her engagement with my work and her kindness always make me feel that she is not only a wonderful teacher and scholar, but also a cotraveler on our journeys in the academic worlds in South Korea and in the United States. Sally Chivers has always offered her brilliant insights and friendship. She taught me the joy of analyzing film and writing about it. Her own engagement with South Korean films on the topic of aging exemplifies a much-needed transnational approach in the field of disability film studies. Katrin Schultheiss helped me think beyond disciplinary boundaries and provided insightful feedback and encouragement. Sharon Snyder's generosity and enthusiasm helped me see the potential in this project. I benefited from her wide-ranging expertise in film, feminist theories, and humanities scholarship. They all offered their generous feedback and provided encouragement when I needed it the most.

Several institutions provided financial support for this research: Syracuse University; the Graduate School at the University of Wisconsin, Madison, with funding from the Wisconsin Alumni Research Foundation and Institute for the Research in the Humanities; Emory University School of Law; the University of Michigan, Ann Arbor; and the Association of American University Women, which gave me an International Fellowship on doctoral research. My days in Ann Arbor at the University of Michigan as a Future of Minority Studies postdoctoral fellow were enriched by the extraordinary mentorship of Tobin Siebers and by conversations with scholars and students in the Global Ethnic Literature Seminar and Identity Matters workshop. I was also fortunate enough to spend two years at Emory University, which afforded me invaluable opportunities to converse with prominent scholars, including Martha Fineman, Rosemarie Garland-Thomson, Sander Gilman, and Benjamin Reiss, who generously offered their mentoring.

I'd like to thank Jade Brooks and the editorial team at Duke University Press for seeing the potential of this project and moving the review and publishing process along smoothly. External reviewers were incredibly helpful and generous in offering encouraging assessments of the manuscript and providing suggestions for revisions. I am deeply indebted to Alice Falk for her painstakingly thorough copyediting and editorial assistance. I couldn't have imagined writing a book without her command in prose and patience to go through my writing multiple times. She not only helped me express my thoughts better but also gently taught me how to write in English more efficiently and clearly. Sarah Groeneveld read the earlier version of the manuscript and offered not just her insights but assistance in improving my prose. Two extremely dedicated research assistants, Eunhee Park and Meesun Kim, helped with finding documents and organizing many materials to finalize references in the late stage of the manuscript's completion. I am also deeply grateful to Jee-Young Park at the Joseph Regenstein Library of the University of Chicago for offering her expertise in transliterating Korean letters according to the McCune-Reischauer romanization system. It was humbling to learn from her and to benefit from her commitment to publications in Korean studies.

Over the years, I benefited tremendously from engaging with the audience at the University of Wisconsin Center for Research on Gender and Women colloquium; annual conferences of the Society of Disability Studies; the University of Michigan Initiative on Disability Studies; the Korean Studies Lecture Series at the University of California, San Diego; the Ewha International Special Education Research Institute; the Envisioning Global Korea from the Margin Symposium at Wellesley College; the University of Wisconsin Institute for the Research in the Humanities; the University of Wisconsin Center for the Humanities; the Department of Gender and Women's Studies at the University of Wisconsin, Madison; the Korea Workshop at the University of Illinois Urbana and Champaign; the East Asia Program Korean Studies Workshop at Cornell University; and seminars at Changae Yŏsŏng Konggam in Seoul. I thank Sheyfali Saujani, who organized the panel for the Berkshire Conference on the History of Women. I'd like to thank Eunshil Kim for supporting my interest in feminist disability studies and bringing many prominent Korean studies scholars and students together to maximize the engagement of our works with one another, a process that helped me think more broadly about South Korean society. I thank Seunghee Park who introduced me to critical approaches to disability and who continues to support my work and career. Her passion, teaching, and scholarship have shown me a model. And I express my deep gratitude to Tobin Siebers, who was my mentor, teacher, and dear friend. His enthusiastic support of my writing, our conversations over our weekly lunches in Ann Arbor, and our video chats kept me focused on my own research and the important issues and topics in the field during an unsettling time. I will hold those memories dear. I'd like to thank Jill Siebers for her warm friendship and kindness over the years. Jane Collins read the drafts of each chapter and sent her incredibly helpful and generative feedback, sometimes within only a few hours. Without her timely comments and encouragement, I wouldn't have been able to finish this book. I am deeply grateful for her dedication, clarity, mentoring, and friendship. Charles Kim kindly offered his expertise and insights as a historian of Korea. I could always rely on Michele Friedner to provide an honest and sharp voice that motivated me to elaborate and clarify what messages I wanted to communicate. Nicole Markotić, Alison Kafer, Michelle Jarman, Mike Gill, Kateřina Kolářová, Eli Clare, and Kang Jin Kyung read my chapters and responded to my writing with their wise, kind, and helpful feedback. Their questions and responses kept me going. I am also grateful for their writings, scholarship, and friendship that continue to inspire my own thinking and writing. Ellen Samuels and Jenell Johnson offered their incredibly brilliant feedback and provided friendship and almost daily support that sustained me in Madison.

I have also benefited from the rich intellectual community at the University of Wisconsin, Madison. I thank Julie D'Acci, Finn Enke, Bernadette Baker, Susan Stanford Friedman, Leslie Bow, Nicole Huang, Stephen Kantrowitz, Steve Stern, Freida High, Janet Hyde, and Sara Guyer for providing support and encouragement. Students at the University of Wisconsin shared their enthusiasm and ideas with me about many topics that are discussed in this book. The fantastic community of fellows who enthusiastically engaged with my work at the Institute for the Research in the Humanities energized my writing. I thank Ayelet Ben-Yishai and Benedict Robinson for providing important feedback. I had the great fortune of being aided by the First Book program of the Center for the Humanities. In the workshop, six extraordinarily accomplished scholars from various fields read and discussed my manuscript for hours. I thank Jill Casid, Leslie Bow, Julie D'Acci, A. Finn Enke, Mel Chen, and Jin-Kyung Lee for granting their time and for helping me to rethink my book's focus in the workshop and beyond. They understood the difficulties of writing for an audience in multiple fields of study and helped me focus on crafting my own interdisciplinary space rather than being constrained by the conventional expectations of each field.

I want to thank those who provided me with helpful and productive information that I included in this book: Vicki Lewis, Stanlie Topple, Byung-sim Bae, Jung Keun-sik, Molly Cook, 홍성희, 배복주, 박김영희, 황지성, and the video-store owner in Myŏngdong, as well as many others working in libraries and in the Korean National Film Archive. I thank Park Young-Sook and others who granted permission to reproduce images in this book.

A wider community of scholars and their scholarship carried me forward, including Susan Wendell, Alison Kafer, Mel Chen, Julie Minich, Nirmala Erevelles, Tanya Titchkosky, Michael Davison, Ann Fox, Sumi Colligan, Carrie Sandahl, Carol Gill, Eli Clare, Katherine Ott, Margaret Price, Catherine Kudlick, Petra Kuppers, Cynthia Wu, Susan Burch, Robert McRuer, Kateřina Kolářová, Louis Cabri, Sara Vogt, Terri Thrower, Susan Nussbaum, Sandie Yi, James Charlton, Roxana Galusca, Aly Patsavas, Megan Milks, Cynthia Barounis, Susan Schweik, Corbett O'Toole, Karen Nakamura, Gayatri Reddy, Anna Guevarra, Ianna Owen, Karli Cerankowski, Nancy Abelmann, Catherine Jacquet, Liam Lair, Ashley Mog, Thuy Nguyen, Todd Henry, and Chris Bell. I thank my colleagues at Syracuse University, who welcomed me to a new academic home in the Women's and Gender Studies Department and the Disability Studies Program.

I want to thank Charles Kim, Jenell Johnson, Mike Gill, and Lynn Itagaki for being my writing partners and holding me accountable for my goals. Writing next to each of them was calming and helped me concentrate. I am fortunate to have Pernille Ipsen and Keisha Lindsay as friends who continue to cheer and care for me. I remember with great affection our times in coffee shops and restaurants talking about the pains and joys of writing a book, and I look forward to sharing more of those in the future. I am deeply thankful to Alison Kafer and Nicole Markotić for their enthusiasm that was vital at the last stage of my manuscript submission. Their friendship, calmness, wisdom, and laughter sustain my thinking. I also thank Elise Nagy, Jessica Cooley, and Paige Hoffmann, who have created a wonderful community at the University of Wisconsin, Madison, and who make the field of disability studies richer. For their support and solidarity, I thank my friends in the feminist, queer, and disability rights activist communities in South Korea: 정형옥, 이효희, 백재희, 원미혜, 강진영, 박순천, 박김영희, 정영란, 나영정, 배복주, 홍성희, 민가영, the members of the trans-ability seminar group, and Changae Yŏsŏng Konggam.

Lastly, I thank Mike and our families for their unwavering support. Words cannot express my gratitude for the love, pain, joy, and support that they give me and the ways in which they all make my life fuller, richer, and sustainable. Thank you.

Any inaccuracy, errors, and incompleteness in this book rest with me alone.

Earlier versions of chapters 4 and 5 were published in *Wagadu: A Journal of Transnational Women's and Gender Studies* and *Sexuality Research and Social Policy*, respectively. Throughout the book, I use the preferred or known spelling of Korean names and provided transliterated names according to McCune-Reischauer Romanization system. Translations of Korean texts are mine unless noted otherwise.

───────────────

Textual description of the front cover: The image on the front cover consists of four acrylic paintings entitled *Daily Happenings* (100cm × 100cm) by a Korean artist Jiwon, who identifies as a contingent laborer. The paintings were displayed as part of Nanjang 2005 in Seoul. On the cover four paintings of different sizes in various shades of red and orange are laid out with light yellow background. In the middle the title reads Curative Violence in black. On the upper left, two faces with the eyes almost closed are joined at the cheek. There is a tiny figure with a human face with wings that look like stairs and a wheel-looking tail. On the upper right, a dog lies on its side and a small cat appears on the edge. On the lower left, a face appears with an extended forehead embedded with a mouth-like shape with red, white, and light yellow. On the lower right, a face with closed eyes is angled on its side. From one eye, matter flows to the side of the face. Liquid-like ruffles wrap around the face. There is another eye embedded on the jaw. Under it, the subtitle Rehabilitating Disability, Gender, and Sexuality in Modern Korea is printed in black and the author's name, Eunjung Kim, in white.

Introduction

Folded Time and the Presence of Disability

In 2005, the South Korean scientist Hwang Woo Suk and his associates published an article in the journal *Science* claiming that they had achieved the world's first cloning of "patient-specific" embryonic stem cells.[1] This success drew immediate national acclaim, as the media lauded him as enhancing national pride and honor. Shortly thereafter, the public television (KBS) program *Open Concert* aired an episode with the theme of the future of science and technology. The concert featured President Roh Moo Hyun's recorded message touting the importance of science and technology and promising his administration's continued full support. After the celebrity singer Kang Won Rae, disabled with a spinal-cord injury, performed in a group and danced in his wheelchair, Hwang appeared onstage with the minister of science and technology. He remarked, "I haven't found the solution to this incurable disease yet. But I hope to make Kang spring to his feet, so that on the concert stage after the next one, he can show us again the quick dance moves he used to have. And I will move forward with all citizens in a search for the path to the day he performs his wheelchair dance to reminisce about old times." In Hwang's view, Kang's pre-injury ability to dance would be restored in the very near future and his wheelchair dance belonged to the future's past. This desire for cure was captured emotionally: while Hwang described the agonizing sadness he felt watching Kang's performance, the frame switched to a slow-motion close-up of Kang dancing in his wheelchair.[2] As the cure rhetoric and spectacle fold past and future over the present, disability surreally disappears. One newspaper captured this disappearance with the headline "No More Wheelchair for Kang Won Rae."[3] Kang merely served as the magician's assistant to prop up the illusion of cure in front of the applauding audience, as if he had already been cured. In these folded temporalities, only his nondisabled past and his cured future become meaningful.

To honor Hwang's success, Korea Post issued a special postage stamp, "Stem Cell Cloning Process and Hope," featuring another kind of temporal folding (see figure intro.1). The images of bodies of the present and the future all appear over the images seen through a microscope. On the left side of the stamp, on top, several cells appear with instruments; beneath this, a needle introduces a nucleus into what seems to be a human egg. Emerging from the left, a figure (gendered as a man) in a wheelchair is shown in progressive changes in his pose within five silhouettes: he is sitting in the chair, raising himself up, running, then leaping, and, at the end, he is embracing another figure (gendered as a woman). This process captures how curative science enables intimate relations, making visible the assumption that normative functioning is the precondition of social inclusion. The right side of the stamp features a bright center, representing the limitless possibilities and hopeful future to which the title of the stamp refers. The curative process is visualized in a way that is similar to the notion of progress in what Anne McClintock calls "pan-optical time," being "consumed—at a glance—in a single spectacle from a point of privileged invisibility."[4] As if filmed in stop-motion, the five figures appear as a single body being fast-forwarded through time. Adding to this effect of animation, a hologram creates depth and glow in the horizontal movement of "progress" to arrive at the privileged, nondisabled body.

In the examples of the concert stage and the postage stamp, the cure that has yet to materialize, the nation-state, and disability are represented on unequal terms to form a nationalist spectacle. Both translate the event that might have happened in the laboratory to a powerful drama of imagined bodily transformation and, by extension, national transformation. Time is folded and contracted with one purpose: to construct the power of the nation by making disability disappear.

Emphasizing the nationalist significance of his technology in its international reach, Hwang also mentioned Christopher Reeve as another example of a life he could transform through his stem cell cloning and claimed that Reeve had contacted him. Much like the singer Kang on the concert stage, Reeve was featured in a curative spectacle—in his case, in the well-known U.S. commercial for an investment company, Nuveen, aired during the 2000 Super Bowl. The commercial is set in the near future and shows the onstage celebration of a "remarkable breakthrough in spinal-cord injuries." The host introduces the special guest who is to present the award, and the camera focuses on the legs and then feet of a man slowly walking forward. The viewers then discover that it is Reeve who is approaching the podium. As the host greets him, the audi-

Intro.1 A special postage stamp issued in 2005 by Korea Post, "Stem Cell Cloning Process and Hope," dedicated to Hwang Woo Suk.

ence rises in a *standing* ovation, welcoming Reeve—who can now stand and walk, and thus provides evidence of the breakthrough—into the normative society. The voice-over addresses the viewers in the present: "In the future so many amazing things will happen in the world. What amazing things can you make happen?" Two frames of text are shown: "Invest well. Leave your mark." This invitation offers the promise of satisfaction from contributing to the cause of curing disability. It entirely omits any image of science, instead addressing the viewers as potential investors and as the benefactors who will shape the future. Reeve becomes the iconic beneficiary, the "mark" of the moralized deed of private investing for profit. This capitalist spectacle of Reeve's virtually cured body covers over his disabled embodiment.

While the Nuveen commercial encourages private investment, in Hwang's case the nation-state emerges as the visible benefactor. Funded largely by the government, Hwang was known to have patriotically refused to accept foreign investment. On the stamp, a disabled person in a wheelchair appears as an object of intervention offered in the name of KOREA, printed alongside the magnified spectacle of life as a site of cure and advancement. The curative power, in turn, fundamentally relies on the presence of disabled bodies framed with a certain emotional effect.

To cure is to properly govern the body and its social relations. *Ch'iyu* (治癒), a Sino-Korean word for cure and healing, is made up of two individual words: *ch'i*, "to govern," and *yu*, "to cure." Disability has long been connected to the imaginary of the colonial Korean body politic during Japanese rule. After Independence, the division, and the Korean War, rehabilitation of the disabled nation, largely tied to capitalist economic development, emerged as the primary goal of postcolonial South Korea. In the new millennium, as the emphasis shifted toward people with disabilities as beneficiaries of the already-rehabilitated nation, the fact that the nation itself was in need of reconstruction began to fade from the collective framework of national identity. Technological, economic, and medical developments confirm the shift in South Korean national identity from a country relying on other countries' aid to one able to govern its citizens through its power to cure disabled others and to offer international assistance to "those in need."[5] The power to physically transform a disabled individual through biomedicine becomes part of the branding effort of the normalized ethno-nation-state.

The magical spectacles of cure on the South Korean stamp and in the U.S. commercial were each contradicted by different realities, however. Korea Post stopped selling the stamp in less than a year, when part of Hwang's research was found to be fraudulent. The national excitement—called "Hwang Woo Suk Syndrome"—turned into shock and shame. He was eventually convicted of various charges, including illegal trading in human eggs, research misconduct, and embezzlement, and received a suspended sentence. And though the commercial featuring Reeve did not claim that the image was real, it similarly misled its audience: people inquired for more information about his "cure."[6] Although no one expects a television commercial to be held to the same standard of truthfulness as a report of scientific research, the realness of the virtual image of Reeve standing and walking was extraordinarily powerful: in effect, viewers were guided to situate this imagined future in their present.

Even the exposure of his scandalous fraud has not stopped Hwang's pursuit of therapeutic cloning to cure disabilities and illnesses. *Nature* recently reported on Hwang's success in cloning animals and on his goals of "producing drugs, curing diabetes and Alzheimer's disease, providing transplantable organs, saving endangered species and relieving grief-stricken pet owners."[7] The continued government funding of and international attention to his efforts show that the drama of cure has expanded from the possibility of curing disability to attempting to "cure" environmental loss, defying the extinction of species and to "cure" the emotional experience of loss, defying mortality itself. It signals yet another way of folding time: an insistence on making the present disappear by replacing it with the normative past, simultaneously projecting onto it a specific kind of normative future. This ironically has the effect of solidifying the status quo, as the assumption embedded in the societal mandate that disability needs to be cured before disabled people can "return" to society is not questioned.

The international debate over therapeutic cloning has been concerned with ethical and moral issues, while emphasizing potential benefits and legal barriers, but it has also been tinged with nationalism and international competition. Following Hwang's alleged success, researchers in the United States expressed frustration at falling behind because of the legal restrictions they faced, which had "given other nations some significant advantages."[8] Technological advances imbued with nationalism threatened to upset existing international hierarchies.

South Korean disability activists spoke up against the emphasis on curing and normalizing disabled people, because the perceived need for cure generally reinforces prejudice against disabled people.[9] Tari Youngjung Na writes, "We shivered whenever we heard the word 'therapy.' When disabled people did music, it became music therapy; exercise became rehabilitation therapy; stage acting became theater therapy; painting was quickly named as art therapy. Even though these activities could be used for the purpose of treatment, we knew that, regardless of specific purpose or content of an activity, they were so easily considered therapies, because of the belief that disability should be cured."[10] The need for cure extends to the activities of life and transforms them into exceptional interventions solely for the purpose of "improvement," with the eventual aim of eliminating disability or of approximating able-bodiedness.

The singer Kang Won Rae seems to have known well that Hwang Woo Suk and the media exploited him as an icon of disability cure to illustrate the significance of biotechnology.[11] Kang stated that he wouldn't wait around doing nothing or put all of his faith on cure but was determined to live his life. He rejected the implied passivity of disabled people in hoping for cure, instead advocating for improving the lives of people with disabilities. He claimed his disability identity when some in the disability community considered him not disabled because of his celebrity status and class privilege.[12] But at the same time he praised Hwang's alleged breakthrough and hoped that it would be developed into a real cure for his spinal-cord injury. His dual desires for cure and for living fully with disability are not represented equally, however. In the same year that he appeared with Hwang on *Open Concert*, Kang released a music video that featured him getting up from an *armchair* and dancing, a scene made possible by special effects, including invisible wires, a body double, and computer graphics. This activity was in fact meant to reenact his past, before his accident, rather than to create an illusion of future cure. But the media emphasized his standing, with one newspaper going so far as to lead with the headline "Kang Won Rae Got up from His Wheelchair,"[13] even though the performance in the video consisted mostly of his dancing in a wheelchair together with nondisabled dancers standing or dancing in wheelchairs in unison. That his album included two songs about the disability movement's push for accessible transportation, and that he produced another music video in collaboration with disability rights activists, which included scenes of large-scale disability protests from the 2002 documentary *Let's Ride a Bus*, received little attention. Though for Kang the need for community recognition of disability identity, the hope for cure, and the commitment to structural changes seem to coexist, for the mainstream media the focus remains on cure.

Seeking Disability in the Spectacles of Folded Time

To cure typically means to restore "health" by removing illness and disability through medical treatment. Figuratively, according to the *Oxford English Dictionary*, it also means "to remedy, rectify, or remove (an evil of any kind)," illustrating that moral judgment about its object as "evil" is an important component of its meaning. The existing critique of cure within disability studies with a Western focus has targeted medical cure and its social impact, tied to criticism of the medical model that sees disability as an individual deficit or pathology to be corrected through professional interventions.[14] The medical model also denies or obscures disability as a valuable element of human difference. Importantly, this criticism challenges the perception that disability needs to be cured and denounces the priority of cure over other social and environmental changes that enable people to live with disability and illness. In other words, the compulsion of cure, regardless of whether any cure is available, preempts social and practical solutions to many of the problems and struggles that disabled people experience. Eli Clare relocates the site that needs "cure" in the context of the United States: "The disability rights movement, like other social change movements, names systems of oppression as the problem, not individual bodies. In short it is ableism that needs the cure, not our bodies."[15] The critique of cure, therefore, has attempted to shift priorities and to valorize disabilities as differences.

Cure entails an individualized approach, which is likely to be determined by the affordability of medical care. Analyzing the Nuveen commercial and the film *In the Gloaming*, directed by Reeve, which depicts a character living with AIDS, Robert McRuer argues that the focus on cure prevents people from having conversations about the systems of power and about everyone's complicity in them. McRuer emphasizes that curative approaches to disability and AIDS are inseparable. He argues that "people with AIDS are not passive observers who are simply waiting for a cure" and it is important to recognize that disabled people are making coalitions with other oppressed minorities and are demanding broad social and political changes.[16]

Disability studies scholars increasingly seek to examine the interlocking nature of oppressions among various marginalized groups and to highlight the importance of making existing medical care and prevention affordable and accessible, of eliminating ableist medical discrimination, and of undertaking efforts at prevention based on proper education and health care. What is problematic in the drive for medical cure is its narrow, simple focus on the gains and benefits that cure may bring, disregarding its associated harms, risks, and disenabling effects. It also closes off ways to support, in the present, "untreated" and "incurable" lives, that is, people who have a disability or an illness, as well as people who refuse or cannot afford treatments. When bodies are pronounced "incurable," they are read as being in a condition of a "nonlife"—without a future and denied meaning in the present. At the same time, cure denies a place for disability and illness as different ways of existing in the present. Cure discourses and imagery operate in political, moral, economic, and emotional realms that go beyond individual medical treatments and personal desires for remedy. An emphasis on cure as the only path forward is damaging, because it obscures the fact that cure is always a multifaceted negotiation, often enabling and disabling at the same time, and may be accompanied by pain, loss, or death.

If cure eliminates disability, why is disability persistently present within the drama of cure? The commercial about Reeve's cure does indeed picture the presence of disability in the future, while rendering it unrecognizable. In addition to those who are watching the broadcast celebration on-screen with a sense of wonder, four people with visible disabilities walk behind Reeve onstage. They may be featured to represent either those still waiting to be cured, once greater sums are invested, or those who, like Reeve, are walking after a long period of using a wheelchair. As much as the image of Reeve's walking surprises the viewers, it also shows new markers of disability, inviting a scrutinizing gaze at his virtual motion, which might seem different. He grabs the arms of the chair for balance as he rises, and he takes each step with care. As he gazes to the side, his neck doesn't turn; the camera focuses on his face, his head (cropped from the image of his disabled body) digitally attached to the walking body. Significantly, this commercial shows a future inhabited by disabled bodies, including that of Reeve. In order for the imagined cure to be meaningful, then, it has to be accompanied by disability. Although disabilities of the individuals and Reeve onstage are read as soon-to-disappear, the very presence of disabled bodies counters the assumption that cure eliminates disability. This may bring us a different understanding about cultural productions that frame embodiments always in reference to one another.

For many, cure demands that we suspend our living in the present and instead wait for a future without disabilities and illnesses, urging us to not live in the present. Alison Kafer calls this temporal framing "curative time": "In our disabled state, we are not part of the dominant narratives of progress, but once rehabilitated, normalized, and hopefully cured, we play a starring role: the sign of progress, the proof of development, the triumph over the mind or body."[17] In the South Korean context, I add to this list the observation that a rehabilitated or cured body becomes a sign of decolonized and sovereign statehood under capitalism, for the colonized and communist state was understood as a disabled and even nonhuman body.[18] Set against the impossibility of inhabiting the present, the promised transformation through cure is enticing enough to make losses and hastened death acceptable, even expected. Kafer continues, "Within this frame of curative time, then, the only appropriate disabled mind/ body is one cured or moving toward cure. Cure, in this context, most obviously signals the elimination of impairment but can also mean normalizing treatments that work to assimilate the disabled mind/body as much as possible."[19] The curative drive also demands an approximation of normality through "habilitation" (the acquisition of skills and abilities) and "rehabilitation" (the regaining of skills and abilities that have been lost or impaired).

If one refuses to read the presence of disabled bodies as always moving forward on the compulsory path to be cured or to die, those four individuals with disabilities who follow Reeve onstage might be imagined as the disability community that congratulates him for his chosen transformation and his belonging to—rather than his departure from—that community. Even though Reeve's focus on cure constrained his relationship with disability rights movements, this kind of imaginative reading attempts to disengage from curative time, which considers one embodiment an improvement from the previous one. This imagining attempts to unlearn the habit of projecting the cure imperative onto disabled bodies, instead focusing on the presence of disability itself and envisioning a future when cure exists as a negotiated transformation.

The presence of disabilities in the representation of cure helps me situate cure in the work of time to examine how cure, even at an individual level, does not always provide relief or advance one's health and functions. What happens when cure promises to take bodies from the category of disability to that of normality, but leaves them in the middle? Can cure coexist with disability? The analysis of cure informs us that disability never simply disappears through attempts at cure; it is recognized, then disfigured and disinvested. The curative attempts also affect gender, age, class, sexuality, race/ethnicity/indigeneity, religion, health status, and nation-state. The temporal and rhetorical politics of virtual cure and the heightened emotions surrounding images of cure—hope, hopelessness, the sense of empowerment, nationalist sentiment, and so on—underscore the need to examine visual and literary cultures of cure beyond medical, scientific, and bioethical frameworks. What do emotional and material investment in cure and the political criticism about cure tell us about our identification and disidentification with disability and otherness? In many cases, curable and cured bodies are disabled, because of the history of disability they carry and because of the unending rehabilitation, up to a certain age, to gain the better bodies that supposedly await in their future. Much as happiness, as explored by Sara Ahmed—who draws from feminist, black, and queer scholars who criticize happiness as a device for oppression—is a wish that keeps "its place as a wish by its failure to be given,"[20] so too cure keeps its place as a destination at which one can never arrive. In that sense, for disabled people normality exists always one moment away, urging us to suspend our life in the present and not to attempt social changes.

Curative Violence turns its focus to the centrality of disability's presence before and after cure, existing in between the past and the future and in between otherness and normality. In these in-between spaces, cure and disability coexist as a process. I examine the suturing together of disability and cure in Korean cultural representations situated in historical and transnational contexts. In this nexus, the violence that is made invisible in the name of cure emerges as an important theme. Focusing on disabled bodies visualized and narrativized in the landscapes of multiply constituted boundaries of otherness and normality in folded time, I explore various imaginations and practices of medical and nonmedical cure in colonial Korea (Chosŏn) during the height of Japanese rule in the late 1930s and in South Korea since the division. The analyses in a given political and historical context are put in dialogue with the concerns of the contemporary South Korean disabled women's movement.

Conceptualizing Cure

Because the workings of cure are complex, close attention must be paid to the interactions among politics, cultural representations, and social movements that all seek various sorts of transformation. Cure operates with the social compulsion of gender conformity and heterosexuality as conditions of recognition and belonging, as well as with normative pressures that vary with context. The imperative of cure is produced by historical and cultural circumstances that make life with disability difficult and unlivable. To deconstruct the oppositional relationship between disability and cure in the societal drive toward normality, I approach cure in two ways: first, as a crossing of times and categories through metamorphosis, and second, as a transaction and negotiation that involves various effects, including the uncertainty of gains and the possibility of harms—caused by what I call "curative violence"—as well as what are considered benefits. These two broadened conceptions of cure help me articulate the multiple ways in which cure is imagined beyond the medical realm.

Hans Christian Andersen's *The Little Mermaid*, a story about a fish-tailed, aquatic being who wants to become an air-breathing human with legs, may be taken as an example of how the two conceptions of cure are narrativized. The mermaid desires to become an ambulatory human being with the bonus (by virtue of her humanity) of an immortal soul. The sea witch tells her, "You want to be rid of your fishtail and instead have a couple of stumps to walk on, just like human beings, so that the young prince will fall in love with you, and then you'll be able to have him and an immortal soul as well! . . . Your tail will part and shrink into what humans call nice legs, but it will hurt, just as if a sharp sword were passing through you. . . . Once you have taken on the shape of a human being, you will never be able to become a mermaid again."[21] In this transaction, she gives up her fishtail and tongue and instead gains legs, pain, and muteness. After the mermaid drinks the potion, "she fainted from it, and lay as though dead."[22] When she wakes up, the lower half of her body has morphed into two legs, enabling her to walk; but with every step she feels pain. What she wants is to live in a different world as a human and to be in an intimate relationship with the prince she loves, desires that all involve corporeal, spatial, and species crossings. This crossing cures her of her previous embodiment through a metamorphosis, but it also disables her. The complete crossing is possible only if she wins heterosexual love and becomes the prince's wife. After the prince chooses another woman for his bride, the mermaid dissolves into foam in the sea. Without marital heterosexual love bestowed by a high-status man, the possibility of her cured, disabled, trans-species embodiment dissolves, forever caught in between the realms of water and air.

Cure appears in this book as an attempt at crossing, involving a transaction with benefits and harms done by curative violence and with other ambiguous effects, often bringing about liminal existence. In addition, the connection between cure and heterosexuality, which is exemplified in the example of the postage stamp, illustrates how the dimension of desire is employed to reinforce the imperative of cure.

Cure as a Crossing

By folding time, cure demands temporal crossings to an imagined or remembered past through "rehabilitation" and "recovery" and to a future without disabilities and illnesses. Cure also attempts to bring about category crossing, altering how a body is classified in ways that may or may not involve actual bodily change. If cure is a crossing from a category of otherness to that of normality, what enables that crossing? What marks the completed crossing to normality, when disability involves bodily, social, and environmental interactions and the histories that bodies carry? Cure appears as an attempt at crossing that can reveal the multiplicity of the boundaries that divide "human" and "inhuman" as well as "life" and "nonlife." Cure seen as a crossing provides an insight not only into disability but also into various thresholds of the normative body, such as race, gender, and sexual and familial relations.

At the same time, curative transitions create a space in between disability and nondisability. In the transformation through temporal and categorical crossing, cure can be incomplete, leaving bodies in borderlands. Together with disability, I find cure in liminal places inhabited and frequented during attempted crossings between categories and times. Here, cure coexists with alterations of disability or with the memory of disability; cure is never a simple erasure. Cure often creates or reshapes disability. One can be cured of a disability and must then readjust to a new body, a change that may generate different sets of disabilities. Karen Beauchamp-Pryor discusses her self-identification as a disabled person who has lost visual impairment. After the cure, Beauchamp-Pryor experiences "anxieties of managing and coping" and "a new learning process," as she deals with "a bombardment of visual information."[23] Moreover, cure often does not eliminate the stigma associated with a history of disability and illness. Many insights that emerge in experiences of transition are lost in the binary assumption that one is either disabled or nondisabled. Thinking about *cured bodies as disabled bodies* owing to their history of disability, shared experiences and communities, and newly created differences might be helpful in teasing out the temporal distinctions of "acute," "terminal," "progressive," "chronic," and "latent" illnesses and their relations to cure.

The mutually constitutive workings of disability, gender, and heteronormativity provide a framework to understand how South Korean disabled women's perceptions of category crossing as cure in the broad sense are enabled by a recognition of their gender without any change in disability. In the television documentary *Thumbelina Wants to Be a Mother* (2007), Yun Sŏn-a, who has a genetic disability, speaks about her marriage: "I thought the categories of human beings were men, women, and disabled people. Even *I* believed so. When [my husband] said I was pretty and lovely and proposed marriage, I realized I was a woman too and worthy of a man's love. I feel like I am living a second life." Yun's crossing from a disabled person to a woman—viewed as mutually exclusive categories—is enabled by the way she is recognized through a heterosexual relationship. She dreams of becoming the mother of a nondisabled child, and she goes through a process of reproductive engineering to select embryos that don't contain markers of her genetic disability. Without this intervention, she considers herself unfit to become a mother due to the possibility of passing on her disability.

Cure is a transitory process, which sets in motion intended and unintended transformations of embodiments, affects, and social and material conditions. This understanding of cure as a transformation can be thought of as in connection to the transition that appears in the practice of "transability," which Bethany Stevens defines as "the need or desire to transition from supposed binary states of physical ability to physical disability."[24] Stevens introduces Sean O'Connor, who desired to be paralyzed and voluntarily transitioned from an ambulatory life to a wheelchair-using life. Stevens explains, "Transabled people are individuals who *need* to acquire a physical impairment despite having been born or living in physically unimpaired bodies."[25] Emphasizing this desire to acquire disability, Stevens views transability "as a catalyst to include disability within the category of body art" created by body modification. In a society that explicitly favors a healthy and normal body, parallels between the transitions from able-bodied to disabled (transability) and from disabled to able-bodied (cure) may not yet be warranted. Alexandre Baril explains that "due to an ableist vision of 'normal' and 'productive' bodies, transabled people's requests are most often considered irrational and are denied," and therefore "a significant number attempt the desired transformations on their own."[26]

It is difficult to think of transitions between disability and nondisability as crossings between neutral and equal spaces, given that the desire for disability is pathologized as "body integrity identity disorder," while the desire for cure is naturalized and mandated. Nevertheless, thinking about cure alongside transability denaturalizes the dogma that disability is undesirable and normality is desirable. It also allows one to imagine crossing the boundaries without violence in a way that can blur those boundaries. In the meantime, the imperative of cure raises important questions: When and how does cure become the only way to make life livable? How does cure preempt the efforts to facilitate various ways to make life livable?

Curative Violence and Cure as a Transaction

Cure involves a transaction with speculative risks that carry the possibility of both gains and losses. Individuals attempt cure with the expectation of functional and social gains that enable them to access other resources. But cure carries a significant risk of unwanted changes or even death. These curative gains and losses are not easily discernible as gains and losses, for what is unwanted by an individual can be perceived as beneficial to one's family, community, and society and vice versa. The determination is already skewed toward normative personhood, gender conformity, and the performance of heterosexuality within an ethno-racial and national boundary.

But is curing disability the same as curing illness? How about chronic and fatal illnesses that involve "pain, functional decline and loss, or reduced life expectancy," which make people pause in their claim that disabled lives do not need cure?[27] In response to disability rights activists' claim that not all disabled people want a cure, Christopher Reeve invoked AIDS to emphasize its importance: "I don't think there is anyone with AIDS who keeps wanting to have AIDS."[28] In his simplistic assumption about the impossibility of wanting to have HIV/AIDS, he did not consider that there might be a difference between wanting to become ill and wanting to be cured from the illness at all costs.[29] What happens when individuals choose not to prevent an illness and when those who are affected by illnesses see medical treatments as unnecessary? What happens when state-enforced medical treatments involve significant violations of a person and their families and inflict material and psychic violence that make people run away from cure?[30] What happens when the line between disability and illness doesn't exist in individuals' experiences? It seems that political and ethical considerations regarding the cures of fatal and progressive illnesses and the ways that they might become available raise more questions than closing off the discussion as Reeve intended. The projected suffering of those with fatal illnesses is not separate from the ways in which disabled and chronically unhealthy lives are imagined. Political judgments about life with fatal illness as an unquestionable "evil" that necessitates cure also inform the discourses about physician-assisted suicide for incurably disabled individuals. An emphasis on the cure for potentially fatal yet fully curable illnesses can be used by those relying on a cost-benefit analysis to dismiss the need for long-term care for people with disabilities. Prognoses and determinations of what is fatal also involve political judgments that influence how we view an individual's life or an individual's suffering as nonlife. Therefore, given how healthiness and suffering are conceived and how the cost of cure is evaluated, there seems to be a significant conceptual and existential overlap between disability and illness.

As a way to govern disabled and ill bodies, cure requires complicated transactions between social and biological benefits and costs, risks of death, and further alienation. Metaphors of war are often used to structure experiences with illness and disability: individuals are said to "battle cancer," "fight against autism," or undergo "invasive treatment." These metaphors tell us about the cost, pain, struggles, and even violence and potential death that accompany curative practices. The idea that illness and disability are enemies is connected to the notion of the body itself as an Other. Simply objecting to cure as a way to affirm disabled embodiment does not capture the way that individuals make complicated moral, economic, and relational decisions to alter their bodies in order to change the meanings of their presence. Disabled individuals might negotiate the potential benefits and costs and decide to go through with various methods of cure. Often, it is not a matter of choice between equally viable options. I use "curative violence" to describe the exercise of force to erase differences for the putative betterment of the Other. Curative violence occurs when cure is what actually frames the presence of disability as a problem and ends up destroying the subject in the curative process. In this sense, curative violence recalls the notion of the *pharmakon*, at once remedy and poison—a remedy that harms.[31] Various kinds of remedy—symbolic, religious, mystical, and medical—and their meanings in culture and public policy make cure a politically charged practice that profoundly influences how we think about bodies and disabilities. The violence associated with cure exists at two levels: first, the violence of denying a place for disability and illness as different ways of living and, second, the physical and material violence against people with disabilities that are justified in the name of cure.

The consent of a given person to any curative intervention may not erase its violent effect. The notion of consent is fraught with ableist judgments about an individual's mental capacity, which is often taken out of its social and relational contexts. For example, the movie *Sex Volunteer* (2009) briefly introduces a woman with a spinal-cord injury, requiring daily care by her parents; she consents to a hysterectomy so that she will no longer menstruate. In an interview, she talks about desiring her menstrual periods. Her story is not uncommon among women with physical and intellectual disabilities. In this case, the hysterectomy is not even read as sterilization, because her reproductive prospect is never recognized; instead, it is considered a convenience-enhancing treatment. Consent to a procedure for family members' convenience, but contrary to one's own desire, illustrates the problem of simply relying on consent to determine violence. The link between cure and violence does not hinge on coercion or the absence of consent but rather on the perceived and material need for transformation, which is premised on the assumption that the uncured status is not acceptable and on the promised results of cure as betterment. This is not to say that all bodily interventions to ameliorate difficulties are violent nor that disabled people are always victims of violence. Rather, consent and cure are based on complicated material, social, and familial negotiations that occur beyond an individual's desire and volition.

Curative violence constructs the normative body by inducing metamorphosis according to its own determination of benefits and harms, as established by how closely disabled bodies resemble and mimic the normative body. Attempts to cure physical, mental, and sensory disabilities and certain illnesses unveil the ways in which disability is enmeshed with gender and sexual norms that serve individual, state, and activist purposes. *Curative violence* adds to the efforts to expose what Judith Butler calls "normative violence"—the significance of transactions between subjects and the institutions that gain power through their ability to normalize certain bodies. Butler recalls, "I also came to understand something of the violence of the foreclosed life, the one that does not get named as 'living,' the one whose incarceration implies a suspension of life, or a sustained death sentence. The dogged effort to 'denaturalize' gender in this text emerges, I think, from a strong desire both to counter the normative violence implied by ideal morphologies of sex and to uproot the pervasive assumptions about natural or presumptive heterosexuality that are informed by ordinary and academic discourses on sexuality."[32] Generating a broader consensus of biopolitical processes, the ultimate ability to cure is to approximate ideal morphologies and to set heterosexuality as a goal.[33] In this transaction, the major goals of the sovereign nation-state are to secure superior ethnicity, heteronormativity, capital growth, and gender conformity. Rather than being commensurate parallels, sexuality, race/ethnicity, and gender intersect as means of curing disability by making it possible to approximate the normative body, even when such approximation cannot be achieved in all respects.

Resisting the primacy of cure offers an alternative ontology of the present that is made possible by disability experiences. A South Korean independent short film, *Mermaid* (2013), presents cross-species identification in between virtual and actual categories in a way opposite to that found in *The Little Mermaid*.[34] A deaf woman challenges her hearing boyfriend, who is reluctant to introduce her to his hearing friends.[35] Confronting his ableist shame about her deafness, she invites him into the pool in which she practices diving and communicates in sign language under the water—a place where hearing is irrelevant. She brings her boyfriend down into the water, into her world imagining herself as a mermaid. The film captures the underwater space where her deafness and sign language are reconfigured into a different ontology. By reframing disability as mystical species diversity, the deaf woman leaves the category of human to challenge the deficit model of deafness.[36]

Even as the meanings of cure remain elusive and expansive, scholars paying attention to small- and large-scale violence agree that "the concept of violence" is also "extremely unstable."[37] Veena Das points out that "contests around the question of what can be named as violence are themselves a sign of something important at stake." Das continues: "The reality of violence includes its virtual (not only actualized) presence in our lives."[38] Scholars have pointed out that gender is central to understanding what constitutes violence; gender also plays a crucial role in understanding what constitutes cure. The compulsion of cure particularly manifests within sexual violence and enables normative recognition of heterosexual femininity. Disabled girls and women are often subject to rape, explained as a curative intervention. In South Korea, in a series of cases of repeated rapes of disabled women, the attackers justified rape as being a favor to their victims.[39] In 2012, the *Global Post* reported that four teenage boys in South Africa were released on bail after raping a girl with a mental disability.[40] In another newspaper article, the presumed asexuality of disabled women is connected to rape by the claim that rape remedies asexuality and would eventually remedy disability,[41] for it is believed that their disability would make it impossible for them to have sex otherwise. Asexuality here is assumed to be an absence of sexual experience, rather than a mode of being. Disability and presumed asexuality are both pathologized, thereby creating the need for remedy. Rape of women who identify as asexual has also been reported in the United States.[42] Similarly, South African activists have named rape of lesbian women "corrective rape,"[43] which aims to punish lesbians and enforce heterosexuality. Revealing the violence of the workings of gendered and sexual norms that require physical and behavioral transformation and identity changes, curative violence involves ordinary and extraordinary violence in history and everyday lives.

In order to discuss the multiple meanings of cure in between times and categories, it is necessary to highlight the multiple meanings of disability. Leah Lakshmi Piepzna-Samarasinha insightfully addresses the difficulty and importance of writing about disability in a multifaceted way: "It is *so* difficult to write both of what sucks about disability—the pain, the oppression, the impairment—and the joy of this body at the same time. The joy of this body comes from crip community and interdependence, but most of all, of the hard beauty of this life, built around all the time I must spend resting. The bed *is* the nepantla place of opening."[44] *Nepantla* is a Náhuatl word meaning "torn between ways"[45]; Gloria Anzaldúa conceptualizes it as an "in-between space, an unstable, unpredictable, precarious, always-in-transition space lacking clear boundaries," in which transformations occur.[46] I situate the cultural representations of cure in the political processes of governing populations, in collective and individual struggles, in liminal spaces between otherness and normality, in times between past and future, in narratives existing in between lived experiences and fictions, and in exchanges between nation-states. This in-betweenness creates displacement yet allows individuals to generate knowledge and take advantage of their unexpected and ambiguous meanings. The temporal and spatial in-betweenness, however, does not negate the importance of recognizing the permeability of boundaries or the responsibility to challenge the institutional effects that boundaries produce, because in many ways liminality is not automatically transgressive. Indeed it might instead be instrumental to maintaining boundaries, if the boundaries are not destabilized together.

Situating Disability and Cure in Time and Place

The study of cure in Korean cultural history requires me to seek a transnational approach that does not uphold the nation-state as a universalizing determinant of how history and embodiment are represented. In *Disability and Difference in Global Contexts*, Nirmala Erevelles proposes a transnational, feminist disability studies perspective that "is neither ahistorical, nor limited by national/ethnic boundaries. It is neither burdened by bourgeois interests nor restricted by normative modes of being."[47] I find myself working in tandem with Erevelles's focus on the material conditions of disability experiences and her effort to complicate Western disability studies by employing both decolonial and nonwhite feminist perspectives. This also requires being open to various manifestations of anti-ableist disability consciousness that may not involve affirmative and identitarian understandings of disability or an anticure perspective. Reframing disability in Euro-American cultures as an affirmative identity—rather than as lack, deficiency, or damage—plays an important role in Western disability studies and the disability rights movement but has also been complicated by scholars who focus on the global mass disablements of people by exploitation, poverty, pollution, armed conflicts, and neoliberal policies in non-Western societies and in marginalized communities in Western societies.[48] It seems impossible to object to medical cure when basic preventive measures and medical treatments are not available to most inhabitants of the Global South. These critiques call for rethinking disability identity both to incorporate multiple intersections—of race/ethnicity/indigeneity, gender, age, nation-state, sexuality, class, religion, coloniality, and more—and to challenge the privileges and hierarchies within which people with various disabilities are located.

Complicating the close alignment of disability with individual identity, Julie Livingston and Jasbir Puar employ the term "debility" to broadly refer to embodied struggles. Livingston, writing of Botswana, uses debility to mean "the impairment, lack, or loss of certain bodily abilities," encompassing "experiences of chronic illness and senescence, as well as disability per se." Her adoption of the word is rooted in her critiques of the way that Euro-American disability studies scholars often rely on "a notion of individual selfhood, complete with an individually bounded body that is itself a social construct."[49] The notion of disability pride, the embrace of differences, and self-identification as a disabled person presume a notion of the individual self that may not fully capture the relationality of the identification of disability. Indeed, Puar claims that the work of depathologizing disability and the "attachments to the difference of disabled bodies may reify an exceptionalism that only certain privileged disabled bodies can occupy."[50] Focusing on "working-poor and working-class communities of color" in the United States, in which, in a neoliberal economy, "disabilities and debilities are actually 'the norm,'" Puar argues, "Debility is profitable to capitalism, but so is the demand to 'recover' from or overcome it."[51] Coming from the systems that disenable, the demand imposed on marginalized communities that they recover from debility speaks to the cure being upheld as an exploitative imperative for survival.

Consider the neoliberal regimes in South Korea and its immediate connection to the need for getting better. In 2008, more than a decade after the economic crisis that led to intervention by the International Monetary Fund, President Lee Myung Bak claimed in front of New York bankers and investors that he was "a CEO of the Republic of Korea, Inc.," reiterating his neoliberal commitment.[52] In the past decade, "healing" (*hilling*) emerged as a key word in South Korean popular culture, along with "cure" (*ch'iyu*) and "therapy" (*t'erap'i*).[53] They have almost replaced the all-purpose term "well-being" (*welbing*), which became popular around the turn of the century and reflected an emphasis not just on economic growth but on quality of life and health-conscious consumption.[54] The proliferation of books, lectures, and services that focus on healing seems to indicate that psychological and physical sufferings have become universal. Healing and cure-oriented discourses consist mainly of psychological consolations about the status quo and calls for self-improvement, when individuals are faced with persistent violations of human rights and failures to adequately provide the resources to which everyone is entitled.

The material conditions of debilities and the operations of cure in South Korean contexts reveal the various appropriations of rehabilitation as a goal and a form of power to govern populations. Under colonial exploitations, wars, and subsequent repressive regimes in South Korean history, then, how do we critically engage with both disability and cure beyond the binary framework of affirmation or disavowal? This question, I believe, is crucial when the overwhelming association between debilities and colonial domination, racism, exploitation, war, and violence makes it easy to simply devour disabled bodies to feed the unchanged desire for health and normality, which is often entangled with the idea of sovereignty. It is important to recognize the complicated ways in which meanings are ascribed onto disabled bodies and to move beyond the cause-oriented framework in which disability is frozen in the moment of its creation only to be seen as the consequence of injustice, while at the same time calling for the elimination of the violence itself.

Disabled characters in literary texts, produced at various times in Korean history during and after the Japanese colonial rule (1910–1945), have been read as a metaphor of colonial conditions deployed to avoid censorship;[55] as markers of outdated values that must be eradicated; as evidence of the costs of the Korean War, of capitalist economic expansion, and of state violence; and as an embodiment of the fate of the lower class generally. If Chosŏn as a nation were disenabled by colonial domination and subjected to violence and oppression, how would the embodied experiences of disabled others represent the national experience? How do fictional works confirm the national and class representativeness of disability, or deny it by presenting disability as a condition of differentiation within the national body politic? Can they contest the preconfigured meanings of disability or offer a glimpse within disabled persons? How do Koreans with disabilities experience the massive historical changes in their everyday lives, and how do they interact with nondisabled and enabled Koreans? Material and corporeal experiences of disabled people may reveal the internal othering within the colonial space. In others words, the othering is not solely done by the colonizer to the colonized, but complexly entangled with the new arrangements within the colonized people. They also allow the imagining of ways in which disabled individuals transgress the metaphorical perimeter. Metaphoric use of disability in literary texts is not exclusive to Korea, and Ato Quayson points out that disability oscillates between being represented symbolically and empirically. According to Quayson, closing this gap between the abstraction of disability as a symbol and the material experiences of disability does not "mean that we must always read the literary representation in a directly instrumental way."[56] Rather, he suggests focusing on the processes of framing and interpreting disability and on the ethical implications of those processes.

Exploring whether a text insists on a metaphorical interpretation and how the details of life with disability and illness in their aesthetic expressions demand the ethical recognition of disability is helpful in analyzing how curability and incurability emerge as a narrative solution or as a result of a set of negotiations between the environment and the disabled body. Disability as nationalized identity produces the mythical experience of shared oppression by the "imagined community" of a modern nation-state that shall be sovereign and autonomous—a community horizontally imagined in the form of an independent, nondisabled body, hiding the creation of the internal Other.[57] The metaphoric depiction of social hierarchy depends on "the *prior naturalizing*" of the social subordination of the allegorized groups.[58] Depicting the national body as disabled and feminized under colonial power depends on the prior devaluation of disability and femininity as dependent and inferior. At the same time, those symbolic bearers of the nation (women or disabled people) are excluded from any national agency. As McClintock puts it, "Women are subsumed symbolically into the national body politic as its boundary and metaphoric limit."[59] Women's bodies, disabled and enabled alike, play a central role in bearing national culture within nationalist metaphors such as "the motherland" or "the national family."[60] Korean "comfort women," those who were sexually exploited by the Japanese military during World War II, have been viewed as the epitome of a Japanese atrocity against Koreans. Hyo-Chae Lee, a prominent feminist activist and scholar, states that the creation of "comfort women" "can only be defined as a crime of genocide against the Korean people."[61] Similarly, Katharine Moon points out that, for the leaders of the movement against sexual exploitation in US military camptowns, "South Korea is a colony of the United States, and the plight of the women represents the oppressed plight of the Korean people."[62] After the Korean War, the raped sex workers "who service foreign soldiers" emerged in literature as an allegory of the nation, as the feminized national identity placed under masculine and imperialist American forces.[63] Because of this symbolic resonance, the women engaging in sexual labor are often erased or vilified.[64] Further, the incidents of sexual violence and exploitation of local women by foreign soldiers were often viewed solely as caused by militarism and the neocolonial power of the United States, while the violence rooted in misogyny, hypermasculinity, and patriarchy in the occupied space was ignored.[65] Nationalism cannot exist without gendered discourses or be "understood without a theory of gender power."[66]

The construction of postcolonial, capitalist South Korea in alliance with the United States depended on an assumption of ethnic homogeneity and normality defined against communist and underdeveloped nations. This construct played a crucial role in bracketing off disabled, poor, feminine, perverted, and racialized Others as outsiders and objects of the empowered nation's "help," which was often exercised in the form of not only symbolic but also corporeal and material violence. The cure imperative simultaneously demands normatively gendered and sexual performances. The familial and social dynamics in performances of cure reveal that one cannot simply focus on disability in imagining a livable life with differences, as such a focus may not challenge the exclusionary gender system and heterosexist demands that render disabled women as desexualized nonwomen, leading in turn to the intervention to sexualize them.

The emergence of the physically disabled women's movement coinciding with the Fourth World Conference on Women in Beijing in 1995 illustrates the importance of gender and patriarchy in the experience of disability. Although many disabled women have actively engaged within various disability advocacies and activisms that emerged in the 1980s, this new gender-conscious disability movement coincided with the focus on the politics of "difference" (*ch'ai*) among feminists on the margins of the mainstream women's movement. Feminist scholarship started paying attention to women with disabilities, sexual minorities, sex workers, girls, and members of labor movements, seeking to challenge nationalism, male-centered labor movements, class-based oppressions, and the able-body-centered system that dovetailed with patriarchy. Disabled women distinguished their needs and experiences from those of disabled men and nondisabled women. For instance, sexual violence in institutions and communities, especially against women with cognitive disabilities, is an issue that has been treated only peripherally by both the women's movement and the disability movement. Disabled women activists who encountered patriarchal and inaccessible, day-to-day operations within the disability movement started organizing women's groups. The disabled women's movement began to culturally reframe disabled women's bodies, challenge ableist norms and social expectations, and provide different perspectives on the body, sexuality, idealized femininity, intimate partner and personal assistant violence, and domestic abuse, alongside inaccessible education and exploitative labor conditions.

Repeatedly finding myself on the edges of acceptable norms of physical and mental health, but always considered nondisabled, I sought a community of women with disabilities and chronic illness to challenge segregation and hierarchy based on normative bodily functions and social expectations, health and disability status, and gender. I joined a nascent group of women with physical disabilities at a disability rights organization. Despite its initial support in organizing the women's group and hosting the first disabled women's conference, the organization showed little interest in supporting political autonomy. The layoff of a disabled woman from the organization led us to form a separate group, which eventually created its own initiative.[67] After a period of exploring how gender and disability experiences coexist and of connecting with other disabled women in Seoul through weekly meetings, we launched the organization Changae Yŏsŏng Konggam (Women with Disabilities Empathy, WDE).

The political emergence of disabled women's activism in the late 1990s has not been monolithic. There are several organizations of disabled women, and they are not all aligned politically on various agendas (including policies regarding reproduction). They are often organized around a particular disability, and their efforts range from promoting specific interests and making resources available for disabled women to broader claims of social justice, human rights, disability coalitions, antiviolence, and cultural movements. For the past seventeen years, under a number of leaders, WDE has expanded to encompass an independent living center for women, a theater group, and a sexual violence counseling center and has defined itself as a disabled women's human rights movement. Many areas of these activities have been funded by the municipal and central governments. During this period of growth, WDE has faced many challenges, including an increasing workload, high turnover rate, low compensation, a range of education levels, and differing disability statuses, as it relied on grant-funded projects that required high productivity from its workers (although some flexibility has allowed women to participate at various levels). While some women have been experiencing difficulty working full-time, because of long hours or because they risk exceeding the income limit for maintaining governmental welfare benefits, others choose to work full-time or part-time as appropriate given their needs or else volunteer to be involved in various activities. Although the diversity of experiences, capabilities, and perspectives has been crucial in its anti-ableist work, the organization's increasingly bureaucratic structure has created an internal hierarchy based on age, seniority, and education, limiting the sustained participation of disabled women. This problem is not unique to WDE, as many disability organizations have been gradually bureaucratized as service-providing agencies funded by the government: Kang Jin Kyung, an activist who works at WDE, explained to me that it became harder in general for people with significant disabilities to be employed by these agencies.

In WDE, disabled and nondisabled activists emphasize "the receptivity of feelings" (*kamsusŏng*), a disability-centered sensibility about experiences that are not one's own and about oppressive social and material conditions. Women with physical disabilities talk about the feeling that comes from familiarity with and responsiveness to women with various kinds of mobility disabilities, mental differences, speech differences, sensory disabilities, or intellectual disabilities. This sensibility, in addition to accessibility and accommodation awareness, reflects the efforts to challenge identity-centered epistemology and to develop interdisability consciousness. The tension between identity-based representation and attempts to transcend the boundaries of identity politics through sensibility provides both opportunities and challenges, raising questions about privilege and power dynamics among people with different bodies and resources. WDE used to have a rule that a majority of executive members should be women with what is called "severe" disability to ensure that it would be an organization led by disabled women, not just an organization for disabled women. The shared sensibility of the experiences of disability, Kang asserts, is generated organically by sharing time in everyday relationships in which individuals invest in each other's lives. Kang explains that the workload and the administrative culture of the organization have made it more difficult to undertake in-depth discussions about differences and that fewer disabled women politically identify as "disabled women," instead seeing themselves as "disabled persons" with specific difficulties that are associated with their gender. Because some workers come to WDE lacking experience of disabilities or familiarity with disability culture, educating them about this sensibility has been necessary, although it can be hard to acquire through a formal curriculum. Despite these difficulties and changes over time, the political activism of disabled women has been challenging the ableist and heterosexist structure of society, providing educations to women with disabilities, and influencing the ways of reading and producing historical and cultural representations of disability and gender, as it provides the space for voicing disabled women's perspectives about how realities are shaped by images interacting with discursive and public understandings of their everyday lives.

Coalitions between various human rights movements and the disabled women's movement have also been forming. In addition, new coalitions based on the alliance of nonnormative families or the movement toward depathologizing asexuality, chronic illness, transgender status, sexual minority status, and HIV/AIDS status have been glimpsed. At the same time, awareness of the needs for an alliance with sexual minorities, laborers, and refugees has increased, and some links have been made as well with organizations for women in the sex industry. The agendas and conversations within these progressive antiviolence, anti-ableist movements and transient communities inform my engagements with texts and historical contexts, as one of the aims of this book is to articulate how the various thresholds of normality—including nondisability, gender conformity, family, and sexuality—constitute and complicate any notion of cure.

Beside these movements and voices, *Curative Violence* closely examines what happens around the necessity of cure, and it conceptualizes cure as a process through which the complicated moral relations between normality and the otherness of disability are produced and reconfigured. To imagine the linkages between various representations that form the repertoire of how different bodies are perceived requires paying genealogical attention to how the present is constituted. In this sense, "Genealogy is a history of events, here understood as discrete, disparate, often randomly connected material conjunctions of things or processes."[68] By unfolding contemporary discourses and tracing them back to prior representations and vice versa, I tease out shifts, resistances, or lineages across persistent images of bodies made aberrant and problematic; explicate the danger that disabled bodies continue to face under the imperative of cure; and glimpse new interpretive and imaginative possibilities that make life livable.

Through the interplays between discursive/audiovisual texts and social contexts, representation constitutes an active process of selecting, delivering, and creating material realities. This meaning-making process shapes experiences, which in turn produce representations. Complex understandings of power dynamics can be revealed when literary and visual representations are read *along* and *within* the social and political contexts identified by examining multiple archives, including newspapers, official documents, policy statements, and activist literature. Rather than evaluating whether we should reject cure or embrace it on the basis of positive or negative consequences of cure in chosen texts or whether the reality in a given time is accurately reflected or misrepresented,[69] I move in and out of representations of realities and fictional narratives, using analysis to construct connections among texts, interpretations, politics, and historical events.[70] Trinh T. Minh-ha's meditation on narrative as a form of political intervention usefully illustrates the importance of *unfolding* time—that is, of imagining the time in between the past and the future—and of claiming presence: "We can rely on the story to tell us not only what might have happened, but also what is happening at an unspecified time and place."[71] Here Minh-ha points out that literature itself is produced by the imagination of the specific historical moment in which it is immersed. Together with discourses, fictions account for the understandings of and possibilities within social realities by communicating with material and immaterial experiences.

Throughout this book, I use specific designations of disability such as blindness, muteness (or speechlessness), deafness, the names of particular impairments, or medical terms for illness to discuss specific communities and their histories. As the term *pyŏngsin* (sick body) became increasingly pejorative and was used to demean or mock certain groups, thereby projecting (and reinforcing) the moral judgment associated with unhealthiness, *pulguja* (presumed to have originated from Japanese) emerged in the early twentieth century as a term for people with disabilities, especially (but not exclusively) those with acquired physical disabilities.[72] In South Korea, the eugenic phrase *simsin miyakcha* (people with feeble mind and body) appeared in laws around the 1960s to broadly refer to people with physical and mental disabilities in addition to those who were deaf, mute, or blind. The Sino-Korean word *changae* has been translated as (and used to translate) "handicap," "disability," "disorder," or "impairments." *Changae* means hindrance, difficulties, or suffering, without any specific reference to ability. Its converse leans toward the notion of normalcy (*chŏngsangsŏng*) or nondisability (*pijangae*), rather than able-bodiedness. "Disability" (*changae*) in this book refers broadly to disparaged and inferiorized bodily characteristics, illnesses, and other differences that are considered aberrant, which includes deviations from historically and culturally specific norms of ethno-racial and gendered personhood in a given historical and cultural context. *Changhaeja* (a person with a burdensome damage) and *changaeja* (a person with *changae*) were replaced by *changaein* (a person with *changae*), today commonly used in both legal and other contexts for people with various disabilities.

Like "cure," in this book "disability" often is a term more theoretical and political than literal, medical, historical, or legal, used to reveal how certain bodily characteristics are broadly problematized. I use "body" (*mom*) not to put it in a dualist relationship with "mind" (*chŏngsin*) but to name an organism, a matter, and a presence that occupies a place and time and is simultaneously physical, mental, affective, emitting, and relational, to distance myself from the ableist determination of personhood. It is easy to picture only physical, mobility-related, sensory, and other visible differences when the body is mentioned, rather than mental and cognitive disabilities, chronic illnesses, and behavioral differences that are not immediately apparent.[73] Nevertheless, I rely on the term "body" to encompass those differences in exploring how various disabilities are situated in relation to abstract notions of "complete" humanity, normalcy, nondisability, and healthiness. To refer to a privileged position without markers of aberrancy, I interchangeably use "nondisability" (*pijangae*), "normative status," "normality," and at times "enabled" or "normalized bodies" (*chŏngsanghwa toen mom*), as to seek cure is to become enabled and gain access to this systemic investment.

Curing the Disabled Spinster:
Gender and Cure in the Premodern Context

Before I enter the time frame of the book, the late colonial period onward, it might be helpful to explore how disability was perceived in relation to gender and sexuality in the premodern context, as colonial modernity is often thought to have demolished the traditional holistic ways of understanding disabilities. From the late fourteenth century to the end of the nineteenth century, the Chosŏn dynasty governed the Korean Peninsula according to neo-Confucianism principles, and people with physical, cognitive, mental, and communicative differences were sorted into three categories (ordered from most to least significant differences): *tokchil, p'yejil*, and *chanjil*.[74] People with disabilities were broadly referred to as *pyŏngsin* (a sick body), with *pyŏngin* or *pyŏngja* (a sick person) used as an overall term. "The sick body" was used for disability and illness alike. At the same time, in the premodern and early modern periods, individual terms were applied to persons with specific physical and mental characteristics, such as *chŏllŭmbari* (a person with a limp); *anjŭnbaengi* (a person who cannot walk); *nanjangi* (a person of short stature); *changnim, sogyŏng, ch'ambong*, or *pongsa* (a blind person); *pŏngŏri* (a mute person); *kwimŏgŏri* (a deaf person); *kopch'u* (a person with a humpback); *kombaep'ari* (a person with one arm shorter than the other); *ŏnch'ŏngi* (a person with a cleft palate); *mundungi* (a person with skin disease or leprosy); *pabo, chŏnch'i*, or *mŏjŏri* (a person with cognitive disability); and *kwangin* (a mad person).[75]

The degree of humanity possessed was inferred from health and disability status. Neo-Confucianism largely constructed the body as a manifestation of moral quality and put forward a notion of "incomplete human beings" (*pulsŏngin*)[76] that was opposed to *sŏngin* (complete, moral persons; adults), thereby hierarchizing bodily differences. This idea of incomplete humanity is also implied in the colloquial term *pantchogi* (a half person), which refers to a person with a disability. A contrary term, *ssŏngssŏngi* (or *sŏnghan saram*, a healthy person), has been used in contemporary disability communities to describe physically nondisabled persons.

Noting that distinguishing features of femininity and masculinity have changed over time, Korean scholars have explored whether categories of disability connected with gender and sexuality were different during the Chosŏn dynasty. In addition to conventional categories of disabilities based on physical, sensory, mental, and cognitive differences—which were organized under a single term, the *pyŏngsin*—intersexed persons, eunuchs, castrated men, homosexual persons, impotent men, conjoined children, and children born with albinism appear in the royal records either as needing protection or as "bizarre" and "ominous."[77] Proper personhood is perceived to be grounded in the two genders, and as a consequence "living up to a human's role" (*saram kusil ŭl hada*) has become a gendered moral judgment in Korean culture.

One example of how the view of gender as binary constructed the individual with intersexual difference as "a sick person" appears in *The Annals of the Chosŏn Dynasty* in 1462. A house slave, Sabangji, who lived as a woman, allegedly had an affair with a widow, the daughter of a high official. This extramarital affair was brought to the attention of the Royal Secretariat. Those conducting the physical examination concluded that Sabangji had both sexes, and officials called for an investigation of her sexual relations. King Sejo intervened with the message that "Sabangji is a sick person [*pyŏngja*], so do not interrogate."[78] Although Confucian officials petitioned repeatedly for permission to interrogate Sabangji, Sejo denied it to protect the widow's family honor. Five years later, Sabangji's continued sexual affair was again brought to Sejo's attention. Royal officials informed Sejo that similar cases were recorded in a Chinese text, and they explained to him that the moral principle of the universe is *yang* and *yin*, which translates to man and woman; thus this person who was neither a man nor a woman was not to be forgiven. Persuaded by this reasoning, Sejo redefined Sabangji as "not of the human species" and ruled that she should be expelled to a faraway place so that she would not be in contact with other people.[79] Given that Sejo, who was a Buddhist, was under pressure from Confucian scholars to enforce moral standards, I can speculate that several factors contributed to Sabangji's transformation from a sick person to a nonhuman: first, the philosophical explanation of binary sexes as a reflection of natural law; second, the perceived subversion of Sabangji's continued involvement with women for whom sexual relations were forbidden, such as monks and widows; and third, the existence of similar people elsewhere, which demonstrated that Sabangji's case was not an isolated personal "misfortune." In addition, Sejo and other scholarly officials understood that intersexed people (*yangsŏngin*) were considered as omens presaging crisis or war.[80] This brief example illustrates how neo-Confucian natural law enforced the rules of heterosexuality and the two-gender system on which the category of humanness was based. The concept of incomplete humanness, connected to the category of illness, could easily fall into nonhumanness (*piillyu*) when combined with gender and sexual transgression, thereby providing grounds for denying individuals a place in society.

In "The Gaze toward Disabled People: In Premodern Literature," Park Hee Byoung traces the usage of *pyŏngsin* in the premodern period and argues that though it was first employed as a neutral description, in the mid- to late eighteenth century it became a colloquial pejorative for "inferior" persons. This term was often applied to the corrupt *yangban* (elite class) while images of healthy bodies and morality helped support the growing power of the masses.[81] According to Park, in the late nineteenth century, *pyŏngsin* began to be associated with the internalized sense of inferiority of the colonized citizenry, the symbol of the old customs, and the defective nation-state without sovereignty that needed to be reformed in order to become a strong independent nation.

To show that the premodern perception of disability, though hardly monolithic, was different from the modern conception of disability as explicitly negative, Park introduces Sino-Korean poetry written by Korean writers, including Pak Chi-wŏn, who describe disability as a relative human difference. Another example of disability consciousness is "A Spinster's Song" ("Nochŏnyŏga"), which Park closely analyzes. This premodern narrative captures how disability cure works with gender roles, heterosexual experiences, and reproduction. Composed in *kasa*, the traditional poetic prose written in Korean, it consists of a narrator's preface, the spinster's soliloquy, and the narrator's epilogue. An anonymous narrator introduces the story to readers and introduces the disabled spinster in her fifties, described as *kajŭn pyŏngsin* (a body that is sick in multiple ways), who agonizes about being a virgin and unmarried: "I don't know what marriage is like, what the taste of husband is like, and if it is bitter or sweet; I'm distressed whenever I think about that."[82] She longs for "the taste of husband," *sŏbangmat*, expressing her desire for heterosexual marriage. Later, she claims that she is not unlike other women and lists her functional capacities in detail. The spinster's emphasis on her abilities reveals and counters the existing prejudice against disabled women and the view that they are disqualified from marriage.

> Even though I am disabled, what can't I do like others. . . . Even though one eye is blind, the other eye can see well. . . . [People] blame me for being deaf; I can hear if spoken loudly to and hear the sound of thunder fine. I eat with my right hand; what is the need for the left hand? My left leg is crippled, but I can use the toilet fine. My nostrils are blocked, but I can smell easily. . . . Large buttocks would rather make me give birth easily.[83]

In addition, she lists her intelligence, demeanor, literacy, and knowledge of feminine virtues as well as her ability to control her body (including not passing gas in public), her hygienic practices in the kitchen, and her skills at sewing and cooking—all qualities that define "a good woman." She then asks why she cannot get married and laments, "How can I not be sad? I alone can't marry when all other women are married and have husbands." In her narrative, her ultimate problem is not with her body but her status as unmarried, especially since being married is crucial for adult women's domestic life and social acceptance. Frustrated by her family's disinterest in finding her a husband, though most marriages were arranged between families, she lists the candidates in the village and picks one name at random. Then she falls asleep and dreams of a beautiful wedding. After waking up with a sense of deep anxiety, she cannot wait any longer to get married. She creates a life-size groom by clothing a wooden stick, which she then uses to perform her wedding. Struck by her sorrow and by her desperation in marrying an object, her family successfully finds a groom—coincidentally, the man she had picked—and arranges the marriage.

Park argues that "Spinster's Song" confirms the presence of counternarratives to the othering of disabled women in the Chosŏn dynasty. Yet the self-affirmation of the spinster also reveals how central feminine virtues and functional capacities are to her marriageability and shows that heterosexuality and reproduction constitute able-genderedness interlocked with gendered able-bodiedness. The story reinforces the link between disability and singleness, for she is cured after consummating her marriage. The spinster is surprised to find that she can move her arm and is no longer deaf. Subsequently she is overjoyed to give birth to twin sons who display "unusual intelligence and beauty." Family fortune and honor follow. The narrator concludes that this story is "amusing and wondrous."

Her cure, as the narrative chronicles her change from a disabled spinster to a nondisabled mother, requires further investigation. In the earlier tradition, the cure of disability shores up religious power. Here, in contrast, the spinster's transformation is framed in relation to her sexuality and the psychosomatic change that sexual relations promise. Traditional Korean medicine emphasizes the healing power of sexual activities, which supposedly strengthen the spirit and circulate positive energy. Marriage and heterosexual experience along with able-genderedness serve as the cultural cure of disability, physically transforming the spinster's body and ultimately leading her to reproduce "beautiful and smart twin sons." That sexual experience is a force curing disability in turn reveals the understanding that disability is intertwined with desexualization. At the same time, the spinster's refusal of low expectations and exclusion suggests that disability indeed functioned as a marker of disqualification from marriage. "Spinster's Song" illustrates the premodern perception of disability, which was intermixed with negative expectations tied to exclusion from marriage and affirmation of agency and its potential to effect changes. I want to propose yet another interpretation of the spinster's transition from disability to normality through able-genderedness. In this case, her "cure" is possible without any change in her body. As she shifts toward becoming a valued wife, disability loses its defining role in her life; the subversive commentary on the disabled embodiment of personhood is incorporated into normative feminine fulfillment housed in marriage.

When the attitudes toward disabled people in premodern Chosŏn are compared to those in modern society, it is difficult to simply posit the premodern as more accepting of disabilities and the modern as introducing negative attitudes toward disabled people. Rather, Sabangji's case and "Spinster's Song" illustrate the existence of exclusionary systems that disqualified individuals from sexual relations and the system of domestic belonging, while also revealing individual resistance and cultural room for exceptions (as appeared in the spinster's arranged marriage). The meanings and conditions of disability have been multiple, and they inevitably challenge its restriction to physical and sensory impairments, mental illness, and cognitive impairments and also exist beyond the binarism of acceptance and rejection.

Constructing the Disabled Others in the Disabled Nation

Japanese imperialism stuck a knife in old Korea and twisted it, and that wound has gnawed at the Korean national identity ever since.
—BRUCE CUMINGS, *Korea's Place in the Sun*

In this section, I briefly document the key moments in Korean history relevant to this book. These moments will appear in chapters that are organized thematically rather than chronologically. Despite the brevity of this description, it aims to offer a sense of how disability was simultaneously constructed with gender and otherness at specific times.

At the end of the nineteenth century, the Chosŏn dynasty was under considerable pressure to change—pressure arising internally from the peasants' uprisings, the shifting economy, and the spread of Catholicism as well as externally from the Euro-American imperial expansion toward East Asia and from developments in Japan, China, and Russia. Chosŏn started its diplomatic relations by signing treaties with Japan in 1876 and soon after with many other Western countries. In 1897, Kojong proclaimed the beginning of the Taehan Empire in order to implement domestic reforms and to build a modern independent state by insisting on equal diplomatic relations with the imperial powers. His attempt to maintain monarchy, sovereignty, and neutrality was short-lived, however, for Japan's victory in the Russo-Japanese War (1904–1905) greatly increased its power in the region. In 1905, the Ŭlsa Treaty transferred Korean diplomatic representation to Japan, leading to full annexation by Japan in 1910. Bruce Cumings identifies this process of undergoing colonization with becoming disabled: "Korea was Oedipus, blinded by Japan's swiftly rising glitter."[84] In this poignant metaphor of disability, colonized Korea is a man who was not only blinded by Japan's shimmer, but also self-blinded as a moral punishment for ignorance about the imperial power. Using another metaphor, quoted in the epigraph, Cumings describes the Korean body being stabbed by Japanese imperialism and suffering a wound that does not heal.[85] In her influential essay on this tendency in literature during the colonial period, Kyeong-Hee Choi notes, "The nation in crisis is likened to a body impaired by sickness."[86] The metaphorical use of disability as a vehicle to represent the violence in national history in effect ties the meaning of disability to the condition of victimization and, in the process, obscures actual violence against disabled bodies within the nation. Some Korean authors sought to use the experience of disablement to represent the social injustice of the capitalism and colonialism imposed on the Korean people. For example, poverty, malnutrition, depletion of local resources, lack of proper medical care, labor conscription, and industrial accidents under Japanese occupation are powerfully illustrated through images of mutilated bodies.[87] In preparing for the 1929 Chosŏn Exposition, which was designed to showcase modern development under Japanese rule, the police arrested and expelled beggars, including homeless disabled people, from downtown Seoul.[88]

Han Man-Soo associates the frequent appearance of blindness in literary texts in the 1930s with the increased use of the term *munmaeng* (textual blindness) to refer to illiteracy. The movement toward the modern sought to improve literacy rates, and the disability metaphor embedded in illiteracy reflected the assumption that the transition from oral tradition to textual culture was a condition of enlightenment.[89] The movement to "eradicate textual blindness" (*munmaeng t'ap'a*) blamed the illiterate public for the loss of sovereignty.[90] Blind people were also associated with superstition, as their traditional role was to engage in fortune-telling—which itself became the target of eradication. From these connections between coloniality and disability emerges the idea of the disabled nation as a cause and result of colonization. The notion of a disabled nation invokes the anticolonial desire for a "return" to a normal, healthy, independent, masculine, patriarchal, and monoracial state.

In order to overcome colonialism, South Koreans, then, must reclaim their proper identity by achieving normalcy and healthiness. This sense of longing is driven by the personal and collective desire for wholeness, or for the idealized, unimpaired body.[91]

As disabled bodies were used to depict Koreans' collective self-image under colonial rule, disability emerged as a social and economic product rather than an individual quality;[92] but the national sense of being disabled did not lead to attention to those living with disabilities or prevent the public from othering disabled people. Rather, it emphasized the national need for disabled people to be controlled so that the national character could be improved. Eugenic discourses—urging that "people with inferior traits" (*pullyang punja*) and the disabled (*pulguja*) must be sterilized and segregated—emerged in the media in the 1930s.

The varied treatment of people with disabilities during the colonial era shows that there was no single paradigm according to which all sorts of disabilities were perceived as products of social conditions. Lee Bang Hyun explains that in traditional society, people with mental disabilities were not removed from their families and that the institutionalization of people with mental illness began during the colonial era.[93] A number of different practices intended to cure mental illness seem to have coexisted during the colonial era, and their processes and outcomes were often violent. Traditional Korean medicine considered mental illness to be caused by weakened organs, by blocked energy flow, or by anger; traditional doctors prescribed herbal medicines. People with traditional religious beliefs thought that mental illnesses were the result of possession by ghosts. Records show that shamans, blind prognosticators, or fortune-tellers attempted curative exorcisms by beating, hanging, or starving affected persons.[94] The colonial regime framed many of these methods as superstitious, barbaric, and inhumane, and it prohibited shamans' activities; it focused on distributing "new" knowledge about how curing mental illness that focused on heredity and social and environmental causes.[95] Lee also found newspaper reports about the Christian practices of curing mental illness through prayers invoking holy spirits and through the exorcism of evil, which also involved beatings. As people with mental illness were described as dangerous and violent, eugenic ideas were promoted by educated Korean elites and Japanese public health officials, who sought to bar people with mental illness from reproducing and who emphasized the need for their sterilization and special protection. At the same time, lacking resources for mass institutionalization, the colonial law of 1912 made families responsible for supervising people with mental illness and fined them when the patients were found on the street. As a result, disabled people were locked up in their homes; there were reports that they sometimes died in house fires, unable to escape.[96]

The colonial Government General established Chesaengwŏn (the Relief Aid Center) to house and to educate orphans and children who are blind, are deaf, or have a mental disability or illness. In 1911, Government General Hospital's internal medicine department treated 1,276 people with mental illness, and the size of the mental ward gradually expanded.[97] The Government General counted 2,498 people in Chosŏn with mental illness in 1926 and 3,013 in 1937, and at least 14 percent of them were described as "dangerous" and needing to be institutionalized.[98] The medical institutionalization policy also targeted people with Hansen's disease (leprosy), and thus Sorokto Chahye Ŭiwŏn (Mercy Clinic) was established in Sorokto in 1916 (see chapter 4).

The unconditional surrender of Japan to the Allied Forces in 1945 brought about Chosŏn's liberation, followed by the occupation of the South by the United States and the North by the Soviet Union. The division was solidified when Syngman Rhee was elected as the first president of a separate South Korea in 1948. The Korean War broke out in 1950, causing large-scale disablement and casualties. The label "disabled" was broadly applied to minority groups, viewed as vulnerable because of a range of conditions, who were subjected to control or protection after the Korean War. The varying conceptions and scopes of disability, along with the often underappreciated racial, cultural, and ethnic heterogeneity of South Korean society, make it impossible for "Korean disabled people" and "Korean disabled women" to be treated as a homogeneous group with fixed status and characteristics. In 1954, the South Korean Ministry of Health and Social Affairs started publishing annual statistical reports on vulnerable populations. The first report included "leprosy patients, mixed-blood children [honhyŏra],[99] widows, drug addicts, patients with infectious diseases, and prostitutes." A year later two new categories—people with disabilities and disabled veterans—were added to the list. In 1961, the first nationwide census of "handicapped" children included "children of mixed racial parentage" alongside children with various physical and sensory impairments.[100]

Rhee's presidency was marked by political repression and corruption from its start until his resignation in 1960, after the April 19 Revolution. A year later, Park Chung Hee took power through a coup d'état, beginning a presidency that lasted until his assassination in 1979. In 1964, Korean troops were deployed to Vietnam for the first time at the request of the United States, and one result was the production of war films featuring disabled veterans. The re-habilitation of these veterans was tied to images of national economic growth and industrial development (see chapter 2). During Park's military regime, the idea of modern eugenics popularized during the colonial era returned with new vigor, bolstered by the aspiration to establish a strong and able nation. Right after Park declared martial law and put the Yushin system in place, so-lidifying his dictatorial power, the Mother and Child Health Act was enacted in 1973. The law justified reproductive control by an appeal to eugenics, while continuing to criminalize abortion itself. It not only stipulated the potential parents' "eugenic or hereditary mental disability or physical illness" as one of the exceptional conditions that would permit abortion but also allowed the involuntary sterilization of people with disabilities (see chapter 1).

After Park's assassination, another military general, Chun Doo Hwan, seized control first of the military and eventually of key governmental institu-tions. He then declared martial law, which in May 1980 provoked nationwide protests and demands for democracy. Chun framed the uprising in Kwangju as a threat from North Korea and used military forces, resulting in mass ca-sualties and disappearances. Estimates of fatalities range from one thousand to two thousand.[101] (So far the commission set up to compensate victims and their families has confirmed around five thousand cases, including individuals injured, killed, or disappeared.[102])

Chun Doo Hwan's regime used the rhetoric of the welfare state to cover up its violent origin. In 1981, the Welfare of People with Disabilities Act was enacted. In the early 1980s, major associations devoted to specific disabilities were formed, including associations of people who are deaf, blind, and physi-cally disabled. Koreans with disabilities also joined Disabled Peoples' Interna-tional. The International Year of Disabled Persons in 1981, together with the declaration of disabled people's human rights and the principles of antidis-crimination, helped fuel an emerging disability movement in South Korea.[103] The human rights of disabled people became its dominant theme. Motivated by the democratization movement, various disability groups, such as the Na-tional Union of Physically Disabled Students, became politically active, fo-cusing their efforts on the presidential election of 1987. In April 1988, disabled people held a public protest in front of the Myŏngdong Catholic Church to urge a boycott of the Seoul Paralympics, because such an international show-case would help the government conceal the severe rights violations and ex-treme poverty experienced by disabled people in their everyday lives.

The disability organizations shared two goals: to amend the welfare law to enhance the social status of people with disabilities, and to enact new legislation to promote employment, special education, and affirmative action in higher education. Activists often viewed disability oppression mainly as a class issue and poverty within capitalism, which considers disabled bodies as unproductive. The disability movement celebrated the passage of the Promotion of Employment of Disabled Persons Act in 1990, which requires eligible work places to meet a 2 percent quota. The Act on the Promotion of Convenience for the Disabled, Senior Citizens, and Pregnant Women was enacted in 1998. The 2000 and 2003 amendments of the regulations for the Welfare of People with Disabilities Act added chronic illnesses to expand the categories of disability to fifteen: physical disability; cerebral impairment; visual impairment; hearing impairment; language disability; intellectual disability; autism; mental disability; kidney, heart, lung, and liver impairments; facial disability; gastrointestinal and urinary impairment; and seizure disability. These specific categorizations of disability based on medical diagnoses continue to limit social assistance and antidiscrimination protection for individuals with various differences including HIV/AIDS status, although efforts are being made to include HIV/AIDS in disability categories. In 2008, the Anti-discrimination against and Remedies for Persons with Disabilities Act was enacted. However, the law is seen as having limited effect in substantially changing the situation of disabled women and children and in supporting disabled people's self-determination. Most cases filed under this law have not been successfully resolved, as the Committee of the Rights of Persons with Disability at the United Nations has noted.[104]

The government created a national registration system for people with disabilities in 1988, and the number of those registered has been increasing. In 2011, the estimated rate of registration rose to 93.8 percent, and disabled people totaled about 5.61 percent of the population. The fifteen categories of disabilities each have three or six ratings, according to the degree of limitation and impairment. In 2000 there were 51,319 people with disabilities living in a variety of institutions (not just for disabled people but also for children, homeless people, women, and elderly people), and in 2011 the number went up to 72,351.[105] Although the deinstitutionalization movement continues to expose corruption and abuses in residential institutions, the number of institutions for disabled people has significantly increased, going from 237 in 2004 to 1,397 in 2014.[106] After activists in the first decade of the century succeeded in gaining some provision of accessible transportation and personal assistance, the disability movement is now focusing on the elimination of the rating system and recertification processes, which rely entirely on medical examinations to determine a person's degree of disability. The system makes medical professionals the arbiters who allocate resources, such as pensions, paratransit use, rehabilitation services, and personal assistance, without taking into account the various kinds of disability and individual needs. For example, a woman with a physical disability was rated as having a first-degree (most significant) disability, which was later downgraded in recertification to a fourth-degree disability: as a result, she lost state-funded personal assistant services, her disability pension, and her eligibility to use paratransit, making it impossible for her to attend college classes.[107]

The launch of the National Human Rights Commission (NHRC) of Korea in 2001 under Kim Dae Jung's administration has been an important catalyst for individuals with disabilities, who can now file complaints about human rights violations without necessarily filing a lawsuit based on discrimination claims. Although the commission's decisions are not legally binding, its recommendations have been made public and have had some impact (in 2009, under President Lee, the commission's autonomy was reduced). The NHRC has funded the production of films to promote a broadened understanding of human rights that includes minority rights. The first in the film series, *If You Were Me* (2003), features a short segment based on a true story that illustrates both the intersection of disability and ethnicity in the context of an immigrant laborer's human rights and the problem of involuntary institutionalization. A nondisabled Nepalese woman worker who did not speak Korean was arrested for failing to pay for her meal at a restaurant. Considered a Korean woman with disability, she was sent to a mental hospital, where she was diagnosed with "depression," "schizophrenia," and "mental retardation"; she was confined for six years and four months in several institutions. The film focuses on the disability identification of a nondisabled immigrant worker as a horrendous violation of the human rights of immigrant workers, but while doing so, it obscures a state-sanctioned, less-visible violation of civil rights by involuntary institutionalizations that remove sex workers and disabled people from the public and domestic spaces.[108] This provides an example of the limitation of singular identity based human rights approach, which requires a significant transformation to create coalitional and intersectional spaces. Critical approaches to disability have emerged to illuminate social discrimination in volumes such as *I Want to Be a Bad Disabled Person* (2002), which challenges the roles of health and normalcy in Korean society. The book problematizes the institutionalization and confronts the myth that people with disabilities possess a kind of innocence because of their isolation from society. It also examines mental disability and the importance of gender and feminism within disability studies and movements.

The sense of disablement of the nation's body continued after the colonial era, while the bodies of individuals with disabilities were inscribed with meanings of inferiority and vulnerability. They were also assigned with the obligation of cure and rehabilitation. After the country's democratization, literary and filmic representations of disability began to focus instead on individual stories of specific disabilities, such as autism, intellectual disability, cerebral palsy, Alzheimer's disease, and deafness, with the goal of raising awareness about the minority experiences rather than serving as political trope. The film scholar Kyung Hyun Kim points out, "Recent cinema in South Korea has produced subjects that extend far beyond standard models of semiotics or Cold War political allegories."[109] Films such as *Oasis* (2002) and *Secret Sunshine* (2007), according to Kim, "continue to exploit the subject of trauma," but "they have successfully moved their subjects away from being allegories of the nation's trauma" into "one that has been privatized."[110] The image of the nationalized sense of disability, while obscuring the oppression of disabled people and othering, shifted to representations of individual disabilities as conditions of vulnerability and violence. However, attending to disability's political presence in these seemingly "privatized" individual narratives of trauma might reveal the larger structural conditions that create different embodiments and construct otherness. Beyond being privatized stories, they shed light on minoritized communities with shared histories and experiences shaped by political and social contexts, demanding specific kinds of recognition and social transformation.

Overview of This Book

In the following chapters, the workings of curative violence appear in cultural representations of eugenics, reproductive control, human sacrifice, suicide, rape, murder, medical isolation, and humanitarian aid as they interact with historical and political shifts. Against these formulations, the book grounds its analysis in the political and economic backgrounds and cultural movements of women with disabilities who advocate for livable lives free of violence.

Chapter 1, "Unmothering Disability," focuses on the ways in which, in modern Korean culture, reproduction has become a major site of intervention for "curing" inherited disability. First, I explore the emergence of a "heredity drama" that exploits the emotions around the revelation of the inheritance of disability, linking this literary drama to the history of the colonial eugenics movement of the 1930s. Second, I investigate how heredity has been invoked as a moral justification for rejecting marriage to a person with disabilities and explore the connection between such justification and the legalization of eugenics in the 1970s. Third, I examine the representation of preimplantation genetic screening in the new millennium. The major texts discussed in the chapter are three short stories, "The Ugly Creature" (1936), "The Kangaroo's Ancestor" (1939), and "A Mountain Valley" (1941); the prominent filmmaker Sin Sang-ok's film about a deaf couple and their hearing son, *The Evening Bell* (1970); a contemporary independent documentary, *Pansy and Ivy* (2000); and finally the three-part television documentary *Thumbelina Wants to Be a Mother* (2007, 2008, 2009). The chapter argues that placing responsibility on mothers not to reproduce disabled children has a history and that the mobilization of biopolitics based on the presumed desire for disability's absence often relies on disability's continued presence at the margins of society to keep reinforcing "undesirability."

Chapter 2, "Cure by Proxy," opens with a discussion of the 1937 film *Sim Chŏng*, which represented filial piety as a uniquely Korean virtue. It tells the story of a daughter who sells herself to sailors as a human offering to the marine deity in order to pay for the Buddhist cure for her father's blindness. I explore the relational and interdependent aspects of cure and familial attempts at extraordinary achievement to supposedly compensate for the presence of disability. I chart the multiple ways in which the cures for disability are presented as miracles made possible by the efforts of an able-bodied family member. I call this person a "proxy" for the cure—someone who is motivated to perform extraordinary tasks for the sake of cure accompanied by supernatural, religious, and moral rewards, including reincarnation, class elevation, and social recognition. Curative dependency created by the familial bind and the desire to sacrifice one's life in seeking a family member's cure are examined in a number of films and literary works: *Sim Chŏng* (1937), *Dutiful Daughter Chŏng* (1972), *The Story of Ongnye* (1977), and *Mother Star in Heaven* (1987)—all of which are based on the story of Sim Chŏng—as well as *Sergeant Kim's Return from Vietnam* (1971), and *Yŏngja's Heydays* (1975), which feature Korean War and Vietnam War veterans. Finally, I discuss *A Tale of Two Sisters* (2003), based on a folktale about a murderous stepmother and two daughters, which creates the patriarchal family as a site of trauma and horror in contrast to the intimate dyad of mother and autistic son in *Marathon* (2005), which emphasizes the mother's effort for her son.

Chapter 3, "Violence as a Way of Loving," addresses the direct link between violence and the discourse of cure—a link based on the condemnation of disabled women for failing to fulfill gender and sexual expectations in the making of the normality-centered, modern, capitalist nation-state. I place the work of activists who address the criminal justice system's failure to recognize the severity of violence against disabled women alongside the curative and violent processes through which certain individuals with disabilities are reincorporated into society. Using literary texts and films, I explore four themes that emerge as a result of the imperative for disabled people to perform normative femininity and masculinity as well as humanity: sexual violence justified to enable "traditional" femininity to return to the past (*The Song of Songs* [2000]), violence as a naturalized response to traditional femininity and its vulnerability ("Adada, the Idiot" [1935], *Adada* [1987]), violence as the price for the transnational purchase of cure and sexual transgression (*Address Unknown* [2001]), and violence as a way to heal the trauma of a nation and as a punishment for incurability ("There a Petal Silently Falls" [1988], *A Petal* [1996]).

Chapter 4, "Uninhabiting Family," takes the case of Hansen's disease (leprosy), which is regularly situated in the past. I examine how the contemporary emphasis on its curability and low transmissibility ironically maintains the stigma associated with the disease to this day. I extend the political aspects of the disease's cure to its cultural history. This chapter first explores the process of removing sick bodies from domestic space during the colonial era (in "The Rock" and "Oksimi," both published in 1936). Second, it examines technology and the benevolence of medical intervention provided in an American-run institution during the Cold War as a gateway into a heterosexual union (*The Litany of Hope* [1962]). Third, it investigates the marriage between a former male patient and an uninfected woman as a symbol of the political healing of historical trauma and of the integration of two separate worlds (*Your Paradise* [1976]). Fourth, it interrogates marriage between former male patients and female medical professionals employed as a sign of cultural rehabilitation the decisive evidence of cured status (*Ah! Sorokto* [2002]). I argue that a more comprehensive understanding of the cultural and social elements of the stigmatization of Hansen's disease, and of its historical interconnections with other disabilities and illnesses, is required before we can begin to discuss the ethical and practical limits of public health measures that discount livable conditions of life without violence.

The final chapter, "Curing Virginity," focuses on the contemporary discourse of disabled people's sexuality as a biological problem that needs an immediate solution. Dealing with the most recent phenomena, the chapter examines the emerging public discourse on the "sex drive" of disabled people, largely focusing on men with physical disability, commercial sex services, and humanitarian rhetoric. It analyzes the films *Pink Palace* (2005) and *Sex Volunteer: Open Secret, the First Story* (2009); the contents of and the reactions to the Korean translation of Kawai Kaori's book *Sex Volunteers* (2005); and the situation of an incestuous rape presented as a cure for a disabled girl's self-harming behavior, supposedly caused by her sex drive, as imagined in the short film *Papa* (2004). The notions of a necessary "release" (*haeso*) and of the charitable gift or humanitarian offering of sexual services in the practice of "sex volunteering" simplistically equate sexual oppression with lack of a sexual outlet.

In the conclusion, "How to Inhabit the Time Machine with Disability," I return to the notion of folding time and discuss how the present continues to disappear through the imperative of cure, habilitation, and rehabilitation. By thinking about the imperative of cure as a time machine that seeks to take us to the past and to the future, I explore the possibility of inhabiting in the present with disability and illness. I also discuss the traps that often appear when discussing non-Western societies in Western academic contexts, denying coevalness or universalizing disability experiences across different cultural contexts. My hope is that the analyses can serve as an investigation of the ways in which we can rethink cure, not as unequivocally beneficial and necessary nor limited to biomedical intervention, but as a set of political, moral, economic, emotional, and ambivalent transactions that occur in social relations. To rethink cure is to unfold the past, present, and future in order to recognize the presences of disabilities and to create spaces for them.

CHAPTER I

Unmothering Disability

An engraved illustration appeared in the newspaper *Tonga ilbo* in 1937 featuring a silhouette profile of a woman in Greek garb sitting on a modern-style chair with crossed legs, holding a mirror in one hand in front of her face and raising her other hand behind her head (see figure 1.1).[1] Above the figure was printed a word, *kajŏng*, "a familial household." The headline read, "Let's not choose a spouse under the dominance of temporary emotion. Know that your household will rise or fall based on whether or not you choose your spouse well." Starting from the problem of young men and women thinking about marriage as matters of their emotions and not reason, the article identified marriage as "an issue not of the two individuals, but of the prosperity of the next generation and the improvement of eugenic traits." As the figure of a modern woman could be misleading, the illustration implies, it would be necessary to examine her hereditary makeup. Exercising reason meant understanding marriage from a eugenic perspective: "A eugenically perfect marriage means that the meaningful marriage is finally achieved." "Surely, the question to consider," the article continued, "is how to select one's spouse, which means asking whether there are certain hereditary traits." The article urged readers to avoid any person associated with mental illness, syphilis, kleptomania, and alcoholism, "because these traits will certainly be passed down" to offspring, constructing certainty about the heredity of certain conditions. Although eugenic propaganda equated desirable physical appearance with good hereditary traits and encouraged "free love," this illustration suggests that because a woman's appearance could mask potential problems, further examination of her hereditary history was required, reflecting the anxiety about modern marriage based on love.

What shift in marriage and family motivated this admonition to investigate the heredity of a potential spouse in colonial Chosŏn? The newspaper article illustrates a trend that Jennifer Robertson also observed in Japan: the "ratio-

일시적감정의지배로
배우자선택은말자
배우자를잘고르고못고르는데
집안의흥망이잇슴을아십시오
庭 家
◆CHOW

1.1 An engraving of a woman sitting in profile looking at a hand mirror under a label, *kajŏng* (familial household). *Tonga ilbo*, October 8, 1937.

nalization of marriage," which became a key feature of a "eugenic modernity" dictating everyday practices on the basis of scientific information.[2] The rationalization in colonial Chosŏn aimed to counterbalance an emergent "emotionalization" of marriage that emphasized modern family life based on a chosen relationship of love, moving away from arranged marriages based on traditional considerations rooted in class. The newspaper article highlighted the individual sense of control for "success" in building a nuclear family household by choosing a spouse without any undesirable traits. This approach, brought about directly by the spread of eugenic information through the print media and lectures and broadly by the social movement toward the modernized life, seeking both the construction and the regulation of selfhood in the name of family, represented a departure from traditional marriage arranged through class-based negotiations.

Reproduction is an important site where curative intervention has been made. Through efforts to control reproductive outcomes in favor of the able-bodied, a particular version of the future—what Alison Kafer called "a future without disability"[3] emerges. However, the desire for disability's absence is not natural or constant; rather, that desire is constructed and reinforced in cultural representations interacting with the material, social, and colonial conditions. The result is specific kinds of dramas that construct and exploit emotional intensity around the reproduction of disabled persons. These dramas present naturalized suffering and maximized social consequences of reproducing a disabled baby to highlight the desire for nondisabled offspring to avoid social and gendered plights.

As discussions of policies and state actions interact with narratives, cultural texts shape desires and produce affects by representing tradition, modernity, and morality. In this chapter, I closely examine literary texts, political and legal discourses, transnational flow of information, cinema, television documentaries, and independently produced film to explore the ways in which reproduction has been framed against disability in modern Korean culture. I traverse three sites: (1) the "heredity drama" and eugenics movement of the 1930s; (2) heredity as moralized justification for rejecting disability and the resultant legal manifestation of eugenics in the 1970s, reproductive surrogacy, and the abortion debate; and (3) preimplantation genetic screening and marriage disqualification based on reproductive prospects in the first decade of the twenty-first century.

Curbing Love with Reason and the Heredity Drama

Eugenic ideas and methods to "fix" and "improve" the "essence" of race were introduced to colonial Chosŏn through Japanese adoption of British eugenics and by Korean elites who studied in Europe, Japan, and the United States during the colonial era. This transpacific and colonial introduction of eugenic ideology and methods, delivered with the powerful seal of civilization in the litany of Western states, heavily influenced how modernity in everyday life was imagined and made material in the peninsula, while conflicting with the traditional idea of procreation as natural instinct and duty. To promote the "enlightenment" of the Chosŏn people, reformers such as Yi Kap-su and Yun

Ch'i-ho seized the opportunity offered by colonial modernity—a modernity in which, as Gi-Wook Shin and Michael Robinson observe, "liberating forces and a raw, transformative power" complexly coexisted with "more nuanced forms of domination and repression in the colony."[4]

The Chosŏn Eugenics Association (Chosŏn Usaeng Hyŏphoe) was launched in 1933 by more than eighty people: medical doctors, educators, politicians, journalists, and Christian ministers who had studied in Japan, China, Germany, the United States, the United Kingdom, and Korea.[5] Yi Myŏng-hyŏk, a professor of medicine who studied at Columbia University, declared in the first issue of the association's annual magazine, *Usaeng* (Eugenics): "Seen from sociological perspective, the security of a nation and the peace of a family do not depend on the population's size but on its character and quality. If society has many deviant elements, such as murder, burglary, fraud, vagrancy, madness, obscenity, disability, they will be not only financially disadvantageous but also pose problems for maintaining public order and for development. . . . One of the solutions is the eugenics movement, which is to radically prevent those who are harmful to society, inferior, disabled by hereditary diseases from procreating."[6] The three issues of *Usaeng* contain information about eugenic practices overseas, including sterilization, translated as *tanjongpŏp* (the method of terminating seed), said to have been in place in the United States, Switzerland, Canada, Denmark, Germany, Mexico, Sweden, Norway, and Finland.[7] The magazine also appeased humanitarian concerns by differentiating eugenics from infanticide.

In the three issues, targets of intervention ranged from people with sexually transmitted diseases, leprosy (Hansen's disease), hemophilia, madness, idiocy, alcoholism, and tuberculosis to those who exhibited criminal behaviors. Articles covered the methods of strengthening Chosŏn ethnicity and health, information on blood types, the appropriate age for marriage, sex education, longevity, venereal diseases, Nazi practices, forced sterilization, and total isolation of disabled populations.[8] Yi argued for abolishing the tradition of arranged marriage, claiming that it caused much harm, including psychological pain and unhappiness. Instead he promoted "free marriage" (*chayu kyŏrhon*) based on love between equals who are superior specimens while suggesting that "people who are disabled, of poor quality and inferior," must avoid marriage and that, "if necessary, forcible isolation and sterilization need to be used."[9] In the effort to regulate marriages based on love, seen as risky, eugenics and the consideration of reproductive prospects emerged as conditions governing the voluntary selection of spouses. The hereditary characteristics could be discovered through a doctor's exhaustive medical workup; through school records, social status, and evidence of intelligence, judgment, and reasoning; through family pedigree, including the parents' social status, alcoholism, and illness; and finally through appearance, physique, and practices regarding hygiene and safety.[10]

Within eugenic thinking, the health of the entire family was contingent on spousal choice—gendered as the selection of the right wife. This view constructed certain behavioral, physical, and mental characteristics as permanent and hereditary aberrations incompatible with family. The ideas of free love and free marriage became popular in the 1920s; so did the call for a "new morality" that demanded of men sexual monogamy and equal relationships with women. At the same time, the stated purpose of marriage was to fulfill each individual's personhood and to improve the Chosŏn *minjok* (ethno-nation).[11] The notion of modern marriage based on love was therefore tied to the rational considerations of heredity, health status, family genealogy, ethnicity, social class, and intelligence.[12] This emphasis on eugenic rationality and new morality paired with individual autonomy required disability to be extracted from the family. Furthermore, Yi Kap-su's remarks in the inaugural issue of *Usaeng* are a discourse that blames human degeneration on high morality, framing eugenics as a new form of moral imperative for a higher purpose invoking Darwin: "As the morality of the human species progressed and knowledge was developed, human physiology worsened and regressed over time. It is because the people who would naturally die owing to their weak physiology were able to avoid misfortune owing to medical developments. It also resulted from the fact that people with diseases could reproduce freely because of benevolent human morality. In other words, it was caused by the survival of the unfit instead of the survival of the fittest as in nature."[13]

Popular magazines and newspapers in the 1930s made references to sex education and genetic principles, and they emphasized the daily practices of health and hygiene. *Sinyŏsŏng* (New Woman) described the archetypal modern woman as having "a healthy body with strong warrior-like sentiment."[14] Another magazine featured an article titled "Birth Control Office" that linked birth control to eugenics: its purpose was to produce a child with superior quality (*uryang adong*),[15] to protect mothers with illness, and to ensure a healthy family life. The article detailed methods of birth control and answered questions from women who were "suffering from the hardships of multiple births." It also disputed concerns about a population decrease by emphasizing quality over quantity and postulating the existence of a class of unproductive human beings with little value—such as those who are "mentally unfit" and "physically diseased," "whose increase in number is the increase in the burden of society." "Quality human beings" and "healthy women" emerged as the ideal colonial and modern citizens.

The description of the Chosŏn people as a homogeneous entity that needed reformulation (*kaejo*) and revival (*chaesaeng*)[16] revealed the imbricated features of a eugenic colonial modernity. The need for reformation justifies colonial intervention and Chosŏn elites' internalized colonial desire for improvement, rather than refusing the dictates of assumed inferiority. Eugenics was translated as *usaenghak*, "the science of superior birth," and *injong kaesŏnhak*, "the science of race betterment." These terms appeared as early as 1920 in the print media. Eugenics in colonial Chosŏn was not simply transplanted whole: it was influenced by traditional values. The effort to revise eugenics was initiated by Hyŏn Sang-yun, who criticized that Western eugenics focuses only on physical bodies; he advocated "the science of superior mind," *usimhak*, arguing that it is important to reform spiritual and mental qualities to improve the human species.[17] In 1926, the *Tonga ilbo* published a column by Ch'oe Hyŏn-bae that ran sixty-five installments portraying Chosŏn as a debilitating nation in need of rehabilitation. The first installment stated, "Dear Chosŏn minjok, do you really have life's freedom and development and do you have the sublime dignity of your existence? It is unfortunate! You only have debility and pain, ruin and grief."[18]

The transpacific importation of European, North American, and Japanese eugenics into Chosŏn evidences a scope beyond the "Eugenic Atlantic" conceptualized by Sharon Snyder and David Mitchell—a construct that focuses on the nation-states of Western Europe and North America and their international collaborations.[19] Snyder and Mitchell point out that a modern state concerned itself with "rid[ding] disabilities from a country's national spaces."[20] Coloniality marks the major difference in the eugenics movements between colonial Chosŏn and the Eugenic Atlantic, because colonial conditions prohibited sovereign nationhood from being the foundation and explicit goal of the eugenics project. In the absence of sovereignty, the efforts to improve the ethno-national constituents were uneasily juxtaposed with the colonial imagery of Chosŏn's inferiority, viewed as undeserving of self-governance and incapable of self-improvement. Within the colonized space, the discursive restraints seem to have led Chosŏn eugenic agents to claim the need to construct desirable traits through education and enlightenment in terms of cosmopolitan world citizenry. In claiming the need for Chosŏn people's rehabilitation, Ch'oe Hyŏn-bae argued, "We are people of Chosŏn. . . . At the same time, however, . . . I am not a person of Chosŏn, or of Japan, of yellow race, of white race, but of the world."[21] Yun Ch'i-ho also introduced the definition of eugenics as improving hereditary traits of future generations through education and urged Chosŏn to follow the trend of the world: "People in the world select the seeds for livestock and plants that are useful to them, but rarely engage in a movement to improve the physical and mental welfare of human beings based on eugenics, because it is believed to be beyond human power. . . . It is deplorable that Chosŏn society lacks such idea let alone the movement."[22]

Historians largely view Chosŏn eugenicists who were committed to public health and to reducing populations with disease and disability as conformists who did not directly resist colonial domination.[23] However, the eugenic project does not seem to have entailed active collaboration with Japanese colonial authorities but might have been viewed as threatening to colonial governance. Continuing the trend between 1910 and 1922, observed by Jin-Kyung Lee, "the anti-colonial positioning of the nationalist bio-political reforms,"[24] the Chosŏn scholars' efforts in the early 1930s to initiate practices to move the Chosŏn ethno-nation toward the modern, healthy, and hygienic body may have been thwarted by the Japanese colonial authorities,[25] making the Chosŏn Eugenics Association inactive in the late 1930s. Yi Kap-su stated that he was arrested by Japanese police while providing marriage counseling intended to improve Chosŏn ethnicity.[26] In 1946, after independence, the Chosŏn Eugenics Association changed its name to the Korean Minjok Eugenics Association (Han'guk Minjok Usaeng Hyŏphŏe) and resumed its activities, opening a National Marriage Counseling Center in the Hwashin Department Store.[27] The tension between Chosŏn elites and the colonial government regarding the promotion of eugenics illustrates the colonial interest in holding the rhetorical power of eugenics in justifying colonial domination that was intended for the international community.

The Public Health Office (Husaengsŏng), established by the Chosŏn Government General in 1938, came to lead the movement toward increasing the physical strength of colonial citizens and justifying the sterilization of people considered inferior and diseased. Kim Ye-rim argues the Chosŏn Eugenics Association's cessation of reporting on the activities was not a sign that eugenic discourses weakened or disappeared.[28] The eugenics ideology and movement continued to be discussed in other popular magazines and newspapers, and their ideas percolated into popular culture and everyday life through the images of healthy bodies in sports, leisure, and entertainment, which constructed what Kim Ye-rim calls "cultural eugenics."[29] The inaugural preface of the magazine *Pogŏn undong* (Public health movement) declared, "For an individual, health and the absence of diseases are the origin of momentum for all businesses and the light for survival. In the same way, for *minjok*, its flourishing future, energy, and outlook depend on the blood rushing in its vessels, the fast reflexes of its nerves, its strength like a swift horse and the flashing light of the whole health. . . . In our womb, we can see only a diseased, anemic populace."[30] In this preface, health appears as an ultimate goal and the tool of Chosŏn's "repair," metaphorized as the light to shine over "a diseased, anemic populace" whose collective blood is the Chosŏn ethnic body politic. Therefore, "scientific research and social practices" of "mass public-health eugenics" were proposed as the cure of the "lethargy" and diseases of the populace.

In colonial Chosŏn, however, eugenics law didn't materialize (although it did in Japan in the National Eugenics Law of 1940 and the Eugenic Protection Law of 1948). Shin Young-Jeon argues that the traditional value placed on reproduction and humanitarian concerns kept methods of negative eugenics, such as infanticide and sterilization, from being enacted.[31] Voices opposed to such methods did appear in the magazine *Usaeng*. The cultural and popular aspects of the eugenics ideal—the healthy life of the body politic—were inevitably far more visible than the consequences of state violence and the destruction of the livelihood of people with diseases or of people who were poor. The discursive emergence of sterilization and a rhetoric that employed vague information about Western nations including Germany and the United States made a powerful impression on the Chosŏn public. Little attention was paid to those who faced removal from the urban, public space and from the Chosŏn populace through incarceration or sterilization. As the Chosŏn Government General prepared for the first Chosŏn Exposition in 1929, *t'omangmin* (people relocated from agricultural villages to the outskirts of Seoul and the urban poor in makeshift houses on unauthorized lands),[32] "beggars,"[33] "burglars," "people with morphine addiction and vagabonds,"[34] and "street vendors" were rounded up, interrogated, and banished from Seoul, because they "harmed the aesthetics of the city."[35] As public anxiety increased to the degree of phobia, threatening the livelihood of people with illnesses, *Tonga ilbo* reported that "lepers" came to the police "boldly" complaining that they would starve to death because people were harassing and rejecting them. The police chief instead tried to calm Seoul's citizens by telling the reporter, "We cannot do anything now. When the construction of Sorokto hospital is not yet complete, what can we do? But I will report this soon to the Kyŏnggi Hygiene Department, round them all up, and banish them to wherever, so please inform the five hundred thousand citizens of this."[36] Leprosarium Chahyewŏn in Sorokto appears as a solution to the public's rejection of people who had "leprosy." This article is a good example of the clash between different understandings of what is to be protected by the state: the patients' safety and survival or the harassing public who perceive them as dangerous. The widespread abuse against people with "leprosy" in urban spaces intensified the need for segregation. Sorokto was later governed under the Leprosy Prevention Act (Chosŏn Na Yebangnyŏng [1935]), legislation that gave its director the authority to incarcerate and punish the residents for their behavior with measures including forced sterilization.[37]

The histories of colonial eugenics are less visible in Western disability studies, especially in their relations to disability politics. Colonial eugenics has often revealed paradoxical framing of "the unity of humankind" and the "intrinsic racial difference."[38] The term "eugenics" has not had a universally negative connotation in contemporary South Korea (this is also the case in Japan[39]); it has not been, in other words, clearly associated with the historical injustices that led to the genocide of people categorized as "subhuman" nor does it immediately call to mind the Nazi Holocaust. Beginning in the 1920s, through channels of local public lectures and printed media, eugenic ideologies came to influence how the future of the Chosŏn people and the desire for a normative family were imagined in the colonial space; this influence continued through the second wave of eugenics in the late 1960s that gave birth to the Mother and Child Health Act under the dictatorial rule in South Korea that aspired to achieve economic prosperity and to empower an independent capitalist nation-state. The word still appears in the Mother and Child Health Act (its latest revision, with updated language, was in 2015) that maintains illegality of abortion but lists eugenics as one of the exceptional justifications of abortion.[40] The colonial and Western legacy of eugenics and the nationalist project of pursuing ethnic improvement for sovereignty inform the ways in which eugenics has been accepted as a scientific rationale.

Heredity Drama

Eugenics served as a cultural logic in the rationalization of marriage and family, the censorship of bodies within the colonial space, and the discourse of sterilization to terminate "bloodlines" carrying undesirable traits. How then did literary texts of the 1930s portray the everyday lives of men and women with disabilities who were negotiating between the perceived need to repair and rehabilitate Chosŏn ethnicity and their reproductive prospects? The contradiction between new ideas of voluntary marriage based on love and the emerging paradigm of rational choice in modern marriage based on eugenic principles generates what I call *heredity drama* around the reproduction of characters with aberrant bodies in literary and filmic texts. Heredity drama exploits the tension created between the discursive certainty of heredity and the uncertainty of reproductive chance. Two short stories of the late 1930s depict a man and a woman with "aberrant" characteristics who encounter the drama surrounding heredity, sexuality, and pregnancy. "The Ugly Creature" ("Ch'umul" [1936]) by Chu Yo-sŏp and "The Kangaroo's Ancestor" ("K'anggaru ŭi chosang i" [1939]) by Kye Yong-muk frame the passing down of disability to the next generation as tragic, not only for disabled children and their families but also for the entire human species. Colonial eugenic imagination appears in these narratives of individual fates involving what was considered improper femininity and the future degeneration of humans.

Chu Yo-sŏp studied in Japan, China, and the United States and mainly wrote stories on poverty and the laboring classes in a realist style. He published "The Ugly Creature" in 1936 in the popular magazine *Sindonga*, for which he worked as the editor.[41] The third-person narrator of this story starts with Ŏnnyŏni's pregnancy, which—considering her looks—even Ŏnnyŏni herself finds hard to believe. The story describes in detail her face with a cleft lip and other aberrancies. From the onset, the narrator sets her appearance against the possibility of reproduction, suggesting that no one would think of her being pregnant even when her body starts to show signs of it. The news of Ŏnnyŏni's pregnancy makes people realize that she is indeed "human," revealing that her disability and her assumed asexuality placed her outside humanity until reproduction occurs. The description of her aesthetic disability follows the genealogy of "the ugly woman" in oral folktales recorded in the nineteenth century, including "The Story of Changhwa and Hongnyŏn."[42] In that tale, Hŏ Ssi is a vicious and murderous stepmother who has multiple disabilities, such as "a double cleft lip," "an impaired arm," and "swollen legs."[43] Ŏnnyŏni's facial and physical disability defies the literary trope in which disability is symbolically potent and indicates moral status. It is neither employed as a sign of her immoral characteristics, as in the case of Hŏ Ssi, nor combined with a kind of agency to reinterpret her disability as an acceptable feature, as in the premodern prose "A Spinster's Song" ("Nochŏnyŏga"), discussed in the introduction. Because of the way her difference is socially perceived, Ŏnnyŏni has to go through dislocation from various spaces—especially marriage, family, and employment.

Ŏnnyŏni was once married through the traditional familial arrangement, in which the groom and the bride were not required to meet beforehand. On their wedding night, shocked at her appearance, the groom ran away. Because their marriage was not consummated, she has no legitimate domestic status within her marital family. After several years of serving her parents-in-law without her husband, Ŏnnyŏni decides to "fix her fate" by leaving the marital family and traveling to the city to visit her relatives. "Fixing one's fate" (p'alcha rŭl koch'ida) is a phrase applied when a woman remarries, suddenly becomes rich, or gains higher status.[44] Ŏnnyŏni's desire in fixing her fate is to create a new relationship between her body and social environment by moving to a city to find a man to marry. Her curative desire manifests in her wish to be treated with admiration and kindness, rather than having a different kind of face.

In Seoul, Ŏnnyŏni hopes to find such treatment in a new, urban environment with diverse people. She goes out to crowded Ch'anggyŏng Palace to see the flower blossoms: "People talk about sightseeing for flowers but in fact one goes out there for people watching. Ŏnnyŏni has never seen that many people in one place, so she couldn't help but stand still with gaping mouth."[45] At the sight of so many people, she is reminded of the shocking news from the village about the bizarre appearance of Westerners, which she had encountered while watching a movie screen showing many of those kinds of people as well as female performers dancing onstage. In a place for displaying diverse bodies as a form of entertainment and the spectacular, she is fantasizing about a man complimenting her beauty. In that moment, she hears a man asking her to go to a quiet space. Waking up to a brutal reality, Ŏnnyŏni hears him say of her face, "Eh, it's damning," as he walks away. Three men in school uniforms corner her to harass her but are repulsed after they see her face and run away, calling her a "monster." That the assault stopped is attributed to the appearance of the targeted woman, which frames the male harassment of women on the street as a heterosexual sanction of femininity. Ŏnnyŏni attempts to fix her fate by coming to a different space in which she imagines a transformation of the social response to her appearance. Lost in the city, she collapses in despair and blames her own mother for giving birth to her. She realizes that she cannot easily fix her fate created by ostracism and abjection.

After repeated failures to maintain her job, Ŏnnyŏni finds employment as a live-in housemaid. The housewife considers Ŏnnyŏni's appearance a plus, because she would not pose a sexual threat by attracting her employer's husband. One hot summer day, when Ŏnnyŏni is seized by her desire for a man, a water supplier makes a delivery; after finding out that Önnyŏni is alone in the house, he locks the door and chases her into her room. Later, she is described as anguished by his disappearance as she had expected to marry him after the incident. She finds out that she is pregnant and experiences hope, depression, and fear, but ultimately she prays for a beautiful girl to prove the cruel world wrong: "She thought even if she had the most unfortunate life, it would be more than satisfying to live with the pride of being the mother of the most beautiful woman. That was the only hope in the whole world. She thought her entire future was depending on it. The wish for a miracle! It is the wish shared by all the ugly, despised, ridiculed, incapable, and oppressed humans."[46]

Here reproduction provides a significant opportunity that might transform the social treatment of marginalized women by disproving the assumption that they are inherently inferior. The narrative thus builds tension about not only the sex but also the appearance of the baby, as the mother's and the baby's fates are bound together. Upon delivery, a midwife murmurs that the baby girl looks exactly like her mother with impairments. Thinking "if that thing grows up, she will again repeat such a life of suffering," Önnyŏni covers the baby with clothes and begins to suffocate her, murmuring, "Die, die." The only cure left for her is to kill her daughter to forestall the girl's suffering caused by the social responses to her disability. She imagines the ridicule she will receive when people find out about her daughter's disability: "The ugly creature gave birth to another ugly creature."[47] Thus, "The new life in front of her eyes was not the hope that would remove her lifelong shame, but the despair that pours new shame upon the shame."[48] When the baby stops moving, however, she is startled and draws back her hands. She imagines that the baby who is breathing underneath the beautiful baby clothes she has made may look prettier when she grows up, although she cannot bear to lift the clothes to see the baby. She rubs and squeezes her breasts and falls asleep touching "the baby's soft skin," establishing a tactile connection without sight. Her motherhood triumphs over her extreme sorrow over the failure of fixing her fate and over her daughter's future.

Önnyŏni's story frames disability as a hereditary fate that one cannot avoid. No miracle could happen under the hereditary principle in effect. It is as if heredity guarantees a perfect phenotypic resemblance between a parent and child, although the language of heredity doesn't appear in the story and is apparently unknown to Önnyŏni. In this framework of perfect heredity, her ignorance provides the ground for the tragic drama in which she is given hope for a cure. The prospect of reproduction provides a chance for her to imagine a different future that would cure her social ostracism, but because of the dictates of heredity, her dream remains unrealized. In the end, however, Ŏnnyŏni does not reject her daughter; instead, she again hopes for a better future in which her daughter's appearance might be improved. "The Ugly Creature" is a story directed toward readers who would know about the theory of inherited disabilities. The story complements the eugenic advice given to the public, providing an example of the kinds of ignorance and irrationality that should be avoided.

While "The Ugly Creature" is the story of a disabled woman mothering another disabled life as a failure to "fix" her life, which is governed by heredity, Kye Yong-muk's "The Kangaroo's Ancestor" depicts a disabled man who knows about genetic principles and is determined to end his engagement so that he does not reproduce his disability. Though the story does not directly address the Japanese colonial rule and racism that produced the notion of Korean ethnic inferiority, it shows individuals negotiating the colonial urban space and eugenic discourse.

Munbo, the protagonist, is blind in one eye. "The Kangaroo's Ancestor" starts with the news of Munbo's engagement to Mija, which in his mind is an unlikely and fearful event due to his family's genetic history of disabilities, because many of his family members have disabilities: deformed hands, limps, hunchbacks, paraplegia, and so on. Unlike literary texts that end by revealing the disability of the main characters, thereby betraying the readers' blanket assumption of able-bodiedness, the upfront placement of information about Munbo's disability and family history together with news of his engagement hint that the narrative will revolve around the couple's uncertain reproductive future. According to Ato Quayson, the sudden revelation of a character's impaired eye in the American novel *Invisible Man* by Ralph Ellison functions as "a discursive punctuation mark": "The suddenness and unanticipated emergence of the impairment with the multifarious metaphors that are attached to it become the means to accentuate the unusualness of the entire event."[49] By contrast, in heredity drama the information about disability is presented together with the reproductively significant event, and the juxtaposition of disability and reproduction—seemingly incompatible—provides tension and anxiety. Much as "The Ugly Creature" starts with Ŏnnyŏni's pregnancy, so "The Kangaroo's Ancestor" starts with the prospective marriage of a man who is self-disqualified from the perspective of eugenics. His previous love, Kŭmbong, had rejected him when she found out about his disability. Kŭmbong is characterized as a modern, rational New Woman who studied in Tokyo. Her beauty, education, and modern appearance are emphasized, providing a contrast to Munbo's disability and Mija's unconditional love. The educated and nondisabled New Woman is set against the disabled man; Munbo understands her rejection of him based on eugenic reasoning as a rational decision that brings him relief.

Munbo believes that the hereditary disability is connected with the future of human species, believing that humans are devolving into a species of kangaroo.

> One scholar professed that the higher animal coming after humans is kangaroos. If this theory is to be believed, isn't the human species in the process of turning into kangaroos like a tadpole turning into a frog? . . . My worthless life should not be treasured, if I were to become only an ancestor of kangaroos, only to mournfully regret the burden of future humankind. If I can't serve as a tool to bolster the sublime history made possible with bloodshed in order to enhance the eternal culture of humankind.[50]

In 1934, *Usaeng* published a New York psychologist's theory that resembles Munbo's fear of a human future characterized by disability. According to the psychologist, madness had increased 30 percent over the preceding ten years; therefore, the entire human species would become mad in two hundred years—in 2139, to be specific.[51] Munbo declares that even if he ignores Mendel's genetic laws, he cannot ignore the hereditary manifestations in his family, which provide genealogical evidence to support viewing the future of the human species as grim. He wants to stop the degeneration into kangaroos by stopping his own reproduction of "disabled, unfortunate seeds."[52] He chooses an abstinent life until he meets a divorced woman, Mija, who admires him as a writer. During their engagement, his fears about the possibility of pregnancy grow. In Munbo's narrative, his heterosexuality comes into conflict with his eugenic responsibility to prevent the perpetuation of disability and eventually to save the human species. Munbo sees himself as one of the main culprits in hastening the spread of disability that will lead to human extinction. Relieved that Mija is not pregnant, Munbo wants the two of them to commit suicide together, thereby sacrificing their lives for the happiness of future generations.

In imagining the future occupied by people with disabilities as dystopic, Munbo also recounts a lesson from Karel Čapek, the Czech author of the science-fiction play *R.U.R. (Rossum's Universal Robots)* (1923): "Early on Čapek prophesied the coming of artificial humans in his piece."[53] The play, which portrays robots destroying human beings when humans do not act with rationality, is here given a eugenic interpretation from Munbo's perspective. Although the author inserts text only fleetingly, even without its title, to justify Munbo's anxiety of his reproduction tied with the human extinction, *R.U.R.* itself was first translated into Korean in 1925 and became influential in Chosŏn in its depiction of class struggles.[54] It provides an important eugenic message and simultaneously the warning against scientific manipulation of life. In *R.U.R.*, robots—a word first coined in the play—are created by male scientists to serve as mechanical slaves that can replace human labor and thereby eliminate class hierarchy among humans, making "the whole of mankind into the aristocracy of the world. An aristocracy nourished by mechanical slaves. . . . And maybe more than man."[55] Helena, who is sympathetic to the robots, provides the key element that robots need to become capable of resisting humans. When she hears about the robots' erratic movements, which are described as similar to those caused by epilepsy, she interprets them as an indication of a soul or internal struggle. She urges scientists to give them souls, to which one of the scientists replies, "That is not in our interest."[56] Eventually Helena convinces the scientist who is in love with her to manufacture robots with soul. From the perspective of eugenics, Helena's sympathy for robots can be interpreted as defying eugenic rationality to maintain hierarchy: it enables the robots to revolt against humans after they realize "that they are more highly developed than man, stronger and more intelligent. That man's their parasite."[57] A handbill says, "Robots throughout the world, we command you to kill all mankind. Spare no men. Spare no women. Save factories, railways, machinery, mines, and raw materials."[58] Because robots ironically lack reproductive capabilities, the play ends with the prospect that the robots will become extinct, since they have killed all the humans who have the technology to manufacture more robots.

In "The Kangaroo's Ancestor," Munbo's comment about the fear of robots taking over the world might reflect a view that, in the play, human extinction is caused by scientists who gave in to Helena. With this cautionary tale in mind, after finding himself disappointed that Mija has dismissed the idea of a suicide pact, Munbo resolves to end his own emotional involvement with her, since their relationship would only end up hastening human degeneration. Mija is "a beautiful evil" who would "gnaw away someone's mind."[59] Her love of Munbo while she knows of his disability is framed as nothing but an emotional temptation that would lead him to fail his mission of nonreproduction.

Much as Helena's sympathy for robots brought humans to their extinction, Mija's sexuality and reproductive potential are a moral threat to this endeavor.

In one poignant scene, Munbo is on a busy street of Seoul, halted at the sight of fast-moving automobiles, streetcars, bicycles, rickshaws, and motorcycles. He finds the moving crowd, made up of individuals with all sorts of physical appearances, chaotic—like a "spilled trash can that needs to be organized."[60] Coming across a beggar, he gives money and notices that other people are just passing by and ignoring the beggar. This observation leads him to the diagnosis that many people are morally disabled. While he affirms his morality to contribute to human evolution by sacrificing himself, he expresses his curative desire for those who are "disabled" in their minds.

> People who are disabled in their minds try to live and those who are disabled in their bodies seek death! If I am to kill myself, shouldn't fairness demand that those people with disabled minds be dead already? If they wish to live so much, I want to replace the disabled parts of their minds. When a clock can't do its job, one has to replace the broken parts inside with the good ones. Before they become kangaroos' ancestors, I want to give them a valuable and eternal life, so that they become the ancestors of a sublime human species and the light guiding the accumulation of human culture. Is there a technician for such human repair on this street?[61]

Not forgetting that he too needs to repair his own deficit, Munbo renews his desire to live. His willed celibacy and removal of himself from the city and from the woman he loves are consistent with the era's dominant social discourses of qualifications for marriage and the social responsibility to reproduce healthy citizens. That Munbo's sacred curative mission to ensure human evolution would be fulfilled by desexualizing himself epitomizes the eugenic justification to sterilize disabled people who may not be as rational as Munbo—who do not have the willpower to carry out the mission of nonreproduction by self-restraint or contraceptives.

Two ideas essential to these stories, "fixing one's fate" and "repairing the human species," rely on reproduction and nonreproduction to "cure" social ostracism and degeneration. A mother with a disability attempts to fix her fate—to ameliorate the social rejection of her aesthetic disability—by reproducing beautiful offspring. That the mother's fate is determined by the features of her child, such as sex, race, and disability status, is a key motif in reproductive heredity drama. A cure effected by reproducing a nondisabled child is in a sense a courtesy cure, in which the disabled persons' association with nondisabled people alters how they themselves are perceived. Erving Goffman explains the courtesy stigma, which attaches to "the individual who is related through the social structure to a stigmatized individual—a relationship that leads the wider society to treat both individuals in some respects as one."[62] The courtesy cure of mothers is, conversely, the remedial effect of reproducing a nondisabled offspring, which Ŏnnyŏni is unlikely to achieve, because her disability is hereditary. Applying the notion of cure to the human species, Munbo sees his genes as causing the degeneration based on the laws of heredity. Removing his germ plasm from the mix by celibacy, if not suicide, would save humans from the fate of being replaced by kangaroos.

Ŏnnyŏni's and Munbo's desires for nondisability in future generations take different turns, however. Ŏnnyŏni's acceptance of her daughter—albeit somewhat distanced, as she cannot look at her daughter's face—in the hopes of her aesthetic improvement is not an affirmation of disabled lives; rather, it is an ambivalent expression of her grief at and hopes for her daughter's future. Framing his charity toward the people in need as an act of moral superiority, Munbo distinguishes himself from the public by establishing another hierarchy. The authors of the two short stories, Chu Yo-sŏp and Kye Yong-muk, take advantage of conflicts between individual desire and the eugenic imperative to eliminate certain hereditary features. Modern marriage based on individual choice and love is framed as being in the public interest and preconditioned by health and the absence of aberrant features. In colonial Chosŏn, outside of institutions in which forced sterilization occurred, discourses of sterilization as a solution to crime and poverty functioned to regulate marriage and portray the reproduction of disabled populations as undesirable.[63]

Yet the existence of eugenic culture and the literary imagination do not illustrate a wholesale rejection of disability. Accommodations and assistive devices, including Korean Braille, were considered to be "cures" for disability. The magazine *Pyŏlgŏn'gon* introduced Braille as a method to make blind people sighted and enlightened; it also addressed the need for Braille education and described the departments for the blind and the deaf in the first special education institute: Chesaengwŏn, established in 1913.[64] A visit by Helen Keller in 1937 sparked interest in the lives of children with disabilities and offered an opportunity to advocate for their education, although Keller herself was a supporter of eugenics. A newspaper article argued, "Who would want a disabled, abnormal child? But seeing society as a whole, even if medicine and hygiene progress, some disabled people cannot ever be eliminated; thus we can never guarantee that no family will have a disabled member. Therefore we need to abolish the old habits of mistreating and despising disabled children and to teach them as humans. . . . We need to make facilities for them to enjoy equal happiness as humans."[65] Although disabled children are problematically cast outside humans in this rhetorics, the care and education of children with disabilities, based on the idea that disability will always be present, and the emphasis on equal happiness pose a sharp contrast to the eugenics goal of eliminating disability and the construction of modern marriage as a site for reproducing only nondisabled children.

Illegitimate Reproduction and the Life Unlivable

Other kinds of heredity drama are formed around infertility and biracial reproduction. In the premodern and early modern Chosŏn, woman's infertility appears as a condition that warrants her expulsion and threatens the woman's belonging in her marital family. A couple's childlessness was attributed to women, and the childless women were labeled *tulso* (a Korean vernacular term meaning a sterile cow) or *sŏngnyŏ* (stone woman) with the accompanying stigma of uselessness and inferiority. Paradoxical to the eugenic emphasis on quality over quantity of reproduction, the traditional emphasis on son-bearing and fertility was adopted and reinforced as the colonial strategy during the 1930s under the slogan of "deliver, increase, and raise" in the preparation for the Pacific War.[66] Kim Hye-su explains that during the 1930s, the pregnancy of women continued from the age of late teens until around the mid-forties and that the average birth rate of women was six to eight children. Women's health was significantly affected by frequent pregnancies, malnutrition, physical labor in agricultural fields, and self-induced abortions during that time.[67] In the social and cultural atmosphere of fertility as the value of women, nonreproductive women's bodies were disenfranchised and considered replaceable in marriage by another woman. Extramarital sexual relation that childless women used as a strategy to increase the chance of being impregnated constructs a drama. One example is "A Mountain Valley" by Yi Hyo-sŏk ("Sanhyŏp" [1941]), which treats the birth of a child fathered by a non-husband as revelations of the woman's sexual transgression and the husband's infertility that have to be erased. Feeling distressed about the blame of the couple's childlessness on her, the wife Song Ssi has attempted to kill herself when she was under extreme stress over the new mistress that the husband brought. While away at a temple to pray for her reproduction, she has sexual relations with another man and gets pregnant. Although she has proven that she is not a *tulso*, her guilt over her sexual transgression—in contrast to her husband's unashamed and legitimized affair—rather makes her wish her own death. After giving birth to a son, she attempts to commit suicide once again. Moreover, she feels relieved when her baby dies suddenly in a month. The husband's infertility is suspected but never made explicit, and his mistress leaves him while being pregnant with another man's child. At the end, the neighbors expect that he would bring yet another woman from the village continuing his pursuit of reproducing his heir. In this story, the assumed infertility of a woman is proven wrong by her mothering a child of another man. However, the successful reproduction of a son does not overcome the gendered moral consequence of sexual violation and illegitimate reproduction.

The unexpected racial difference of a newborn may also endanger mother's life, generating heredity drama interacting with sexual morality and family honor in a complicated way. Yu Chu-hyŏn's "Inheritance of the Sun" ("T'aeyang ŭi yusan" [1958]) depicts a man who is proud of his family heritage and honor, while living in poverty. He is waiting for his daughter returning from the city. The whole narrative proceeds to the revelation of the baby that his unwed daughter brings home and how it would clash with his pride about his family's reputation. When the father looks at the baby's face with black skin, he almost faints and immediately expels his daughter with the baby. The mark of black heredity is constructed as abject together with his daughter's prostitution with a black American soldier after the Korean War.

The fact that the newborn's characteristics can threaten the mother's status constitutes the narrative climax of heredity drama. Disability, gender, race, and sexual violation of monogamy in the culture of preferring nondisabled son with Korean ethnicity born in wedlock all comprise vital components of social and familial rejection of the mother and the child. Notably, in "Inheritance of the Sun," a sexually uninhibited shaman with physical disability witnesses the father's violence and his destructive morality. Her presence serves to reveal the familial violence coming from the father's adherence to the traditional ideology of gendered sexual morality and racism.

Heredity, Morality, and the Codification of Eugenics

From the time of the division of Korea and the Korean War, the South Korean government encouraged births; it suppressed the dissemination of information on birth control methods until the 1960s,[68] when it received international aid to promote birth control programs from the International Planned Parenthood and the U.S. Population Council. The Korean birth control movement, led by women's rights activists, revived the discourse of population "quality over quantity" to gain national support.[69] The famous slogan of the Park Chung Hee regime, "Physical strength is the foundation of national power," captures the eugenic equation of individual fitness, health, and able-bodiedness with national economic growth and political power.[70]

The process by which eugenics was codified into Korean law in the 1970s—specifically targeting disabled women—is directly connected to the eugenics movements of the 1920s and '30s, but this time with a pronounced emphasis on strengthening the sovereign nation-state. The legislative revival and intensification of the eugenics movement in the 1960s under the repressive military regime were considered necessary for postcolonial national reconstruction and economic development. The reemergence of the baby contest is one illustration of this movement. During the colonial era, judging and giving awards to healthy babies began as a way to raise awareness about nutrition, hygiene, and child development. One of the earliest baby contests was held at a Christian hospital in Kongju. Babies were measured and rated on body size, weight, clothes, and cleanliness, and fifteen of the selected thirty-five "superior babies" received awards.[71] Beginning in 1927, the Government General had examined babies in T'aehwa Women's Clinic and given awards to those that were healthy to emphasize the importance of physical well-being.[72] After the Korean War, healthy baby contests were held by various private and public agencies, and they gained more prominence in the 1970s.[73] In 1971, the Namyang Dairy Company and the Munwha Broadcasting Company launched the National Better Baby (*uryanga*) Contest. This highly competitive popular contest, which emphasized the nutritional quality of baby formula, used babies' height, weight, shape, and other developmental indices to determine the winner. The results were compared with the averages of children in other nations. Some critics argued that the competition had become too fierce and had commoditized babies "as if they are being graded in the meat market."[74] In addition to commercial interests, the healthy baby contests reflected the desire for a nation-state constituted with more desirable physical traits and Westernized physiques combined with internal class distinctions.

Within this context of the national promotion of eugenics, population control, and economic growth, the need to determine genetic quality before marriage appears in the film *The Evening Bell* (*Manjong* [1970]), directed by the prominent filmmaker Sin Sang-ok. A significant portion of the film is solely in Korean sign language, depicting conversations between the deaf couple with no subtitles or indirect translation by the hearing interlocutors. The decision to not translate the sign language positions the internal culture of deaf society at the center of the film and thus throws into relief the effort to avoid deafness. At the same time, it invites an othering gaze by highlighting the failure of communication between deaf characters and the hearing audience. In doing so, it presents the heredity drama of a hearing child of a deaf couple, a liminal figure between these two seemingly separate worlds.

This hearing son, Yongsik, falls in love with a hearing woman, Mia. The prospect of Yongsik's marriage and the role of his deaf heritage build narrative tension. Yongsik's uncle has a plan to arrange his marriage to a deaf woman for a sizable commission from her rich family. As Yongsik's uncle sees it, that Yongsik is hearing and has deaf parents, though lower class, makes him a good match for a deaf woman with an upper-class background. To end Yongsik's relationship with Mia, the uncle goes to Mia's brother, who is a physician, and reveals that Yongsik's parents are deaf. At the same time, Yongsik also informs Mia of his parents' deafness. Shocked by the news that would have an implication for her reproduction, Mia goes to the deaf school, sees a group of deaf children communicating in sign language inside fences, and runs away in terror at the unfamiliar sound and spectacle. The deaf children are seen through her horrified and alienating gaze with her eyes shown in an extreme close-up as she hides behind a tree and seeks spatial separation from the deaf world.

Worried that the deafness in Yongsik's family is hereditary, Mia meets a physician and asks what would happen if a hearing son of deaf parents marries a woman "who is healthy and has very clean blood"—rhetorically framing deaf heredity as tainted blood. The physician, a friend of her brother, disingenuously confirms her fear that the children will be "deaf with no exception" and adds, "You can't let your emotion deal with health issues." The prohibition against reproducing deafness is made obvious by Mia's brother when he tells Yongsik, "Mia would have to be childless if she marries you." These events disenable Yongsik under the medical description that he possesses an atavistic trait that will surface in the next generation. Dramatizing this point, Yongsik pretends to be deaf at a bar as he drinks alone. Much like Munbo, who internalizes eugenic ideology and desires to remove himself from the gene pool in "The Kangaroo's Ancestor," Yongsik becomes a self-sacrificing martyr of antidisability ideology when he attempts suicide. At the end of the film, it is revealed that Mia's brother and her physician colluded to lie to scare

Mia away from Yongsik: there was no scientific basis to believe that Yongsik's offspring would be deaf. Mia's brother did not want her to marry Yongsik simply because his parents were deaf. The heritability of deafness is employed to conceal social prejudice against disability as if the former is a justifiable cause of rejection: Yongsik is disabled by a courtesy stigma created by his proximity to deafness.

Faced with rejection and his own disablement by his heritage, Yongsik decides to accept the arranged marriage by his uncle with a deaf woman, and his family receives a lump-sum dowry from her family. The mother reveals ambivalence when she signs to him that a deaf woman has "much sadness in her life" and is therefore not appropriate for him, a remark indicating that she herself disqualifies deaf women from marriage. Yongsik's mother is determined to make her son's love come true and persuades Mia to accept her son. In the narrative's climax, Yongsik's mother runs out to return the dowry, meets Mia, and communicates in writing that her son loves her. She then is hit by a truck and dies at the hospital holding Mia's hand. Mia is so touched by her sincerity and integrity that she tries to convince Yongsik that even if they do have deaf children they can raise them to be like his mother. This is the only moment of the film when parenting deaf children is presented as a possibility. In his grief and prejudice, Yongsik encourages Mia to marry a man from "a pure and good family."

In *The Evening Bell*, genetics is employed as the indisputable reason that the couple should not marry (or live without any biological children), while the real reason for disallowing marriage is simply that others wish to avoid being associated with deaf people. Thus, disproving the heritability of deafness does not lead to the social acceptance of difference. Once the prejudice against persons with disability and the imperative that they not reproduce are established, only a significant sacrifice, the deaf mother's death, makes room for reconsidering cultural and social rejection of disability. Mia's tenuous acceptance of the idea of mothering disability is brief, as her brother confesses that he lied about the genetic prospect of her future children and affirms that they would never have a deaf child. The news is given as if morally rewarding her for embracing the possibility of deaf children. After this "blessing" of normative reproductive prognosis from the bride's patron and the medical doctor, the film ends with their wedding, affirming the narrative closure with the ableist message that denies the place for reproducing deafness.

The 1970s were a decade marked by writing cultural eugenics into law and implementing it through the involuntary sterilization of people with certain disabilities who were institutionalized. As a way to limit population increase, Congressperson Pak Kyu-sang suggested the National Eugenics Bill (Kungmin usaeng pŏban) in 1964. This bill would have legalized abortions for disabled mothers and their permanent sterilization, called "eugenic surgery" (usaeng susul). Pak Kyu-sang argued that the goal of such legislation was "to modernize the family and population." The legislation included provisions for sterilization because of hereditary disease in a family and the legalization of abortion "for women who had given birth to three or more children and whose poor health renders them unable to raise another child and for women who have given birth within the past two years." "Eugenics" became the euphemism that could persuade the public to accept harsh-sounding sterilization and abortion based on the prospect of reproducing disability. The opposition therefore employed moralist and religious perspective on abortion and sterilization broadly or focused on the harm of such practices to women's health and framed abortion as murder, rather than attempting to discredit eugenics.[75] Although this legislation did not progress, it paved the way for the Mother and Child Health Act (Moja pogŏnpŏp) of 1973.

A year after the National Eugenics Bill was put forward, debates reemerged in the National Assembly and newspapers about the draft of the Mother-Child's Health Protection Bill. Proposals submitted to the Ministry of Government Legislation were withdrawn several times in response to objections raised. The bill as initially proposed permitted abortion for economic reasons and mandated reporting all pregnancies to the authorities by the twenty-fourth week. Under the notorious Yushin system of dictatorship, the Constitution was suspended and the National Assembly was dissolved. Without those articles, in 1973, the revised bill was passed into law by the Emergency National Affairs Committee as the Mother and Child Health Act. Article 8 of the law permitted abortion—which had been defined as a crime since 1953[76]—with the consent of both the person and her spouse under the following circumstances: (1) the pregnant person or the spouse had a eugenic or hereditary mental disability or physical illnesses specified by executive order (these were "hereditary schizophrenia, hereditary bipolar disease, hereditary epilepsy, hereditary feeblemindedness, hereditary neuromuscular diseases, hemophilia, mental illness with overt hereditary criminal tendency, other hereditary illness that had 10 percent or higher inheritance rate"); (2) the pregnant woman or her spouse has a contagious disease specified by the Infectious Disease Prevention Law (cholera, plague, smallpox, tuberculosis, sexually transmitted diseases, leprosy, etc.); (3) the person was impregnated by rape or sexual assault; (4) the person was impregnated by a blood relative to whom it is illegal to marry; or (5) the continuation of pregnancy harms the mother's health and threatens her life.

The enactment of the law allowed the de facto legalization of abortion in medical facilities before the twenty-eighth week of pregnancy.[77] Abortion was largely available in clinics, showing no need for women's movements to pursue legalization of access to abortion, until the recent emergence of the pronatalist Christian movement became visible and Korea's low birth rate was highly politicized. These pronatalists have targeted abortion by arguing that doctors who perform them should be prosecuted, but they have left abortions justified by disability as an exception. In 2012 the Constitutional Court confirmed the conviction of a midwife who performed abortion,[78] indicating that women's access to abortion, indirectly permitted, can be easily taken away. The Mother and Child Health Act has been amended many times since it was passed, but the article (which was 8 and now 14) retains much of the same language; there were only minor changes in the executive orders.[79]

The 1973 law also included Article 9—a provision that required physicians "to report to the authority without any delay when a patient is found to have the designated illness and if the physician determines that sterilization is necessary for preventing the illness from being inherited or infecting others." Upon receiving the report, the Minister of Public Health and Social Welfare could assign a doctor to sterilize the patient. This article was in effect—although authorities maintained that it was never enforced[80]—until its removal in 1999. The law promoted involuntary sterilization as the duty of medical professionals under state authorization.

In 1975, under this article, twelve women were subjected to intense public debate and scientific scrutiny because of their disabilities, and nine of the women were found by the authorities to have "hereditary disabilities" that require involuntary sterilization. The head of Chŏngsimwŏn (Right Mind Institute), the institution where the twelve women resided, requested authorization for their sterilization under Article 9. The circled image of one of the women's "chromosomal anomaly" was published in the newspaper as clear evidence that their disabilities were genetic, with opposing and affirming opinions about sterilization placed on both sides of the image.[81] The reproductive rights and perspectives of the women were never mentioned or considered. A few days later, the newspaper Chosŏn ilbo published a photo of the institution's gate under the headline "Feeble-minded Children, Puberty a Divine Punishment." Creating the impression that women with developmental disabilities have dangerously uncontrollable sexual urges, the caption reads, "With awakened desire for the opposite sex, they lurk in front of the men's ward and even forget their meals."[82] These discourses constructed the sexuality of disabled women as dangerous and their reproductive ability as needing to be removed.

The language of *tanjongpŏp* (the method of terminating seed) used in the 1930s changed to *purim susul* (sterilization surgery). *Chosŏn ilbo* reported that coercive sterilization was also called "health and welfare surgery" (*husaeng susul*) and printed the opposition to the sterilization of the women, but not against eugenics: "Coercive sterilization is done for the sake of public interest and eugenics, but it impairs the human instinct to reproduce and is expected to face opposition. Especially as our country has little awareness of public interest and eugenics, the first coercive sterilization will face numerous attacks."[83] The most vocal opposition came from the Psychiatric Physicians' Association, which contested the hereditability of certain conditions.[84] The objections to sterilization focused on the possible misidentification of disability and on the possibility of developing a future cure for disabilities, rather than affirming that people with intellectual disabilities and other hereditary features have a right to reproduce and be born.

Chŏngsimwŏn was not granted permission in the end, because of the intense objections from psychiatrists and religious leaders as well as the public; nevertheless, the institution was later found to have sterilized fifty-seven men and women without authorization, although some local authorities were informed of the surgeries. In 1999, Congressman Kim Hong-sin revealed that sixty-six men and women had undergone illegal sterilization in six residential institutions since 1983.[85] Following this exposé the same debate over the pros and cons of mandatory sterilization recommenced, although Article 9 was abolished prior to the report. The sole defender of coercive sterilization was Chi Kwang-jun, a law professor who repeated the eugenic line: "People with mental retardation may not feel inconvenience themselves but impose inconvenience on many people around them and cause harm to society. They have hereditary genes with high probability of giving birth to mentally retarded children; thus, they can give birth to tragedy and bring misfortune to their offspring." Just as in the eugenics discourse of the 1930s, he cited the Kallikak family in the United States as a tragic example of hereditary disability; he also noted that sterilization was practiced in the United States, Sweden, Italy, and France, implying that mandatory sterilization was therefore not a barbaric practice. Chi Kwang-jun not only lacked an understanding of reproductive rights as human rights; he was also unaware that the methods and findings of Henry Goddard's *The Kallikak Family* had come under attack in the United States and had been completely refuted in 1940.[86] Chi claimed that state-authorized sterilization was more humane for those people with "mental retardation" and argued that Article 9 should be reinstated.[87] In order to stir up old debates about mandatory sterilization without considering the voices of people with disabilities, the newspaper *Sŏul sinmun* legitimated Kang's opinion by publishing alongside that of Yi Tong-ik, a Catholic priest who opposed coerced sterilization of people with disabilities as a grave human rights violation. Yi argued that involuntary sterilization ignored human instincts for procreation and that society has the obligation to protect the weak and the vulnerable. Almost seven decades after the idea of eugenic sterilization was introduced in Korea, the same debates about the reproduction of people with disabilities were repeated once again with almost no change or explicit challenge to discourse of the dangers of disability.

Institutions and complicit local authorities were not the only proponents of coerced sterilization. Two institutions out of six in Kim's report revealed that they had acted with permission from the parents of those sterilized. Under the aggressive regime of population control, the state set regional quotas of contraceptive surgeries, and public officials often visited the institutions to increase the numbers.[88] People who were institutionalized testified that they resisted so fiercely that they were beaten and restrained prior to the surgery. Furthermore, manipulation and threats were also employed by the superintendents, posing as patriarchal figures within the institutions.[89] Analyzing the biopower operating in sterilization abuse, Ch'oe Wŏn-gyu explains that disabled people in institutions put up much resistance, and some succeeded in avoiding surgical procedures. He points out that Chi's position is no longer acceptable in South Korean society, because of the resistance mounted by disabled people and human rights activists.[90] However, while coerced sterilization has been strongly denounced from a humanitarian perspective focusing on suffering, little efforts have been made to support reproductive rights of people with disabilities including legalized access to abortion, and more efforts have to be made to condemn the very basic eugenic premise and its nationalist and utilitarian basis. As a consequence, the desire to control the results of reproduction seems to have grown stronger in the early twenty-first century, while at the same time the pronatalist attack on women's reproductive rights overall has also grown. The feminist challenge to pronatalism has been focusing on (1) legally allowing all abortions by twelve weeks of pregnancy and (2) limiting abortions, by twenty-four weeks of pregnancy, only allowing abortions based on economic reasons and in the instances of maternal or fetal infectious disease, rape, incest, the mother's health, or a fetal deformity that threatens fetal viability or maternal life.[91] Although the proposed revision eliminated "eugenics" as a cause for allowing abortion, it takes the path of listing the permissible conditions for later-term abortion by exceptionalizing fetal and maternal diagnosis and their prognosis and poverty rather than fully guaranteeing nondisabled and disabled women's rights to choose.

The violation of disabled people's reproductive rights that the Mother and Child Health Act made legal in the language of eugenics reveals an extremely problematic conceptualization of maternal health. It automatically disqualifies disabled women from reproducing at all. The involuntary sterilization of women with disabilities needs to be fully critiqued and halted to ensure disabled women's reproductive rights. But simply prohibiting abortion is not a solution to the problem of the selective legalization of abortion based on the disability status of parents or a fetus, because the illegality of abortion itself poses a significant problem by limiting women's reproductive rights. Because women do not have the right to access safe and legal abortions, problematizing disability-based abortion can have the result of simply perpetuating the state's control of women's reproduction. The disabled women's movement calls for a careful approach that pays attention to the marginalized voices of disabled women before joining the chorus of anti-abortion rhetoric, illustrating the complexity of reproductive issues, the important claims of disabled women's rights to access abortion, and the history of violence told from disabled women's perspectives.[92] While pro-life activists do not object to disability-based abortions, the opposition to disability-based abortion has gained prominence within the contemporary disability rights movement without considering the importance of decriminalizing abortion, and an activist, Kang Jin Kyung, explains that some disabled women's organizations also join this position.[93]

Consider the controversy spurred by a remark made by the former South Korean president, Lee Myung Bak, in an interview before he was elected. He stated that he was mainly against abortion but that some abortions are unavoidable to prevent the birth of babies with disabilities.[94] In response, disabled activists launched protests and occupied Lee's campaign office. They argued that his comment casts "the parents of disabled children and parents who are expecting a child as potential murderers who could have had or could have an abortion" and reveals that he regards disabled people as people who can be killed without consequences.[95] Equating abortion to murder, male activists emphasized the right for disabled people to reproduce and for disabled babies to be born. In reporting the voices of activists, an article in the *Han'gyŏrye sinmun* covered the history of the Nazi's T-4 euthanasia program targeting disabled people as well as the colonial history of sterilization of people with Hansen's disease under Japanese colonial rule, suggesting that the same eugenic rationale underlay Lee's remark and these programs.[96]

While the reproduction of women with disabilities continues to be socially discouraged, the reproductive ability of disabled women has also been exploited. In 2002, with the help of a disability rights organization in Chŏllabukto Province, a group of middle-aged blind women told their life stories, which were published in *Chŏnbuk ilbo*. Four women said that, when they were young, they were sent to other families to serve as mistresses and bear children.[97] These blind women were so-called *ssibaji* (seed receivers). Their status was dependent on their ability to produce sons, which the nondisabled wives were unable to do. The stories in the newspaper suggest that, following childbirth, their status as mothers was temporary. One of the women was called "aunt" by the child she mothered; others took on the roles of nanny or maid. Various commentators framed this as the remnant of an inhumane traditional practice that made women instruments for reproducing male descendants and as a human rights violation, which was consistently called "shocking" to modern thinking.

Of the four women featured in the newspaper article, two were blind at birth and two became blind later in life. By and large, blindness doesn't appear in eugenics literature's lists of disabilities to be prevented by prohibiting reproduction. It is quite possible that not framing blindness as a hereditary condition enabled the reproductive exploitation of blind women to become surrogates. A short story written by Hwang Sun-wŏn, "In the Institution for Blind Children" ("Maengawŏn esŏ") refers to this practice of reproductive surrogacy by blind women in the 1950s. The narrator explains, "There were occasions when a blind girl was smart and virtuous; she could go to be a mistress of a man who wanted to have a child."[98]

Following the newspaper report, several television programs aired testimonies by blind women about their lives. The news documentary *Uri Sidae* (Our times) featured "I Was a Surrogate," an episode that introduced a blind woman in her fifties.[99] She became blind after the death of her mother; her stepmother, who wanted her to leave the house, told her that if she married the man introduced to her, he would be able to cure her blindness. Her family took her against her will to the house of an older man who was already married and had five daughters. The blind woman became a surrogate expected to reproduce a son. She explains that after finding out that the promised cure was a lie and knowing that she had no home to return to, she had hoped to give birth to a son in the belief that her life would change for the better. However, she gave birth to a daughter and her life became more difficult. Even though she ultimately bore two sons, her life didn't improve, and the children couldn't call her their mother. Later she attempted to leave the home with her daughter and the younger son, but her "husband" took her son away from her. For her, unmothering occurred even in the context of her biological motherhood and her care and labor of child-rearing. The cure of blindness (by providing the cost of medical treatment) was offered as a compensation to lure her into such exploitation.

These stories reveal that blind women were used as tools of reproduction and as a solution to wives' infertility to preserve patrilineage and illustrate that disabled women do not have a simple relationship to reproduction. For some disabled women, reproduction is forbidden because of the assumption that their disability is hereditary and because of the imperative not to reproduce disabled children; for other disabled women, fertility was perceived as a resource that could be exploited and instrumentalized owing to their marginalized status.[100]

Curing Risks

Unlike involuntary sterilization of the twelve women in the institution and the anti-abortion position taken by male disabled activists in response to Lee's remark, the emergence of reproduction made "risk free" through preimplantation genetic screening was marked by the relative absence of debates regarding its ethical implications. In May 2007, *Thumbelina Wants to Be a Mother* was aired on television as a Family Month prime-time special, enchanting the South Korean public with an emotionally charged story of a woman of short stature, Yun Sŏn-a. Her life was shaped by the experiences of osteogenesis imperfecta (OI), commonly known as brittle bone disease. The documentary was extremely popular, eliciting such responses from viewers as "I cried the whole time while I was watching it" and "It was the most touching story that I have watched on television lately."[101] This quasi-medical documentary depicts Yun's journey to become a mother through assisted reproductive technology that removes the chance of disability.

The documentary differentiates itself from many television documentaries that introduce the lives and struggles of individuals with disabilities and their family's "sacrifices" and that seek to evoke pity by focusing on the difficulties and pain caused by their disability as well as their social exclusion. The departure from the common image of individualized suffering reflects a growing emphasis on the desire of disabled people to live as "ordinarily" as possible. It is not the usual portrayal of the "human victory" of a disabled person who overcomes disability by accomplishing difficult tasks. Rather, the documentary presents a disabled woman whose reproductive chance of disability to be "cured" through extraordinary measures have enabled her to become an ordinary mother. As Yun explains that she was a disabled person and had become a woman after marriage, her heterosexual relationship ushered her into the gender system, constituting her "rebirth." "Men" and "women" are understood as exclusively able-bodied privilege; unless and until a disabled woman gains intimacy with and recognition by a man, they remain outside the binary gender system.[102] After achieving marriage, which had seemed impossible, she pondered if she could also earn another seemingly unreachable title, that of mother. The documentary frames this journey toward becoming a mother as a journey toward having a child without disability, through technological intervention.

Two years before the documentary was filmed, a magazine introduced the love story of Yun Sŏn-a and Pyŏn Hŭi-chŏl and mentioned that the couple had discovered that in vitro fertilization (IVF) might make her pregnancy possible. IVF is deemed necessary not because of the difficulty of conception but because of the possibility of passing down her disability.[103] *Thumbelina* opens by showing Yun wearing a patient gown as she awaits a pelvic exam in an infertility clinic, then wincing with pain on the exam table. The scene effectively reframes technologically unmediated fertility with a chance of fetal disability as conditional infertility. The inheritability of her disability makes her an "unmother" in contrast with "unwomen"—the term applied to infertile women in Margaret Atwood's *The Handmaid's Tale* (1985). Yun is not an unwoman in this sense: instead, she is an unmother rendered incapable of reproduction because she has a 50 percent chance of reproducing a child with her disability. In this way, *Thumbelina* redefines motherhood as preconditioned on the status of the child as able-bodied. Unless the possibility of hereditary genetic disability is eliminated, there will be no mother or fertility in this framing. In order to become a mother, Yun goes through IVF, a preimplantation genetic diagnosis (PGD) to screen for "aberrant" embryos, and the implantation of selected "nonaberrant" embryos.

After the first *Thumbelina* ended without a successful pregnancy, news media speculated about a sequel.[104] In August 2007, several months after its airing, Yun appeared on a talk show to break the news of her pregnancy,[105] and the newspaper coverage of her announcement illustrated the public's interest in her reproductive project. Two subsequent documentaries, airing in May of 2008 and 2009, covered the drama around the birth of her son and his first birthday. What is striking in the trilogy covering three years of her life is the absence of ambivalence about the technology of PGD and screening to select certain embryos, the high risk she assumed in undergoing the process, and the ultimate payoff embodied by the nondisabled son. In addition to the spectacle of Yun's different body, often shown in X-ray images, this trilogy of themes constitutes the heredity drama, one that exalts the desire for a nondisabled body and naturalizes certain emotional responses, such as the grief over "failing" to get pregnant, the anxiety over giving birth to a disabled baby, or the joy over "succeeding" to reproduce an able-bodied baby, as the main motif to draw reaction and identification from the audience. The rhetoric of risk-free reproduction through PGD frames disability as a risk while making other risks invisible. Yet this heredity drama is formed around a tension beyond that provoked by the chance of disability, as the screening process already intervened to ensure the birth of a baby without OI. The tension arises not from the disability status of the child but from the possibility that the mother might die during a Caesarean section, as her disability puts her at an extremely high risk of hemorrhage or bone fractures. The doctor informs the husband of the reported fatal cases of a person with the same disability. With the camera in the operation room, the audience sees the entire process of the C-section and the birth of her son presented with a dramatic music.

In the documentary series, the preference for having a nondisabled over a disabled child is presented as a moral and natural given—not as her or the family's choice. Becoming a mother without question appears to mean becoming the mother of a nondisabled child. After birth, nondisability has to be confirmed once again even after it was guaranteed before the implantation. After examining the newborn's genetic tests, the doctor delivering the news calls it a "gift" to the couple: not only does the baby not have the genetic disability, but he is not even a carrier of the OI gene, meaning that his own reproductive future of nondisability is diagnosed at birth as secure. The doctor cheerfully declares, "Genetic illness ends in your generation," another preemptive remark—here, erasing the option that the son might have a child with a partner who has a genetic disability. The documentary praises the PGD that prevents Yun's disability from being inherited and offers cured reproduction, while dramatically exploiting the suspense about the possibility of harms that the mother would experience as well as the possibility of other disabilities of the newborn.

Only after becoming a mother does Yun gain narrative power in the first person through the voice of the celebrity actress Kim Hŭi-sŏn, who recently gave birth, although the narrative in this third documentary is still written by the writers. The voice-over narratives of the first two documentaries were from the perspective of her husband. In the opening of the third documentary, the voice narrates, "I want to become a *good* mother." The documentary includes many scenes of Yun crying—sometimes from the happiness of having a "perfect family" but sometimes out of frustration at being unable to carry out the physically demanding activities expected of an able-bodied mother taking care of her child. Moreover, because her spine curved further and her bones weakened during her pregnancy, she experiences severe pain. As a result, she needs to decide if she should undergo a major surgery that would render her immobile for three months and that she has only a 10 percent chance of surviving. It is not surprising that many newspapers praised the touching story of Yun's decision to risk her life to become a mother. She quickly became a symbol of the greatness of the maternal love that overcomes disability. A women's newspaper, *Yŏsŏng sinmun*, selected her as one of twenty women leaders who inspire hope.[106] Encouraged by Yun's "success," one newspaper commentator wrote about the need to provide government funding for genetic testing and screening and to lift the legal limit on testable and eliminable genetic conditions (currently restricted to sixty-three conditions), which the commentator criticized as violating the equal treatment of patients and reducing their self-determination.[107]

There were few significant debates about the ethics and social implications of using PGD to screen out disabled embryos, and the media discussion of PGD and the impact of the documentaries do raise some concerns. One newspaper praised PGD as a solution that could replace abortion and reduce suffering and social expenses: "Genetic illness is not curable, therefore preventing birth is the best solution. It can be prevented by terminating pregnancy after genetic illness or chromosomal anomaly is detected through existing prenatal diagnosis, such as amniocentesis or chorionic villus sampling, but mental and physical pain is inevitable [following an abortion]."[108] The opposition to abortion rights is embedded in this critique, while at the same time it considers an abortion in cases of detected fetal disability an unquestionable mandate. One of the few cautionary voices was that of *Tonga ilbo*'s science columnist, Yi Ŭn-hŭi, who wrote that *Thumbelina*'s story might lead to the desire to find and prevent all diseases that can be passed down.[109] Yi reminded readers that PGD is not a treatment of disability but a screening process to eliminate the birth of babies with disability and concluded with the dystopic vision presented in the Hollywood film *Gattaca* (1997), which depicts a future in which genetically engineered reproduction becomes the norm. Yet this minority opinion is not a significant sign of controversy or debate about the use of such technology, at least not with the same intensity shown in the debate about sterilization in the 1970s and '90s. In public discourse, pointing to the film *Gattaca*, with its genetically engineered people labeled Valid (in vitro birth) and naturally conceived people with genetic flaws labeled Invalid (in utero birth), appears a meager warning about the dangers of genetic engineering.

Thumbelina depicts reproduction made possible for disabled women and at the same time demands that their reproductive "risk" of passing down their disability be "fixed" through an engineered reproduction in order to achieve motherhood. This enabled motherhood, however, continues to provide challenges to Yun's life in her effort to become a "good" mother and to live with her disability.

Recent research by Hwang Ji-sung, based on interviews of women with disabilities, reveals a direct connection between the popularity of Yun's successful reproduction through PGD and hostility toward disabled women who chose not to undergo PGD but instead bore a child with an inherited disability. For instance, Hyŏnmi, a woman with OI, gave birth to a baby with OI and was sent to the genetics department at the hospital for further testing, where she faced a series of accusatory questions. Hyŏnmi told Hwang, "They asked why I gave birth, when there was a way to prevent [my disability] from being passed down genetically. They were talking bluntly. They mentioned IVF and the television program. 'There is a way to prevent [OI] from being passed down. Why did you give birth without checking things out?' the genetics doctor said."[110] The feminist disability studies scholar Susan Wendell points out that, although the screening of fetuses and selective abortion based on disability status may initially be voluntary, such practices fairly quickly become social mandates, creating an atmosphere in which being born with a disability is viewed as the evidence of a mother's culpability of not preventing disability.[111]

Silence in Wedding Gowns

In the midst of the drive toward curing risks in the heredity drama, an independent documentary by Kye Un-kyŏng, *Pansy and Ivy* (*P'aenji wa tamjaengi* [2000]) deconstructs the marriage fantasy from a disabled woman's perspective and reveals how the imperative of unmothering disability oppresses disabled women. *Pansy and Ivy* presents a series of short episodes featuring two sisters with short stature, Yunjŏng and Sujŏng. Opening with a casual party scene where many men and women gather, drink, and sing together at the bar, the film shows Sujŏng and a seemingly nondisabled man, Sŏngju, becoming intimate. In a key three-part subsection, "Preparing the Wedding Gown," the two sisters are seen contemplating the possibility that Sujŏng might marry. The social script of courting that is familiar to nondisabled audiences appears unfamiliar, awkward, and embarrassing from the perspective of Sujŏng.

The sisters visit a married friend with a physical disability who encourages Sujŏng to be more active in pursuing a romantic relationship with Sŏngju. The film shows a close-up shot of the friend's left hand and her wedding ring as she prepares a meal for her guests. She works as a mentor to the sisters, helping Sujŏng overcome the hurdles to marriage placed before her. The fleeting shot of the friend's wedding ring makes an important point: marriage is presented as an important immediate goal for Sujŏng, who at thirty-six years old is believed to have little time left before becoming too old to marry, even though she is shy and unsure of her own and the man's feelings. Sujŏng unwillingly admits her feelings toward Sŏngju in front of the inquisitive sister and their friend. The friend convinces her that she has to hold onto him, adding, "He is disabled, too, but he is better than us." In this way the audience learns that Sŏngju has a disability that is not obvious (later explained as an amputated leg), which means he occupies a "higher" status than Sujŏng in society's hierarchy of disabilities based on heritability and visibility.

In growing expectation of an intimate relationship with Sŏngju, Sujŏng decides to learn about sexuality. The two sisters bring a pornographic video to the friend's place in "Preparing the Wedding Gown 2." The camera captures the discomfort and worry shown on Sujŏng's face while in the background exaggerated moaning sounds are playing on the television. Sujŏng's friend advises her to see a gynecologist to learn more about her body and risks and whether sexual intercourse is "possible." They are very concerned about the physical danger posed to the sisters by sexual intercourse, pregnancy, and delivery. As marriage appears increasingly possible, Sujŏng visits a gynecologist with her sister. It is their first visit to a gynecological clinic, and they seem uncomfortable and embarrassed in front of the middle-aged male doctor. The doctor explains, "You two have some special problems. That is why you're worried. We doctors sometimes may sound a bit cruel. But because your children may develop the same problems, you don't want to pass the sufferings on to them in this situation. An option for you may be to adopt a child." While the doctor avoids referring to their disability directly, he makes it clear that children with the same disability should not be born. Because he assumes that people of short stature suffer, he treats reproduction for them as necessarily prohibited, not as a matter of their decision. The doctor then tells them that he has to physically examine them in order to answer more questions. The sisters leave the clinic feeling awkward and perplexed, faced with the paradox that they have to undergo a physical examination by a doctor who at a quick glance judged that they should not give birth.

In order to emphasize marriage as the goal even more strongly, the film inserts an episode in which the sisters attend the wedding of their night-school teacher. Sujŏng and Yunjŏng visit the dressing room of the nondisabled bride, standing on either side of her chair as she sits in her wedding gown. Later, they sit at the back of the hall watching the bride and groom and listening to the officiant. The camera zooms in on their faces as they are looking forward impassively. However, the film supplies no guidance on what they are feeling: the interpretation of their faces is left to the viewer, who must weigh the juxtaposition of this wedding and their chances of getting married.

The film compellingly represents the sisters' ambivalence at various cultural sites of marriage. It also shows them in other settings: they participate in singing contests, they tan at the beach, and Yunjŏng accompanies her mother to a photo studio. Though presented as part of the flow of their daily lives, these activities do not strike viewers as meaningful ways of living as singles, because the sisters appear alone or only with family members.

Finally, in "Preparing the Wedding Gown 3," a long take captures a dialogue between Sujŏng and Sŏngju, her love interest. She begins the conversation by asking about their relationship in a way that hints at troubles, and she says that speculations about their relationship have been bothering her. He responds at length why he cannot marry her:

> You have to get married and I have to get married too. I especially feel that way since I'm the oldest son; I don't know what you will think about what I have to say. I'm the first and only son; I have to have a son for my mother.

I'm concerned about my mother feeling lonely so I have to choose a wife who has disability that is similar to mine. Maybe a person who has a more similar disability would be better. Yeah, that's what I think. That's how I feel. I'm getting old and you're getting old too. It's more serious for you because you're a woman. It's a bit easier for me [to marry later] because I'm a man. You have to get married before you turn forty. You have to hurry. The days are going by quickly. If you get too old, you can't get married. Everyone has to get married once in life.

Sujŏng sits next to him silently, saying nothing and expressing no anger or disappointment. She lets him talk out his justification as if it would make her understand. His breakup speech encapsulates sexist, ableist, and ageist qualifications for marriage that work against disabled women on multiple levels: first, the obligation to produce a son in order to preserve the patrilineal line; second, the hierarchy of their disabilities (acquired versus genetic); third, the double standard of marriageable age; and fourth, marriage as a mandate.

Sujŏng's silence is a powerful response. It allows the audience to speculate about what she might be feeling but offers no closure. Her silence is a tool that resists the dominant narrative of such scenes and frustrates the audience's expectation of seeing it play out once again. But the silence is also a manifestation of the fact that there is no language available through which she can express herself.

As one of the few independent films on the topic of disabled women's sexuality, *Pansy and Ivy* makes an important contribution to the growing genre of disability documentaries. And according to the film scholar Kim Sŏn-a, by incorporating narrative drama style, it blurs the boundaries of drama and documentary.[112] Kim explains that although the documentary does not attempt to speak for the marginalized people, it is filmed from the marginalized position of its subjects. The camera shots are consistently taken from a low angle to equalize the imbalance of power between the filmmaker ("I") and the subjects ("them"). Unlike most television documentaries on disability, there are no interviews and no voice-overs providing a master narrative, as seen in *Thumbelina*. The audience hears only the actual conversations among people in their daily settings.

Yet the camera's quiet presence is felt through the somewhat rigid faces of the main characters, who are conscious of its gaze. In fact, the film does not focus on the dialogues but combines several short scenes into sections. These seemingly fragmented pieces are connected under the theme of marriage, depicted as a topic somewhat alien to the two disabled women. The columnist and filmmaker Ryu Mi-rye points out that the film is made more appealing to nondisabled people by framing the two sisters not as persons with disabilities but as women who dream about marriage.[113] Ryu's categorical distinction between persons with disabilities and women is worth contemplating. According to her, being a woman is emphasized through the connection to marriage, confirming the distance between the categories of people with disability and gender that Yun Sŏn-a described. Although the film spends quite some time following the sisters' daily journeys—as they use public transportation that involves dangerous and slow stair lifts and are stared at by people in the city of Pusan—the topic of marriage is read as explicitly identifying their femininity. The two women's efforts to achieve marriage, not their experiences of physical and attitudinal barriers, their lack of employment, and the daily difficulties they experience, are connected to their gender.

The dramatized ending of *Pansy and Ivy* presents another provocative silence, as the sisters are shown sitting on a small boat on the sea wearing wedding gowns (see figure 1.2). The only sound is from the seagulls, cawing loudly and eerily, that surround them. They are sitting close to each other, expressionless and looking away from the camera, which is fixed on them in a long take. Viewers finally can see the wedding gowns that, as the section titles implied, were in the making throughout the film. The sisters fulfill the imagined desire of wearing wedding gowns without actually getting married. By suggesting another reading—that the gowns were never meant to be worn in actual weddings—this fantastical scene demystifies marriage. The stillness of Yunjŏng and Sujŏng grabs the attention of the audience, showing that their strength exists outside of marriage. The failure of their arduous efforts to attain a cultural cure through marriage is transformed into a demonstration of the unreality of such a cure for the two sisters.

The final image of two sisters in a boat in their wedding gowns provides a powerful refutation of romantic love as a basis for marriage. Two women's opportunities to reproduce are preempted and positioned outside of marriage that is reserved as a reproductive institution for mothering nondisability. The refusal or inability to enter into marriage for disabled people ought to be considered against gendered and ableist expectations surrounding reproduction and marriage.

In the interdependent construction of disability and binary genders, the institutions of marriage, sexuality, reproduction, and the nuclear family become sites for rehabilitating disabled persons by mitigating disability's stigma. This

I.2 A still from the documentary *Pansy and Ivy* (2000). Two sisters wearing wedding gowns sit in a boat looking away. Reprinted by permission of Indiestory. Image courtesy of Indiestory.

mitigation leads to the illusion that disability can be erased in accordance with patriarchal cultural customs of fulfilling gender expectations and heterosexuality. Such narrative formulas reflect and reinforce the normative orders that regulate the intimate lives of disabled women. However, the medical cure that aims to enable the reproduction of nondisability (*Thumbelina*) exists alongside attempts to deconstruct this reality (*Pansy and Ivy*), highlighting the disruptive potential of disabled bodies that exist outside of the gendered imperative.

In Korean culture, placing responsibility on mothers not to reproduce disabled children has a history of eugenic campaigns and postcolonial nation-building and of cultural representations of heredity drama. The mobilization of biopolitics based on the presumed desire for disability's absence often relies on disability's continued presence at the margins of society to remind people of its "undesirability" by providing evidence of social and material costs. Reproduction has been framed within the notions of a nondisabled mother, of mothering nondisabled newborns, of family, and of morality in ways that forbid the continued presence of disability. In these restricted spaces, it is not surprising the authors and the filmmaker imagine that the characters like Munbo,

Ŏnnyŏni, Song Ssi, and Yongsik resort to undoing their lives by attempting either suicide or killing the newborn. And the documentary depicts the silence of the two sisters as the only possible response. Cure thus represents the denial of different bodies not only in the form of prevention but also in the form of the elimination of disability. While disabled and nondisabled mothers with disabled children and their children themselves may live with accusations of irresponsibility, ignorance, and immorality, their presence and experiences challenge moral certainty of an imperative to engineer nondisability together with women with disabilities who choose not to be mothers, who therefore remain not fully incorporated into the binary gender system. The curative violence is directed not at disability but at reproduction with the possibility of disability, or rather at reproduction of disability configured as harm. Cultural texts become legible vehicles for navigating the complicated scientific, medical, historical, moral, and emotional terrains invested in a reproductive futurity of unmothering disability.

CHAPTER 2

Cure by Proxy

Considering articulations of the body's ends makes it possible to learn that we are not alone in our bodies.

—TANYA TITCHKOSKY, "The Ends of the Body as Pedagogic Possibility"

In 1937, the film *Sim Chŏng* (*Shim Chung*), based on a well-known folktale, was screened at the Tansŏngsa theater in Seoul and in 1938 at the Liliha theater in Honolulu. The discourse inside and outside Chosŏn about the overseas screening highlighted the unique Koreanness of the story, especially the Koreanness of the imagery, at a time when filmmaking was increasingly thwarted by Japanese censorship.[1] *Tonga ilbo* reported the first overseas screening of a Korean film with excitement, remarking that the film would provide a chance to showcase Chosŏn's "unique ethics," "traditional morality and aptitude," and "unique devotion and sentiment of utmost filial piety."[2] In Honolulu, the film was advertised with such descriptions as "special Korean, all talkie" and "Korean photos in pure Korean language, pure Korean actors, pure Korean director, made in Korea, pure Korean landscape, Korean film."[3] One Korean-language newspaper in Honolulu sketched the film's plot: "The model of filial piety presented in the story is a pious daughter who sold her life to sailors to open her father's blind eyes. Owing to that sacrifice—the sacrifice of her life into the dangerous stormy ocean—her father could see. With his eyes, he sees his daughter's spirit fly on the cloud."[4] The first screening was popular among Koreans in Hawai'i and led to the demand that it be shown again.[5] The discourse surrounding the screening of the film illuminates the strong cultural attachment to the value of filial piety (*hyo*) in Chŏng's sacrifice to cure her blind father; it is viewed as a quintessential value that represents an authentically Korean ethos and is a source of significant pride.

Sim Chŏng is based on the well-known premodern folktale "The Story of Sim Chŏng" ("Sim Chŏng chŏn"), which has numerous variations and multiple origins; it can be traced back to a similar story from the Silla Kingdom recorded in the twelfth and thirteenth centuries.[6] In an English version, translated in 1889 by the American Presbyterian medical doctor Horace Allen, a man Sim becomes blind while grieving the loss of his wife, who died after giving birth to Chŏng.[7] When Sim falls from a bridge into a stream and asks for help, a Buddhist monk rescues him and says, "True, you are blind, yet not incurably so."[8] Then the monk instructs Sim to make an offering of three hundred sacks of rice to his temple, an act that will restore his eyesight and bring the family status and nobility. Sim promises to make the offering but realizes to his dismay he doesn't have so large a fortune. His fourteen-year-old daughter, Chŏng, finds out about her father's promise and takes the opportunity to sell herself to the sailors who are visiting the town to buy a virgin as a sacrifice so that they may have safe passage over the rough water. After she is thrown into the sea, she meets the Sea King, who sends her back to life on land as a reward for her selfless filial piety and sacrifice. She is found inside a lotus flower by the king of the land; she marries him and becomes the queen. In an effort to find her father, who has left his hometown, the couple invites all the blind men in the kingdom to the palace. Reuniting with her father, who is still blind, she explains what happened to her. He says, "'Oh! My child, can the dead come back to us? I hear your voice; I feel your form; but how can I know it is you, for I have no eyes? Away with these sightless orbs!' And he tore at his eyes with his nails, when to his utter amazement and joy, the scales fell away, and he stood rejoicing in his sight once more."[9] Sim's blindness is suddenly cured, and he is able to see his daughter in her royal status. This folktale shows that the daughter's reincarnation and their reunion directly cause his cure, linking the two bodies and thus forming an intercorporeal cause and effect between death/rebirth and cure.

Unlike other cure stories recorded in the Koryŏ dynasty, in which the cure of disability evidences the sacred power of Buddhism,[10] in the folktale the healing power of the Buddha purchased through an economic transaction is obscured, as Sim is not cured after his daughter has made the offering. His cure is delayed until his daughter sacrifices her life and is then reincarnated and reunited with him. As Chŏng's birth is identified as an origin of Sim's blindness, her sacrifice warrants the restoration of his eyesight. Family members' moral status and nondisability are mutually constructed through this intercorporeal cure effect.

In exploring the relationship between family and cure in this chapter, I take literally Tanya Titchkosky's poignant observation that "we are not alone in our bodies": also present are normative criteria for what counts as "human." In examining disabled bodies located on "the edges of humanity" in Western context, Titchkosky argues that disability is seen as a "limit without possibility": "Once recognized as limit and at the end of what counts as human, disability is emptied of life and its grounding as a cultural (not natural) production is obscured."[11] Titchkosky says, for example, that blindness is understood solely as an inability to see rather than as perceiving the world differently. I rely on the multiplicity of corporealities within an individual to show how cure makes it obvious that disabled bodies are bound to other bodies, seen as not simply "limit without possibility" but also as waiting to be transformed and providing the opportunity for transformation to others. The relational and gendered aspects of the experiences of disability call upon nondisabled family members to work as curative agents whose behaviors would directly and indirectly affect disability. I call this agent a proxy for cure. Cure by proxy creates the conditions that produce curative dependence, resulting in a disabled person's cure being determined by the actions of their family. In order to uphold the transaction of cure that her father initiated with a Buddhist monk, Chŏng becomes a proxy who acts on Sim's behalf to consecrate the offering to the temple, eventually making her own life an offering. In other words, proxies are motivated to perform extraordinary tasks in order to cure the disability or illness of another under the belief that, by supernatural and religious means, their actions will be rewarded.

I use the notion of proxy to capture the interpersonal dynamics around the socially constructed obligation to *do something* when disability is present in the family. A proxy does not directly cure disability or illness but exhibits devotion to cure and the continued manifestation of the desire for a painless, normatively shaped and functioning body, as if to stop wanting a normal body is itself morally corrupt, even pathological. The curative labor includes praying and prioritizing the goal of "improving" the state of the disabled others to self-interest. Rather than representing a disabled person's needs, the proxy enforces compulsory normality and carries a responsibility to work toward cure, simultaneously rendering the disabled person as a receptacle for their rewards. The logic of cure by proxy denigrates disability and denies a disabled person the opportunity to live without transformation. At the same time, proxyhood provides a way to complicate the notions of agency and subjectivity, which assume an individual who acts on one's behalf and promotes one's best interest. Instrumentalizing the person involved in the cure by proxy (a family has to sacrifice something to cure a disabled person) within both supernatural and realist realms points to the need to interrogate how the family operates as an exclusive community for survival, in order to challenge the imperative of cure that devitalizes disabled embodiment.

The binding of multiple bodies of family members and a disabled person motivates the desire for cure in the interest of the collective entity and forges the belief that what one person does with one's body cures another's disability. When cure is perceived to be necessary for the survival of a patriarchal family, cure practices move away from the binary—cast as either individual choice or social coercion—to a transactional realm of negotiating over collective bene-fits and sacrifices. The moral values of selflessness, virginity, chastity, and reli-gious piety; the socially constructed mandate of devotion; and the emotional need to do something impel putatively altruistic actions. The rhetoric of the "burden" of disability has highlighted the economic, physical, and emotional costs of care. The assumption that disabled persons become "burdens" to their families and to society as a whole supports the death drive of disabled persons and undergirds ableist ideologies that justify the refusal to provide necessary resources to all as a social entitlement. In this chapter the focus on the mul-titude of familial corporeality elaborates how the burden of cure is imposed on disabled persons, so that the family can achieve a normative moral status.

The term "proxy" invokes its popular culture reference of the disputed clin-ical diagnosis, Münchausen syndrome by proxy: a caregiver, usually a woman, falsely claims or induces illness or impairment in a proxy, usually a child, often resulting in direct harm.[12] The fifth edition of the *Diagnostic and Statistical Manual of Mental Disorders* includes "factitious disorder imposed on another," defined as "the falsification of physical or psychological signs or symptoms, or induction of injury or disease, in another, which is associated with identified deception."[13] The person who lies about or actually creates health problems in the proxy's body may receive sympathy and also attention from medical professionals. If I reverse this rhetoric of proxy by replacing an imposed injury or disease with imposed curedness, another notion of proxyhood emerges in addition to the formulation of the proxy as a nondisabled family member who works for a cure on behalf of a disabled person. A disabled person can be a proxy here whose body needs to be cured through the actions and the desire of nondisabled family members. A family member may use a disabled per-son's putative or induced physical improvement as a proxy for their own self-interest, whether that be surviving, achieving familial normalcy, or gaining social rewards for their actions. In other words, the blind father, Sim, becomes a proxy whose cure is necessary for elevating Chŏng's filial piety to be upheld as an ideal. This reversal of proxyhood is not to simply denounce the family member's urge to cure or to pathologize it as an equivalent form of mental disorder or to construct disabled persons as passive victims, but to reveal the socially scripted nature of actions and the gendered expectations imposed upon others and to think about curative violence existing within relations.

I move back and forth between these two coexisting formations of proxyhood—first, the cure of a disabled person through the actions of a nondisabled proxy and, second, the imposition of cure on a disabled proxy to serve the ends of a nondisabled family member—in arguing that curative violence is embedded in this intercorporeal bind created through proxyhood within the family under the imperative of cure imposed as a collective moral goal. The role of society disappears in the emphasized need for familial transformation. This argument may run against the valorization of the "Asian" cultural emphasis on collectivity and relationality often praised over the "Western" focus on individuality and the liberal notion of autonomous selfhood. Unlike the interdependence formed in a reciprocal and equal caring relationship that does not demand the "improvement" of a disabled person, the binding of bodies within a family creates the "disabled family"[14]—and as the family feels the pressure to achieve normalcy for its material and reputational survival, disabled members are compelled to be cured or removed. In the representations of the disabled family, disability framed as a family's problem turns the body of the disabled person into property to be dealt with or hidden, regardless of what that person desires.

The need for cure by proxy can be compared with the persistent social expectation for nondisabled mothers to directly cure and improve their disabled children with extraordinary care and direct interventions. When the eugenic imperative of unmothering disability—illustrated in the previous chapter as disqualifying disabled women from motherhood and preventing births of disabled newborns—fails, mothers are often blamed for the disability of their children. In *Unstrange Minds*, a cultural history of autism and the parents of children with autism, Roy Grinker discusses one study where mothers of disabled children in South Korea are criticized as bad mothers, and how discourses of *hwapyŏng* (*hwa-byung*; fire disease) are used by the researchers to explain the mother's bad parenting.[15] *Hwapyŏng* is constructed as a Korean culture-specific disease with psychosomatic manifestations caused by the sense of unfair accusations and unresolved anger often caused by the disempowerment of women. Blaming a mother for a child's disability gestures toward the difficult bind that mothers experience in South Korea: either being blamed for not being available when they work full-time or being blamed for caring too much. The imperative of cure and habilitation can be obligated and pathologized at the same time.

The well-known film *Marathon* (2005; dir. Chŏng Yun-ch'ŏl), which significantly raised awareness of autism in the South Korean public, constructs a mother's desire for normalizing the disabled son as her pathological drive for cure. The mother, without the support of her husband, focuses on teaching her son in an effort to habilitate him. His swimming and running are seen as having a curative effect on his disability, such as improving his attention and removing problematized behaviors. When people with low expectations of the son's ability to participate in ordinary activities tell her not to be obsessed with his running, because he is different from other people, she screams back, asserting his sameness with others and his normalcy, at least during his running. When she finally realizes that he cannot be the same as others, she violently prohibits him from running ever again. Her realization that she cannot cure him completely goes to the other extreme by blocking him from doing what he was encouraged to do for years. When he shows his own initiative to participate in a marathon, she is finally able to accept the fact that she does not have to force him in one way or another. Significantly, this realization leads to the recovery of her distanced relationship with her husband and her nondisabled son at the end of the film.[16] The dramatic participation of his running in a marathon and the mother's acceptance of her son's differentness suture the divided family. The mother's compulsory curative efforts to enforce sameness as a gateway to inclusion and the mother's compulsory exclusion based on differentness illustrate a rich and prominent archive of a mother–disabled son relationship in South Korean film for disability studies examination.

Taking a different entrance into the familial relationship through a father and daughter's curative proxyhood, I first explore the nationalist formulation of curative ethos by relieving itself from the duty for social assistance. The promotion of *hyo* (filial piety) in the interests of nationalism, briefly noted above in connection with the Honolulu screening of *Sim Chŏng* (1937), also appears in two other films based on this folktale: *Dutiful Daughter Chŏng* (*Hyonyŏ Chŏngi* [1972]) and *Mother Star in Heaven* (*Hanŭl nara ŏmma pyŏl i* [1981]). Next I closely examine how cure is exacted from the visual transference of the father's disability to his daughter's body, and how she becomes a curative proxy not only for him but also for the entire nation. In *The Story of Ongnye* (*Ongnye ki* [1977]), it is the nondisabled wife whose faithfulness is tested and who succeeds in proving her devotion and in bringing about both the rehabilitation of her disabled husband and the recovery of her ill mother-in-law. To deepen the analysis of the link between the nation-state and rehabilitation, I examine the relationships between demobilized war veterans as curative saviors of disabled women in *Sergeant Kim's Return from Vietnam* (*Wŏlnam esŏ toraon Kim Sangsa* [1971]) and *Yŏngja's Heydays* (*Yŏngja ŭi chŏnsŏng sidae* [1975]). Heterosexual marriage is tied to the corresponding disability status of the couple (possible only between two disabled individuals or two able-bodied individuals). The miracle of curing or rehabilitating a disabled woman is completed when she forms the normative nuclear family by giving birth to a nondisabled child, also demonstrated in the previous chapter.

Lastly, I discuss the 2003 film *A Tale of Two Sisters* (*Changhwa, Hongnyŏn*; dir. Kim Jee-woon), whose title refers to the premodern tale of Changhwa and Hongnyŏn to exploit cultural anxiety about the vicious stepmother with disability who kills her stepdaughters. In the film, when an ill mother is taken care of by a female nurse, the presence of this outsider poses a threat to heterosexual marriage and the nuclear biological family, evoking the deep-seated horror of violence against the daughters. This horror manifests in the form of the mental disability of one of the daughters, who, to cure her trauma, invents a proxy—an alter personality who is responsible for the death of her mother and sister. In the conclusion, I chart the connection between the representations of a gendered familial bind and their legislative counterparts that deny eligibility for social welfare to unemployed disabled persons who have productive family members. This enforced dependence on and relation to the family has a devastating effect on the ability of disabled persons to survive.

Nationalizing *Hyo* as Feminine Virtue

The story of Sim Chŏng has functioned as an ideological apparatus that reinforces gender hierarchy by suggesting that daughters should work and sacrifice to empower patriarchs and the nation. Feminist critics of the folktale have pointed out that the ideology embedded in it demands women's sacrifice for modern nation building[17] and that the blind father is a morally corrupt figure who sells his daughter for his own gain.[18] Building on these critiques, Jung Ji Young traces how the story was used as an educational tool to exhort women to actively sacrifice for the nation in the name of *hyo*.[19] The story appeared in the textbook *Chosŏnŏ tokpon* (Korean language reader [1924]) during the colonial era and continues to this day to be reprinted in elementary and middle school textbooks.[20] Even though disability is central to the story as a condition that naturalizes the practice of *hyo* through sacrifice, these critiques have not interrogated the central role of disability or questioned the reasoning by which a man's cure for blindness is considered a reward to his daughter.

The history of Korean migration to Hawai'i might explain why *Sim Chŏng* was the first Korean film screened overseas. Domestically the film *Sim Chŏng* wasn't as successful as *Spring Fragrance* (*Ch'unhyang chŏn* [1935]), the first sound film, which was based on a folktale involving romance and chastity.[21] Koreans moved to Hawai'i to work on sugar-cane and banana farms starting in the early twentieth century, following a period of Japanese migration that began after the Chinese Exclusion Act was enacted in 1882. In 1921, by one count, the Korean population in Hawai'i was near six thousand.[22] American missionaries, including Horace Allen who translated the story of Sim Chŏng promoted this migration, convincing Americans in Hawai'i that Koreans are "easy to control from their long habit of obedience."[23] Between 1910 and 1924, almost a thousand Korean women moved to Hawai'i as "picture-brides," a term that refers to women whom marriage brokers introduced to workers in Hawai'i via photographs.[24] Newspapers in the 1920s frequently reported on scams, divorces, and violence experienced by women who migrated through this marriage arrangement.[25] The film *Sim Chŏng* may have been more pertinent and representative of Korean values than another popular film on the love story, *Spring Fragrance*, to many migrant women living in Honolulu who perhaps identified with Chŏng, having left their country on a ship without much information to an unknown island for the promise of better future.

In the folktale, the father–daughter dyad is configured as one body that needs to work toward a cure for blindness. One manifestation of this in the cinematic version is that disability and the imagined effect of disability is transferred from father to daughter. Though only fourteen minutes of the film have been recovered, a still image from one scene reproduced in a newspaper provides a glimpse of this transference (see figure 2.1).[26] In this scene, Chŏng is trying to find her friend while wearing a blindfold. A movie review by Sŏ Kwang-je describes this scene as the most creative invention: "The most praiseworthy scene in the film is the part when Sim Chŏng plays hide-and-seek. This seems to be the director's best idea inserted to the adapted storyline of the traditional Sim Chŏng story."[27] Sŏ thinks that the film, however, does not adequately capture the imagined emotional suffering of Chŏng, when it shows her walking home while crying when she realizes how difficult it is to be blind. He underscores that the imagined suffering of blindness should have been visualized by Chŏng's more dramatic bodily expressions with emotional intensity, such as collapsing in despair or running home to her father. Even

2.1 A still from the film *Sim Chǒng*. Chǒng is wearing a blindfold and playing with two girls. *Tonga ilbo*, November 10, 1937.

with his dissatisfaction, Sǒ calls this scene the director's "best idea," because Chǒng's simulated experience of blindness and her emotional reaction served an important function in motivating her to cure Sim's blindness at all costs. This brief simulation is supposed to adequately convey the struggles of the father to the daughter and the audience, without considering the embodied skills and adaptability of Sim, who has been blind for more than a decade and has successfully raised Chǒng as a single parent with help from others. This scene also appears in the 1972 film. This transference of disability to the daughter deputizes her as a proxy for the cure of the father's blindness, projecting her desire to him. Chǒng's performance of blindness in the film, therefore, is a key moment for her in becoming a surrogate disabled body whose death would lead to the cure of her father's blindness.

The restored footage from the 1937 film shows Chǒng's devotion and her daily labor to cure her father's blindness. She prays at night outside, kneeling down in front of a bowl of water, a religious practice of prayer. Kwidǒk Ŏmŏm, who was a friend of her late mother, praises Chǒng for her piety and good behavior, and she hands Chǒng a bottle of elixir, procured at the Buddhist temple, that might cure her father's blindness. She also gives Chǒng a talisman for her to carry to effect his cure. A religious network devoted to pursuing cure is maintained around the proxy, in appreciation of her virtue. Chŏng's every-day life is dedicated to visiting her mother's grave, serving her father, sewing to support them both, and praying for a cure, before she finds another way to make her wish come true by selling herself.

Chŏng's willingness to sacrifice herself for the cure is central to her cross-ings from the submarine realm to the terrestrial and later to the celestial one, described in the Honolulu newspaper *Kungminbo* as her flying up on the cloud, leaving her father behind.[28] Water signifies that the crossings are re-births. It is in the stream that Sim hears the news that his blindness is curable, and Chŏng drowns and is reincarnated in the sea. In the versions found in Allen's translation and in *Kyŏngp'anbon*, the King of the Sea explains Chŏng's past life in heaven to her. There she was in charge of the wines; and because she and Sim were lovers, she gives him access to them all—and he unknowingly drinks the forbidden wine cherished by the king. This is revealed to Chŏng later: "As punishment, the King decided to banish you to earth, but fearing to send you both at once, lest you might be drawn together there, he sent your lover first, and after keeping you in prison for a long time, you were sent as daughter to your former lover. He is the man you claim as father. Heaven has seen your filial piety, however, and repents. You will be hereafter most highly favored, as a reward for your dutiful conduct."[29] This previous life makes her filial piety and duty of cure interchangeable with a wife's duty.[30]

In Allen's translation, the failure of reproduction is presented as a psycho-somatic cause of Sim's blindness.[31] Sim married an ideal woman named Kwak, who possessed both beauty and grace, but his distress over not having a son weakened his eyesight. He became completely blind when his wife died after giving birth to a daughter. By connecting his blindness to his sin from a past life in heaven and his lack of a son, this version frames his metamorphosis into being a sighted person as the restoration of moral status. That the cause of disability was the absence of a male child sets up a logic in which hav-ing a son would become an important component of the cure narrative. This sonlessness is remedied in the *Kyŏngp'anbon* version as Sim gains eyesight, remarries, and has sons, thereby demonstrating the cure's ultimate success. Allen's version ends with another component of success, class elevation: "His Majesty was overjoyed to have his lovely Queen restored to her wonted happy frame of mind. He made the old man an officer of high rank, appointed him a fine house, and had him married to the accomplished daughter of an officer of suitable rank, thereby fulfilling the last of the prophecy of both the aged priest and the King of the Sea."[32] All of these changes are brought about by Chŏng's sacrifice of her life.

When disability is thought to diminish one's presumed wholeness, "betterment" is imagined as requiring moral, spiritual, psychological, and physical transformation. Disability then is not contained in one's body but becomes a family attribute, which a larger familial body has a duty together to support, improve, and remedy. Linking the story to nationalism—as an example of what it means to live as Koreans with Korean values—contributes not only to the demand that women sacrifice for the family's collective interest but also to the imagination of disability as a target of endless intervention, a moral test of family members. Cure prevents individuals with disability from being perceived as embodying a livable life. That this tale has been retold so many times illustrates the lasting cultural weight of cure narratives and their significance in reinforcing the daughter's role as "selfless and dutiful."

Although Chŏng's offering is made without Sim's knowledge (and many versions of the story highlight his ignorance to protect him from being accused of trafficking his daughter), he symbolically becomes a devotee, offering his daughter to the higher power in exchange for cure. In their theory about sacrifice, Henri Hubert and Marcel Mauss argue that the transformation of the person who provides the offering is religious in nature: "The devotee who provides the victim which is the object of the consecration is not, at the completion of the operation, the same as he was at the beginning. He has acquired a religious character which he did not have before, or has rid himself of an unfavorable character with which he was affected; he has raised himself to a state of grace or has emerged from a state of sin. In either case he has been religiously transformed."[33] The father, Sim, would be morally and religiously transformed by gaining eyesight; conversely, his blindness is constructed as "an unfavorable character" and unbearable sin that needs to be rectified. Because Sim's reckless promise to pay the monk for the cure can be kept only after the sailors purchase Chŏng, the folktale treats the offering of Chŏng to the sea as a corrupt blend between worship of a marine deity and Buddhism, as both elements collude in exploiting the villagers' poverty. The vulnerability of the father to the lure of sightedness, fame, and honor and the vulnerability of Chŏng to the ideological command of filial piety enable this transaction. As illustrated in the discourse associated with the Honolulu screening, the ideology of *hyo* and the image of disability and its cure are constructed to represent unique elements of Korean culture that need to be celebrated and maintained.

Saving the Nation

The cure by proxy seems to be not always limited to family: it can also structure imagined relationships among disabled bodies, national politics, and sovereign territory. Jung Ji Young points out that the scene of reunion between father and daughter in Sim Chŏng's story has been invoked for various political purposes. One example is a remark made by the novelist Ch'oe In-ho in a newspaper. In "Open Your Eyes, Our Nation," an essay marking the Independence Day reunion of divided families from the North and South in 2000, Ch'oe writes poetic lyrics metaphorically identifying the cure of blindness with the reunification of North and South Koreas. He says, "This is the time for our nation. It is the time to come out of the delusion of three hundred sacks of rice and to see the face of our daughter. In our dreams, we have missed her, the desire of our nation, unification, the face of Sim Chŏng, by opening to the light the eyes that were closed like those of Sim, the blind."[34] Ch'oe identifies himself and the Korean people with blind men who need to be cured to witness the symbolic reunification, while separating "we" from the daughter. Gaining eyesight thus signifies enlightenment and a hopeful future, leaving blindness in the realm of "ignorance," "darkness," and the past. In the 1972 film *Dutiful Daughter Chŏng*, directed by the prominent and prolific filmmaker Sin Sang-ok, at the moment of the father's magical cure rain starts to pour down, curing the drought-stricken land and all the people with disabilities that it touches. As the disabled body is metaphorically read as a "national body," the cure of all people with disabilities and the restoration of the environment signify a prosperous, unified, and sovereign Korea.

It is perhaps not surprising that several literary creations based on the folktale depict Chŏng's trafficking as involving sexual labor, reminding readers of the many rural women who, during the rapid industrialization of the 1960s and 1970s, had to go to cities to work in red-light districts to support their impoverished families.[35] For example, in the novel *Sim Chŏng* (2003) by Hwang Sŏk-yŏng, the daughter Chŏng is trafficked as a mistress and becomes a prostitute traveling through China, Singapore, Taiwan, and Korea. Jung Ji Young points out that the author establishes the daughter's status as prostitute to symbolize fallen East Asia under the coercive force of Western modernization.[36] Both the disabled father and the trafficked daughter provide metaphorical opportunities, for blindness is understood as misfortune that creates conditions for the daughter to be traded and victimized. Similarly, Jung herself reads the trafficked daughter as a figure that summons painful collective memories of exploited women in Korean history: "Sim Chŏng operates as a medium of narrating the trauma of 'selling daughters' during colonial rule and the modernization process. In other words, it is circulated on the one hand as a story of extraordinary filial piety, and on the other hand as a medium of evoking uncanny memories of daughters who went to factories, became 'comfort women,' and joined brothels to make money, and as a story of the fathers who sold their daughters."[37] This memory can also be simplistically connected to the image of "picture-brides" in Hawaiʻi, an image that erases women's agency in partaking in the transactions.

Perhaps it is this image of exploited women in Korean history that required the cure of all people and the land in Sin Sang-ok's film. Toward the end, Chŏng is found on the shore by the king, who recently lost his wife and out of grief had been neglecting his duties. Seeing Chŏng as the reincarnation of his deceased wife, the king wants to marry her. The officials are first hesitant, unsure whether she is a marine princess or a ghost, but they agree that the king's marriage to her would be his only chance to restore his power and ability to take care of his kingdom. The signs of the kingdom's trouble are shown in scenes of scorched land and people fetching water and pouring it onto the fields for their crops. Searching for the new queen's father, soldiers arrive in her hometown and are greeted by a man with a speech disability and a woman with a limp. The introduction of these two disabled characters foreshadows that they will later be cured. Soldiers find out that Sim's blindness has not been cured and that, after running through all the money the sailors gave him, he left the village with a woman named Ppaengdŏk and began working as a fortune-teller, a vocation common for blind people in the premodern period.[38] After Ppaengdŏk leaves him penniless, Sim walks into the sea to kill himself, telling the soldiers, "I am a sinner who sold my own daughter to the sea. I need to follow her."[39] His self-incrimination, regrets, and suicidal gesture do not appear in many versions of the story, but here they have the important function of framing him as responsible for his daughter's death and as in need of moral redemption before the cure occurs. Throughout the film, Sim is depicted as reckless, shallow, and vulgar. He promises to give three hundred sacks of rice to the monk out of pride, because he was offended by the monk's judgment of his poverty and not because he so strongly desired to become sighted. Sim hurries to sign the document promising to donate rice toward making a new bell to the temple, knowing that he will not be able to afford it.

The daughter's proxy role in finding the lump sum to buy the rice requires not just her willingness to die but also her virginity, because sailors believe that only a virgin will calm the sea. Her lack of sexual experience becomes a commodity that carries supernatural value as a consecrated offering. At first the family's poverty, not the cure itself, requires her death. But her willingness to become an offering to the sea is translated into her becoming an offering for the cure. For this reason, another person cannot pay the money to the temple. When the villagers find out that Chŏng is about to be taken by the sailors to be killed, a villager volunteers to donate the rice to the temple for Sim's cure. Chŏng explains that someone else's donation would not effect the cure, as she would be breaking her promise to the sailors. In order to spare Sim from feeling responsible, Chŏng lies to him, saying that she is leaving forever because a rich family has adopted her. On the day of her voyage, the new bell is rung to celebrate the Buddha's birthday. Imbricating her sacrifice's multiple layers of syncretism, the bell consecrates her death and signals that she will be saved by religious power. Her sacrifice is a representation of her faith in religious and seductive power to cure, undertaken in the belief that disability is caused by karma that creates the need for absolution. The father's guilt and his willingness to follow her path function as morally redeeming characteristics before he reunites with his daughter and becomes sighted.

When Chŏng, now the queen, meets Sim, she is extremely saddened that he is still blind and feels that being a queen is meaningless if her father can't see her. In great distress and frustration, Sim rubs his eyes vigorously. The dramatic music crescendos and then suddenly stops with an out-of-focus shot of his eyes. The camera slowly returns to focus and cuts to his point of view, as he is able to see the face of his daughter; at that moment the thunderstorm and rain start. It is the rain that serves as a curative medium for all people with disabilities, reminding the audience of the beginning of the film, which showed the birth of Chŏng during a nighttime thunderstorm. As the rain touches the other blind men gathered in front of the queen, they instantly gain their sight.[40] In Sim's hometown, where people are celebrating the rain, the woman with a limp finds her leg cured and the man who had a speech disability starts to speak. The rice field is full of water, and the ship of the sailors who threw Chŏng into the sea returns to the harbor safely, signifying prosperity.

The curative power generated by the pious daughter's willing sacrifice works in multiple dimensions: her own reincarnation and the elevation of her status as a moral, supernatural, and secular reward; the king's recovery of his ability to rule the kingdom as a restoration of patriarchal governmentality; the father's sightedness as a transformation for the daughter's happiness and for his repentance and willingness to sacrifice his life; and the restoration of all other disabled people, becoming able-bodied through the king's paternal grace and prayer. The environmental cure for the drought would also prevent the national disaster of famine. The cure is constructed as requiring sacrifice and commitment to normality, which are rewarded by the total disappearance of disability in the kingdom, imagined as a utopian outcome.

What is at stake in this representation of female sacrifice and male cure and the disappearance of all disabilities as an idealized national space? As I discussed in chapter 1, in the early 1970s the eugenic ideas surrounding the reproduction of disabled people provided an indication of how public health and export-driven industrialization under the dictatorship set the disabled citizenry against the postcolonial nation, which was itself set against communist North Korea. The presence of disabled bodies in a given family and political space was a sign of moral degeneracy and an obstacle to modern and capitalist prosperity. The visual transformation from disabled bodies to enabled bodies violently disavows the presence of disability without the possibility of cure, constructed as a symbol of the moral corruption of the family and nation.

Taking the need and desire for cure for granted, family members may be compelled to find ways to cure disability at all costs as a moral imperative, with the behavior of family members seen as directly linked to the bodies and health status of disabled individuals. In Sim Chŏng's story, cure is not a simple reward for self-sacrificing acts but a complicated process that resolves the conflict, including the separation of daughter and father. Proxy then operates within the moral economy in representations of the collective effort to remedy disability for collective gain. Much as in Talcott Parsons' concept of the "sick role" in modern Western society—which highlights the sick person's right to be exempt from ordinary activities and responsibility but also deprived of a claim of full legitimacy and seen "in need of help" to get well[41]—in the formulation of proxy, the needs and contributions of persons with disabilities and illnesses are not recognized. Exemption from ordinary activities means that the person cannot live an ordinary life until attaining the cured status. The proxy role mandates a family member's dedication to cure, and this emphasis on cure and functional enhancement precludes finding ways to live with disability. This cure appears in a gendered way when a nondisabled daughter—or the wife of a disabled man whether or not she herself is disabled—goes through the sacrifice of trafficking herself, ultimately accepting death as the price of enabling the man. Authorizing oneself as a proxy for another is a manifestation of relational agency beyond individuality that is required by the cure imperative and the proxy's passivity to abide by that imperative. This imperative provides a justification of one's action and hides one's desire, which obscures the ableist ideology that disfigures disability.

Medicalizing the Miracle Cure

In addition to the continuing insertion of the tale of Sim Chŏng in textbooks to teach filial piety as a national ethos, the folktale has been repeatedly made into films in the twentieth and twenty-first centuries.[42] The mystical cure of blindness in the folktale changes to a surgical cure in a 1981 film with a contemporary setting, *Mother Star in Heaven* (dir. Yi Yŏng-u). The film depicts that a daughter's wish to cure her father's blindness by sacrificing herself motivates institutional interventions of medicine, charity, and the Christian church. The film depicts a teenage girl, Minsun, and her blind father, Tuchŏl,[43] and is based on the true story of a girl, Kim Min-sun, who received a presidential award in 1981 for her filial piety, a story that attracted sufficient donations to pay for surgery on her father's blind eyes.[44]

In mimicking the folktale, the film differs from the real story that was described in newspapers in crucial ways. *Tonga ilbo* reported that Kim Min-sun's mother had left the family when she was two years old and her father was a street vendor who became blind after a traffic accident.[45] In the movie, Tuchŏl is blinded by an industrial accident in a quarry, and her mother is fatally struck by a train while saving Minsun from injury. By making the mother's death a sacrifice for her daughter's life, the film paints her as highly virtuous in contrast to the woman who left the blind husband and her daughter behind. The cause of Tuchŏl's disability makes him a heroic worker and thus connects him to the first National Land Development Plan (1972–1981), which was intended to spur rapid economic growth. In the film, Minsun works at a chicken farm and a brick factory as the sole support of the family while attending primary school; in reality, the father and daughter sold taffy on the street and resorted to begging.

The movie fails to show any kind of social services, worker's compensation, or possibility of employment for blind people: the teenage daughter and blind father are on their own in their struggle for daily survival, relying wholly on Minsun's wage labor. She refuses to accept money collected from fellow students and charity offered by her neighbors. When Minsun is accused of stealing money from a classmate, she doesn't defend her innocence in order to protect her friend who actually stole the money. Her pursuit of independence and her altruistic acceptance of responsibility appear to prove her moral character. In a modern and industrial setting, the experience of blindness remains the same as the folktale. Tuchŏl is isolated at home; when he does leave the house, he falls off a bridge like Sim into a stream of water. He has to rely on his daughter to bring food home. When her hard labor makes her ill, however, Tuchŏl is motivated to find a way to earn their living. Soon enough, with his new determination, he is able to generate income by collecting firewood and weaving bamboo baskets. This rehabilitation is set up as an important moral precondition for his being worthy of free surgery as a charity case.

At her school play on Parents' Day, Minsun plays the role of Sim Chŏng onstage. While performing the crucial scene in which Chŏng reunites with her father and he regains his sight, Minsun is overcome with sadness at the thought of her own blind father. She blames herself for not being able to provide a cure for his blindness. She comes out of character; running off the stage to Tuchŏl, who is sitting in the audience, she tells him, "Father, I will die like Chŏng. I want to open your eyes." The theatrical performance of the cure drama frames Tuchŏl's blindness not as his embodied difference but only as an "uncured" or "yet-to-be-cured" condition that demonstrates Minsun's insufficient *hyo*. Even though Tuchŏl had never displayed any wish to be cured, this incident successfully communicates Minsun's deep desire for her father's cure and motivates her teacher to find a way to provide him medical treatment. Tuchŏl consoles Minsun, "I don't need eyesight anymore. I can see the world with my mind better than with my eyes." But in their determination to find a cure, both Minsun and her teacher ignore this voice. When Minsun visits a clinic and learns that the surgery is expensive, she asks the doctor if her own eyes could be used to cure his blindness. Her teacher visits various places, including the local hospital, to seek help. To get the money for the surgery Minsun decides to leave the town to find a lucrative job in Seoul, mirroring Chŏng's decision to sell herself to sailors.

Minsun's agony at being unable to cure her father makes it obvious that layers of cultural representations have so powerfully shaped the film's reality that Minsun identifies with Chŏng and embraces self-sacrifice for her father's transformation. In scenes that did not make it into the film, Minsun's emotional turmoil over the role and the need for her proxyhood were further underscored.[46] When Minsun is distressed at being unlike Chŏng, because her father is still blind, her teacher tells her, "Who knows, God may bless you, if you think about what you can do for his cure like Chŏng." But later this teacher regrets the cruelty of making Minsun play the role of Chŏng, because the folktale makes the family feel directly responsible for uncured disability.

In the film's original screenplay, predatory recruiters from Seoul played the role of the folktale's sailors, luring Minsun to Seoul by telling her that in just a month she would be able to make enough money as a maid or secretary for her father's surgery.[47] The film's omission of this exploitative scam—with its suggestion of a social problem—provides evidence that *Mother Star in Heaven*, like *The Story of Ongnye* (discussed below), was intended as a government propaganda film to influence citizens' behaviors. It serves a nationalist project, presenting the rehabilitated father who overcomes obstacles and the hard-working devoted daughter and depicting South Korean society as compassionate and charitable. In the final version, it is Minsun who decides to leave her hometown to make money and asks the owner of a brick factory for a job in Seoul. On the day she is about to leave for Seoul, the teacher stops her at the train station and tells her that her father would receive the surgery for free. To heighten the sense of dramatic urgency, this scene is intercut with shots of her house, as medical personnel forcibly remove Tuchŏl and take him to the hospital in an ambulance. During the surgery, Minsun prays at the church; viewers see a statue of Jesus hanging on a cross. When the surgery is over, Tuchŏl is able to see his daughter. The folktale's syncretism—mixing Confucianism, Buddhism, and animism—is replaced with Christianity and modern medicine, which do not appear at odds as they together generate a miraculous medical cure. The government-enforced modernization movement (*kŭndae-hwa undong*) recasts institutions such as clinics and churches as playing a crucial humanitarian role in improving impoverished agricultural communities. At the school playground, the now-sighted Tuchŏl, wearing a modern suit for the first time, and his joyous daughter, Minsun, are surrounded by a crowd of children who chant, "Hurray, Minsun; hurray, Minsun," making his cured status as her achievement through the practice of filial piety. Minsun's voice is heard saying, "The world is beautiful. I am so happy to live in this world."

Multiple layers of proxyhood are operating in this celebration. Minsun's teacher worked on her behalf to solicit donations for the surgery. The teacher's point about the "cruelty" of making Minsun play the role of Chŏng emphasizes that inability to cure blindness is an abject condition to bear for family members. What motivates the teacher and the donors is Minsun's deep desire for the cure and her guilt at not fully becoming Chŏng to make possible her father's cure. This process makes the father Minsun's proxy as she imposes cure on him and is celebrated for her virtue upon its success.

In this contemporary remake of the folktale, which contains direct inter-textual references to it, the disabled subject becomes deserving of the gift of medical intervention by first becoming a productive citizen through his own willpower. After a long period of poverty and reliance on his daughter's labor, Tuchŏl is suddenly rehabilitated and starts to generate income to support his family without any change in his circumstances or resources. In the 1980s, the Chun Doo Hwan government promoted individual rehabilitation through will-power and diligence by emphasizing "the will to rehabilitate" (*chaehwal ŭiji*) and created the Award for Overcoming Disability. With the United Nations' declaration of 1981 as the International Year of Disabled Persons, the human rights of disabled people and their need for social integration received more attention, but the emphasis on the need for individual rehabilitation by overcoming disability also increased. In response to the International Year of Disabled Persons, the Ministry of Health and Social Affairs developed the Welfare Law for the Mentally and Physically Disabled, which served the military government's "welfare state" propaganda. At the same time, the number of disability institutions increased. In 1973, there were 25 institutions for disabled people housing 1,718. A decade later, the number of these institutions had significantly grown to 82 with 8,021 residents.[48] These numbers don't include institutions for people with mental disability, elderly people, and Hansen's disease and tuberculosis patients or orphanages that had disabled children. (In 2014, there were 1,397 disability institutions with 31,152 people. Separately, 59 mental institutions housed 11,048 people.) Custodial care began to be supplemented by medical rehabilitation, therapy, and vocational training in the institutions.

In this structural removal of disabled people from the community by institutionalizing and segregating them, Tuchŏl's disablement caused by an industrial accident is counteracted with his sighted normality after surgery constructed as a necessity, rather than by his adjustment after becoming blind with the provisions and accommodations that can sustain him to live as a blind person in the community with his daughter. This way, the endeavor of rehabilitation does not reduce the need for cure. As *Mother Star in Heaven* suggests, cure appears as a reward for overcoming one's disability and gaining productivity, for proxy's willingness to sacrifice one's education, and for the family's never ceasing to desire cure.

Marital Cure and Chastity

As filial piety is gendered to emphasize the need for daughters to serve their fathers, so too marital piety is gendered and its object is broadened, so that nondisabled wives serve their in-laws, husbands, and their children. Marital piety involves sexual surveillance and proof of chastity. Another film of the 1970s—a period of rapid economic growth and political repression—*The Story of Ongnye* (*Ongnye ki* [1977]), directed by Im Kwon-Taek, illustrates the crucial role played by female care and chastity in mitigating the family crisis of a disabled husband and an ill mother-in-law.

The film historians Yi Myŏng-ja and Hwang Hye-jin argue that *The Story of Ongnye* displays the archetype of the self-sacrificing daughter-in-law and wife rooted in filial piety that produces a "maternal nationalism" (*mosŏng minjok chuŭi*) calling for women to serve the nation through their role of mothers.[49] Yi and Hwang classify it as a governmental propaganda film to support the New Village Movement, a state-run campaign to modernize rural (and later urban) communities that had an ideological emphasis on diligence, self-help, and cooperation. Women who have been marginalized within the patriarchal system, they contend, can speak only as wives and daughters-in-law in the practice of *hyo* in their marital families. Building on their argument about the state's construction of women as moral workers for development, I pay attention to the way that disability and illness in the family necessitate this kind of patriarchal ideology and activate the agency of nondisabled women.

Set in a rural village in the late 1960s, the film hints at the Cold War politics between the Soviet-led communist bloc and the United States–led capitalist bloc by referring to Sputnik 1 (the first artificial satellite) and Apollo 11 (the first manned moon landing) as signs of modern progress, thus propelling a traditional kinship council to alter its traditional Confucian governance. The title character in *The Story of Ongnye* is a young woman from a poor family in a fishing village. She has been supporting her family by diving to catch fish and other seafood to sell. When she was seventeen, her parents arranged her marriage to a man, Kŭnsik, from a family of the *yangban* class in a rural mountain town. The marriage broker promises Ongnye's family that the groom's family will pay a fortune, because he walks with a limp. Payment is apparently required to make possible the marriage of a nondisabled woman and a disabled man, constructing disability as a deficiency for which compensation is owed. (In *Adada*, another film by the same director that is discussed in chapter 3, a woman with a disability marries a nondisabled man after giving him valuable agricultural land.) Because Ongnye's father has been ill and she has four siblings to support, she accepts this marriage transaction. Here the negotiation of marriage involves heritage, wealth, physical ability, and deception. Seeking to ensure the birth of a son to inherit the family name—since Kŭnsik is the only heir—the council of elders of Kŭnsik's kin commissioned the marriage broker to minimize his disability by concealing his quadriplegia and impoverishment. That quadriplegia needs to be disguised shows that a certain level of mobility is constructed to be crucial for marriageability.

While journeying to the groom's family with a relative and the marriage broker, Ongnye hikes toward a rocky mountain blocking her path, which foreshadows the struggles lying ahead of her. Her migration from the fishing village to a mountain town to marry an unknown man echoes the journeys taken by "picture-brides" and by Sim Chŏng. Realizing that she has been tricked upon arrival, Ongnye dreams of running away; in fact, when her father visits her and finds out that the marriage was arranged under false pretenses, he takes her back home. However, she returns voluntarily to her saddened and apologetic husband and her appreciative parents-in-law. She pledges to her husband, while massaging his disabled arm, "I will never leave. I am telling the truth. Believe me. You will be able to use your hand, if we try hard enough. Let's try." Her loyalty to her marital family is demonstrated in her taking on the mission of improving her husband's function, in the belief that her hard effort will be rewarded by his cure.

Before her marriage, Ongnye viewed the sea as a space of freedom and resources that makes possible her family's livelihood. Her moral and physical testing begins when she moves to the mountain town, which naturally limits her ability to work and travel. Although Ongnye misses her hometown, she needs to be devoted to her husband and mother-in-law and to work for their improvement. Physical care and reproductive labor are not consecrated offerings to be rewarded by cure, as in the case of Chŏng, but they are duties embedded within the roles of wife and of daughter-in-law. The film emphasizes Ongnye's willingness to fulfill these duties and points to their necessity not only within the family setting but also for the community.

Taking into account the political atmosphere and social conditions when the film was made in the 1970s, Yi and Hwang point to its politically motivated construction of the ideal wife and daughter-in-law whose hard work inside and outside the household enacts the ideology of filial piety in an agrarian economy. The nationalist interest in such an agent for rural reform and economic development led to a focus on women's physical labor and morality: the need to enforce sexual regulation and discipline to soothe patriarchal anxiety about women's participation in public affairs.

Kŭnsik's rehabilitation becomes the ultimate goal of Ongnye's labor, which includes therapeutic massages as well as physical and emotional care. The film's emphasis on Ongnye's positive attitude in supporting two families makes disability the ultimate "test" of her virtue. The challenge intensifies when her father-in-law dies and her mother-in-law has a stroke while Ongnye is pregnant. During her father-in-law's burial procession, she goes into labor. The ending and the beginning of life are shown in intercutting scenes; the film signals that a change in her life is near. As the family's economic situation continues to worsen, Ongnye becomes its only productive member. Highlighting the absence of male power, these circumstances frame Kŭnsik as totally incompetent, burdensome to the family, and morally corrupt in his suspicion of his wife's faithfulness—suspicion that restricts her movement at the family's time of greatest need. Kŭnsik distrusts her interactions with Sudol, a man who has been helping the family, and feels that the aid of this productive nondisabled man threatens his marital sexual security. The film contrasts the bodies of the two men; the camera angle tilts up from Sudol's feet from the point of view of Kŭnsik, making Sudol look bigger. Kŭnsik's doubts about Ongnye's fidelity make him abusive and violent toward her. By portraying the tension around Ongnye's self-directed agricultural work, the film presents women's economic activity as exceptional and contingent on husbands' inability to work, obscuring the fact that agricultural production depends heavily on women's labor, an unremunerated contribution to the domestic economy that is often overlooked.

Although the villagers are tightly connected and help each other, Ongnye's presence in the public sphere heightens the family's anxiety about her sexuality. This anxiety limits her appropriate role to domestic spaces alone. On the way to the temple to pray that her husband and mother-in-law be cured, Ongnye visits a neighbor's house to collect payment for socks she sold her. The woman is not home, and her husband insists on giving more money than Ongnye is owed. After forcing money on her, the man sexually assaults her until Sudol stops him. To retaliate, the man claims that he caught Ongnye and Sudol having a sexual affair, and his lies create a scandal in the entire village. With family honor at stake, the family council of elders—the village's patriarchal judicial and governing body—decides to expel her from the family. They blame her lower-class origin for this dishonor. Although Kŭnsik wants his wife to stay, he is unable to speak his opinion in front of the elders.

The council's decree transforms Ongnye into an assertive agent with a strong voice, who speaks against the decision. Rather than challenge the false accusation of infidelity, she argues that expelling her will threaten the family's survival. She delivers a speech to her husband that echoes her resolution upon her return to him, but this time her focus is on her mother-in-law's cure: "Even if people blame me, I will stay in this house. Do you know why? Mother does not recognize people. Didn't she even fail to recognize you? But she recognizes me. The family council cannot save her. I am the only person who can save her. It's not because I am her daughter-in-law and she is my mother-in-law. It's not because I want to be praised as a dutiful daughter-in-law. What is important to me is the fact that she recognizes only one person in the whole world, me." As she utters the last sentence, the camera shows Ongnye starting to feed her mother-in-law. Then, as the music swells with sublime sadness, her extraordinary curative activities are shown in a montage of quick cuts. She climbs around the rocks in the mountain to gather medicinal herbs and goes into ice-covered water to catch frogs to be used as medicine. Kŭnsik is shown to be engaging in manual work for the first time, indicating that he is also being transformed into a productive family member in response to Ongnye's curative determination. Ongnye starts the hundred-day prayer by kneeling down in front of a tree with a bowl of water and wishing for the cure of her mother-in-law, an animistic practice and spiritual labor also seen in Chŏng's praying for her father's cure in the 1937 film.

The solutions to all the family's problems arrive all at once. Right after her prayer, Ongnye is shown assisting her mother-in-law, who is standing and walking out of the house, signaling her recovery from the disabilities caused by her stroke. In the background, Kŭnsik is in the yard doing carpentry with his hands. The family council withdraws the accusation of her infidelity and delivers the news to her that Sudol, who had to run away from the village after the incident, was interviewed by the police and contradicted her assaulter's false testimony about their affair. As a result, the council reinstates her and gives her an award as a true paragon of filial piety and spousal chastity.

The Story of Ongnye purveys the ideology that women should work within the traditional boundaries of their role but also be capable of supporting the family without disrupting the gender hierarchy. To prevent Ongnye's empowerment as head of the household outside of the domestic sphere, sexual regulation operates as a form of surveillance.[50] Her husband's disability and her father-in-law's absence legitimize her proxy role as head of the household, but she is allowed to function as such only within the contradictions of domesticity and the demand of public engagements.

Ongnye's turmoil is depicted as a result of her having to play the role of head of the family in place of her husband. It is assumed that her marriage to a disabled man would have been unlikely and undesirable had her family not been poor. Although Ongnye and Kŭnsik grow intimate, the film portrays her commitment to the marriage as based on her sense of moral responsibility. Yet their scenes together invite the audience into the everyday life and interactions of a disabled person with his family. Ongnye and Kŭnsik's sexual intimacy and reciprocal commitment are important if understated components of the film, taking it beyond the simplistic depiction of arranged marriage as abusive to women. However, by keeping its primary focus on ideal womanhood, the film turns this sexual intimacy into yet another stereotypical relationship between the active, nondisabled caregiver and the passive, disabled receiver.

In *The Story of Ongnye*, the nondisabled woman is presented as a role model who embodies the ideal of femininity in a shifting society, a woman who can act to eradicate the impractical remnants of old gender roles but does so in a way that upholds their spirit. She confirms the importance of chastity and self-help. Male disability serves as a motivation for women's self-sacrificing yet modern practical, productive femininity.

The Cold War and political repression from the 1960s to the 1980s provided an important social context for the film industry's cultural emphasis on selfless femininity. The 1970 amendment to the Film Law established film censorship. Article 11 required reporting and submitting the screenplay to a government office before filming began. Article 13 listed the criteria for censoring a film: a film would be entirely suppressed or would be permitted to screen only with modifications if it was judged to violate the Constitution, harm the authority of the nation-state, disrupt social order, damage international relations, or lower citizens' morale. In 1972 Park Chung Hee declared "Korean-style democracy" and defended the new Yushin system by stressing the acute crisis that had arisen from international developments, specifically the United States' withdrawal from Vietnam and the fear of its subsequent plan to disengage from South Korea as well. This change signaled the beginning of "full-blown, formal authoritarianism."[51]

In the process of enforcing censorship, Yi and Hwang argue, Park Chung Hee tried to construct a dichotomous image of the Occident and the Orient in cultural representations and looked for measures to modernize South Korea in a way that would overcome the hegemony of the West by emphasizing the spiritual roots of Korean tradition.[52] Through films, the regime promoted Korean traditional values adopted in practical ways to aid the development process; in these formulations, rural life emerged as the root of the collective memory of the Korean people, while the material conditions of life and the roles of women inevitably changed. These tensions appear visually in *The Story of Ongnye*. As a text, it not only operates as a story of chastity or cure by proxy but also reflects the project of the authoritarian government and its efforts to construct the image of a modern nation through women's labor and cured bodies while upholding *hyo*.

The daughter's and wife's labor of cure—including prayers, economic activities, the procurement of medicine, and physical and emotional work—leads to physical and moral changes in disabled men in the films, and it places the rehabilitation and survival of disabled persons inside the self-contained family as an exclusive unit of care. The sexuality and leadership of women threaten patriarchal power, generating violent responses against women inside and outside the family and serving as a test for women to show their true, self-sacrificing devotion. When the conflict is resolved, the cure of family members follows: the health of both Ongnye's father and her mother-in-law improves as does her husband's physical function, making him a productive worker. All of these corporeal changes signal cure by the proxy, including the character transformation of a disabled person.

Vietnam War Veterans and the Nuclear Family

If the success of cure by proxy has so far relied on curative caring for disabled men and the economic and spiritual labor provided by nondisabled women as well as on their sexual morality, how do the films construct masculinity in relation to curative proxyhood? The films featuring disabled and nondisabled Vietnam War veterans that depict their relationships with disabled women provide a rich opportunity to examine how gender, sexuality, and nationalism play central roles in rehabilitative and curative drama. Upon the request of the United States, South Korea sent a total of three hundred thousand troops to Vietnam between 1965 and 1973,[53] which generated substantial gains to the national economy.[54] Vietnam War veterans returned with and without traumas, and their struggles to adjust and to survive economically appeared in films, such as *Sergeant Kim's Return from Vietnam* and *Yŏngja's Heydays*, which did not question Korean participation in the war itself.

Sergeant Kim's Return from Vietnam, named after a hit song, features four veterans who served in the Tiger Division, including one with an amputated arm, who arrive home from Vietnam on a ship—thus echoing the opening of the classic Hollywood film *The Best Years of Our Lives* (1946), which depicts the return of three servicemen from the battlefields of World War II, including one who has lost both arms below the elbows. It presents male camaraderie, women's support, and heterosexual relations as the key to veterans' reintegration into civilian society. To this list, *Sergeant Kim's Return* adds a nationalist message of the duty of veterans to cure a disabled family of a fellow soldier and contribute to the nation by independent self-making. The film portrays the sudden cure of the mentally disabled widow of the platoon leader as a key event, establishing that the veterans can now move on with their lives. Similarly, in *Yŏngja's Heydays* a nondisabled male Vietnam veteran attempts to rehabilitate Yŏngja, whose arm has been amputated by an accident and who is working at a brothel. In this section, I will examine how the two films frame the veterans' effort to cure and rehabilitate disabled women—thereby recuperating themselves—as altruistic actions outside the bounds of the family.

These two films take a path for incorporating veterans as empowered agents for nationalist development by curing disabled women, differing significantly from the earlier period's social commentary of poverty and post–Korean War struggles without any successful resolution or rehabilitation. *The Aimless Bullet (Obalt'an* [1961]) depicts a Korean War veteran and his destitute family, offering an important refusal of curative drama. The veteran Yŏngho, who survived multiple gunshots from the battlefield, is asked to be in a movie that depicts a veteran with an almost fatal gunshot wound who miraculously recovers by the care and the sheer will of a loving nurse. When the film crew asks him to show his scars, he gets extremely angry and refuses to partake in such an exploitation of his trauma. His repudiation of sensationalization contributes to the film's emphasis on the social and structural elements of the family's ailment. Moreover, disabled characters in the film are never cured or rehabilitated. As the only breadwinner of the family, Yŏngho's older brother is a passive law-abiding citizen who would not do anything about his own toothache. He lives with his mother who has psychological trauma from the war, his sister who decides to engage in prostitution with American soldiers, his daughter, and a pregnant wife. Feeling trapped, Yŏngho decides to rob a bank in an attempt to dramatically transform the financial future of his family and ends up in prison. At the end of the film, his brother, whose wife has just died in childbirth, aimlessly rides in a cab while bleeding from his mouth.

Class marks an important distinction between the tragic ending in *The Aimless Bullet* and the prosperous future in *Sergeant Kim's Return from Vietnam*. In *Sergeant Kim's Return*, the father of Sergeant Kim Ch'ang-ho plays the role of an uber-patriarch who demands that the four veterans pull themselves up by their bootstraps. A successful businessman who owns a hotel, he serves ramen noodle soup to his son upon his return. When Ch'angho complains about the meagerness of the food to welcome a returning son from the battlefield, his father tells him, "The real battles begin now," delivering the message that the successful adjustment to civilian life requires militarized masculinity and frugality. The veterans visit the wife of their platoon leader—who was killed in battle—and his son and find that the widow has become mentally disabled out of grief and has no family members to provide care. She appears unresponsive, endlessly rubbing her late husband's iron helmet. The veterans gather in the basement of the hotel of Ch'angho's father, drinking to keep themselves from feeling guilty and to escape from the difficulty of adjusting to civilian life. The father barges in with a baseball bat and beats them, lecturing on the need to reflect on what they can do for the nation. After the father's lesson, the veterans move from the basement to the rooftop and collectively remember the battle that caused the commander's death and Chinyŏng's loss of his arm. After facing this traumatic memory, they resolve to reunite in one year, after they have found their own place by contributing to society. The corporal punishment by the father transforms the veterans, pushing them to overcome alcohol abuse and their emotional pain and ultimately to become productive patriarchs themselves.

The Ministry of Patriots and Veterans Affairs, who sponsored the film, inserts itself into the plot as caring for the family of the deceased officer. It initiates the widow's hospitalization in the National Mental Hospital and pays all the costs of her treatment. Because Ch'angho feels responsible for the commander being killed when the Vietcong ambushed the platoon, he takes on the role of helping the widow and her son. Rather than relying on his father to provide employment at the hotel, he works at a construction site, where sounds of explosions—mimicking the battle scenes—continuously refer to the metaphor of the war at home. While the widow is being treated at the hospital, he takes care of her son. When his girlfriend asks about plans for their marriage, Ch'angho tells her that it is his duty to cure the widow first.

Despite the doctor warning against exposing the widow to any overly stimulating environment, Ch'angho takes her and her son out to an amusement park. The unresponsive widow suddenly bursts into unstoppable laughter, takes off her dress, and wanders into the street. Ch'angho saves her from being hit by a car, but he is struck himself and falls to the ground. In this crucial moment, the son shakes his mother as he cries over Ch'angho's fallen body. At the sight of Ch'angho on the ground, which perhaps reminds her of her husband, the widow stops laughing and suddenly becomes lucid as she attends to the situation. Ch'angho clearly becomes a proxy for the widow, as she had mistaken him for her husband prior to this incident. His sacrifice and bodily injury inexplicably lead to the cure of her mental disability, much like the mysterious corporeal transference between Chŏng's death and resurrection and the cure of her father Sim's blindness. The stereotypical perception that a mentally traumatized person would just "wake up" when exposed to a shock problematically echoes the scene in the film in which the father's corporal punishment transforms guilt-ridden and disabled veterans into moral and productive subjects.

After the widow's cure, the focus then shifts to the recovery of Ch'angho, who is now disabled with an injured leg that requires multiple surgeries. On the day of their reunion, Ch'angho walks toward the other three veterans; his successful recovery from the disablement that occurred on a domestic "battlefield" completes the adjustment drama. Through the cure of the widow by his proxyhood, Ch'angho fulfills his brotherly duty, frees himself from guilt, and becomes engaged to his girlfriend. At their engagement ceremony Ch'angho's father ushers all of the veterans into the capitalist future as partners in his new land development and construction firm, now that they have proved that they are fully adjusted. The film ends with a spectacle of economic development: the three veterans are lined up, each driving a semi on the newly built expressway, as they follow a path toward the successful future. Chinyŏng, who used to be a pianist and now has a prosthetic arm, is on a plane looking down at the road; he is the director of a children's choir, and they are flying to a performance overseas. The vehicular positioning of all four veterans in motion toward successful careers is couched in terms of national economic development under the Park regime's aggressive economic policy.

The absence of any sentimental focus on Chinyŏng's lost arm and the relative ease of his relationship with his supportive girlfriend pose a contrast to *The Best Years of Our Lives*, which capitalizes on the disability of Homer, the double amputee, and the melodrama around his adjustment to his new body and the vexed social responses to his disability. *Sergeant Kim's Return* squarely fits into the mold of government propaganda films that depoliticize the U.S.-led involvement in the Vietnam War and its cost and instead emphasizes economic benefits and patriotism by exploiting curative transformations. The homecoming of the veterans is completed through cure by proxy: the widow appears as an instrumental proxy for Ch'angho's moral recovery from the debt of being saved by his commander, and he is her proxy, whose self-sacrifice and disablement results in her cure, thus establishing the intercorporeal connection between the two bodies in the absence of her husband.

In *Yŏngja's Heydays*, Ch'angsu, a nondisabled veteran, strives to rehabilitate his lover, Yŏngja. This is the first of the three films based on the 1974 novella of the same title, written by Cho Sŏn-jak.[55] Critics have read Yŏngja's life trajectory from housemaid to a rape victim, garment-factory worker, bus-fare collector, and disabled sex worker as representing the experiences of many undereducated rural women from poor families whose exploitation fueled rapid economic growth and industrialization. In contrast to *Sergeant Kim's Return*, with its patriotic message, this film has been seen as presenting a strong social commentary, in which Yŏngja's "disability represents the disability of the time."[56] However, unlike *The Aimless Bullet* with no "happy ending" in the postwar urban space, *Yŏngja's Heydays* ends up reproducing the rehabilitative drama made possible by a dedicated selfless veteran.

David Mitchell and Sharon Snyder explain that disability often "serves as a metaphorical signifier of social and individual collapse," creating the need for rehabilitation or cure.[57] Constructed as a discursive and visual symbol, however, disability does not simply conform to the social scripts assigned to it; rather, it also creates unexpected possibilities.[58] The visual presence of a disabled body emphasizes its materiality and lived experience. In her room in the brothel, Yŏngja keeps a large copy of the statue of Venus de Milo to reframe her body with its amputated arm as beautiful to the customers. One male patron is repulsed by the presence of "double cripples" in the room and runs out, demonstrating that the reframing can work in the opposite direction: her resemblance to the statue has turned Venus into an undesirable disabled figure. Nevertheless, the statue provides insight into her effort to survive the representational, social, judicial, and economic restraints that dominate the space of sex industry and that define her class and body status.

The film opens with the police raid of a brothel in a narrow back street, captured by a handheld camera; in a montage of women in their underwear being rounded up by male police officers, the film title runs over the freeze-frame of a medium close-up shot of Yŏngja moving away with her hand raised to stop the police (and the camera) from approaching her. Her posture of ineffective resistance to the forces rushing toward her sets the tone for her powerlessness and repeated victimizations. Like the ironic phrase *The Best Years of Our Lives*, the title *Yŏngja's Heydays* is subverted by her image in this frame, as Yŏngja experiences violence, exploitation, and disablement. The portrayal of her not-so-innocent vulnerability, then, necessitates a savior to bring her happiness, to protect her, and to "tame" her unruly sexuality and "self-destructive" alcoholism, seemingly produced by the cruel social conditions of the times.

Yŏngja and Ch'angsu fell in love before he went to Vietnam. When he returns and finds her disabled and working at a brothel, he demands an explanation. Treating him as she would any customer, she demands money. Angered by her vulgarity, he tosses money on the floor, yells at her to undress herself, and throws her down, but he is repulsed by her willingness to turn a trick. Her flashback gives the audience the answer to Ch'angsu: Yŏngja was repeatedly raped by the son in the family for which she worked. Eventually, she was expelled from the house; she found a job first at a garment factory and then as an onboard bus-fare collector. She lost her arm when she fell off the crowded bus and was hit by a car.

Her rape, her exploitative and unsustainable labor in the sweatshop, her disablement, and her suicide attempt on the railroad function to explain her entry into the sex industry, framing her as different from other sex workers who are condemned as avoiding hard work in order to seek easy money. Ch'angsu's emotional commitment torments Yŏngja, because she feels she doesn't deserve his care and love. Although Ch'angsu appears caring and protective, he often uses violence to compel her to accept his care. When both of them become infected with a sexually transmitted disease, Ch'angsu slaps her without explanation. When Yŏngja resists his forcing her to go to the clinic, he yells at her, "Your body is rotting." When she accuses him of infecting her, he slaps her face again, then drags her into the clinic and pays in advance for two weeks of treatment. His physical violence against her is seen as necessary to cure her sexually transmitted disease and problematically does not seem to invalidate his role as a self-sacrificing healer. He is also her regular customer, giving her most of the money he makes at the bathhouse. As part of his curative intervention, he makes her a prosthetic arm, so that a dangling sleeve does not immediately announce her disability. When she wears the prosthesis in front of a mirror, she weeps for joy. The scene transitions to the clinic, where the doctor tells her, "You are completely clean now." In the next scene, Ch'angsu brings her to his empty bathhouse. As he washes her body, she confesses that she now feels ashamed of herself because of him. It seems that he has restored her lost sense of "shame," and this confession is depicted as a signal that her sense of sexual morality has been restored. While Ch'angsu cannot cure her one-armed body, his interventions in curing her STD and making her prosthetic arm turn him into a savior, naturalize his repeated violence—in the name of cure—against her body that is "violatable" due to her sex worker status, and justify his moral judgment of her efforts at economic survival as contaminated.

When a customer offends Yŏngja on the street by not paying her for her services and calling her an "arm cripple" (p'al pyŏngsin), Ch'angsu gets into a fight with him, which leads to his arrest and imprisonment. While Ch'angsu is in jail, his friend Kim—in his effort to save Ch'angsu from "ruining his life" by having a relationship with a prostitute—visits Yŏngja and says, "Go in and pack. You're coming with me." Yŏngja meets Kim's crude attempt to intervene with fierce resistance: "How dare you tell me what to do! I know you have pity on me but do you think I am a beggar? I am going to earn money myself for Ch'angsu and me." He responds, "You better shut up right there! So, is this what you mean by working hard? Do you think a woman's body is some kind of meat? It is not to be sold for money. You are not doing Ch'angsu any good." Although she fights back against this violent harassment (of a kind frequently experienced by sex workers), saying, "It's none of your business; just leave me alone," she runs away into the street in agony. Affected by this brief conversation, she drinks heavily and apparently ponders committing suicide by looking down the railroad over a bridge, as a way to release Ch'angsu from his proxy effort to rehabilitate her from her sex work and the negative effects of her disability.

Then somehow a dramatic transformation occurs. After a considerable span of time, Ch'angsu finds Yŏngja near a housing construction site, working and holding a baby daughter; she is married to a disabled man. Ch'angsu tells her that her new life is "a miracle awarded by God." In the scene that ends the film, her husband and Ch'angsu are riding motorcycles side by side, indicating that a male bond is being forged between those who care for Yŏngja, whose face is superimposed with her daughter looking over the two men and the expansive urban landscape.

The film portrays Ch'angsu as a hardworking man, emphasizing both his physical labor of scrubbing peoples' bodies at the bathhouse and his compassion for Yŏngja and his desire to save her from her "self-destruction" and to compensate for the harms she went through during his absence "serving" the country. This is a careful refashioning of the novella's character, the Man (Ch'angsu in the film), who is located on the margins of society in poverty, whose sexual pleasure depends solely on purchased sex, and whose memory of the war and of his violence in it is still vivid. The novella depicts the Man, in his first-person voice, as focused on his own gratification: he enjoys a sense of power in his relationship with sex workers. Caught up in his identity as a veteran, he brags that he had killed seven Vietcong. He throws cash to Yŏngja for the perverse pleasure of seeing her hastily collect it from the floor. He remembers "buying" a girl in Vietnam with a box of emergency food: "How happy I could have been, if I were cruel enough not to know the girl's sorrowful resistance."[59] The author thus shows the Man thinking of himself as a sympathetic savior of women selling sex, unaware of his own cruelty while raping the starving girl. He goes on to describe paying an "ugly girl" to turn tricks out of "compassion," even when he thought he could easily get the same sexual gratification from better-looking women in the village. The author seems to criticize this distorted compassion, which is a front used to justify self-aggrandizement, exploitation, and violence. Unlike Ch'angsu in the film, the Man does not try to rescue Yŏngja from the brothel; instead, he supports her line of work by helping her recruit customers. The purpose of the prosthetic arm that hides her disability is to solicit customers on the street into her room, where they are less likely to reject her when they first see her disability. Ch'angsu's moral characteristics are emphasized in the film to provide a contrast to those of Yŏngja, who thinks that she is not good enough for his love. Yŏngja's rehabilitation is thus possible only through her relationship with a disabled man and not with Ch'angsu, who witnesses her new life as an indirect reward of his devotion and compensation for the loss of his love. Yŏngja exists in a different domain, as an Other of society who cannot cross the divide between disabled heterosexuality and nondisabled heterosexuality. It is worth noting that in the 1982 remake of the film, Yŏngja is portrayed as a nondisabled woman who marries Ch'angsu in the end, an alteration underscoring that for her to have a relationship with Ch'angsu in a film narrative, she cannot be physically disabled.

The film's omission of Yŏngja's life between the time she leaves Ch'angsu and the time she reappears with a husband and daughter makes her domestication appear more sudden and dramatic. The shot of Yŏngja hanging laundry outside her house with her baby on her back depicts the normalization of a disabled and prostituted woman and provides a contrast to the street outside the brothel, where women are considered out of order, contaminated, and dangerous. In the novella, Yŏngja does not make this dramatic transition to a normative life by forming a nuclear family. After leaving the brothel to live with the Man, she returns to collect what she is owed by the pimp and dies there in a fire. After the fire is extinguished, the Man is able to identify her corpse only by its lack of an arm. The novella's death by fire and the film's transformation to a mother and a wife after a suicide attempt are opposite solutions to the narrative crisis brought about by the juxtaposition of curative and violent Ch'angsu and disabled and resisting Yŏngja. The director commented that the ending was altered based on his intention to provide "redemption" to Yŏngja and to increase the chance to pass censorship, because he thought her tragic death would be considered too critical of society.[60] While her marriage and the reproductive family eschew the tragedy of violence and social consciousness, the two opposite solutions are serving the same political message: Yŏngja cannot survive with her disability without male protection.

In both *Sergeant Kim's Return* and *Yŏngja's Heydays*, disabled women's cures and rehabilitation by male proxy agents occur outside of heterosexual marriage. Casting the masculine effort as patriotic duty, serving the nation imagined as an extended patriarchal family, redeems male citizens through their humanitarianism; the workings of proxy and masculine altruism are nationalized and function to maintain gender hierarchy through disability status, domesticity, and curative violence. In this scenario, disabled women's bodies need to transform to shore up masculine paternalism and national benevolence.

Unremembering Trauma:
Multiple Personalities and Ghosts as Proxies

Cure operates as a way to share social responsibility for normative bodies within national Korean kinship—imagined as consisting of a single ethnic group—or family kinship wrapped up in morally enforced relations. Cure by proxy can therefore determine who is kin and who is not. Highly acclaimed for its horror-genre aesthetics and its unsettling gothic twist, *A Tale of Two Sisters*[61] draws on a well-known traditional story written in the early nineteenth century, "Changhwa Hongnyŏn chŏn" (The story of Changhwa and Hongnyŏn),[62] which helped produce the strong Korean ethos against the stepmother as an immoral other. Though the two sisters are named Sumi and Suyŏn, the original Korean film title uses the names of the two sisters in the traditional story—Changhwa and Hongnyŏn; the audience is thus deliberately misled into expecting a plot focusing on a malicious stepmother and victimized daughters, only to have those expectations ultimately betrayed.

As briefly mentioned in chapter 1 in the analysis of "The Ugly Creature," the story of Changhwa and Hongnyŏn depicts the stepmother Hŏ Ssi as a villain whose disability is read as external signs of her internal immorality. She is also called "the Ugly (or Evil) Woman" (*hyungnyŏ*); she has a double cleft lip, an impaired arm, and legs whose swelling affect her walking.[63] This disabled stepmother is supposed to interfere with the attachment between a father and his daughter after his first wife died. To get rid of Changhwa, the stepmother pretends to have found evidence of premarital sexual activity by faking her miscarriage—she plants a skinned rat in the girl's bed. The father sends Changhwa away in order to protect the family honor. Hŏ Ssi's son, who escorts her out, drowns her in a lake. Her sister, Hongnyŏn, is drawn to the lake by Changhwa's spirit and also drowns herself. The sisters then appear to a local police chief as ghosts and petition him for justice. Hŏ Ssi and her son are executed, and the father gets married to a new wife who gives birth to twin daughters, the supposed reincarnations of Changhwa and Hongnyŏn.

The 2003 film *A Tale of Two Sisters*, however, does not depict a stepmother or follow this story line. Rather, it imagines the destructive threat that a young nondisabled nurse poses to two daughters whose mother is ill and commits suicide and takes the threat to the level of abject horror. *A Tale of Two Sisters* provides unique manifestations of the proxy within oneself—in the form of an alternate personality and ghostly figures who work to cure one's mental trauma. This self-curative mechanism, however, becomes a sign of mental disability that is seen as endangering oneself.

Tracing the constructions of multiple personality and memories as objects of knowledge in Western science, Ian Hacking points out that severe and repeated child abuse was considered a cause for multiple personality disorder, which was seen as a coping mechanism involving amnesia that needed to be treated by recovering lost memories of pain.[64] Fitting with this theory, the film presents the traumatic experience as causing multiple personalities and amnesia as a coping mechanism of the traumatized subject. Early Western studies of multiple personality disorder in the late nineteenth century assumed that each personality was visible in one's physical presentation, such as posture. As Hacking points out, "Photography was part of the initial rhetoric of multiplicity"; that place has now been taken by quantitative tests of the degree of dissociation.[65] The presumed visual differences of an individual's multiple personalities are cinematically exploited in *A Tale of Two Sisters*, which presents an alter personality, performed by another actor and leading the audience to mistake her as a different character. In the following analysis of the film, rather than engaging with the clinical framework of multiple personality disorder (or the new diagnostic construct that has replaced it, dissociative identity disorder),[66] the multiple personalities are understood as the multiplicity of selves within one body revealing a relationality that reinforces the Korean ethos about family, kinship, and national bounds mandating curative dependency.

Unlike the traditional story, which introduces the stepmother into the girls' life after the death of the birth mother, the film places the ill mother in the same house with a young nurse, Ŭnju, a friend of her husband who is a doctor.

The nurse's presence worries the daughters, Sumi and Suyŏn, who fear she may take over their mother's place. Their mother lives on the second floor with the girls. Ironically the medical doctor does not work as a familial proxy to care for the wife; the outsider care provider poses a threat to the marital relationship, which is already constructed as in peril because of the wife's illness. Later the mother is found hanging inside a wardrobe—and when Suyŏn finds her mother's dead body, the wardrobe collapses on her. As she struggles to escape from the weight of the wardrobe and her mother's corpse, the nurse, Ŭnju, comes upstairs and sees what is happening. Sumi, unaware that her sister is dying inside the room, blocks Ŭnju and shouts that she is not allowed upstairs. Ŭnju tells her, "You may regret this moment someday"; enraged, Sumi storms out of the house. This is the traumatizing moment of losing two family members that haunts Sumi and disables her mind; in response, Sumi develops an alter personality of *Ŭnju* (also acted by Yum Jung-ah who appears as the nurse Ŭnju), a violent stepmother to whom she can assign blame. In this alternate reality, Sumi thinks that Suyŏn is still alive. (In the following analysis, to differentiate the characters in the film's diegetic reality from Sumi's alternate reality, I use *Suyŏn* in italics when she is a hallucination that Sumi sees, and *Ŭnju* in italics when she is clearly Sumi's alter personality, shown to the audience as the stepmother who used to be the nurse.)[67]

The film starts with a bird's-eye view of clear water in an old-fashioned hand-washing bowl on a table, as if the bowl functions as a crystal ball, in front of two large windows in the large, sterile space of a mental hospital. A man who is a doctor and Sumi, with her head down, sit across the table from each other. The scene's unrealistic space and eerie monochromic hue turn the domestic drama into a psychiatric mystery focused on accessing Sumi's shut-down mind. The doctor begins by saying, "First tell me about yourself. Who do you think you are?" He then shows her a family picture of parents with two girls and the nurse, Ŭnju, standing awkwardly behind the father. Pointing at Ŭnju's face with his finger, he asks, "Do you know who she is? It's your family photo." The doctor's questions frame the nature of her mental disability as centered on Sumi's and Ŭnju's identities and on the problem of who belongs to the family.

Sumi does not engage with him, as the doctor continues to ask her about "that day" and presses her to tell him what happened. She slowly turns her head up toward the window, shown in a tight frame. In a flashback (or an alternate memory of Sumi), the scene then transitions with music to *Suyŏn's* and Sumi's arrival with their father at an idyllic two-story modern house near a lake. The beautiful natural scenery provides a striking contrast to and visual relief from the tension in the hospital room, where Sumi's face is mostly blocked by her hair (much like traditional images of female ghosts who harbor resentment). Sumi and *Suyŏn* sit on the dock on the edge of the water, which eerily evokes the lake in which Changhwa and Hongnyŏn drowned in the folktale; its darkness represents the unknown of the mind in contrast to the clear water in the hospital space. Sumi and *Suyŏn* are greeted awkwardly by *Ŭnju*, who used to be a nurse for their mother and is now their stepmother. When *Ŭnju* finds old family photos with her face ripped out or marked over, she goes into a violent rage. *Ŭnju* runs to *Suyŏn*'s bedroom, wakes her, and finds her bird dead underneath the blanket—a scene that recalls Hŏ Ssi's planting of a bloody dead rat in Changhwa's bed—and starts to beat *Suyŏn*; finally, she locks her up in the wardrobe. After discovering that *Ŭnju* abused *her sister*, Sumi appeals to her disengaged and distant father. He tells her quietly that her sister is already dead, giving the first clue that what the film is presenting as real may not be what it seems. However, her alternate reality continues. As morning light breaks in through the window, *Ŭnju* drags out a bloody body bag, indicating that she has murdered *Suyŏn*. Finding a blood trail on the floor and *Suyŏn*'s body in the bag, Sumi fights with *Ŭnju* (note that she is fighting herself) until she drops on the floor. When Sumi opens her eyes, the camera shows from her point of view the blood on the floor disappearing, providing further evidence of her hallucination.

Knowing that blaming *Ŭnju* is only a temporary solution, Sumi wants to end her pain by making *Ŭnju* kill her (that is, by attempting to kill herself). While Sumi is on the floor, exhausted after their physical altercation, *Ŭnju* tells her, "Do you know what is really scary? You want to forget something. Totally wipe it out of your mind. But you never can. It doesn't go away, you see. And it follows you around like a ghost." Sumi pleads, "Help me," and the alter replies, "Sure, I will help you," holding a large statue over Sumi's body. The role of the alter as a proxy is thus to end the trauma by ending her life rather than by providing any cure. With the sound of plaster breaking, the father enters and finds Sumi on the floor, surrounded by debris. When the nurse, Ŭnju, comes into the room with him, the camera rotates around Sumi's alter, *Ŭnju*, who transforms into Sumi in the eyes of the viewers. Realizing that what she experienced with *Ŭnju* was not real, Sumi takes the pills given by her father to stop her dissociation. In the hospital room, Ŭnju says to Sumi, "It's all over now. You'll feel better here." Sumi, with unfocused eyes, grabs Ŭnju's hand and won't let go, signifying that there is unfinished business between them beyond Sumi's imagined resentment. When Ŭnju goes back to the house and sits alone in the dining room, she hears sounds coming from upstairs and feels the presence of a ghost. This shows that Ŭnju herself was also culpable for Suyŏn's death and the death of the girls' mother. The ghost exists not only as a hallucination in Sumi's mind but also as a separate entity haunting others.

The pills that the father has been giving to Sumi stop the transitions between the alter personalities and the hallucinations in which she sees *Suyŏn*. Because the alter, *Ŭnju*, is a proxy for remedying her own trauma and guilt, the pills that address her psychiatric symptoms of dissociation and hallucination are in direct conflict with the cure that her traumatized mind requires—a proxy villain and the sister whom she needs to protect.

The self-sacrificing nondisabled proxy, like pious Chŏng who ultimately cures a family member's disability as a moral reward, cannot be sustained here, for the existence of the curative proxy is pathologized as a symptom and needs to be eliminated by medical and pharmaceutical intervention. Sumi's unresponsive state in the hospital room that is supposed to be the place where she would feel "better" implies that her cure or living outside the hospital is not possible, because the two different conceptual worlds are working against each other. Instead, her father chooses to hospitalize her in the catatonic state seen in the beginning of the film. Sumi's past exists as her present in her alternate reality. Adding to the film's circular temporal structure, the hospital scene at its end shifts to a scene of Sumi sitting alone at the dock at the lake where she was shown together with Suyŏn (or perhaps *Suyŏn*) in its beginning.

Ghosts are important figures in the South Korean film—one shaped like Suyŏn and another resembling the body of the mother—disrupting the psychiatric resolution of the story that would explain the supernatural phenomena as symptoms of Sumi's mental illness. Ghosts also are memories that constitute mental trauma. The impossibility of the coexistence of the proxy for cure and the medical cure reveals that curative frameworks compete with each other for the dominant explanatory power of the presence of disability. Sumi's failure to prevent the death of Suyŏn and her ill mother from committing suicide becomes disabling trauma, and her only solution to rehabilitate herself is to create a proxy to bear the responsibility. The fact that her mother could not imagine living in the family with her illness and had to end her life, and Sumi's hospitalization, confirms the construction of family as for exclusively nondisabled members.

I read *A Tale of Two Sisters* as providing two insights about the cure by proxy and curative dependency. First, the proxy effort to work for the cure of disability can be enacted by disabled individuals themselves, making one's cure attempt (with medical, religious, or supernatural means) itself a sacrifice of oneself for the purpose of collective benefits. Second, regarding the relational duty to protect and serve one's family members, cultural imageries of folktales provide gendered references to which society resorts in order to justify the removal of disabled persons from the space of family in the name of incurability and self-harm.

The Death Drive of the Corporeal Bind

As a way to conclude, let me return to "The Story of Sim Chŏng," with which I began this chapter. In 1936, the writer Ch'ae Man-sik took a different moralizing approach to cure and disability in his refashioning of the story. His play, *Sim the Blind* (*Sim pongsa*), focuses on the blind father.[68] In this play, Chŏng never comes back to life after the sailors drown her in the sea. The queen of the kingdom, who thinks highly of Chŏng's sacrifice, hosts a party for blind men and plots to arrange for Sim to meet a woman who would take the place of Chŏng and care for him. In the moment of reunion with this surrogate daughter, he does gain his eyesight and finds out that the woman in front of him is a stranger. Out of extreme guilt over Chŏng's death, he gouges his eyes out and heads to the sea. After achieving the cure, Sim violently undoes it by self-injury to morally punish himself, because his desire for cure led to his daughter's death. The example of Sim's re-disablement and implied suicide in order to free himself from the moral burden of the proxy's sacrifice necessitates further violence as part of emotional consequences of the intercorporeal bind between the father and the daughter. In this case, relationality and the interdependence of family and a larger kinship group formed around disability operate to support the oppressive imperative of the "betterment" of bodies for the survival of collectives, ending with deadly results.

The obligation of the family to support members with disabilities has been established by the South Korean nation-state, which considers itself rooted in unique Korean values, such as *hyo*. This legal obligation of care exempts the state from its duty to provide social assistance, which has deadly effects. In 2010, a construction worker was found dead, hanging from a tree in a park in Seoul. On a note, found in his pocket, he had written, "When I die, those who work at the precinct office, please help my son to get benefits."[69] An ex-convict, he had done daily labor as work became available. He learned that his income level made his disabled son ineligible for state benefits for medical insurance and a stipend. Falling into the crack between sufficient income to afford medical care and eligibility for welfare, he thought that becoming an orphan would leave his son better off.[70] His suicide occurred under a system in which the income-earning ability of family members prevents children and parents from receiving state support, even when the income is not sufficient for the survival of others (especially disabled relatives). The questions of whether his action was reasonable or beneficial to the son and whether eligibility could have been determined some other way should be set aside, because the father might not have been aware of all legal options for the son's eligibility. The reasoning behind his decision is familiar to disabled people who have to negotiate a bureaucratically dictated balance between their own income, welfare eligibility, and the income of their family members.

Taking the man's suicide as one of many signs of the systemic violations of their right to life, Korean disability rights activists launched a campaign to abolish the laws that obligate immediate family members to support disabled persons.[71] Several laws, including the Civil Law and National Basic Living Security Law,[72] are written based on this principle. Unemployed disabled adults cannot receive support from the state if their parents, children, or the spouses of children are gainfully employed above a certain income cap. The person with the duty to support can refuse that obligation and be declared by the authorities "incapable of providing support,"[73] but a disabled person cannot forfeit the right to be supported by a family member able to earn an income[74] and thus is forced into the condition of familial dependence. Calls to abolish this law emanate from activist camps that have been set up in Kwanghwamun Square in Seoul since August 2012; participants in these camps hope to win politicians' support and raise public awareness about the law that unjustly transfers state obligations to family members and denies the individual rights of persons with disabilities. The corporeal and financial bind linking family members creates the demand for curative labor or institutionalization rather than sustainable care. The exclusive nature of the family for care and survival is under challenge by disabled activists demanding that they be recognized as individuals separate from their family members. This corporeal bind is connected to the frequent depiction in films of the sacrifice of the proxy and the suicide of individuals with disabilities.

There are many cases of individuals' suicides upon the loss of their basic state welfare support, due to the increased income of their family members with the obligation to support.[75] In 2011 in the city of Namhae a seventy-four-year-old person who was living in a nursing home lost state welfare benefits, when their five daughters' incomes were revealed, which would require them to pay the nursing home monthly. In order not to burden the daughters, they committed suicide. In Chŏngju, a man in his sixties was notified that he would lose benefits because of his children's increased income, although he had been estranged for more than thirty years. Even though there is a possibility to petition to prove family estrangement, he killed himself. In 2012, a seventy-eight-year-old woman killed herself when she was no longer eligible for welfare, due to the increase in the incomes of her estranged daughter and her husband.[76] In 2011 the South Korean suicide rate reached 33.3 (out of 100,000 people), which is almost three times higher than the low- and middle-income WHO member states' average of 11.2 (as of 2012).[77] These statistics provide one indication of the difficulties that people with disabilities experience in their struggle for survival and the need for expanding social provisions. They also provide contexts for approaching cultural representations of violence interacting with the factors that shape these statistics. Lisa Stevenson explains, regarding Inuit people in the Canadian Arctic, that "suicide is sometimes invested with the desire to live differently."[78] It is important to acknowledge that disabled individuals may utilize cure or suicide with the desire to live differently. In contrast to the national investment in futuristic biotechnology, living with disabilities demands eradicating the conditions that make lives with disabilities unsustainable.

Through the familial bind—as the family members' bodies are bound together through affect and corporeal influences—the family becomes an enclosed space for survival and calls on self-sacrificing female agents to navigate the gendered system of moral reputation. This familial bind intertwines with the imperative of cure or the removal of disabled bodies. Another form of the violence is that of concealment of a disabled member to avoid stigma and the sense of shame. The short film, *Continental Crossing*, a part of the Human Rights film series *If You Were Me* (*Yŏsŏtkae ŭi sisŏn* [2003]) depicts the social and sexual alienation of a disabled man. It features a scene where he is left alone at home on the wedding day of a family member. It is taken for granted that he is not supposed to attend the event, as everyone in the family is busy getting ready for the outing. This is a commonly shared experience for people with visible physical disabilities. To protect the reputation of the family the presence of disabled persons is erased. In these texts the family is constructed as a space where embedded violence upholds the gendered and normality-centered hierarchy. The colonial and postcolonial nation-state takes advantage of this exclusive familial unit by urging nondisabled and disabled women to be devoted and to support the family without any social provisions.

CHAPTER 3

Violence as a Way of Loving

Since 2001, the Disabled Women's Sexual Violence Counseling Center, a non-governmental advocacy organization based in Seoul, has been running an anti-sexual violence campaign with the slogan "Disabled women do not want to be an object of sexual violence."[1] The campaign works to counter the belief that sexual violence is a type of compassionate "cure" for women with physical and intellectual disabilities, a belief that rests on the assumption that sexual violence against disabled women—who are assumed to be "undesirable" and "unrapable"—is a favor to them. In this account, rape is associated with the sexual recognition of disabled women as women and is thought to transform them into sexual beings or satisfy their sexual needs that have been ignored. In the other account, violations of disabled women are often represented as an expected consequence of their vulnerability, illustrating the need for sheltering them.

The complexity of sexual and asexual lives of disabled women under oppression is erased by the binary logic—that sexual events are either the external recognition of sexual needs or victimization. In a popular film, *Oasis* (2002), a man named Chongdu gets released from prison, visits Kongju's family, finds out that she has a physical disability with a speech difficulty and is living alone, and, the next time, breaks into her apartment. He sexually assaults her, and when she loses consciousness, he runs away. Later, Chongdu and Kongju start a romantic sexual relationship. While they are having sex, Kongju's brother and his wife enter her apartment and accuse Chongdu of raping her. At the end of the film, Chongdu is put in prison, and Kongju is left awaiting his release. The false rape conviction for consensual sex in effect underwrites a fantastic retelling of the initial sexual assault as a genuine gesture toward unlikely intimacy between two outcasts.

A typical response to the rape of disabled women is poignantly captured in a scene from *Oasis*. When Chongdu is arrested, the interrogating detective reproaches Chongdu in front of Kongju: "Are you a pervert? How do you even get aroused seeing that kind of woman?" The gender disqualification and sexual repulsion expressed in "*that* kind of woman" enable the violence of denying the sexuality of disabled women and the dangerous assumption that violence is an indication of sexual desirability. Kongju attempts to communicate that she was a willing participant in the intercourse, but both the detective and her family ignore her voice, because they cannot imagine that consensual sex is possible for a disabled woman. Her frustration and speech difference are interpreted as signs of her emotional trauma. The film, however, does not problematize the violence of his initial assault or depict any trauma that might have been caused by the attack. Rather it highlights the family's neglect and the violence of the social denial of her sexuality.

Following the real-life acquittal of a man who was initially convicted of raping a disabled woman, the newspaper *Tonga ilbo* published a column titled "Oasis."[2] The columnist laid out the case: the defendant, N, had run into M, a woman with a mental disability, whom he met before. After having dinner together, N had taken M into a nearby motel, where they had sexual intercourse. M initially testified that she was scared, so she followed what she was told. He was convicted of "rape of the feeble-minded and -bodied," then appealed. The columnist writes that in front of the chief justice, M testified that she was not forced to have sex and that the sex was "refreshing and eliminated her stress."[3] The Taejŏn High Court reversed his conviction. Here two testimonies are taken to frame the event as either rape or a pleasurable experience that does not involve any pressure. Although it is unlikely that either of these discourses fully captures her experience, the columnist criticizes her family and the activists who assisted her to report the incident, arguing that M could not speak the truth at first because of her family's judgment: "The people who should have been convicted in this case perhaps are those normal people around her. They wanted her to testify that she was raped; they denied that she has an instinct to feel refreshed and has the right to release her stress. They viewed her life in terms of their honor and reputation. They may be the real disabled people with the incurable disability of hypocrisy and arrogance."[4] By assigning to the family members and activists the label of disability, the columnist deploys the stigma attached to disability to attack their attitude toward sexuality, but does not challenge the widespread sexual violence against disabled women. The column connects the case to the movie not just by invoking the movie's title, but also by employing its figurative interpretation of the sexual interaction as M's oasis, erasing its representation of sexual assault. Another justice on the panel wrote that the chief justice for N's appeal mentioned the movie during their deliberations and asked, "Have you seen the movie *Oasis*? If we listen to only the defendant's story, this is a perfect *Oasis*."[5]

Contemporary activism against sexual violence and for disabled people's self-determination illustrates the importance of examining cultural images of disability and how they frame the ways in which South Korean society understands, and even adjudicates, violence and sexual agency. The Counseling Center's axiomatic declaration that disabled women "do not want to be an object of sexual violence" directly challenges the myth that rape is a favor that recognizes their sexual needs. However, the determination of violence as violence is already constrained by the binary framework of universalizing disabled women as always victims or presenting a sexual event as a positive acknowledgment of ignored sexual needs. The approach that challenges both the widespread impunity for sexual violence—and its justifying rhetoric—and the assumption that disabled people should not be sexual is paramount.

Complicated social scripts of violence assume the undesirability of disabled women and demand their transformation in order to conform to a specific kind of gendered femininity that undergirds patriarchy and the capitalist modern state. Violence ironically enables the violent subject's power to recognize the othered subjects as humans, as if disabled women are otherwise inhuman. Medical cures for disability are also seen as endowing humanity, as recognized by specific behavioral and linguistic abilities as well as heterosexual conformity to the perceived binary gender, thereby situating disabled bodies as prehuman. The imperative of transforming bodies to become socially legible as human beings is closely connected to what Robert McRuer and Alison Kafer articulate as compulsory able-bodiedness and able-mindedness interwoven with heterosexuality in a capitalist society.[6] I explore in this chapter the physical interventions that are putatively intended to better disabled individuals and the material and immaterial lived consequences of those interventions. These interventions guide disabled bodies inside the systems of gender and heterosexuality or deny life when our bodies do not conform.

Concerned with the problems of the juridical and social responses that have been failing to address or contributing to the violence against disabled adults and children,[7] this chapter charts the psychic and physical violence through which certain individuals with disabilities are incorporated or erased in the name of compassionate cure. The vulnerability of disabled bodies is often constructed to represent colonial, national, and transnational oppression, and as they become metaphors, the political nature of the interpersonal violence against them is concealed. I lay out four themes that emerge as a result of the imperative for disabled people to perform desirable femininity and masculinity as well as humanity in literary texts and films: sexual violence justified to enable femininity (*The Song of Songs*); violence authorized as a naturalized response to traditional femininity and its vulnerability ("Adada, the Idiot"; *Adada*); violence as the price for purchasing cure (*Address Unknown*); and violence as a way to heal the trauma of others and as a punishment for incurability ("There a Petal Silently Falls"; *A Petal*).

Curative Sexual Violence and Nostalgia

A traditional agricultural community in the early twentieth century is imagined as an inclusive place for disabled individuals in *The Song of Songs* (*Aga* [2000]), a contemporary novel by the prominent conservative writer Yi Mun-yol.[8] By drawing on nostalgia for an "ideal" past, the author criticizes modern society for driving people with disabilities out of communities into institutions—not to aid the deinstitutionalization movement by disability activists seeking the right to live in their communities, but simply to advocate a return to an unproblematized traditional past. This nostalgia effectively reframes the villagers' sexual violation of a disabled woman as compassionate acceptance and a way of loving. In a 2011 interview, Yi said that he had a special affection for the novel, which was finally being translated into English, because it "seeks to evoke the aura of the old Korean culture which disappeared long ago from our society."[9] Yi had earlier created controversy and provoked feminist criticism with *A Choice* (*Sŏnt'aek* [1997]), which tells the anachronistic story of a woman from the Chosŏn dynasty in a first-person voice, deploring the changes in modern women's roles, and presents her Confucian womanhood as a noble choice. Published at the time of the 1997 economic crisis and the cultural movement to restore male authority in the family, *A Choice* represented a significant backlash against the women's movement.

After pointing out that *A Choice* made the author "the most prominent antifeminist in the land," Ji-moon Suh adds, "He then wrote [*The*] *Song of Songs* (*Aga* 1999 [*sic*]), which takes a nostalgic look at the old days when even halfwits were humored and given a haven and a role."[10] Although in Suh's description the novel seems to be a benign parable, *The Song of Songs*' portrayal of a woman with multiple disabilities and of the villagers' violence also has drawn serious criticism. Park Young-hee, an activist with a disability, connects the novel's romanticized depictions of the main character's rape to a real case of sexual violence in a rural village. In her essay, "I Do Not Want to Become an

Object of Sexual Violence," Park introduces the real-life case of Kim Myŏng-suk, a woman with an intellectual disability who was subjected to sexual violence at the hands of seven men in her village for seven years until their actions were exposed in 2000.[11] The village men began raping Kim when she was thirteen years old. Park challenges the façade of compassion in an agricultural village in which, Yi fantasizes, various groups of people live in harmony within their proper place. In the old days, according to the novel's male narrator, villages were structured in multiple concentric circles, each inhabited by people according to their ranks and roles.[12] Kim's victimization undercuts the novel's romanticization of a rural community, which, Park notes, does not guarantee disabled women's human rights and safety. As the political movement for the rights and visibility of disabled women took shape in the late 1990s, disabled and nondisabled activists viewed the romanticization of violence in *The Song of Songs* (and in the film *Oasis*) as endorsing and promoting violence against disabled women.

As *The Song of Songs* begins, three men are recalling Tangp'yŏni, a disabled woman who entered their old hometown in the 1940s. In her mid-teens Tangp'yŏni was abandoned in front of the house of Noktong, a village elder; her origin was unknown, but it was generally understood that she was from the lowest nomadic class, lacking a family name and hometown. The three men construct the feminization of Tangp'yŏni, who otherwise could not be thought of as a woman or even a human being. She was referred to as "one trembling life form," which later develops into "an organism which can move itself" and then becomes more like "a big worm."[13] The narrator says, "Her appearance made it difficult to determine not only if it is a man or woman, but also if it is a human being or not."[14] In the novel, being human becomes a status to be endowed by physical interventions, such as sexual violence, as a form of the social recognition of gender. The narrator explains that her gender depends on external responses to behavior and bodily events. Underlying this position is the author's belief not so much that gender is socially constructed as that disabled bodies are disqualified from essentially conceptualized gender. The narrator presumes that one is recognized as human by displaying biological markers of normative maleness and femaleness, but disability creates an exception. The narrator explains, "A signifier is possessed not by its subject but by its perceivers, as was Tangp'yŏni's gender signifier. The fact that she was a woman was revealed by many distinctive signifiers. But in order for them to achieve meaning, the signifiers had to be noticed."[15]

When Tangp'yŏni has her first menstrual bleeding, which the narrator calls "her signal sent out to the world outside,"[16] the whole household panics, thinking that she is seriously ill. One woman in the house finally realizes that the blood is her menarche and murmurs, "Well, that thing is a woman too."[17] Menstruation functions as an unexpected sign of her gender and her reproductive capacity: "After that, Tangp'yŏni was recognized as a woman not only by her appearance but also by her inner body and that recognition expanded beyond the household."[18]

A year later, Tangp'yŏni is sexually assaulted on a mountain by a man who probes her genitals with a stick. The narrator describes the assault as "the first external response provoked by Tangp'yŏni's femininity."[19] The women in the village find out about the incident, identify the man, and threaten to force him to marry her. The narrator describes Tangp'yŏni's reaction to the assault: "Even though the guy apologized over and over again, Tangp'yŏni could not stop crying. I am sorry for speculating this way, but might her lament have been caused by the sadness she felt—caused not by a virgin's anger and humiliation at being exposed to a young stranger, but by the fact that the member of the opposite sex left her alone, even after he recognized her as a woman and approached her?"[20] The speculation of the narrator illustrates the dangerous myth that Tangp'yŏni wanted to be raped and was angered that the man refused her. The narrator adds that an assault that usually would have harmed the reputation of a woman did the opposite for Tangp'yŏni, sending the message that she was a single woman of marriageable age, as matchmakers contacted her every month after the incident.

In the novel, the voice of the narrator frequently interrupts the flow of the story with his praise for the traditional rural village as a humane and inclusive space for everyone, which also preserves hierarchy. At the center of multiple concentric circles, he argues, "there was a core where people with healthy normal mind and body lived."[21] This "stable and unified core"[22] allowed people with various abilities to be included under its care. He decries the way in which modernization created institutions, mental hospitals, rehabilitation centers, and custodial centers to remove people with disabilities from communities because they are unproductive and need to be hidden. The narrator points out that the new medical and legal designations of people with disabilities, such as "people who need relief" (kuho taesangja), "patients with mental illness" (chŏngsin pyŏngja), "feeble-minded and -bodied" (simsin miyakcha), and "disabled people" (changaein), have replaced the traditional terms, such as dwarves, deaf, or blind—indicating individuals who could be part of the community (on its periphery) in their own places along with "lepers, butchers, and beggars."[23] After being criticized for his sweeping attack on modernity, the author defended himself by claiming that the perspective is the narrator's, not his own.[24] Yi also stated that he believed that "the exceptional nature of the body and the mind" of Tangp'yŏni would effectively prevent the novel's being read as indiscriminately condemning modernity and as idealizing the past as a "vanished paradise." However, as the feminist scholar Kim Ch'ong-ran notes, in fact the narrative does not depict Tangp'yŏni's perspective: it is the author who determines her experiences of being an Other alienated by modern development.[25]

The nostalgia for a past as displaying a compassionate charitable attitude toward disability, while its violence against disabled people is hidden, reso-nates with the widespread myth of traditional harmony and communal care in Asia that was supposedly demolished by Western individualism and mod-ernization or that stands in opposition to individualized Western societies. The disability historian M. Miles points out the tendency to idealize past Asian cultures: "*in the old days*, before the pale foreign devils sailed up in their little ships, disabled people were cared for in their families and were integrated and accepted in their communities."[26] As Miles warns, although modernization did indeed promote institutionalization in Korea, nostalgia "provides simple and misleading answers to highly complex questions" about disabled people's experiences.[27] Reviving this idealized past in contemporary discourse is espe-cially dangerous, because it is almost always constructed from the perspective of nondisabled people, ignoring disabled people's memories and experiences of violence in the community and family. As the analysis of the short story "Adada, the Idiot" will show in the next section, rural communities where disabled people lived side by side with nondisabled people without institu-tionalization in the 1930s were imagined differently as cruel places for disabled women to inhabit.

Yi Mun-yol's strong desire to valorize the traditional village community by portraying its conflation of sexual violence with belonging also appears in his short story "An Anonymous Island" ("Ingmyŏng ŭi sŏm" [1982]), featuring a disabled man, which was translated and published in the *New Yorker* in 2011. The label of idiocy grants moral immunity to the man named Ggaecheol [Kkaech'ŏl], an outsider who makes sexual advances to women in the village. Sexuality becomes a resource that provides him with shelter and food, thus ac-tualizing sexual subversion associated with his disability. The story opens with the first-person narrator listening to her husband complain about the ano-nymity that accompanies urbanization; in his view, it causes "the moral failing of our generation, a major factor in the corruption of women's sexuality," and he misses his hometown village where no one could be anonymous.[28] The rest of the story is the woman's recollection of a one-clan island where ten years earlier she had taken her first teaching job. Shortly after arriving on the island, she notices a man watching her with a "clinging gaze"; this is Ggaecheol, and she soon observes how strangely he interacts with the villagers.[29] Ggaecheol wanders around the island without a home or a job, but he is fed and provided for by people. She eventually realizes that he is having sex with women in the village, whose opportunities for any extramarital affair are severely limited because all but Ggaecheol are connected by blood or marriage. Considered infertile by the men, never becoming attached to any one woman, and never talking about the affairs, Ggaecheol is accepted by "all," though they treat him like a child (and occasionally a man beats him). Ggaecheol is portrayed as serving the unique role of providing women with sexual release, aware of exactly when they need him. Though known to everyone, Ggaecheol is a perpetual stranger who doesn't belong, protected by the difference that puts him in a different moral dimension. He functions as a solution to preserve the façade of sexual morality and patriarchal order in the island and possibly—as suggested by a whispered comment that a newborn baby looks like him—a solution to infertility. The anxiety about his reproduction is suppressed as the villagers remind each other, as if his disability guarantees his infertility, "Ggaecheol just an idiot."[30]

The teacher herself becomes part of this dynamic. On a day when she is disappointed that a much-anticipated visit by her fiancé fails to happen, and her "body burned even hotter,"[31] she takes shelter from a cloudburst in a storage shed—where Ggaecheol attacks her. After the initial shock, she recalls, "I did not resist as I fell into a dreamlike state—I just let go of everything. I'm embarrassed even to remember it, but I didn't feel victimized. I'm not so sure that I didn't enjoy it, as if he and I were having an illicit love affair."[32] This fantasy that a sexual attack by a hypersexually portrayed disabled man is a favor to a woman resembles the fantasy about the sexual attack in *The Song of Songs*, narrated by a nondisabled man. In both fantasies women want to be attacked: in one, the disabled status of an aggressor exempts him from responsibility and in the other, the disabled status of a victim denies her victimization. Ggaecheol serves as a sexual "oasis" to the village women, whose extramarital affairs would otherwise disrupt ties of kinship. His disability is the key to maintaining his role: "The men all treated him like a half-wit or a madman, but it seemed as if they were trying hard to mask their anxiety that perhaps he wasn't really like that."[33] Yi Mun-yol imagines that sexual violence provides a positive function for an anonymous aggressor (Ggaecheol) and a victim (Tangp'yŏni), ultimately enabling them to inhabit the community.

In "A Gracious Love Song? *Aga*? The Degenerate Worldview of Yi Mun-yol," Kim Chŏng-ran considers Yi's choice of a disabled *protagonist* itself a deliberate move to eliminate women's agency and subjectivity. Kim finds *The Song* similar to *A Choice* in that Chŏnggyŏng Puin from the Chosŏn dynasty voluntarily subjects herself to male domination, and Tangp'yŏni has to depend on male benevolence because of her disability. Even though Kim problematically equates disability to the absence of agency, she frames disability as difference, thus challenging the author's view of disability as occupying the lower rank: "From his hierarchical perspective, the author cannot understand, even if he tried, that Tangp'yŏni is not inferior but different."[34] Kim criticizes the author as arrogantly interpreting the sexual assault as a sign of human compassion and points out the danger of the author's employment of nostalgia as political ideology: such nostalgia not just valorizes the community of the premodern times but also promotes the return of a caste-based hierarchy that denies democracy.

However, in addition to Kim's imposition of "degeneracy" to denounce Yi, a eugenic term used to promote the hostility against disabled people, Kim's support for modern institutionalization of people with disabilities as a counterposition to Yi is problematic. Toward the end of *The Song of Songs*, the narrator describes with sadness that Tangp'yŏni could no longer live in the community but had to be sent to an institution. Kim asks, "Is looking at [Tangp'yŏni's] path to the institution through sad eyes going to solve the problem? Is it so deplorable that the niche she was occupying has disappeared because communities have been dismantled?"[35] She argues that it would be better to improve the conditions of places where people with disabilities could be protected more humanely and efficiently, than to abolish institutions altogether. Uninformed of the disability rights movement, Kim defends the need for institutionalization by invoking the vulnerability of disabled people, which frames living in the community as dangerous. Nondisabled feminists who raise concerns about the uncompensated labor of women in the community who care for people with disabilities and illnesses or for the elderly may share this perspective, often ignoring the fact that institutionalization itself is the unjustifiable segregation of people with disabilities whose right to live in the community with proper resources is violated. Disability rights activists advocate for in-home care and personal assistance, for expanding social support to enable people with disabilities to stay in the community, for making communities safe places without violence, and for acknowledging the various contributions that disabled people make and the care that they provide.[36]

In *The Song of Songs*, after the Korean War, Tangp'yŏni meets a man named Pŏnho. He, too, is an outcast, whom the villagers perceive to be impotent. Pŏnho repeatedly rapes Tangp'yŏni, and she screams and bleeds every night. Noticing that Tangp'yŏni is hurting, the villagers ask the doctor to treat her injuries, and they arrange a wedding between the two as a solution to the sexual assaults. The narrator portrays this as another gender-signifying process, which begins with the recognition of her menstruation and sexual assaults and ends with a physically and socially coerced marriage.

Later the narrator confesses that he had met Tangp'yŏni and on numerous occasions had joined a group of men in harassing her:

> Tangp'yŏni was a woman who was not beautiful or sexually attractive. And she lacked reproductive ability and was unable to sensuously enjoy sex. Even though we were immature at that time, it could seem cruel and mean to tease her by approaching her sexually, when she had nothing as a woman.
>
> But we already prepared our excuses in case we were accused, even if they may seem senseless. The reason why we were obsessed with her sexuality was not our sadistic taste for enjoying her despair. We intended to supplement her imperfect sexual signification. We genuinely approved of her femininity and we loved her as a woman even though our way of loving was different. That is why we happily conferred on her the title of a queen and called ourselves her knights.[37]

The narrator reasons that violence has the power to endorse femininity, and therefore it is an intervention that "cures" the supposed gender imperfection. The presumed undesirability and deviance from normative femininity of disabled women are constructed as conditions that can be cured by sexual violence. This rhetoric endangers disabled women's lives, while at the same time distinguishing their sexuality from that of nondisabled women.

In the activist magazine *Konggam* (Empathy), three disabled women activists criticize *The Song of Songs*, asserting, "It is a gross mistake to assume that disabled women have difficulties in having a sexual experience; that it is right to make them experience sexual activity, ignoring what they want and what they think; and that doing so is the most important and wonderful thing. That is absolutely not the case. Assaulting women with disabilities sexually and coercively, ignoring their volition and thought, is sexual violence, not charity."[38]

The contemporary patriarchal nostalgia for the "old times" idealized as being inclusive of disabled people authorizes nondisabled men as "knights," justifying sexual violence as a curative intervention to transform a disabled body into a heterosexual woman.

Reifying Traditional Femininity and Morality and Its Violent Erasure

"Mute for three years, deaf for three years, and blind for three years" is traditional advice given to a bride about her conduct in her marital home during her first years of marriage. This saying succinctly encapsulates the collapse between disabilities and the performance of desired femininity. An oral folktale from the late Chosŏn dynasty tells the story of a woman who acted as though she had a disability after being told by her mother that "she must pretend that she does not see the things that are to be seen, that she does not hear the words spoken around her, and she must speak as little as possible."[39] Obeying her mother, she does not speak a word for three years. Her husband's family "thought she was deaf and dumb, and so they decided to send her back to her father's house."[40] The figurative suggestion to presumably able-bodied brides that they act mute, blind, and deaf was a warning against expressing their own opinion or bearing witness: instead they should serve unnoticed. However this folktale suggests that married Chosŏn women face a dilemma: disability should be performed as part of their domestic demeanor, but they should not be actually impaired if they wanted to stay married.

A traditional rural village during the 1930s is imagined as a ruthless place where a disabled woman cannot survive facing the imperative to transform into an "enlightened," able-bodied "New Woman." One of the best-known disabled figures appears in a short story by Kye Yong-muk, "Adada, the Idiot" (1935). It focuses on a married woman who is described as mute (*pŏngŏri*) and has an intellectual disability (*chŏnch'i*) in a rural village that is transitioning from traditional agricultural society to modern capitalist society during the colonial era. Her name is Haksil, but everyone calls her Adada, mimicking the sound she makes when she tries to communicate. The narrator explains that her disability makes her undesirable for marriage and "her own parents had not even considered her as a human being, because she was a 'worthless child,' or more to the point that she was a 'wicked child' who was disgracing the family's good name."[41] In order to arrange Adada's marriage, her parents give a parcel of land to the poor family of the groom as a price for taking her.

The groom is happy to marry Adada for the labor she will perform and the land she brings: "Not that the idea of marrying a mute had been particularly appealing, but otherwise he never could have married without actually buying a wife. . . . [His parents] lost no time in performing the nuptials, lest they lose her to someone else. A daughter-in-law who would support them for the rest of their lives! Why, they could not help but want Adada. On top of that, Adada was a good worker. She docilely did whatever she was told and had never complained in the least."[42] But after five years of good harvests generated from the land, her husband grew impatient with her clumsiness and became violent.

With the money accumulated from speculative investments in Manchuria, in the emerging capital market, Adada's husband brings home a woman he considers "a true love for his perfect wife," a woman who is "intelligent and gracious."[43] Because the land Adada brought is no longer needed, not only does the husband become crueler in beating her, but her in-laws also grow ashamed of her and her disability. The relationship between her husband and his mistress, based on love, is set up as the antithesis of the traditional arranged marriage based on economic merit, and thus Adada loses her place in the family: "No longer in favor with her in-laws, with no one to take her side, and unable to bear the beatings of her insensitive husband, she was finally driven out."[44] Adada is sent back to her mother, who curses at her every time she makes mistakes in her house and brutally beats her.

Not able to withstand her mother's beating anymore, Adada flees to Surong, a poor man in her hometown who does not have any family. His affection toward her is sincere, but this relationship, like her previous marriage, reflects a negotiation between Adada's status as disabled and his status as lower class: "Although Adada the mute did leave something to be desired, he would never have gotten himself a wife without buying one, so even though the wife he was getting for nothing was dumb, he was satisfied."[45] Surong and Adada leave the town for an island where they try to start their lives as wife and husband. However, when Surong shows her some money he has saved to buy land, she becomes fearful, believing that money brings unhappiness. While Surong is sleeping, she throws all of the money into the sea. Furious, Surong kicks her into the deep water and watches her drown with the money floating around her body. "Adada, the Idiot" narrates the tragedy of the disabled woman whose domestic belonging and life itself are tied to the value of money. To prevent Surong from changing into a cruel man like her first husband, Adada throws his money away—and as a result she is murdered by him.

This short story is the best-known text by Kye Yong-muk, making Adada represent the traditional value of humanity with her resistance to modernizing materialistic culture. Humanity in this interpretation rests on nonmaterialist, traditional femininity. The literary critic Chŏng Ch'ang-bŏm reveals his problematic perception of intellectual disability as he downplays its role to emphasize the moral meaning of Adada's action. Chŏng comments that even though her decision to discard Surong's savings "originated from the typical characteristics of idiots, who are prone to act out impulsively when they are provoked," it is also an act of defiance based on her belief that happiness does not depend on money as well as her claim of human rights.[46] In addition, Chŏng finds that Adada symbolizes the value of the human and the exploitation of peasants under colonial rule: "Adada's struggles and resistance are not merely those of a mistreated disabled person, but are by implication those of the peasants, who finally fight back after long periods of forbearance and obedience after being robbed of their lands under Japanese rule."[47] The critic separates the meaning of Adada's action as a disabled person, which is deemed only misbehavior and foolishness, from the moral lesson that Adada provides through the brave action that costs her life. But what warrants her death, and who is spared responsibility for it? In this conventional reading of the story, Surong's violence in killing her, not to mention the violence of both families, is not questioned: it is presented as a natural response to her disabled existence and action.

The short story was made into the film *Adada* (1987) by Im Kwon-Taek who emerged in the 1980s as a commercially successful filmmaker internationally recognized on film festival circuits.[48] In an interview, he mentioned that he wanted to "capture the look of Korea as a specific region . . . [and] our stories that no one else can tell, the stories that are inconceivable unless you're Korean."[49] In portraying this uniquely Korean story, the director erases "the idiot" from the original title and depicts Adada as a deaf woman who is fluent in sign language.[50] The film highlights Adada's traditional femininity as authentically Korean and uncorrupted, connecting her morality to the rhetoric of mental health. The film begins with the image of a hand spelling out words with the following subtitles: "I, the mute, am disabled but mentally healthy. The people around me are physically healthy but mentally disabled." "Mentally healthy" constructs Adada's moral superiority, which is made incompatible with "idiocy" or unhealthiness, while the immorality of nondisabled characters is understood as mental disability. This is the only scene in which her sign language is translated into subtitles for the sign-illiterate audience. The film thwarts communication between Adada and the hearing audience and sign language users alike by not including the translations of sign language and by often putting her signs outside of the frame. The film transforms Adada "the idiot" into a conventionally desirable sexual woman from a high social class who is deemed pure and innocent and whose language is not understood.

Pyŏn In-sik, a film critic, writes that the film's removal of Adada's intellectual disability is intended to make her a "complete woman," because in Pyŏn's perspective, "idiocy" is connected to the difficulty of overcoming challenges through her subjectivity. According to Pyŏn, the director invented Adada's *yangban* (elite class) heritage, literacy, intelligence, and eroticism in order to portray Adada as mentally unimpaired, a "complete woman" with an "uncorrupted mind."[51] Her being deaf and mute is interpreted not as a disability but as a symbolic representation of traditional womanhood constructed from the perspective of modern society in the 1980s. In Pyŏn's framework, Adada's goodness (interpreted as mental health) transforms her death into a willed martyrdom that preserves traditional value, which is becoming lost in materialist culture and modernization: "Through her death, Adada recovers the meaning of human life. This is the message of [Im's] films, the recovery of the human."[52] This reinvention of the character reveals the disability hierarchy based on its symbolic possibility and the prejudice against intellectual disability.

The film deliberately makes Adada erotic through its voyeuristic gaze on her virginal, resisting, and pained body on her wedding night. When the husband loses interest in Adada, her father-in-law asks her to cut her traditional hair and to get permanent curls "like a New Woman," so that she can make her husband attracted to her. Adada follows those directions, and she changes her hair, wears makeup, and serves drinks to her husband, only to get kicked out of the room by her husband. Adada's inability to successfully transform into a modern-style woman to win the husband's love through her attractiveness emphasizes the economic transaction of their marriage.

Whereas the original short story says little about the mistress, the film portrays Miok as a New Woman, wearing Western attire and supplying the household with modern objects, such as a record player and tobacco. "In the articulation of the New Woman (*sinyŏsŏng*), the Old Woman (*kuyŏsŏng*, which literally means 'old-fashioned woman') was indispensable as the antithesis," Choi Hyaeweol explains, "providing a contrast between the imagined ideal of woman for the new era and the old (read 'backward'), 'tradition-bound life of woman during the Chosŏn dynasty.'"[53] As Choi notes, "The Modern Girl was something of an icon, discursively constructed in the mass media as a caricature with her short haircut, silk stockings, make-up, Western shoes, jewelry, and other accessories. If this outer appearance represents the Modern Girl's materiality, she was also portrayed as decadent, morally depraved, and money-hungry."[54] In winning the love of her in-laws with trendy gifts and gaining the status as a wife of the head of the household, she is seen as possessive and controlling of her husband. In one scene, when Adada is kneeling on the floor begging Miok to help her not be expelled from the house, Miok is sitting on a Western-style chair, domineeringly looking down on Adada and showing annoyance at the difficulty of understanding Adada's expression and signs. The two women are set against each other, for each depends on the husband for her livelihood. The film clearly shows that it is Adada who must be removed, as her status as wife is a remnant of the traditional arranged marriage that requires money to compensate for "undesirable" femininity, as opposed to a modern marriage based on love and desirable femininity.

Adada's in-laws, who have been superficially sympathetic to her, morally unburden themselves by giving her a payment matching the value of the land Adada brought as dowry as they send her away.[55] This proves that her marital status has always been dependent on the value of the land. It is this money that excites Surong, because once he adds it to his small savings he can finally purchase land and stop hiring himself out as a manual labor. When Surong is sleeping, Adada has a vision of him wearing a Western suit with Miok by his side, just like her ex-husband. As the film highlights Adada's moral determination to discard money, Surong's violence is portrayed as the natural consequence of her action, making it possible to describe Adada's death as "self-destruction."[56]

The film's aesthetic portrayal of Adada's death is intertwined with its treatment of disability as both a source of tragedy and a moral lesson.[57] Adada's submerging body is seen as evidence of her resistance to land ownership and capital accumulation, rather than as Surong's punishment for her nonconforming action and resistance to violence. The film shows that her failure to become a desirable woman and her efforts to free herself from the influence of wealth are punished by murder, thus emphasizing the imperative of transformation that is imposed on the disabled subject. Seeing the murder of a disabled woman as her sacrifice and resistance to capital values depoliticizes the multilayered erasure and rejection of her disabled, incurable body as an outdated and incompatible mode of femininity within the colonial space.

The Political Transactions of Cure and Sexuality

Violence plays an important role in enforcing bodily transformation, often disfiguring and reconstructing disability. The film *Address Unknown* (*Such'wiin pulmyŏng*, dir. Kim Ki Duk [2001]), set in the 1970s in a rural village near Camp Eagle, a U.S. Army base in South Korea, clearly displays the transactional dynamics surrounding cure during the Cold War. Curative technology involves the exchange of money, power, sexuality, and values such as gratitude and morality. The cruelty in the film generates shock effect on multiple levels, and it is important to unpack the meanings of disability and cure that are constructed to enable such cruelty. These images of violence often serve to justify, rationalize, and naturalize violence against certain bodies that appear to warrant violent treatments. Violence is an embodied experience connected to images of disabilities in various ways.

Address Unknown presents Ŭnok, who is a high school student living in the village near the camp town. She has an eye impairment: her brother, using a pistol made with the materials from the base, had shot her in the eye. The gun is marked with the letters "US," linking the violence that caused her disability to the military presence and American hegemony. Although the film emphasizes that the military presence is what facilitates the violence by repeatedly inserting shots of military aircraft flying in the sky, it also highlights the cruelty and banality of everyday violence committed by individuals. Disabled bodies are repeatedly represented as bringing despair and disorder. Children ridicule and taunt Ŭnok about her disabled eye, which she keeps covered by her bangs. She is raped by two male students in the neighborhood, gets pregnant, and is later dragged to a clinic by her mother for an abortion, which leads to her expulsion from the school. Under these conditions that construct her life as "nonlife," Ŭnok thinks of the possibility to cure her eye as a chance for a better future.

Two main points emerge in the film's depiction of cure and disability. First, a physical transformation by medical cure does not automatically allow for a successful category crossing from disability to normality because of existing hierarchies and the debt that comes with cure. The cost of cure includes financial and emotional debt or gratitude, creating the curative institution and the benefactor's power to dominate the cured protagonist. The debt of cure compels the cured individual to undo the cure in order to return to disability. Second, the history of colonialism and war, combined with the compromised state sovereignty through the imperialist military presence, intensifies oppression and hierarchies based on nationality and race, sexual intimacy, gender, and disability status. Moreover, the ability to speak the dominant language of English, access to military power and medical resources, anticommunist and nationalist ideology, and human and nonhuman animal status also create a system of hierarchies and values. The system motivates individuals and families to take speculative risks to change their bodies, because they find the system unchangeable and existing life unlivable. The violence is constantly imposed *on* them *by* others as well as exerted *by* them against *themselves* and against those who are more marginalized.

In one scene, Ŭnok's boyfriend, Chihŭm, presents her with his painting as a gift. After looking at it, Ŭnok tears it apart and throws it on the ground. Chihŭm puts together the pieces to reveal a portrait of her face with unimpaired, symmetrical eyes. His desire to cure her eye by creating able-bodied imagery clashes with her anger over his aesthetic erasure of her disability and her sense of rejection. This scene unfolds in front of the inaccessible territory occupied by the foreign army: the sign reading "US government property. No trespassing" delivers a sense of spatial and political dispossession. His desire to imagine Ŭnok's normative face then parallels the desire to reclaim the land that is taken by the U.S. military in the name of international peace and security. This national metaphorization of disabled embodiment poses a problem for Ŭnok as the villagers' resistance to and cooperation with the military play out on her body, thereby imposing violence and cure.

The opportunity for cure is unquestionably connected to the presence of the American military. Ŭnok befriends a white American GI, James, who is abusing drugs. His interaction with the villagers is constantly monitored by military police to protect the reputation of the army. Contrary to the predominant image of American GIs as domineering and crass in South Korean films, the director attempts to depict, albeit unsuccessfully, James as one of the victims of the Cold War politics who cannot find the purpose of his life in the middle of an isolated foreign town.[58] Noticing her eye, James rips a picture of a white model's eye from a pornographic magazine and puts it over Ŭnok's eye, telling her that she would be "a shoo-in for Miss America." Both Chihŭm's portrait of her, with its normative aesthetics, and James's transracial mask, which erases racialized disability, serve as visual markers of the transformation and possibilities that cure can offer. James says, "Do you want eye surgery? It's easy enough for a good old American military hospital to take care of. If I help you, you'd be my sweetheart?" Ŭnok asks, "Can you fix my eye, really?" and nods. In fact she has been motivated to study English ever since she heard a government benefits officer tell her mother that the hospital at the base might be able to provide a cure. The paper eye doesn't just signal her postcure able-bodiedness but also functions as a racial mark on her body, forged by her sex trade with the GI. Before agreeing to the exchange of cure and sex, Ŭnok had found out that the benefits her family had received on account of her father's status as a soldier who died during the Korean War were revoked because he had been found alive in North Korea. This reminds the audience that the Korean War has never ended but has remained in a state of truce. As their status plummeted from the family of a decorated soldier to the family of a deserter under surveillance for communist alliance, they lost their means for their life. Ŭnok's cure and alliance with the American military are deemed necessary for increasing the chance for the family's survival.

Another family in the film is that of Ch'angguk, a biracial man, and his nameless mother, whom villagers call "crazy" and having "a fate of a dog." The mother is known to villagers as a *yanggongju* (Yankee princess or Western princess), a derogatory term for a sex worker within a camp town. They live in an abandoned military bus in a field, away from other houses in a liminal state of un-belonging to their community. Daily, Ch'angguk's mother sends a letter and a photo of Ch'angguk to her GI husband, Michael, who left Korea. She waits for his reply, only to receive the returned letter stamped ADDRESS UNKNOWN. Without hesitation, she changes the envelope and mails out the same letter again. Living in a vehicle that cannot move and sending a letter that cannot arrive, she desires to go to the United States and refuses to talk to the villagers in Korean, instead speaking in English, which offends them. Her desire parallels Ŭnok's desire for a cured eye; through their relationship with the GIs, both seek an escape from the unsustainable life.

Both Ch'angguk's biracial status and his mother's cross-racial sex work constitute disability in a South Korean historical context. After the Korean War, South Korean annual statistical reports on "vulnerable populations" listed "mixed-blood children" and prostitutes along with people with impairments or infectious diseases, disabled veterans, "leprosy" patients, drug addicts, and widows. A year later people with impairments and disabled veterans joined the catalog.[59] The first nationwide survey of "handicapped" children was conducted in 1961 by the Korea Child Welfare Committee.[60] It classified biracial children as having "social handicaps." The survey defined "children of mixed racial parentage" as "those children born of Korean mothers and foreigners (Chinese and Japanese not included)."[61] The survey report addressed the issues of the children born outside of marriage to Korean women engaging in sex work and foreign servicemen in the military services.[62] Sex workers, biracial children of sex workers, and disabled people exist alongside and within the intersectional space of marginalized identities. The so-called protection meant mainly sending biracial children to the United States through adoption. Some of these children were placed in a special school and taught English to prepare for their adoptions in the mid-1960s. This stigma-based definition of disability in the postwar context was changed to more medically defined impairment categories in the mid-1970s.

Ch'angguk's mother desires to go to the United States to make her son's life possible. Villagers despise and mistrust him, as he is the child of a black American GI and a stigmatized Korean woman; as the result, the only job he can find is working for a man who slaughters dogs for meat. When he cannot bear the cruelty of pounding the body of a dog as it hangs from a tree nearing death and refuses to do so, the butcher brutally beats him. The shot of him riding in a dog cage on the back of a motorcycle driven by the butcher on their way to pick up a dog from a seller links his body and animal bodies, not in a way that simply degrades him in a conventional sense, but in a way that forms the shared marginality of and intimacy between animals and biracial and disabled people at the bottom of the village hierarchy.

Kim Ki Duk situates dogs at the center of his film's representation of violence among characters, and he constructs dehumanization as a way to forge an alliance with nonhuman animals beyond the fraught category of the human. In fact, the film's opening disclaimer, "No animal was harmed in any way during the making of this film," underscores that violence against animals feels often real and tantalizing rather than mimetic—as goes without saying in the case of violence against the actors' bodies.[63] The statement makes it clear that acts of violence against animals in the film are and will be felt as "significant in and of themselves" rather than serving "as an allegory or symbolic complement to help illuminate the issues of violence against humans in the plot."[64] In addition to their becoming objects of direct violence, dogs share intimacy and bond with marginalized people in the film. Ŭnok gains a sense of sexuality by watching dogs copulate in front of her, and she also takes pleasure from her puppy orally stimulating her genitals. Chihŭm also has a close attachment to his dog. As interpersonal violence continues in the village against Ŭnok, Ch'angguk, and his mother, dogs are also beaten, killed, sold, and burned almost to death. Later, to exact revenge, Ch'angguk puts a rope around the butcher's neck and then makes the dogs kill him by pulling it tight. His action effectively "humanizes" dogs by making them agents who are capable of paying back the violence. At the same time, they are used as his instruments of revenge.

The film's representation of nonhuman animals deconstructs the concept of dehumanization as a necessarily degraded status that licenses violence. Instead it problematizes the comparable violence against animals and against human beings who are marginalized by racial and physical difference, sexuality, and gender. By showing victimization and the infliction of violence, the director constructs strong interspecies affinities, rather than assuming intraspecies commonality and anthropocentrism. Furthermore, by juxtaposing the common sight of dog-meat soup in a village restaurant, served as a traditionally nutritious meal, with the brutal practice of beating dogs before killing them in order to make the meat more tender and delicious, he presents a particular Korean culinary culture as one of the many causes of violence against (and among) those who are considered disposable and consumable bodies.

Hiding his yearning for his father and his desire to escape the town, Ch'angguk severely beats his mother every time she runs into trouble with the villagers by stealing food, rudely speaking English as she brags about her American husband, and screaming her question about her husband's address at the gate of Camp Eagle. Ch'angguk's violence against his mother poses a contradiction to his refusal to participate in beating dogs, blurring the boundary between victims and perpetrators of violence. One day in what his mother eerily perceives to be a caring moment of his washing her bruised body, he takes out a knife and starts to cut off the tattoo of his father's name on his mother's breast. By assaulting his mother's body, he attempts to free her and himself from the inscription of the American father as the origin of their denied life and her mental difference. The removal of the tattoo from his mother constitutes curative violence as an imposed symbolic remedy that physically harms. After erasing the mark of their collective disabilities from her body, Ch'angguk ends his life. Leaving his mother in bloody water, he drives a motorcycle into the muddy farmland and kills himself. Mourning her son's death, his mother in the end sets her bus and herself on fire, testifying to the unlivability of their lives.

Ŭnok's cure, enabled by her relationship with the GI and the military, poses a conflict with her Korean boyfriend, who questions the need for cure albeit ineffectively. When James, the American GI, is taking Ŭnok to the base for surgery, Chihŭm stops her by seizing her arms and says, "I like the way you are." She is unconvinced and confronts him, asking, "Are you sure you could smile at this for the rest of your life?" As Chihŭm falls silent, Ŭnok pushes him away and leaves with James. On the way home, while her eye is still bandaged after the surgery, James drives into the middle of an open field, where he has sex with her. The scene shifts: now her mother is removing the bandage, finding her eye completely cured, and grabbing James's hand in gratitude. After she is cured, Ŭnok runs into Chihŭm and looks at him with sad eyes, as the military chopper flies overhead, reminding the audience of the military domination of the place and people. The film portrays Chihŭm, who is in love with Ŭnok, as a disempowered perpetual voyeur circling around Ŭnok and as the victim of repeated extortion and harassment by the two men who raped her. To live up to the patriarchal expectation of protective masculinity, he later seeks his revenge against James and the two rapists and ends up with a leg injury that disables him, just like his father who became disabled during the Korean War. The two generations' disabilities testify to the continuing geopolitical struggles on the Korean peninsula, producing bodily transformation as their consequences.

In their relationship after Ŭnok's surgery, James inflicts sexual and physical abuse on Ŭnok. He attempts to tattoo his name on Ŭnok's breast with his knife, creating another parallel between Ŭnok and Ch'angguk's mother. In order to escape James's violence and the debt of cure, Ŭnok grabs his knife and stabs her own cured eye. This transactional entanglement of cure and violence is no coincidence: the larger economic system of values in the village depends on hierarchies involving disability status, race, gender, sexual relations, and military presence, all of which foster interpersonal violence. Ŭnok chooses cure and later disability as a way to survive in the midst of conditions that foreclose her life. Although restoring the impairment in the exact same way through self-injury would be as unlikely as achieving complete normativity by corrective surgery, her face becomes exactly the same as the face before the cure. However, through this exact restoration of disability, the film does not present her disabled embodiment as desirable, but rather makes the nationalist point that the cure is a corrupt status based on the sexual collusion with the GI, which she has to undo.

Although many villagers' lives are in one way enabled and disabled by the presence of the base, women's relationships with GIs are morally condemned and seen as violating the nation's sexual boundaries. In this denial of life, Ch'angguk's mother and Ŭnok enact violence against themselves.

The village is a product of Cold War transnational politics, in which speaking English signifies power or enables exploitation—as the butcher who used to work on the base says that the ability to speak English makes one a slave to Americans. At the same time, it occasionally serves as a sign of madness and antinational complicity with the imperialist force. Ŭnok is not only disabled by her brother with the weapon whose markings highlight the U.S. military presence, but is also violated by the young village men who brag about their English and are even called "English-hungry" by Ch'angguk, whose own American-accented English was learned from his now-disappeared father. The career of killing "commies" during the war is also presented in the film as conferring moral authority. Chihŭm's father brags about his disabled leg as a symbol of his exploits. Later he is awarded with a decoration for his military achievements, which had long been unacknowledged. To save Ŭnok from violence, Chihŭm shoots an arrow into James's genital region. His action of using a traditional weapon rather than a gun to symbolically castrate James only leads his father to submit his medal at the police station, where he begs the police officers—who are outraged by Chihŭm's daring act of attacking an American GI—to let go of his son. The father's surrender to the police, which acts to protect the American hegemony, illustrates that the Korean War was not just between North and South but was a surrogate war carried out on behalf of the larger forces after World War II that generated the Cold War, which still dominate the national space.

The crip and queer theories scholars Robert McRuer and Alison Kafer both show that compulsory able-bodiedness marks the nonnormative bodily presence itself as unsustainable.[65] In Ŭnok's case, able-bodiedness becomes unsustainable because of its price, which she continues to pay. Her cured body continues to be embattled because of gendered, sexual, and racial hierarchy and the ideological division between North and South. She has to renegotiate for a chance for life by reacquiring a disability. Cure provides the solution for the problematized bodily difference, and it is based on speculative risks that involve the possibility of loss and gain to the degree that cured bodies sometimes need to be re-disabled to stop the harms that come with the cure.

Trauma and Mental Disability

Violence on a massive scale, collective memory, disability, the trauma of guilt, and interpersonal violence interact in cultural representations. One of the common representations of women outside the bounds of normalcy is as madwomen, or women with a mental disability or mental illness.[66] The image of a wandering woman with mental disability, always wearing a flower in her hair, who has left the safe, livable boundary of society, appears frequently in the South Korean cultural imagination of the natural landscape.[67] The madwoman does not live in the attic, but in wilderness, often outside the livable boundary of society.

Ch'oe Yun's novella "There a Petal Silently Falls" ("Chŏgi sori ŏpsi hanjŏm kkonnip i chigo" [1988]) centers on a nameless teenage girl with mental trauma who has been journeying alone ever since the day of the massacre in Kwangju, which occurred during the armed struggle for democratization that lasted from May 18 to May 27, 1980.[68] After the assassination of Park Chung Hee, Major General Chun Doo Hwan rose to power in 1979; many protesters demanded that a direct presidential election take place in Seoul and other cities and were countered with martial law and the arrest of the opposition leader, Kim Dae Jung. Troops were sent to the southern city of Kwangju to suppress the protests by students and other citizens, and they fired indiscriminately into the crowds, causing an estimated five hundred civilian deaths and injuring more than three thousand.[69] The sociologist Keun-sik Jung argues that "the post–Cold War world order contributed to South Korean authoritarianism," as evidenced by the United States' approval of "the deployment of Korean military forces before and during the Kwangju uprising."[70] This involvement in Kwangju led to anti-Americanism in the democratization movement as "a new form of nationalism."[71]

In 1994 Chang Sŏn-u made the novella into a film, *A Petal* (*Kkonnip*). Together with the novella, the film is one of the most important texts representing the Kwangju massacre, created before those responsible were convicted of their crimes.[72] According to the critic Koh Boo Eung, however, the novella "depoliticizes" the historical experience of the Kwangju uprising and democratization movement by focusing on a girl's interior narrative.[73] One layperson's response to the film shows similar dissatisfaction, even though the film depicts the historical events by inserting documentary footage—recorded by a German cameraman, Jurgen Hinzpeter, during the uprising—and reenacting the mass protests and military violence. The author of a letter sent to the film magazine *Cine 21* opines that *A Petal* did not show the story of Kwangju that audiences wanted to see but instead had used "an adolescent girl with a mental disorder as a spokesperson."[74] The letter writer added that those who experienced that history could speak of Kwangju only when intoxicated: "We could talk about that day, only when we became someone else." In separating "we," the subjects who were collectively traumatized by the event, and "a girl with a mental disorder"—a fictional character who is directly affected by the violence but is assumed to be speaking for others—this viewer presupposed the existence of some single story that accurately represents the historical memory of the Kwangju Uprising. If the girl is a spokesperson, whom is she representing? Whose voice can directly represent the political and historical significance of the violence of Kwangju? Viewers might have preferred the speaker to be the girl's brother, a young man who took part in the student democratization movement, was harassed by the authorities for his political activity, and was killed, or the mother who had lost her son and joined the protest, not a teen-age girl with a mental difference who is cast out of the political realm. In the novella, the girl is aware of her discredited status as a "dull-witted" girl even before the trauma, as her mother yells at her, "You don't have a clue, do you? When are you going to understand? Idiot!"[75] The girl tells herself, "No wonder why people made fun of you and cussed you out," indicating that she has long been marked as different.[76] If the girl cannot represent the political and histor-ical "truth" of Kwangju, and if her mental state before and after the massacre makes her an "unfit" spokesperson, is she telling a story of Kwangju at all? If so, whose story is it and in what way does it become political?

In Anglo-American feminist literary criticism, the madwoman has come to have a particular status as a metaphoric figure of feminist rebellion. In their influential book *The Madwoman in the Attic*, Sandra Gilbert and Susan Gubar read the madwoman as the female "*author's* double, an image of her own anx-iety and rage. Indeed, much of poetry and fiction written by women conjures up this mad creature so that female authors can come to terms with their own uniquely female feelings of fragmentation, their own keen sense of the dis-crepancies between what they are and what they are supposed to be."[77] Later in *The Madwoman Can't Speak*, Marta Caminero-Santangelo offers a counter-narrative to Gilbert and Gubar's argument: "My theoretical starting point is the suggestion that a search for the subversive madwoman in literature not only involves some violent repressions of its own . . . but also is fundamentally misguided, since the symbolic resolution of the madwoman as an alternative to patriarchy ultimately traps the woman in silence."[78] In response to the ques-tion posed by the National Women's Studies Association in 1995 regarding the use of madness as a strategy for transforming "the sex-gender system and ideologies of gender," Caminero-Santangelo poses another: "How does this strategy in fictional texts hold up in the face of the chaos of violence, abuse, battering, rape, political unrest, and discrimination that affects real women's lives?"[79] She observes that madness and violence are similar in "their contri-bution to a dominant order" and that madness "provides the illusion of power while locating the mad (non)subject outside any sphere where power can be exerted."[80] In assessing "the value of madness itself as a metaphor for resistance" in American women writers and their texts on madness, Caminero-Santangelo emphasizes the opposite: "As an illusion of power that masks powerlessness, madness is thus the final removal of the madwoman from any field of agency."[81] She points out that, in the literary texts that she examines, characters of women writers "retreat into silence" and that "insanity is the final surrender to [dominant] discourses, because it is characterized by the (dis)ability to produce meaning—that is, to produce representations recognizable as meaningful within society."[82] She interprets insanity as existing outside the registers of meanings and considers silence nonresistance. Shoshana Felman similarly argues, "Far from being a form of contestation, 'mental illness' is a *request for help*, a manifestation both of cultural impotence and of political castration. This socially defined help-needing and help-seeking behavior is itself part of female conditioning, ideologically inherent in the behavioral pattern and in the dependent and helpless role assigned to the woman as such."[83] Embedded in the dichotomous interpretive paradigms in English literature of madness as political rebellion or as helpless surrender without meaning are assumptions about the primacy of speech, actions, coherence, independence, and intentionality as providing evidence of agency and subjectivity. They do not ask how the representations of the madwoman interact with—and produce meanings pertinent to—women living with mental disability, whose realness and realities are ejected from the general category of women. Furthermore, any judgment of the political efficacy of madness as a response to—or a product of—a social phenomenon assumes the basic subject position to be sanity, which does not allow for the existence of mental disability as difference.

Formulating a feminist disability studies approach to madness/mental illness, Elizabeth J. Donaldson grounds her analysis on the corporeality of mental illness as physical impairment, without reducing it to the purely biological.[84] Donaldson emphasizes the materiality of mental illness as "the thing-in-itself" and approaches the representation of the madwoman phenomenologically, arguing that "critical approaches which view mental illness as symbolic or as primarily socially constructed often seem to deny the material conditions of the body. Corporealization recognizes a more complex, tangled relationship between the somatic and the semiotic."[85] How would the analysis change if we take mental disability as a point of departure and as a subject position that experiences "violence, abuse, battering, rape, political unrest, and discrimination," rather than as a symbol removed from reality or as a by-product of reality?[86] Here, my main interest is in the relationship between violence that demands to be perceived as meaningful and curative transformation that supports the able-bodied imagination of agency that is grounded on sanity, and which disallows different ways of inhabiting a space.

The girl's mental disability in the novella "There a Petal Falls Silently" and the film *A Petal* is not always contained in a trope of larger political violence committed by the state and the collective historical memory of injury, because such a reading inevitably turns her into a vehicle—a wound and the site of the nation's healing—thereby erasing her existence with its difference before and after the traumatic event. The violence that the girl experiences also cannot be fully contained as her individual story or as some kind of evidence of human cruelty against the weak. Rather, the repeated violations of her body after her mother dies are connected to those experienced by other women with mental disability, who are attacked not only because of the perceived threat of their incurable aberrancy and gender, but also because violence is deemed necessary to "awaken" them or "cure" them.

The girl's embodiment of mental disability is not entirely a metonym of Kwangju's traumatic memory. It is not a wholly subversive political rebellion, or simply an apolitical individual cry for help. Instead, the girl's existence reveals social hostility and cruelty within and outside of institutions and homes, prompted by the conditioned response to her difference. The search team following the traces of the girl in Taechŏn far north from Kwangju reports, "We had found to our surprise that in this region there were several people just like the girl who, if not necessarily for the same reason, were wandering around in the grip of some compulsion."[87] Chang, one of the main characters, similarly had "seen plenty of girls stumbling around drunk like this one. They might have had a reason, but why should he care? There was no need to shoo her away; in his mind these girls might as well have been nonexistent."[88] The girl's existence provides an invitation to imagine many other women with mental disabilities who are exploited for the meanings others assign to them and at the same time fail to be understood in the present, and who therefore cannot safely inhabit domestic and public space as who they are.

"There a Petal Silently Falls" urges us not to take for granted that one's status before a trauma is a normative "wholeness" that comes to be damaged by force, and that therefore after a trauma one needs to be fixed to be accepted again. I am compelled not to read the girl as a fallen petal, in silent, lost innocence. Not withering away, the girl instead literally eats petals to survive: "I found petals to eat, shoots, every once in a while a piece of unripe fruit, and very rarely some cabbage roots or a sweet potato. One day I devoured some pink petals and bush clover shoots and threw it all back up. But the very next day I was up and down the slopes looking for more flowers to eat."[89] The petals in the novella are *pharmaka*, which poison and nurture her body. The girl decorates herself with petals and lays them on an anonymous grave, engaging in the labor of living, caring, and mourning the dead. Instead, I read the girl's vulnerability as the powerful condition that subverts the understanding of living.

Mel Chen's discussion of the term "feral" helps illuminate the contesting ways in which the girl's presence in wilderness can be interpreted as commenting on domestic (both familial and national) spaces: "The notion of feral also brings up ambivalent identifications with antihomes, since it both rejects the domicile and reinvigorates a notion of public shelter. As a moving target, the sign of the feral also invokes diaspora and its potential to naturalize nationalisms and capitalist geopolitics."[90] Closely interwoven with the day of the massacre, which was the result of domestic and international Cold War politics and anxiety about communism, the everyday violence against a girl who has become feral actively denies her the possibility of continuing a life with a mental disability outside the home, unless she can produce a coherent and meaningful narrative about national trauma and move toward cure.

In the girl's nonlinear internal monologue in the novella, memories of the news of her brother's death, her mother's change over time, and the day her mother died are mixed and repeated. Having lost her sense of time and of the distinction between the past and the present, moving in and out of her dream under the "black curtain" draped over her traumatic memory, the girl finds herself in a village. People demand that she tell them everything she has seen and threaten her: "You won't move an inch unless you talk."[91] She then goes into a cave and fights off monstrous beetles. When she becomes unconscious, she is dumped in some bushes and left at the foot of a dark mountain, where insects attack her. Refusing to sleep, she sets out to find her brother to tell him what happened to her mother. She is following the voice inside her head, which will take her to where her brother is waiting for her. She wakes up to find a mute fisherman looking down at her face. He makes a "weird sound," just like her mother, who "acted like the mute: all she did was croak and pound her chest."[92] She finds herself able to understand what the mute man is trying to say: "It wasn't the first time I'd talked with a mute."[93] She discerns muteness from the absence of communication. Here the girl engages in a nonverbal conversation with the man as she did with her mother and with another mute man in her village. Faced with being coerced into producing a narrative, she desires muteness, so that she won't be pressured into speech about her being:

"The more tightly I shut my mouth, the worse some of those people attacked me. Somehow they knew I could talk. Would they have bullied me if I were a mute, like that man I met in the mountains?"[94]

In depicting violence mixed with kindness and care, Ch'oe Yun employs disabled subjects who do not resemble hyper-able military masculine bodies: the mute fisherman; Chang, who is described as having a stutter (and in the film is shown as limping and becoming mentally disabled at the end); and the man named Kim Sang-t'ae, who is chronically ill and who rescues her from a farmhouse. But disabilities do not create a connection between these men and the girl. After feeding her for three days, the mute rapes her: "Right before nightfall, just as I was falling asleep, a bluebird came between my legs and entered me."[95] The girl continues,

> It was then that I realized I was slowly turning into a stone. I found I was holding pebbles in each of my hands. And then I seemed vaguely to understand, like the fuzzy outlines of a bad dream I couldn't remember, why that bluebird was pecking inside me. Maybe it was all an illusion. . . . When that bluebird forced itself inside me it hurt badly, but I didn't make a sound. That kind of thing is nothing to me now. Thousands of those birds could attack me, but I'll never cry out, I'll never get down on my knees, I'll never ask for mercy.[96]

Immediately after telling of rape, she is taken back to the day her mother died, the day she "lost everything forever. When I woke up in the shadow of the mountain that night, I didn't know. I didn't know that in a single instant I had undergone a terrible change."[97] In moments of violence, she does not focus on those who are doing harm but on the bodies that carry the marks of harm. The girl describes rape as bluebirds entering and remaining inside her, indicating the ongoing corporeal experience of violence. Conversely, she is described as "a bird" that can be plucked in Chang's urge to attack her.[98] In the slow process of changing into a stone with pebbles in her hand, she withholds her own critical judgment of various responses from animals and from the superficial and fragmented encounters with those described as "faces," which cannot become relatable persons.

Nonhuman animals and things, such as insects, beetles, dogs, birds and stones, appear as agents and tools of violence invading her but also permeating her body. In addition, she is afraid of growing green wings and antennae. Her interspecies permeation illustrates her phenomenological practice of the critical suspension of victimization.

> Along the river I met more people than I can count. Men and women who
> fled at my approach, children who grabbed my long streams of hair from
> behind and giggled. Dogs didn't bother to chase me, but just barked and
> bared their teeth. . . . And along the river more birds entered me with their
> sharp beaks. There must have been dozens of them inside me, each in its
> nest. If I kept still and closed my eyes I could hear them chirping, and I
> would start trembling. What did they want? Freedom? Their provider? If
> only I could give them what they wanted! I opened my mouth so wide my
> jaws hurt, I gagged, I struggled to get those birds out, but not one of them
> flew out, unless it was while I slept.[99]

Her inability to get the birds out of her throat and free them makes her body
a cage, indicating her failure to enunciate speech to describe her experiences.
As she wanders from the mountains to fields and comes down to villages when
she is hungry, she forgets why she is walking: "I stopped thinking about where
I was going, and like someone in a trance I took whatever those people offered
me, including a place to stay for a night, two nights, or longer."[100]

Chang's perspectives and experiences are represented by a third-person
omniscient narrator; three sections are devoted to the several months he
spends with the girl until she disappears. Days spent with Chang do not appear in the girl's narrative. He is a construction worker, part of the disenfranchised working class, and he lives in a shedlike basement room. He finds the
girl following him at the riverside "like some mad dog" who "turned halfway
toward him, produced a chilling smile, and a few words tumbled, indecipher-
able, from her lips."[101] Soon enough he attacks her body out of fear to stop her
from giggling and (he thinks) mocking him. The rape does not chase her away,
as she continues to follow him. Chang's descriptions of the girl more clearly
frame her as a (non)human animal living in a nest, curled up, crawling on the
bare floor, moving "like a mouse," and needing to be locked up.[102] While Chang
lives with her in his place, his violence surges multiple times at her silence,
at her unresponsiveness, and at the sight of her body; he rapes her again and
beats her down, until he realizes, "The more he had abused her, the more
miserable he had felt the next day. His slapping, instead of producing a change
in her behavior, had merely drained his energy."[103] Chang is unsettled by the
failure of his curative violence and by the impossibility of understanding her.
The urge to cure her and make her into a human instead possesses him: "Her
utter lack of response pained him. What could he do to awaken her? He hadn't
a clue. If he couldn't return her to normalcy, wasn't there at least a way he could

transform her into something resembling a human being? It was maddening."[104] And after violence fails, he attempts—with an equal lack of success—to bring about her transformation by transforming himself into a caring man.

Revealing what was hidden behind the black curtain in the girl's confession in front of an anonymous grave, Ch'oe Yun emphasizes the girl's psychological trauma caused by her own physical violence against her dead mother's body, stressing that from the girl's perspective there is no clear line between who is culpable and who is not. Not knowing who authorized the violence during the massacre, and not identifying who and what created the wounds, she can see only her mother's wounded body and recall her own violence against her mother. When the girl tells the story of the day from the beginning, the first-person voice changes to the second person when she approaches the death of her mother, as if someone else is addressing her and telling her what she had done. Then the first-person narrative resumes: "I can never return to that day. To the place where I committed that terrible crime. Where I stamped on Mama's hand, her arm, her empty gaze, so that I alone could live."[105] Her guilt, rising from a deep conviction of her own violence, poses a stark contrast to the impunity enjoyed by those who are actually responsible for the killings and for rape.

Recounting the painful memory of the day is far from being a resolution or cure for her trauma. Chang witnesses the girl at a grave sitting down, swaying, and going from silence to mouthing sounds, screaming, and shrieking, before returning to silence and rising again with a few flowers in her hair: "The man imagined her lips beginning to move. Her swaying gradually intensified in time with the movements of her mouth. The man heard nothing, but knew that even if he did, he wouldn't understand."[106] After following her for several days, he realizes that her journey to the grave is repeated daily, which shows that the confession is not serving as a curing moment that resolves her trauma, as often imagined in the psychoanalytic narrative of recovery. (The film, however, does employ her confession at a gravesite as its final resolution.) She then arrives at the marketplace, as part of her routine. The uncanny banality of repetition horrifies Chang and frustrates the reader's expectation of a dramatic and meaningful cure in the moment that she internally confronts and overcomes her traumatic memory. Chang observes "the nether world occupied by the insane" that is marked by her giggle, "the happiness of utter oblivion," the "beginning of a living death," and "her vacant gaze," making it impossible to fulfill his desire "to identify with her, to enter her and repair what has broken inside her."[107] The description of her entering into a living death makes humanness depend on social registers of sanity. As she escapes the significations of vitality and the human species, the girl embodies an ontology of intense vulnerability.

The last voices heard in the novella are those of a group of college students who have been searching for the girl after learning that their dead friend's mother was killed at the protest. As they follow her journey north, away from Kwangju, they meet a man in his mid-twenties named Kim Sang-t'ae, who has been chronically ill. Kim had found the girl in the rubble of the abandoned farmhouse. It was rumored that

> a girl had been living at a farm and many a man from Sŏch'ŏn had gone there to violate her, apparently with impunity. The girl charged nothing for her services and was fair game for all who visited. Several versions of the story made the rounds: she was a sweet young thing; or she was just a kid; or she was a bit older, and ripe for the plucking. She'd been kicked out by her husband and in-laws; she was a prostitute who had escaped from a red-light district; or else she was simply a madwoman.[108]

Identifying with her as a victim of rumors, because he himself had been harmed by the rumor that his ill health was somehow responsible for his young girlfriend's death, Kim rescues her from the farm and takes her to a clinic. Though he hoped that rescuing her would clear his name, now the local talk is that "the spirit of Kim's dead sweetheart had returned, intent on revenge."[109] Revealing the local understanding of mental disability, the villagers condemn the girl's presence, thinking that she is unclean and possessed by a spirit, and they gather at the entrance to the clinic: "Rocks were thrown through the window of the girl's sickroom. [Three] days later a delegation of local people confronted the clinic director and demanded that he turn her out."[110] Fears about Kim's health and the death of his young lover combine with the anonymous girl's unintelligible presence to provoke the villagers' violent rejection, making it impossible for the girl to receive medical care and to live alongside them.

As if betraying Chang's hope that "she would be recognized no matter how many transformations she had undergone" by someone who had known her,[111] after hearing of the girl's state from Kim, the search group thinks, "It would surely be more painful for us to see her alive than dead," because she "had been trapped in a chamber of insanity, a chamber darker than death, which offered no possibility of bringing her life to completion."[112] They are ironically afraid to actually encounter her:

What torture for us the living to see a person in a state of walking death! People often describe such a person as utterly mad. It sounds so simple. Just call someone mad and there, the world is back in order again. You gather with others, bring up familiar names, slap your knee and say you've just heard that poor so-and-so has lost her mind, and put on a sad face. Maybe it was better, as Kim had said, if the girl was dead and gone; maybe it was better if she didn't reappear before us.[113]

They fear facing the corporeality of her wound and of mental disability. The violence she had endured made her humanness unrecognizable, as if inhumanness automatically authorizes more violence against her body.

Finding her photo in a newspaper advertisement placed by Chang, the search team visits him only to find out that the girl is no longer there. The team listens to Chang's long monologue of self-reproach. At the end of the novella, only the image of a smiling girl wearing her maroon dress with a withered flower in her hair lingers in their imagination. After realizing that they had a collective illusion of seeing the girl on the train, the students start to probe their own motives for searching for her. In a series of reflective questions, they reveal that they desired to locate and transform the girl ultimately for their own sakes:

To comfort our lost friend with the knowledge that we had found her? To pacify the soul of their departed mother? To fulfill our sense of obligation to do something after what happened that day in that city to the south? Or had we set out because we couldn't live with ourselves if we did nothing? Did we want a quick cure for the suffering that we in our immaturity felt? Were we motivated by a masochistic desire to find in that girl concrete vestiges of that horrible day? In wanting to protect a girl who was already wasted psychologically, were we merely indulging in a cheap excuse for humanitarianism?[114]

These questions are the author's warning against the interpretive temptation to metonymically turn the girl into something that represents the massacre or a blank page on which one's own meaning can be projected. They also provoke questions about my own motive. In my desire to connect her to othered bodies without nationalizing her trauma or reading her as a quintessential victim of patriarchal violence, might I also be turning the speechless, physically wounded, feral, mentally disabled girl inhabiting various public spaces and the wilderness into a body providing evidence of everyday violence against othered bodies? Does the students' wish to find her come from the desire to contain and tame her feral ontology? What would have happened if the students had found her? Isn't any attempt to find meaning in her pain a violence that denies her presence as is?

One sentence reveals in passing that after she hurt herself on a train she was sent to some sort of institution—what she calls the "gray building"—from which she escaped, following her own face from the past: "Not the twisted, convulsed face, but the plain yet wonderful face with the rosy cheeks and the flower in her hair. The face that Mama would recognize, and Brother too. That face had guided me all along, growing ever distant as it drifted over the horizon. Floating in the sky, smiling faintly, it had shown me the way out of that gray building where I was kept with other girls my age after the incident on the train."[115] Her escape to continue her journey challenges medical and custodial institutionalization imagined as the solution to the nomadic existence of women with disabilities. Out of fear that her present self will not be recognized by others, the girl chases her own image as remembered from the day before she went out with her mother—from before the trauma—and tries to fight off her own face's transformation into the "monster."[116] The flower in her hair—which is read as a marker of madness—that she remembers from the day before her mother's death connects her pre- and posttraumatic existence.

Unlike the search team's attempt to bring her back to her social network of the past in order to satisfy their own desire, the opening—which could be in the voice of a member of the search team who ultimately couldn't find her—directly instructs the addressee on how to engage with her presence without acting on curative desire, fear, or on what Petra Kuppers calls "the diagnostic gaze," which "reduces the presence of bodies to texts that need to be read and categorized."[117]

As you pass by the grave sites scattered throughout the city, you may encounter her, a girl whose maroon velvet dress barely covers her, a girl who lingers near the burial mounds. Please don't stop if she approaches you, and don't look back once she's passed you by. . . . You need not be afraid of her; you need not threaten her and rush off. . . . Please don't raise your voice, and when she reaches for you with dirty fingers, try not to make fun of her or curse her. Don't be too quick to sympathize with this wasted girl who longs to escape the shadows for the sunlight, and if she retreats from your indifference or from a smile or gesture you may have let slip, don't spit on her footprints as if she were bad luck—even if she blocks your path for a moment, even if you feel a blind urge to escape your predicament by assaulting her, knocking her down, stomping on her, strangling her, disposing of her without a trace.[118]

The narrator tells men who might encounter her about the conditioned violent responses to her presence, listed one by one. The narrator also warns that resisting the incomprehensible presence of the women would not eliminate the relationality of copresent bodies in a given space. The fact that the girl's brother does not exist makes random graves and young male bodies replacements for him, demanding the shared ethics of recognition that goes beyond the family surrounding the girls who have been traumatized and living with differences.

In the film *A Petal*, the director shortens the novella's prologue and uses it as the final voiceover, spoken by a member of the search team; it begins as another from the search team weeps in a bus. The camera quickly cuts to Chang, wandering around gravesites, looking for the girl: "Just pretend that you don't see her. . . . All you have to do is to look into her face for a moment and show some interest." Unlike the novella, the film does not appeal to viewers to withhold the impulse to annihilate the madwoman's presence. Denying the presence of unknown women with mental disabilities in the here and now, daily interpersonal violence functions as a visual and symbolic portal into the national suffering caused by massive state violence rather than exposing the brutality of the conditioned curative response to the girl's nonconforming existence and inexplicable silence. The film's emphasis on state violence erases this gendered, disability-based politics of everyday violence.

In the film, the girl becomes a victim of "spectacularized violence,"[119] whose psychic and physical pain functions to inflict pain on those who are watching her, unable to protect and rescue her. The audience's suffering becomes more important than the girl's. The film uses the girl's pain and vulnerable body to force viewers to relive the atrocity of the massacre, relying on the male gaze to bring voyeuristic pleasure and catharsis.[120] Chang Sŏn-u, the director, describes her weeping at a gravesite acting as the shaman's ritual called *ssitkimgut* of healing and of "washing" away guilt.[121] The film scholar Saito Ayako points out that *A Petal* fuses the violence of Kwangju and everyday violence against the girl through rape scenes: "The film repeats violence in order to criticize the fundamental trauma of the origin of the nation-state."[122] Saito rightfully criticizes the film for legitimizing violence as a necessary tool to summon the pain of the historical trauma: "The girl is a sacred sacrificial lamb and a shaman in the film. She becomes the director's hardworking shaman who delivers the tragedy of the ethno-nation."[123] Other scholars also criticize the film, as it inscribes its own language on the girl's body and constructs its own memory of the day, which is different from that of the girl.[124] Through the scenes of the demonstration in Kwangju, military violence against citizens, and dead bodies, the Kwangju massacre is projected on the girl's body. As her trauma is shown to be rooted in the day of her mother's death, the violence she experiences subsequently loses significance beyond functioning as a visual entrance into her traumatic memory. As Saito points out, the film's focus on the trauma of the past erases political and gendered meanings of the curative violence against the girl's disabled and nonconforming body occurring in the present.

During this process of erasure, the film treats her humanness as contingent on her condition—as if, in her disabled and victimized body, she had already left the category of the living. Her body changes into such nonliving forms as a haunting ghost, a corpse, a disembodied spirit, and an illusion. In an animated scene, she is shown as a spirit with a transparent body; she visits her home, thinking that everything in the house is feeling so lonely, which evidences her affinity with the objects. The empty home represents a space and time before the violence to which she cannot return. In another scene, the girl is in a train and sees a monstrous ghost in the window of the door; the ghost she sees is her own face. The ghost whispers to her, "What did you do to your mother? Speak to me, speak to me." She screams to mask the voice and strikes the glass with her head until the window cracks. In another scene, the troopers throw her body first in a truck on top of a pile of corpses collected from the street and then into the hole dug to bury the bodies, hers included. Kim's description of her to the search team is revelatory of the way humanity is signified in a way that denies it to victimized bodies: "She seemed more broken than what I had heard from the rumors. Her body was covered with bruises and had a terrible odor. So I thought she was dead and that would be the reason why it smelled so bad. If her finger hadn't twitched, I would have just turned away. I was scared. I was so ashamed that she and I were in the same category as humans." Despite his shame, Kim does not deny the fact that she is a live human being, setting aside the notion of humanity defined by ability—and what is considered dignity— and refusing the notion of dehumanization triggered by bodily condition. As Giorgio Agamben observes, "No ethics can claim to exclude a part of humanity, no matter how unpleasant or difficult that humanity is to see."[125]

The film shows Chang raping the girl three times at length. In the beginning of the film, when the girl starts to follow Chang at the riverside, he rapes her in the wooded area and then chases her away. After the rape, she continues to follow him and sits next to him, mumbling "mother," "holes here," and "brother," as if the rape has had no effect on her. Rather, she has a strong attachment to Chang, which is explained when the search team finds that Chang has a build similar to that of the girl's brother. After the first one, the scenes of rape are interwoven with black-and-white flashbacks of the massacre's violence and animated fantasy scenes. The second rape scene is preceded by her running away from troopers in a chaotic street after shots are fired. She falls down and the audience shares her point of view on the ground, watching the feet of approaching troopers. In this sequence, her face with its unfocused gaze is intercut with her mother's face at the moment of death. The third rape scene occurs after Chang comes home drunk, finds out that she was cooking a meal, becomes outraged by her strange attachment to him, and brutally beats the girl. He shouts, "Why did you come here? Who are you? Speak to me!" She shouts "Brother!," and he becomes more violent, screaming, "I am not your brother!" The face of the girl lying on the floor leads to a flashback of her lying on the pile of corpses. After Chang finishes raping her, the close-up on her face cuts to her crawling in the bushes and then into an animated sequence in which a giant insect is attacking her. The images of a man's legs in military boots and a military helicopter are inserted, establishing a clear link between the insect and the military. When she yells "Brother!," an exclamation visible in a speech balloon rather than audible in her voice, a man in premodern warrior attire appears on a white horse, kills the insect with a sword, and rescues her. They fly away together on the winged horse.[126] The camera shot abruptly cuts back to the girl lying on the ground in the dark corner of Chang's shed, a stark contrast to her dramatic ascent with her brother. The conflated scenes of the violence reduce the rape that occurs in sight of the audience to a mere visual segue into her traumatic memory shown in her dissociated state, separated from her corporeal experience.

The animated fantasy scenes do not simply represent the girl's longing for rescue in the moment of rape: the attack by a giant insect links her terror to the violence on the day of the massacre. In her fantasy, the rape instead brings about her rescue; the disturbing suggestion is that Chang, the girl's surrogate brother, is saving her by inflicting violence that makes her memory of violence surface.[127] The next morning, the light and calm around the shed denote a kind of change in their relationship after the violence. Chang goes to work and then to the market to buy clothes for her, pretending to be her father. When he cannot answer the seller's question about her age, he walks away with an obvious limp; the seller cusses at him, "Cripple, he doesn't even know his own daughter's age," forging a link between the girl and Chang as outcasts. Chang's transformation after the violence suggests a logic alarmingly similar to that presented in *Oasis* (described at the beginning of this chapter), in which disabled women serve as a device for transforming alienated men into relational subjects.

The central question in the film about whether the girl can be cured is combined with the question of whether she will ever be found by the search team. The director imagines the audience to be part of the search team, and he himself appears onscreen as a passenger in the bus with the team.[128] Only if she is located by those who can bring her back to her previous relations before her trauma would she regain her subjectivity. The film critic Kim Ch'ang-hwan instead sees the history of the Kwangju uprising through the girl's disability: "Our mind is cracked open as we are watching her irreparably open wound. Through the medium of her body, our bodies wander around the time and space of Kwangju."[129] In this imagining, the nameless girl's wounded body becomes an avatar of the viewers. As the girl's narrative is turned into a metaphor for the healing of the national trauma of the Kwangju uprising, the site of cure is switched from her madness to the audience's pain.

However, the impossibility of curing her disability and of locating her prevents her from becoming a stable vehicle of historical storytelling. Rather, the ubiquitous presence of madwomen "whose bodies have been violently read for clues to their 'abnormal' minds"[130] haunts this story, especially in the novella. The focus on the hostility toward the presence of women with mental disabilities is not an argument against metaphors themselves. Metaphors can provide an opportunity to examine what they conceal in order to stably deliver salient messages and how they can lead to what Elizabeth Grosz calls "the patriarchal effacement of women."[131] Ch'oe Yun writes about these women's stories not simply as the representation of the violent history of Kwangju inscribed upon the girl's bodies, but also as the representation of the people who are labeled insane and are not allowed to inhabit the spaces outside institutions. *A Petal* emphasizes the violence and anger shown toward a disabled woman in Chang's desire to fix her, and this violence plays an important role in bringing out her traumatic memory and in transforming him. This productive function of interpersonal violence against the already-traumatized body, which continues in everyday life, hides itself behind the process of generating meanings about state violence.

Unlike *A Petal*, another well-known film about the Kwangju massacre, *Peppermint Candy* (2000), does not other the disabled subject as a way to represent curative violence; instead, it demonstrates a masculinized self-erasure. It traces the memory of a man named Yŏngho who was a private in the military deployed in Kwangju. He is shot in his foot and accidentally shoots and kills a girl who was going home. The film shows scenes from Yŏngho's life, moving backward from 1999 to 1979 when he first met his love. In the famous scene of 1999, he stands on a railroad bridge in front of an approaching train, shouting "I am going to go back!" with his arms spread to accept the force that will end his life. The implication of his suicide, the desire not to inhabit the present, and his psychosomatic limping, however, do not meet with the intervention of his cure from others, as the tragedy of his life originated from his forced participation in the massacre. Instead, he holds the narrative power and subjectivity and is determined to travel in time to the past before the trauma to undo its memory. Compelled by his desire to cure himself by suicide, he denies the possibility of the presence of himself with disability in the present.

While Yŏngho in *Peppermint Candy* is presented as mentally ill, the more common reference of madness connected to trauma is of women like the girl in *A Petal*. One photograph captures the image of madwomen that is common in the imagining of this Korean landscape, tied not specifically to a historical event like Kwangju but to the general experience of women's oppression. The feminist photographer Park Young-Sook connects the images of madness to patriarchal oppression, which labels women who are rebellious as insane and at the same time produces mental disability. This feminist image can subtly turn disability into a vehicle. As if in response to the call in "There a Petal" to look at a madwoman with some interest and a nonthreatening gaze, Park created the *Mad Women Project*, producing images of performed madness. Park explains, "The feminists, who played 'mad' women in the photographs, are speaking for all women."[132] The models are the photographer's "close friends, who are well-known artists and activists in the art and feminist circles in Korea."[133] In order to avoid the stigma attached to real mental illness, she emphasizes that the models are not *really* mad. Nondisabled feminists simulate and perform the madness they have imagined, experienced, and encountered in their lives. Performing madness in a sort of "drag" becomes a tool to show women's experiences that cannot be explained through coherent narratives, yet their bodies are seen as telling an everywoman's story. In this way, the performance of mentally disabled bodies by nondisabled women becomes yet another appropriation of mental disability as metonym. Reified as a symbol, madness loses its own existence independent of the message it is made to carry: the consequences of oppression in the case of the *Mad Women Project*. The material body of madness is read as representing an identifiable cause, generating distanced sympathy without identification.

In one photo, a woman tightly holding a pillow in her arms in an empty abstract space—as if she were holding a baby—stands on the right side of the frame, much as the girl in *A Petal* holds a bundle of her clothes from the day she lost her mother (see figure 3.1). The body of the woman in the photograph is turned to the side, and she looks at the camera/viewer. Her look is defensive but wary, trying to protect something from the outside world. The framing of the woman on the right and the direction of her gaze—toward the front, not to the right or the center—suggest that no space or exit is left open for her. The photo is a simulation of a "real 'mad' woman" whom Park saw at a mental institution she had toured. Park recalls, "We saw a woman in the hallway. She was holding [the pillow] so tightly to her and appealing to the doctor. She seemed very pitiful."[134]

Park adds that the woman had lost custody of her child after her divorce, and the desire to see her child "made her go mad."[135] Extracted from this unnamed woman's situation, madness expresses the harms of women's oppression. This process may render invisible the continuing alienation experienced by disabled women in institutions and communities. The disabled body in this image crystallizes the injustice and suffering that causes wounds, while at the same time obscuring the complex components of material and social interactions that continue to shape experiences after disablement. Thus, after disablement, the focus of intervention shifts from social structures to individual bodies, and the question of why disabled women are considered to be degraded, removable, and cut off from their community is not raised. Accordingly, a static concept of disability as a tragedy replaces the dynamic social relations that construct it. The social configuration that removes women with mental disabilities from the community where they might find proper accommodations and care is not always recognized in this kind of feminist imagination.

Even if rebellious feminists in a patriarchal society are accused of being mentally ill, the differences between the woman in the hallway of the psychiatric ward, the impersonator in the photo, the girl onscreen wandering by the gravesites and following her rapist, and the photographer who intends to reclaim the label are more complicated than the image suggests. Calling someone "mad" might also be exercising violence against women who in fact do exist outside "normalcy." For example, the film A Petal includes a scene in which the clinic's doctor rotates his index finger by the side of his head—making a stereotypical gesture signifying "crazy"—after the village women who are angry at the girl's presence throw rocks through the window. The women shout indistinctly, but the viewers see the dismissive gesture of the male doctor calling the women crazy for believing that the girl is possessed by an evil spirit. Nondisabled women's experiences of being associated with madwomen do not automatically open the way to understanding how women who exist outside of "normalcy" are violated and erased or to improving the possibility of social justice and ethical responses.

3.1 *Mad Women Project 1* (1999). 120 × 150 cm, C-print. A woman stands holding a pillow and looks at the camera. Photograph by Park Young-Sook. Reprinted by permission of the photographer. Image courtesy of the photographer.

3.2 *Mad Women Project: A Flower Shakes Her* (2005). 120 × 120 cm, C-print. A woman lies on a bed of pink wildflowers with her eyes closed. Photograph by Park Young-Sook. Reprinted by permission of the photographer. Image courtesy of the photographer.

In the performance of madness, the continuing life with a disability without cure and the experiences of continued oppression and violence are not explored, as the harm is seen as already done. However, another photo in the series (see figure 3.2) provides a glimpse of the ways in which Park Young-Sook's collective art project may challenge the ableism that sustains the otherness of disabled people and may start to uncover the presence and the power of women with mental disabilities.

A woman is lying on a bed of pink wildflowers in bloom, with her eyes closed and a slight smile on her face. For a moment, at the risk of romanticizing mental disability, I try to imagine this woman as the future of the girl in *A Petal*, an imagination that is not allowed by the film. The woman inhabits the space without the demand for narrative and the compulsion of cure. An absence of such demands is an ethical response not only to traumas but also to an ontology of disability. No longer clenched hugging the bundle of the dress she wore on the day of massacre, her arms are now thrown open. The simulation of disability by a nondisabled woman in this photo delivers the desire for lived disability; it is not an exercise (of the kind often criticized) to mimic what it is like to be disabled, which ends up further othering and distancing disabled people with pity. The descending slope from left to right creates for the viewer a sense of the frame's instability, providing a contrast to the woman's undisturbed presence in the middle. Park states, "The images of 'madwomen' speak for their grandmothers or mothers. The feminists who performed as madwomen represent all women and vicariously experience their situations. This experience is the experience of sharing, the work of sharing itself."[136] The universalizing language and the potential exclusion of women living with mental disability when speaking of "all women" gives me pause. Yet I sense the affinity toward embodied mental disability and intense silence in the photograph. This performance of madness occurs outside of what Kuppers describes as "the 'normal' images of people with mental health problems: hysterical displays of bodies out of control, fits, excess, and 'being outside one's body.'" Instead, much like Kuppers's performance of people with mental differences in *Traces*, the woman's body in the photo is "unknowable. Closure is denied. The spectator is not given access to the truth about [her] experiences and thoughts."[137] Silence here is not the absence of language, as the physicality of mental disability involves many different kinds of communication that might represent various meanings and meaninglessness.

Private Justice and Ethics of Nonviolence

"Perhaps our society itself is the crucible."
—BAE BOGJOO

I opened this chapter by describing the activist campaign objecting to disabled women's victimization, engendered by the fantasy constructed in cultural representations that violating disabled people is a form of communicating interest and caring that benefits them. *The Crucible* (*Togani*, released overseas with the title *Silenced*), a 2011 film on sexual abuse by teachers of deaf children at a deaf residential school, illustrates that representations can also play the opposite role of generating social changes. The film is based on the novel of the same title by Gong Ji Young, which was inspired by actual events in Inhwa School in Kwangju. In the novel, the fictional city is named Mujin, "the mecca of democracy"—an allusion to the city of Kwangju and its history. While the media reports about these events over the years and the popular novel did not garner significant public attention, the film was a box office hit and became the epicenter of what was called the Togani Wind, the Togani Syndrome, or the Togani Effect. The film depicts a corrupt criminal justice system in which the school principal who raped a deaf boy and two other teachers who also sexually abused and physically tortured deaf boys and a deaf girl with an intellectual disability receive suspended sentences and serve no prison time. After a series of legal measures, including appeals, prove to be ineffective in bringing justice, one of the victimized boys takes matters into his own hands: he stabs one of the teachers and throws the teacher and his own body under an approaching train. The film ends by noting that some of the perpetrators in the real case have resumed teaching deaf students.

The public anger at the sexual victimization of deaf children and corrupt criminal justice system generated by the film was palpable and widely covered in the media. The rather hurried response by authorities included the reinvestigation of the perpetrators and their prosecution under different charges, which resulted in them being convicted and sentenced to prison time; amendments to laws and new policy mandates; efforts to reform how prosecutors investigate crimes and to provide adequate assistance and accommodation to disabled victims; increased supervision of boarding schools for disabled children and institutions; and the permanent shutdown of Inhwa School for deaf children.

Amidst this righteous rush, the organization Changae Yŏsŏng Konggam (WDE) released a statement asking the public to contemplate their anger and compassion. The presumably able-bodied public was outraged by the perpetrators' cruelty and felt compassion for the helpless, innocent deaf children who were segregated from mainstream education and society, remained invisible in the public realm. In the film, when Inho, a new teacher, arrives at the school, he discovers the violence and becomes a whistleblower. WDE critically reads the hearing character Inho as a "savior," "spokesperson," and another "guardian" of vulnerable disabled people, thereby functioning to maintain a safe distance between the audience and disabled people. WDE points out, "From an early age in the institution, the children's human rights have been violated by those who were their sole and significant guardians. The children have been excluded from 'commonsensical' experiences and from the 'normality' of society. It is worth questioning the assumption that the children expect 'commonsense' and the legal system to normally recognize them as the victims of violence and to provide the most important resolution of the whole event."[138] WDE calls for an acknowledgment of the public's complacency in supporting ableist social segregation: "When the distance between 'them' and 'me' is lessened, we can move beyond *The Crucible*." What needs to be questioned is the violence embedded in the segregated education system and in the institutionalization of disabled people, as well as the public's general rejection of the presence of disabled people in communities. The statement also underscores the forms of violence that have become invisible: the abandonment of disabled babies, the sterilization of disabled women, and the lack of education and unemployment that make disabled people vulnerable to violence committed by family members and neighbors and to institutional abuse. Indeed, the antiviolence measures should not be limited to the criminal justice system but should address the systematic violence of ableism that has become acceptable and naturalized.

The Crucible does not question segregated education in a custodial institution; it reflects that many families abandon deaf children or prefer to send them away, lacking the means and support of raising them in the communities. The privatized form of justice in the form of revenge in the film becomes the only imaginable response to the interpersonal and systemic violence that makes the lives of disabled individuals impossible. The deaths of disabled individuals in the pursuit of justice in self-annihilation also occur in Unknown Address, as Ch'angguk and his mother kill themselves. The murder-suicide that concludes *The Crucible* is the filmmaker's invention: it did not occur as part of the events at Inhwa School. Rather it is an ending designed to convey a sense of protest. Ending one's own life as the only way to end violence is an act that turns one's vulnerability into the political claim that life is not possible without changes in the conditions that authorize violence.

The idea that vulnerability causes violence deprives disabled bodies of power and naturalizes violence. Revenge and suicide practiced as a form of private justice defy distanced anger and depoliticized compassion toward the images of victimized disabled individuals, as self-violation is one of the few instances wherein disabled people's agency can be made visible in cultural representations. As a *pharmakon*, the violence against oneself and others becomes a conceptual and practical response to violence committed in the name of cure. In this crucible of violent interactions, the ethics of nonviolence, intense vulnerability, and self-reflection shown by the mad girl in *A Petal* may provide a beginning of working toward life with disability and without violence.

CHAPTER 4

Uninhabiting Family

Contemporary campaigns to combat the persistent stigma associated with Hansen's disease (leprosy) focus on disseminating the scientific information that it is neither hereditary nor highly contagious, but completely curable. A 2009 campaign poster by the Korean Hansen Welfare Association celebrating World Leprosy Day states, "Make a Note: The distorted history of people with Hansen's disease needs to stop" (see figure 4.1).[1] Above the slogan, three note-pads are pinned on the light peach background, each with a word in English and an illustration: "touch," with two joined hands in the shape of a heart; "take," with two pill capsules; and "open," with four hearts, pointing inward and placed over a circle. The emphasis on touch addresses the misperception that the disease is transmitted by skin-to-skin contact and urges the public to abandon their prejudice that has constructed people with Hansen's disease as untouchable. The pills indicate curability through multidrug therapy as the key to inclusion in an open and loving society.

The "distorted history" refers to the forcible segregation of people with Hansen's disease, labor exploitation, physical violence, massacre, and reproductive violations throughout the past century and the social exclusion and prejudice that continue in the present. The poster presents the state-sponsored organization as engaged in remedying historical injustice, effectively hiding the fact that the history was also shaped by the nation-state, humanitarian organizations, and medical authorities that falsely warned against the danger of the disease under the banners of promoting cure and protecting the public. After the Korean War, South Korea reenacted the policy of forcible segregation (1954–1963) through the Infectious Disease Prevention Law. Later, the government focused on placing people who were cured into segregated settlement villages, which were often run by religious organizations.

Another effort to eliminate the disease's stigma involved changing its name from "leprosy" to "Hansen's disease," after the Norwegian physician Gerhard

4.1 The fifty-seventh *Segye Hansenpyŏng ŭi Nal* (World Leprosy Day) poster, Korean Hansen Welfare Association, the Ministry of Public Health, Welfare, and Family (2009). Three symbols of hands, pills, and hearts are printed with the words "touch," "take," and "open." Reprinted by permission of the Korean Hansen Welfare Association. Image courtesy of the Korean Hansen Welfare Association.

Armauer Hansen, who discovered the bacterium, *Mycobacterium leprae*, that causes the disease.[2] In the 1940s Stanley Stein, the editor of the *Star Magazine* in Carville in the United States, advocated using the term to emphasize scientific knowledge over the biblical associations of leprosy. In South Korea, the name "Hansen's disease" (*Hansen Ssi pyŏng*) was introduced in the 1950s,[3] and in 2000 the term "leprosy" (*nabyŏng*) was replaced by "Hansen['s] disease" (*hansenpyŏng*) in the Infectious Disease Prevention Law. Internationally "leprosy" continues to be used by global health communities.[4] In his medical and cultural history of the disease, Rod Edmond argues that some present-day patients prefer "leprosy" because the name "Hansen's disease" "sanitises their condition and obscures the victimization it has traditionally provoked."[5] There is profound irony in associating "Hansen" with neutrality to undo historical violence, given that Dr. Hansen was found guilty in 1880 of inoculating—without her consent—a woman who had a neural form of leprosy with the material drawn from a nodule of a patient with the cutaneous kind in an attempt to prove that the disease was caused by the bacilli he discovered. Moreover, the fears he roused helped lead to the passage of laws that mandated the separation of patients from their families.[6] Nevertheless, I primarily use "Hansen's disease," consistent with contemporary advocacy around it; I also use "leprosy" (*nabyŏng*) and "lepers" (*mundungi*) throughout this chapter to reflect usage in the primary sources as well as the often-conflicted ways in which language is tied to image, power, and the politics of cure.

Although the World Health Organization (WHO) declared it globally "eliminated" in 2001,[7] Hansen's disease is not a thing of the past. For the past violence has not been remedied with acknowledgments and reparations; the stigma of Hansen's disease persists even when it is cured; the descendants continue to experience stigma; the disease itself persists in certain regions; affected people may avoid diagnosis and treatment; and Hansen's disease co-manifests with HIV in certain cases, "not as one from the past and one in the present, but both in the now."[8] Despite what antistigma campaigns suggest, information about biomedical treatment and low transmission has not provided an easy antidote to fear and stigma. Nancy Waxler, a social scientist of health care, asks, "Why are the stigma and fear of leprosy still prevalent in many countries when an effective treatment is readily available?"[9] Writing about AIDS, which is often likened to Hansen's disease,[10] Paula Treichler argues that its social dimension is "far more pervasive and central than we are accustomed to believe. Science is not the true material base generating our merely symbolic superstructure. Our social constructions of AIDS . . . are based not on objective, scientifically determined 'reality' but on what we are told about this reality."[11] How have the cultural representations of people with Hansen's disease been shaping the ways in which the reality of the disease has been experienced, understood, imagined, and distorted? How do gender, family, and marriage play a role in rehabilitating cured subjects?

A few facts might illuminate how knowledge about the disease has undercut justifications of the lifelong segregation of patients. First, doubts about the need to segregate patients emerged as early as 1897 at the International Leprosy Conference, before Hansen's disease was cast as an international problem affecting imperial enterprises. Second, that the disease is not hereditary was publicized in Korea as early as 1928.[12] Third, the sulfone drug dapsone was first developed in the 1940s to successfully treat Hansen's disease. More effective multidrug therapy (dapsone, rifampicine, clofazimine), recommended by the WHO in 1981, has been made available globally at no cost since 1995. Given that the disease has been curable for more than half a century, its subsequent history raises several questions about the role of biomedical knowledge/ technology and cultural representations in sustaining discriminatory policies and prejudice: What would have been the "right" course of history as opposed to the "distorted" kind? When social "solutions" to the disease emerge, how do they reshape relationships among affected people, family, and communities? When the scientific and biomedical "facts" change, what happens to the cultural images and social understandings on which people rely to make sense of an illness?

Even when violent treatment has been justified in the name of cure, political and medical managements of a disease are not supported by scientific consensus. In addition, medical curability does not automatically provide any cultural cure, creating the need for representing cured bodies being normalized by heterosexual marriage and other gendered processes. While the medical cure is available, the perception of curedness has to be culturally enforced through various interventions, while curedness itself becomes a marker of disability. The emergence of institutions to treat and isolate patients transformed the domestic space and the family itself as requiring healthy bodies. I explore how curative institutions are at the center of familial and domestic dramas around sick bodies and create the meanings of cure. I examine, first, the process of violently removing the sick bodies from the domestic space and of representing the sick bodies as dangerous, reshaping the family exclusively for the able-bodied (in Kim Tong-ni's "The Rock" and Kim Chŏng-han's "Oksimi," both published in 1936); second, technology and the benevolence of medical intervention by an American-run institution during the Cold War by forging a quintessential cure narrative by the poet Han Ha-un (Yang Sŭng-ryong's *The Litany of Hope* [1962]); third, marriage between a former male patient and an uninfected woman as a symbol of the political reconciliation of historical violence and the integrability of two separate worlds (Yi Chŏng-jun's *Your Paradise* [1976]); and fourth, marriage between male former patients and female medical professionals as the ultimate evidence of a cured status (Kim Hui and Kim Myŏng-gon's *Ah! Sorokto* [2002]).

Relying on curability to eliminate the stigma of an illness constitutes "normative violence," which justifies the rejection of incurable and not-yet-cured bodies and fails to address the erasure of the humanity of bodies whose life is suspended even after the cure is completed.[13] The repeated appeal to scientific information in the hope that curability will remove social antagonism toward disabled bodies does not recognize the fear and othering constructed by cultural discourses. The poet Han Ha-un writes of the ontological distance between the certified status as cured, which seemingly guarantees a return to society, and the denial of humanity that cured people continue to face:

우리는 종이쪼가리 인간
문서상의 완치
서류상의 사회복귀

We are human beings made of a scrap of paper
Completely cured, written on paper
Returned to society, written on record[14]

As Han writes, the moment of complete "cure" may never arrive for those who are cured of Hansen's disease unless the nature of cultural dramas around the illness and remaining disabilities is transformed—a transformation that cannot occur while they are segregated.

Problematizing Leprosy

In *Madness and Civilization*, Michel Foucault writes that leprosy disappeared from the Western world at the end of the Middle Ages, suggesting that "lepers" and "leprosy" were concepts that rose and fell with the Catholic Church's power and that this disappearance did not necessarily represent an actual decline in the disease's prevalence.[15] The historian Zachary Gussow argues that leprosy "re-emerged" in the non-Western world as a result of political activities that situated leprosy as a "disease of 'inferior people,'"[16] a designation that invited European and American intervention in Asia and Africa to serve colonial interests. The disappearance and "re-emergence" of leprosy from the Western perspective reflect nothing about the disease except its political visibility. International movements of immigrants and missionaries and colonial migration to Asia and Africa during the age of high imperialism coincided with the more intense international dialogue about leprosy control, such as that which occurred at the International Leprosy Conference in 1897.

At the conference, Hansen presented his method of using uninfected people as guards who identify and isolate the patients, although there was no consensus regarding the need for segregation. Hansen encouraged the compulsory segregation of "lepers" and incited fears of contagion to win support for the policy in Norway. With eugenic interests in mind, Hansen equated national advancement with leprosy treatment: "What I desire is that Norway shall rise to take her place on an equal footing with other advanced nations."[17]

Hansen proposed reforms to existing laws that barred patients from being placed in regular hospital wards. "Then, in 1885," Hansen wrote in his memoir, "we obtained a ruling that compelled such patients to live isolated from their immediate families. If this were not feasible or acceptable, they could be placed in a special leprosy hospital."[18] However, because most Norwegians understood leprosy as a sign of God's will, beyond the control of human beings, his policy of segregation drew anger and strong opposition. In response, he changed the grounds of his argument to safety and patriotism. Dividing "the sick" and "the healthy," Hansen urged "healthy people" to exercise power largely on behalf of the nation: "I maintained that healthy people must have the same humane treatment as the sick. If the fit found that the diseased could be a danger to them and consequently to the community as a whole, they had the right and duty to isolate them as long as it was done compassionately. Fortunately the healthy were in the majority and ultimately were prepared to responsibly exercise their power."[19] His strategy shows how leprosy can be used to impose a dichotomy and turn segments of the population into adversaries: "the healthy" and "the sick."[20] Assigning nonaffected people to enforce a patriotic vigilante mission—that is, to find and isolate leprosy patients—was an effective tactic in expanding legislative power with violent consesequences.

Hansen became an international campaigner for the segregation of leprosy patients and was the central figure in discussions regarding the disease's prevention. The emphasis on controlling leprosy carries a specific transnational meaning: as Hansen's patriotic commitment to Norway's standing demonstrates, it helped create a hierarchy of nation-states based on how well diseases were managed and epidemics were controlled. At the Berlin conference, Hansen made several recommendations. First, he argued that leprosy could be prevented through isolation; second, he proposed a "system of compulsory registration, control and isolation," as practiced in Norway; and, third, he insisted that "in each country, the sanitary authorities must be allowed to make regulations according to their 'particular social conditions,' with the permission of their governments."[21] Meanwhile, the French dermatologist Ernest Besnier denied that segregation was necessary to control leprosy; he believed "that isolation was appropriate where leprosy was 'largely spread' or focalised."[22] Although Besnier's amendment was accepted in the final statements of the conference, Shubhada S. Pandya suggests that the first International Leprosy Conference set a tone that supported endorsing segregation, promoted by the British in their interests in India. Pandya's assessment is borne out by the Third International Leprosy Conference in Strasbourg in 1923, which approved "a proposal to prevent and deny entry of 'alien' lepers by countries."[23] The Second International Leprosy Conference in Bergen in 1909 had recommended the removal of children from "leprous parents" as soon as possible.[24] Pandya claims that the attempts by the civilized countries of the West to internationalize the problem of leprosy in the last decade of the nineteenth century were motivated by the fear that leprosy would "invade" their nations via immigrants and expatriates returning from former colonies. For the first time, leprosy was constructed as a problem of Asia and Africa, and immigrants to Western countries were considered a threat that would spread the disease.

This Western intervention in Asia provides a backdrop to the medical institutionalization in Korean history. In the 1900s, the number of missionaries grew significantly, and in 1911 the American Presbyterian doctor Robert M. Wilson established the leprosarium, Aeyangwŏn, in Kwangju. Concerned about the expansion of Christian medical charity, the Japanese colonial government actively sought to catch up to Western missionaries' management of leprosy in East Asia. Finally, in 1916 the Government General established the hospital Sorokto Chahye Ŭnwŏn as a predecessor to the full-scale hospital and leprosarium that eventually expanded to the entire island in the 1930s. The hospital served primarily as an instrument of international propaganda to justify colonial occupation, the sociologist Jung Keun-sik explains, rather than to provide treatment to patients.[25] The colonial government started to gain overall dominance in leprosy management with the Chosŏn Leprosy Prevention Act, enacted in 1935. Sorokto Hospital was built and expanded mainly by the forced labor of the patients who were under the special jurisdiction of the hospital authority. In the 1940s the total number of patients exceeded six thousand. Forced labor, punitive confinement, forced sterilization and abortion, massacres, the state appropriation of the land reclaimed by the patients, the separation of children from their patients, and lifelong segregation in settlement villages constitute only part of the colonial and postcolonial violence experienced by people with Hansen's disease throughout the twentieth century.

People with Hansen's disease and those who are cured of it call themselves *Hansenin* (Hansen people), forming a biosocial identity and political constituency with shared histories of violence, human rights agendas, and demands for reparations and better treatment. To emphasize their status as cured, another category, *Hansen hoebokcha* (people who are cured from Hansen's), appeared more recently. Aside from *mundungi* (a Korean vernacular term whose connotations are similar to "lepers"), the terms *na hwanja* (used by the government from 1954 to 1999) and *lep'ŭra hwanja* (leprosy patients) were also used in the past; their medical overtones cast the individuals as perpetual patients, even if they are cured. In Sorokto, *Mun Ssi* ("Mr. and Ms. Mun," using the first syllable of the Korean vernacular term for leprosy, *mundungpyŏng*) and *Han Ssi* ("Mr. and Ms. Han," using the first syllable of *Hansenpyŏng*) have been used among the patients.[26] This practice indicates that the patients formed a new kinship around the illness after being disinherited from their own families, and it was common for patients to change their names upon receiving the diagnosis. More broadly, *Hansenin* also includes unaffected family members, especially children. Because of the erroneous assumption that leprosy is hereditary yet latent, the children of *Hansenin*—labeled as *migama* (children who are not yet infected)—were segregated into special schools, such as Ŏjŏng Elementary School Tongjinwŏn pungyo, which closed in 1999. Teachers who taught children from *Hansenin* families received incentive pay to compensate for the alleged added risk.[27] Institutionalizing these children immediately after birth, and thus separating them from their parents, still occurred in the 1960s as a necessary way to control the disease. The children of leprosy patients and children who themselves had leprosy were recognized as having a disability, as were biracial children of unmarried parents and children born out of wedlock.[28] In the *Handicapped Children's Survey Report* of 1962, Sung Joon Bang advocated that the children of "lepers" be removed and institutionalized in orphanages. Bang states, "The doctors in turn, have the greatest responsibility to assure that the parents fully understand what their own possessiveness (selfishness) would mean in the life of their children in refusing to release them."[29]

Jung Keun-sik points out that newspaper depictions of fearsome *mundungi* as vagabonds added to their social alienation. A saying popular in nurseries, "If you don't stop crying, lepers will take you," reflected and contributed to leprophobia: the very real fear generated by the media, leading many accusations of "lepers" of kidnapping and using their victims' flesh and organs to cure their disease.[30] This threat was used commonly as late as 1960 to discipline children, according to Jung, along with warnings about tigers and Japanese police officers. In 1922, *Tonga ilbo* reported that a "bizarre rumor" that *mundungi* kill children had been circulating in the Iri region. It led villagers to violently attack and beat leprosy patients in their communities, and patients suspected of such crimes were arrested on numerous occasions in the 1920s and 1930s.[31] In one case, twenty patients with leprosy were detained and interrogated when a six-year-old child disappeared and the family believed that he had been taken by "lepers" for his liver.[32] The child was found in a relative's home, and the patients were released. In the mid-1930s, around the time that the Chosŏn Leprosy Prevention Act ordered compulsory internment of the patients, head-lines included "A Leprosy Patient Exhumed a Rotten Baby Corpse, Distilled It into Alcohol, and Drank It," "Superstition Is to Blame! A Leprosy Patient Killed and Ate a Ten-Year-Old Child," "A Leprosy Patient Who Ate Raw Liver Sentenced to Death as Requested by Prosecution," and "A Leper Who Ate a Child Sentenced to Death."[33] In the meantime, the Sorokto rehabilitation fa-cility (Kaengsaengwŏn) was depicted as a "paradise" (chŏn'guk) or a "different world" (pyŏlchŏnji) for patients. In 1939, its expansion was completed and its capacity raised to 6,020 patients, making the institution a "world-class" facility that perfectly combined safety and crime prevention.[34]

Sŏ Chŏng-ju's well-known poem "The Leper," published in 1936, captures and reinforces the image of "lepers" as "child-eaters."

The leper grieves
Over the sun and the blue sky.
When the moon shines on the cornfield,
He murders a child and eats,
And weeps all night his flower-red weeping.[35]

The vivid visual imagery of "the leper" eating a child and his bloody tears evokes the sense that leprosy drives the infected person to kill babies in order to be cured. The poem constructs the image of eating the baby as a fated con-dition of mundungi: their existence originated from what Tonga ilbo called an "obsession for life."[36]

Earlier records of affected people seeking such cures also exist. At the end of the 1880s, James Gale, who was appointed to the new Presbyterian mis-sion post in Wŏnsan, remarked on "lepers" and tigers strolling through his frontyard—"errant lepers 'who might at any time seek the traditional cure for their complaint, the flesh of children.'"[37] Paralleling Gale, who described Ko-rean "lepers" as racial Others who embrace superstition, Koreans feared white Westerners when they first arrived in Korea at the end of the nineteenth cen-tury and viewed them as people who take children away and remove human organs in order to make medicine.[38] People with "unfamiliar" bodily features confronted curiosity and fear that they would take children away. An article in the Korea Times offers a succinct account of the event. "There were the Baby Riots, a series of riots against Westerners brought on by rumors that the West-erners were taking Korean children and using their body parts for medicine and for developing photographs. In addition, there were rumors that Protestant missionaries had established their schools and orphanages so that they could use the children for immoral purposes. Several Koreans had been killed in the streets during the riots and because of the apparent danger; foreigners had to suspend their worship among the natives."[39] This threat of cannibalism by Western medical missionaries and people who had leprosy was constructed as a response to bodily, racial, and religious differences, which manifested the fear of curative interventions and of imagined curative impulses.

The image of cannibalism and its association with leprosy had roots in the medicinal use of body parts in the fifteenth century. In *The Annals of the Chosŏn Dynasty*, several entries record the use of human flesh to cure diseases such as epilepsy and leprosy.[40] For instance, the "Chronicle of the King Sŏngjong" mentions a woman named Tŭkpi; upon hearing that flesh could remedy sickness, she cut off her finger, dried it, turned it into powder, and fed it to her husband, who had what was called *nabyŏng* (leprosy). Although it was questionable if this term was referring to the same disease of leprosy, as a result, it was said, he was cured. The officials requested that Sŏngjong approve a reward to her for her loyalty to her husband.[41] In the King Sŏnjo period, the chronicle records that vagabonds attacked and kidnapped people to steal and sell their gallbladders, which were known to be effective in curing a skin disease (*ch'angjil*). Sŏnjo ordered the arrest of these organ snatchers.[42] Other diseases are also involved in accounts of human bodies being consumed. In 1922, a woman with syphilis was accused of exhuming a corpse from the grave and eating parts of it to cure her disease. But this incident was not generalized to all syphilis patients; it did not become part of their image, as happened to "lepers."[43]

Nevertheless, people with visible skin diseases were not universally treated as threats to their communities. Several mask performances popular during the late nineteenth and the early twentieth centuries included a *mundungi* character as an important narrator, along with other disabled individuals who expose the cruelty of Chosŏn's caste system.[44] In *Kasan Five Jesters*, five *mundungi* are mixed in a group with other beggars and gamblers.[45] *T'ongyŏng Five Jesters* includes a dance performance of a *mundungi* who is in the *yangban* (elite class).[46] Another *mundungi* laments that he became sick because of his ancestors' sins, and he bewails how useless his *yangban* status and money are to his sick body.[47] Leprosy was interpreted as a manifestation of one's ancestors' moral status. In the late 1910s this moral interpretation changed, and the sick bodies were instead perceived as a danger to the community.

While the collective image of "lepers" as cannibals spread through print media available to the public, the discourse of infection and heredity started to emerge as the sterilization and institutionalization of patients were promoted in the late 1930s. Not surprisingly, public hostility toward leprosy patients who were viewed as criminals coexisted with a fear of infection. In 1992, in the well-known case of five missing boys who went to the mountain to collect salamander eggs, also known as the Frog Boys (*Kaeguri Sonyŏn*) case, the police received a tip that they were buried in Ch'ilgok Farm, a village where former leprosy patients had settled. Newspapers reported on these suspicions, for which there was no evidence.[48] People living in the village were outraged and protested against the prejudiced media coverage; the journalists, in turn, described the protesters as violent mobs threatening the freedom of journalism and assaulting reporters. For more than a decade, the suspicion persisted that the villagers were connected to the children's disappearance, as the case remained unsolved even after the children's bodies were found elsewhere, buried on a mountain. This rush to implicate *Hansenin*, which so angered the people of the settlement village, demonstrates that leprophobia is still deeply embedded in South Korean society.[49] The image of the affected people as potential criminals, believed to be obsessed with a cure based on superstition, made their existence incompatible with that of the unaffected public. The imperative of cure, therefore, created the need for segregation, supported by the assumption that the patients' desire to be cured might make them dangerous and uncontrollable.

Family and Motherhood

Kim Chŏng-han's short story "Oksimi" (1936) provides a way of viewing the effect of leprosy on the complicated negotiations within a patriarchal family structure, the emergence of modern femininity, and the socioeconomic transformation of a rural community. Through Oksim, the nondisabled protagonist, the narrative portrays dynamic changes in gender hierarchy. Most importantly, the family's survival depends on sending Oksim's husband, Chŏnsu, who has leprosy, to Sorokto.

Kim Chŏng-han's works, in general, offer powerful socialist critiques of a changing Korea, written in a realist style. They expose and problematize the hardships and abuse endured by peasants under colonial rule, even at a time when censorship increased greatly. In his debut work, "Village under the Temple" ("Sahach'on" [1936]), he portrays corrupt monks who are landowners exploiting peasants after the Manchurian Incident in 1931. Bruce Cumings explains that, in the 1930s, nearly four out of five peasants were tenants who rented all or part of the land they worked.[50] In the year before the publication of "Oksimi," peasant resistance movements sprang up.[51] The exploitative nature of the Buddhist monks' landownership also appears in "Oksimi" as a backdrop to the economic downfall of Oksim's family.

The story starts with Oksim's sexual feeling surfacing in spring, while she is working at a construction site with male laborers. Mandu Halmŏm, an older widow working next to Oksim, goads her further by asking, "Are you gonna just grow old like this?"[52] Mandu points out that the current situation will not improve, adding that chastity and the honor attached to it are pointless. Mandu's complaint against patriarchy addresses the difference in how a disease is lived by men and by women. When women have an illness, she argues, they are more likely to be thrown out of the family. The conversation makes readers wonder about the nature of her husband's condition, as Oksim's life is presented as akin to that of a widow.

The possibility for a widow to remarry, called "fixing one's fate" discussed in chapter 1, signaled a radical cultural change in the early twentieth century. Oksim briefly wishes for her husband's death so that she can pursue a new life, but she immediately feels guilty. When Oksim tells Mandu that everything is fate, Mandu responds, "What is fate? If you fix it, that's fate too. A fool like me couldn't fix it."[53] The conversation among women during their lunch hour is set against the repeated blasting of the mountain to build a road. The setting's turbulence mirrors the changing morality and shifting social structure.[54] Mandu convinces Oksim further:

> I feel like I am confusing you even more by saying this, but I have to say something, because your life ahead is so dark—just like my past. You don't live your life twice; women are the most foolish people. Let's say, if you became like him, and if your husband were healthy, would he live alone not doing anything [like you]? We know life is deceitful but it is foolish to be deceived when you know.[55]

Mandu's encouragement makes Oksim consider seeing An Sipchang (Manager An), her childhood crush, who works at the same site.

After the day's labor, Oksim comes home to yet more work: feeding her entire family, including her sick mother-in-law and two young sisters-in-law, as well as her son Subok. Her father-in-law tries hard to care for his son, who is now living in a hut apart from their house. Such isolation of leprosy patients appears frequently in literary texts in this period. The hut is a temporary solution: it hides the patient and protects the family's reputation rather than preventing family members from being infected, a possibility that does not appear to be a primary concern. "Oksimi" provides some explanation of the growing importance of surveillance of and hostility toward leprosy: "Given the conditions at the time, when the disease came to be known to the neighborhood, he couldn't help but move into a hut."[56]

The mother-in-law's complaints about how much the father-in-law spends on medicine show that the disease's main burden is the economic hardship it causes: "Everything is because of having a sick son. If it had not been for him, this household wouldn't have gone bankrupt and our daughter wouldn't have been sent to a factory."[57] In addition to Oksim's wage labor in construction, the narrative introduces yet another change in agricultural society: women emigrating for factory labor. In the 1930s, peasants started to leave the countryside to look for factory work because the family budget needed wage income. As Cumings notes, "The combined effect of the depression and the industrialization of the peninsula shifted large populations off the farms and into new cities and industries."[58] Kim Chŏng-han captures this change in rural villages and shows how the agricultural family could survive without owning land. Registering practicality and coldness, the mother-in-law blames her husband's dedication to curing their son for their need to "sell" their oldest daughter (and, in the future, two other daughters) to the factory to pay their debt. In the 1930s, the movement of young women from rural areas to the urban centers for factory or service labor increased more than that of men.[59] Curing the son is the father-in-law's priority, at least until he is faced with a critical choice about sending his son to Sorokto.

Although "Oksimi" does not mention the colonial situation and the new law that mandated the forced institutionalization of all leprosy patients, enacted the year before its publication, they serve as a general backdrop to the story. As Oksim has an affair with An Sipchang, he suggests running away to start a new life, in view of her husband's disease. He insists, "If your husband had any other disease, you wouldn't dare to dream of running away, and I wouldn't have dared to sin."[60] It appears that leprosy is different from any other disease, mainly because it draws community antagonism and state surveillance. The diminished sway of traditional values, including Confucian principles of chastity and marital loyalty, and the fear of the disease coincide to provide an opening for Oksim to pursue sexual pleasure and other life options.

The original title of "Oksimi" was "The Immoral Woman" (p'aedŏngnyŏ),[61] which was changed by the newspaper Chosŏn ilbo before it was serialized. Even though the unused title highlights the judgment of Oksim's affair, the story itself does not take a moralizing gaze; rather it portrays the husband as extremely violent. She draws away from Chŏnsu, but his own actions estrange her even further. When he gains firsthand knowledge of her affair, he chases her and screams, "I knew what that bitch wanted from the beginning. Did she ever go to the construction of the new road, because she wanted to work? She got horny so she went to pave her path herself."[62] She flees with An at night without any of her belongings. After Oksim's departure, the family's economic hardships increase, and Chŏnsu's and his mother's conditions worsen. His father works for other tenants, as he is deprived even of his own tenancy.[63]

The story's silence about Oksim's life in flight makes clear that its focus is the survival of Chŏnsu's family while he is ill, not her transformation from a rural wife into an urbanized modern woman seeking love and liberation. Out of the blue, Oksim comes back and hugs her son like a "hungry animal."[64] This maternal yearning effectively casts her past pursuit of exile with her lover as regrettable. Her return is followed by Chŏnsu's brutal assault on her. Whereas her mother-in-law remains furious at her, reflecting society's judgment of her as an immoral woman for having had an extramarital affair, her father-in-law unexpectedly turns against Chŏnsu: "You get out, dirty man. Otherwise, rather kill me. Are you so scared of Sorokto? You, jerk, a cow."[65] The need to preserve the patrilineage explains why the father sends his daughter to the factory to pay for the cost of Chŏnsu's medicine; it similarly justifies the family's choice of Oksim to support the family and raise her son. Never having seen his father so furious, Chŏnsu withdraws. Shortly thereafter, Chŏnsu's hut, which had tentatively served as a refuge between the family and the institution, is set on fire. The author's unsympathetic attitude toward Chŏnsu's patriarchal violence against his wife works to vindicate the family's choice of Oksim over him. Signifying the important shift away from the traditional emphasis on morality and women's duty to provide care, the narrative emphasizes the removal from the family of the sick and unproductive person, whose violence upon his loss of power makes him incompatible with his income-earning wife. Having won her father-in-law's support, Oksim promises her loyalty to him and to the family.

The key to understanding Oksim's return is to think of it as a move to compensate the family suffering economic hardship as much as a signal of the limit of her sexual emancipation. The literary scholar Ch'oe Wŏn-sik judges Oksim's return to be a brave action, for she has to face prejudice and punishment.[66] Oksim and Chŏnsu can no longer inhabit the same domestic space: it is the caring and practical patriarch who accepts the daughter-in-law. The presence of leprosy threatens the family's survival. However, this disruption of the family is resolved by Oksim's reembrace of her role as a dutiful daughter-in-law and mother. In this narrative structure, the Sorokto institution—an alternative introduced rather suddenly—appears to be the solution for the family crisis. The exit of Chŏnsu suggests that maintaining the family necessitates his institutionalization. In analyzing the story, Ch'oe Wŏn-sik asks whether Oksim's return is the author's compromise with and reinstatement of rural patriarchy.[67] He proposes that even if it is seen as a compromise, there would be no other choices available for a rural woman who runs away with a modern man.[68]

At this juncture, the transformed family in an industrializing economic structure revives women's domestic role of caring for the family and engaging in wage labor in place of an ill husband. The father-in-law's acceptance of Oksim, his grief at watching his son depart for Sorokto, the existence of the institution, the community's increasing hostility, and the colonial state's surveillance of the illness together all identify the family as an unsuitable space for an unproductive and ill person. The modern transformation of the rural community accidentally and momentarily opens up a possibility for a woman to seek escape; however, Oksim does not successfully merge into modern life free from responsibility toward the extended family. Whereas Chŏnsu never displays any affection toward his son, Oksim's affection toward the boy functions to naturalize motherhood and to discipline her sexuality.

"Oksimi" did not draw the same kind of attention from critics for its realist reflection of Korean society as did the author's other works, because its power dynamics—the struggle between a nondisabled woman who starts to be influenced by a more liberated atmosphere and a man with leprosy who turns violent because his authority in the family is waning—are made ambiguous. "Oksimi" shows that the old values and social order are subject to change as modernity and different economic relations emerge in the village, and as the state begins the process of removing from the community its leprosy patients, constructed as a threat.

In the same year that "Oksimi" appeared, Kim Tong-ni published a short story titled "The Rock" ("Pawi" [1936]). Depicting a woman with leprosy, "The Rock" displays not only domestic violence but also heightened surveillance and the increasing hostility toward ill and unruly bodies under the Japanese system of medical policing. Homeless people—including "cripples, beggars, and lepers"—gather beneath a railroad bridge at the outskirts of the village. While the beggars are practicing their routines, singing and dancing, the "lepers" congregate for a quiet discussion. "They say the Japs are going to kill off everyone suffering from paralysis. 'You mean to say they're going to kill people who've done no wrong?' It was the latest arrival who answered—the woman who had come from the village."[69] "Paralysis" here is translated from the word *p'ungpyŏng*, a broader category that includes leprosy-related physical disabilities and stroke-related paralysis. This English translation is from the author's revised version of 1947, but the 1936 original goes into much greater detail about the rumored Japanese policy:

> I heard that military police will soon come to kill off all paralyzed people like us with guns. A young leper murmurs with worries. Even if it was an absurd saying, they came to pay great attention to it. And they all thought inside "that can't be." As "that can't be" was their only weapon. "It can't be true that they're going to kill people who've done no wrong, can it?" A woman who came from the village murmured. All of them whispered the same thing several times. For a long time, no one opened their mouths.[70]

After the "lepers" hear that the government has given the order to send military police, the anxious hope voiced in the expression "that can't be" is soon replaced by silence. Indeed, their only resort is denial: "They believed that their 'that can't be' was based on the absolute authority of something like the sky. But they were not intelligent enough to articulate what that authority was."[71] By deleting this collective recognition of the injustice and fear existent within the communal space, the author shifts the reader's attention away from the growing hostility and public health surveillance of the 1930s. In the revised version, the narrative instead quickly flows into the flashback of the woman's past, the story of her son, and her yearning for the reunion with her son.

Her son Suri is an important figure in the narrative by virtue of his absence. Sons were believed to be the future and carriers of the family lineage, and the author describes how his future—and so too the family's future—is transformed by his mother's disease: "In all probability, they say, he would have got himself a wife and lived out a quiet, respectable life, had not the dread hand of cursed disease reached out to his mother."[72] The costs of medication lead to a financial crisis for the son, his loss of hope, and his disappearance, signifying the end of the family lineage. According to the 1947 version, "After he lost his son, the old man became more coarse and violent with every passing day. He came home drunk every night and beat his wife."[73] This is a shift in emphasis from the original, which described his violence as frequent even before his son's disappearance. The author appears to emphasize that the woman's illness and her "failure" as a mother cause both the loss of the son and her husband's change. The old man urges her to die and brings rice cakes laced with poison to her hut, as it becomes harder to hide her existence and as the rumors about wandering "lepers" and disappearing children intensify.[74] The growing communal antagonism toward leprosy patients, perceived as kidnappers, removes any habitable space for the patients within the domestic arena and the community, leaving death and institutionalization the only options for the family to pursue. In "The Rock," the woman eats the poisoned rice cakes despite knowing that they will kill her. "In the end she ate the rice-cake all right but death wouldn't come easily. Eventually she just had to go somewhere and, they say, she left the rice-cake thrown up all over the hut."[75]

Fleeing her murderous husband and her hut, the woman builds another hut on the outskirts of the village, where she joins other outcasts. There she awaits a chance to run into her son, near the Rock of Blessings on which she can pray; she believes "that by rubbing the rock she would get to meet her beloved son."[76] To her disbelief, she briefly encounters her son, and he leaves with the promise to visit her again. She keeps rubbing the Rock of Blessings, eager to reunite with him, but to avoid people she goes only after dark. "With the passing of time her whole faith and trust became more and more bound up with the rock. It was as if she would always have the hope of meeting her son again as long as the rock stood on the ground, and perhaps even for all she knew—her own illness might somehow be completely cured."[77]

As her prayers at nighttime are not answered, she takes the risk of praying on the rock during the day. Villagers find her, drag her off the rock so violently "like a dog, her legs trussed up in the rope, her whole body burst into one bloody wound,"[78] and beat her until she loses consciousness. Her efforts to seek a cure and find her son are punished with severe violence. A workman washes off the rock as if the woman has tainted it. This religious symbol lies at the core of community living, and the woman can no longer access the means to bring her son back; her pursuit of the son through the rock's power instead has a fatal end. As she overhears the villagers talking about her son's being in prison, she also witnesses her hut engulfed by the flame. She collapses on the rock, rubs her face against it, and is found dead the following day. The villagers' comments reveal the depth of their rejection of her: "The dirty thing would have to die here"; "A leper dying with her arms around the Rock of Blessings"; "Our precious rock."[79] The juxtaposition of the detested human body and the revered supernatural object powerfully illustrates the context-bound nature of human values. As the family transforms into a space of physical antagonism, her desire for her son and a cure is projected onto the rock, which later becomes a tool complicit in her death.

Han Hye-sŏn, in her study of disabled characters in literature, argues that the rock serves as a substitute for the son.[80] Just as the woman cannot live with her son, so she cannot approach the religious symbol guarded by the villagers. "The Rock" reveals how the family as a physical and relational arrangement becomes antagonistic toward an ill mother as part of the social alienation of people with leprosy and stresses the community's participation in that process. With the emergence of institutions to which leprosy patients are consigned, isolated and removed in the name of cure, the family again appears as an uninhabitable space, and the community feels threatened by the presence of the demonized others, often characterized as nonhuman species. Like "Oksimi," "The Rock" allows for the interpretation that the disease's harmful effects are primarily social. Survival is impossible because of the depletion of finances and familial and communal violence, rather than the danger and suffering from the disease itself. However, in both stories, women are assumed to be the keepers of family, though the fates of those families are quite different. One family survives because the nondisabled woman, Oksim, returns; the other is destroyed seemingly by the woman with leprosy. In "The Rock," motherhood is exalted as being similar to the rock's supernatural power, but the villagers' violence prevents her from fulfilling her role.

"The Rock" and "Oksimi" show the process of the patients leaving familial spaces; one results in the departure to Sorokto, and the other results in death. Huts outside of the home serve as a temporary place of exile and hoped-for cure, only to be demolished—leading to further banishment to a place from which there is no promise that they will return.

Curative Power and the Cured Subject

While segregation and human rights violations of *Hansenin* continued, the campaign to eliminate prejudice was combined with the U.S. government's interest during the Cold War in promoting its own image as possessing scientific, curative, and humane power. Jane Kim argues, "As leprosy provided the most compelling picture of Christian compassion, humanitarianism and moral authority, the emotive characteristics of the discourse on leprosy provided the means for neutralizing resistance, naturalizing power and ultimately legitimized the anticommunist Christian characteristics of the post-colonial nation-state in South Korea."[81] As part of the propaganda effort, the United States Information Service (USIS)-Korea was established in 1949 to improve foreign relations and promote U.S. interests overseas in line with what Frances Saunders calls the "cultural Cold War."[82]

In 1962, the Motion Picture Section of the USIS produced a semibiographical film about a well-known poet associated with leprosy, Han Ha-un, called *The Litany of Hope* (*Hwangt'otkil* [Yellow dirt road], dir. Yang Sŭng-ryong, dubbed in English). For five days the film was screened in the Citizens' Center in Seoul for a general audience together with a comedy. Despite its claim of being based on the poet's autobiography, the film is largely a dehistoricized and depoliticized re-creation of his life: the spatial and historical specificities of Japan, China, and North and South Korea where he lived are conspicuously absent (except for one scene signaling the beginning of the Pacific War). The fictional elements in the film construct a quintessential cure narrative through an iconic figure, to enforce meanings of a physical cure made possible by American aid.

The narrative proceeds from diagnosis and despair to medical treatment, physical restoration, and achievement as a poet, and finally, the cure is completed by the heterosexual union. The film continually emphasizes the importance of rationality, science, and modern institutions in contrast to superstition, ignorance, tradition, and family care. For example, a scene of Han's mother making snake soup for his cure is accompanied by a voice-over:

Medicine that was replaced with the false cures of the past
through a mother's desperate urging
Cures born in the midst of man's ignorance
Cures which match loathing with loathing
Cures which can damage more than disease
Cures that reject science for the ways of ignorance and fear
Cures which can kill by causing delay

The often lethal effects of what were once thought to be cures are set against the real cure that brings hope for change. When Han lands on Sorokto for treatment, the soundtrack shifts from traditional music to a cheerful Western tune. The voice-over continues, "Who could not hope in a community given meaning and being by the chemicals which heal?" Comparing the treatment there to his mother's superstitious attempt at cure and his lover's untrained care, the narrator says, "In this place of healing . . . I found hands guided by devotion, but given strength by knowledge and skill. Skill smelted in the crucible of time. . . . To the sanitarium of a man named Wilson, guided by pity across the seas from the U.S. when this century began." Stating what he calls the overwhelming truth that the disease can be cured completely by the drug, he says that this future lacks only his lover, Haegyŏng. After he is cured of leprosy in Sorokto, he is referred to the American-run sanitarium, Aeyangwŏn, for another form of cure that can bring a new and better life: plastic surgery to repair the "ravages" of the disease. As he exits the Sorokto hospital, an extreme long shot shows him walking down a dark hallway, moving away from the camera and toward the light. The modernity of the institutional architecture represents a pathway to further corporeal transformation. The music transitions once again from a traditional Korean to a Western tune as he arrives at Aeyangwŏn.

After taking a quick look at Han's hands and face, a Presbyterian missionary, Dr. Stanley Topple at Aeyangwŏn (played by himself), says in Korean, "I can fix these four fingers and eyebrows completely." Although he promises the complete cure of erasing the marks of the disease in this scene, in a conversation about his memory of the filming, Dr. Topple told me that his remark in the scene was scripted without consultation and he was dismayed by the line's claim of complete cure given to him by the director. He also said, "We can certainly improve the deformity a lot. But no surgeon makes the claim that we can bring the patients back to complete normalcy. That is not an honest medicine."[83] Topple's recollection provides the context of the film's exaggeration of medicine's capacity to bring back normality, presented as a precondition toward integration into society and blocking out the possibility of living with disabilities after the disease's cure.

The film moves on to show Dr. Topple attending to his patients. These are the only scenes in the film that feature nonactors, in order to portray the medical relief work done in Aeyangwŏn. Providing a "litany of hope" for those who are recovered from the disease but whose bodies need "repair," the narrator lists the names of sanitariums and hospitals that are "built on the charity of a government and its people, and on those from other lands," and built on "pity and compassion." The bodies of *Hansenin* in this scene become platforms on which American modern technology and compassionate care are displayed. In the following scene Dr. Topple and a nurse make a home visit to a *Hansenin* who has visible bodily marks. There are close-ups of hands and feet of patients in the hospital room and of a man at his residence looking down as his hand runs over his face, shielding it from the camera as he talks to the doctor. Emphasizing the compassionate humanity and religious dimension of the institution, the places of cure are constructed as "havens of hope" and "homes of miracles." The erasure of traces of the disease through "repair" is elevated beyond scientific and medical intervention to the status of what the poet-narrator states as "Miracles that let us show our faces without shame. Miracles that let us return to the home, the villages, we had known."

Plastic surgery to remove any signs of the disease constitutes the most visible part of the cure: it signals that without a normalized appearance, the cure is neither complete nor effective in bringing about real changes. As the nurse unwraps the bandages from Han's face, the camera zooms in and the narrator dubs it a miracle, a term repeatedly used to assign supernatural power to medical technology. Han looks down at the mirror in his hand and bows to the doctor. The medical science that cures disease here leaps to a mystical realm that enables a return to full humanity and the erasure of shame through plastic surgery. It is only after his eyebrows and nose are restored that Han launches his successful career as a poet, as shown in the scene of newspapers containing his most popular poem, "Barley Stem Flute," coming rapidly off the press. The next scene, which shows the hand surgery performed by Dr. Topple, fades to a shot of two women walking through a gate of Aeyangwŏn to visit Han. His lover, Haegyŏng, joins him and the doctor in the garden. The film ends in a wide-angle shot of Haegyŏng and Han walking on the beach, the very scene with which *The Litany of Hope* started. The written statement that ends the film, "From the faith and hope of the individual stems the strength of the nation," foreshadows the legislative codification of eugenics led by Park Chung Hee, who often said, "Physical strength is the foundation of the national power."[84] Furthermore, it casts a U.S.-Korean alliance as necessary in the Cold War geopolitical landscape. Curability and the hope for reintegration into society successfully depoliticize the colonial and postcolonial management of the disease and the violence done in the name of cure. For example, even at a time when the hereditary theory of the disease was already disproven, patients were allowed to marry only if they were sterilized while at certain institutions.[85]

The cure that testifies to the power of science and medicine can be completed only when all markers of disease are erased, thus enabling a heterosexual union with a nondisabled person. Thus, in this sequence, cure can develop into inclusion only after the patient is visually transformed through aesthetic surgery that supposedly averts scorn and removes stigma. The poet's actual ambivalent experiences of cure are glossed over by this seamless transition from the disease's cure in the film; Han's getting his eyebrows, nose, and hands "repaired"; professional success; and rejoining the love of his life. Unlike what is portrayed in the film, he was not treated at Aeyangwŏn. He received nose reconstruction surgery at a university hospital (not at Aeyangwŏn), and he later underwent another medical procedure to undo it. He wrote in *New Literature* in 1958, "Now my face is uglier than that before the surgery. It changes its color to red or blue according to the temperature."[86] Alarmed by this failure, Han decided not to receive an eyebrow transplant. Rather, he described taking off his hat to face people's stares as revealing his "top secret, modesty with no eyebrow."[87] Furthermore, he never reunited with his nondisabled lover. Both of them were arrested in the North during the Soviet Union's occupation as they were suspected to have assisted his brother's political work. He was bailed out of jail due to his illness and went to the South to find the new medication. Later he returned to the North to look for his lover, but without success. Instead, he was put in jail, escaped, and went back to the South.[88] Eventually, in the settlement village where he lived, he married a woman who had Hansen's disease.[89]

Believing that full integration of people who had Hansen's disease could not be achieved, the poet dreamed of building a self-governing independent nation of people called Muha Republic to efficiently control leprosy; ironically, his purpose was to "purify blood and promote ethnic eugenics."[90] Addressing the reality of people affected by the disease—the denial of their right to life and the violence against them—Muha Republic, he imagined, would be "a new welfare paradise" (*pokchi nakt'o*).[91] Similar to Han's dream of forming a separatist community rather than seeking an unlikely return to the society outside the curative institution, beginning in 1962, more than three thousand *Hansenin* who had been in Sorokto started a land-reclamation project on Omado Island where they could live self-sufficiently and sustainably. After three years of hard labor, this project was crushed when the government forcibly seized the reclaimed land and distributed it to the nearby villagers who opposed living close to *Hansenin*.

The transnational power to cure as pictured in *The Litany of Hope* is presented in humanitarian rhetoric that focuses on the visibility of cure: a removal of the markers of the disease that leads to literary success and heterosexual union. The forging of the paradigmatic cure narrative for transnational propaganda and for the antistigma campaign based on curability connects to my last site of analysis: legal and cultural advocacy for *Hansenin* and the representation of marriage as the ultimate symbol of curability.

Marriage as Reconciliation

The trope of marriage as a reward that follows a cure has been prevalent Korean cultural imaginations. Until recently, critics have read Yi Chŏng-jun's best-selling novel *Your Paradise* (*Tangsindŭl ŭi chŏnguk*) mainly as a political allegory, one that uses Sorokto Island and the hospital's sovereignty over it as a way to describe the Park Chung Hee regime. The literary critic Kim Hyŏn writes, "When it is impossible to directly show the theme of a piece due to restrictions of the period, an author can and should express the theme discreetly and euphemistically."[92] The author himself has commented in various writings and interviews that the novel was intended to allude to the military regime.[93] In the novel, the arrival on the island of the hospital's new director, Colonel Cho Paek-hŏn (a character based on a real director, Cho Ch'ang-wŏn), wearing a military uniform evokes the image of Park Chung Hee after his coup d'état. His status as a medical doctor and a military colonel underscores that the hospital's medico-juridical authority rules the island.

Although the novel can be read as a political allegory, it is not limited to that allegory; indeed, it became an effective narrative of the history of people with Hansen's disease on the island. That the novel was inspired by an extensive exposé of the situation on the island, written in 1966 by the journalist Yi Kyu-t'ae, adds to its historical significance.[94] The novel focuses on Director Cho's effort to build a self-sufficient territory for residents by reclaiming land for farming. Hwang, the elder among the patients, initially does not trust Director Cho, given that all previous efforts to create a paradise have ended up elevating the status of the "reformers," while hiding violence against the residents and the suppression of their civil and political rights. Hwang later reverses his position and supports the Omado reclamation project. In contrast, Sangguk, who works at the hospital and is an adult child of patients (classified as *migama*), remains skeptical about the project and escapes from the island. By fleeing, Sangguk disavows the fantasy that such a "paradise" could exist under its medico-militarized control. The author remains ambivalent toward Director Cho's character and his deeply political endeavor.

Director Cho's reclamation project mirrors the Omado project that was shut down by the government, for which proper resolution and reparation are still pursued. In the novel, this gross violation of the residents' rights to the land they created is blamed on Director Cho. When he later returns to the island as a civilian, he attempts to put right his failed integration project by finding another way to symbolically connect the island and the mainland:

a marriage. With Director Cho's encouragement, Haewŏn, a man who was formerly a patient, is about to marry an uninfected woman, Miyŏn. A reporter, Chŏngt'ae, who is deeply interested in writing about such an unusual marriage, visits Cho and finds out that Cho has been deliberately lying about the bride, who is a *migama*—her parents had been affected—and thus has the status of a patient. This information is unknown to the groom: "Even to this day, he thinks that Miyŏn is a normal healthy person, unaware that her parents were lepers."[95]

> The director told Chŏngt'ae that he and Miyŏn had agreed to keep her past a secret in order for Haewŏn to overcome his belief that only patients were able to live together. It was necessary if he was to gain more self-confidence. Then the director asked Chŏngt'ae to wish them happiness and encourage them in their proud union. . . . "Please let Haewŏn and the islanders think this marriage is between a former patient and a non-patient."[96]

The marriage clearly becomes a tool of Haewŏn's cultural rehabilitation, moving him toward integration into society. Cho aims to change Haewŏn's internalized identity as "leper" through his marriage to a woman who belongs to the dominant group.

While practicing his speech for the wedding, Cho reveals his political intention to use the marriage to replace his failed project of geographical and material unification. When territorial connection between the island and the peninsula through the reclamation has failed, Cho tries to find a symbolic integration across the remaining divide:

> "Looking at this situation, we might come to the conclusion that a union of hearts is much more important than the material connection of muddy embankments. In that sense, the marriage of Yun Haewŏn and Yi Miyŏn is a meaningful union of two people from two very different stations in life. The embankments, which were built by rock and soil and only exist as physical entities, are only today being truly connected before our eyes." . . . Sangguk's face, which had been tense, began to relax and he wore a faint smile. Yet Chŏngt'ae could not read the meaning behind his smile. Either he had been moved by the director's direct and pure thinking or he was jeering at his pathetic ambition.[97]

In an interview thirty years after the novel's publication, the author revealed that Sangguk, who overhears the speech with a grin on his face, is the figure who represents society's intellectuals—those who suspect everything and need to reflect deeply, even if it means that they cannot act politically.[98] That the speech was never delivered in the actual wedding ceremony but was heard only by a skeptic signifies the failure of Cho's discursive substitution: the symbolically constructed wedding cannot remedy the historical injustice of land appropriation. The author explained, "I intended to distrust and suspect the character with a political conviction. That's why I ended the novel with the speech rehearsal. There is no more political person than a speech maker."[99] The interviewer, U Ch'an-je, asked the author, whether he considered depicting Miyŏn as a "purely healthy person," not a *migama*. Yi answered that he would have done so, if he were in political office and not a novelist, because historically the marriage between a patient and a healthy person was unthinkable: "It would have been too naïve, too romantic, or too fantastic a conclusion, wouldn't it?"[100] Yi added that he wanted to be on the side of *mundungi* rather than a ruler, no matter how noble the ruler's intentions and goals, because a real paradise cannot possibly be founded upon segregation.

One key point made by the novel is this warning against dictatorship and the belief that true utopia, however well planned, can be built by one person's power; another focuses on the possibility of altruistic intentions not swayed by the corruption of power. Although the author intended to problematize the use of marriage to represent a symbolic solution to a historical injustice, the marriages between male *Hansenin* and female non-*Hansenin* are nevertheless employed as evidence of the social integration of *Hansenin* that will be discussed in the next section.

Hansen's Disease in the Twenty-First Century

On October 11, 2004, in Seoul, the Korean Bar Association hosted the Forum on the Human Rights of People with Hansen's Disease. The media reported on the forum, "the Sea of Tears," and claimed that this was the first public appearance of *Hansenin*.[101] More than four hundred people with disabilities who were cured of Hansen's disease gathered, voiced their experiences, and called for special legislation to redress the extreme discrimination and lifelong stigma they had suffered. These collective voices of *Hansenin* attracted widespread attention to the violence committed throughout the twentieth century. As a result, at the beginning of the twenty-first century the human rights of *Hansenin* emerged as an important sociolegal issue in South Korea.

A well-publicized Japanese court case provides a clear explanation of this seemingly sudden public emergence of *Hansenin* advocacy. In 2001, the Kumamoto court of Japan ruled that the Leprosy Prevention Law was unconstitutional, and it ordered the government to compensate the 127 plaintiffs who were institutionalized in Japan.[102] Prime Minister Junichiro Koizumi publicly apologized for the forced institutionalization and sterilization based on "scientific" beliefs that had since been discredited. The Japanese parliament approved a bill to compensate those who had suffered decades of systematic civil rights violations by the state.[103] Encouraged by this legal success in Japan, 117 Koreans who had been institutionalized during the colonial period on Sorok Island sought compensation in 2003 and 2004.[104] Though the Japanese government initially rejected their claims, the Korean *Hansenin*'s requests for compensation began to be approved in 2006 after persistent advocacy.[105]

The journalists reporting on these developments focused on the need to eradicate prejudice against *Hansenin* by disproving the beliefs that had originally justified institutionalization and sterilization.[106] Because any discourse on the human rights of *Hansenin* relies heavily on the fact that leprosy is neither highly contagious nor hereditary, questions regarding what forces and knowledge were used to isolate *Hansenin* are left unanswered. The South Korean government continued this process of isolation even after a cure was developed, and it covered up several mass murders of *Hansenin* by military police and civilians. In 2007, the Hansenin Incidents Law (*Hansenin sakkŏn pŏp*) was created in South Korea to investigate the postcolonial victimizations and to support affected people. In the recent rulings, the Seoul and Kwangju courts ordered the government to compensate *Hansenin* who had been forcibly sterilized and had received forced abortions in national hospitals.[107]

In response to the Japanese court case, the Munhwa Broadcasting Corporation aired a two-part documentary on prime-time television, *Ah! Sorokto* (dir. Kim Hui and Kim Myŏng-kon). Part I, "People Standing on the Edge of the World," opens with scenes of researchers excavating a site where an atrocious massacre occurred in 1945 after Korea's independence from Japan. The survivors, standing around the site, deliver testimony about the massacre of eighty-four patients. Leaving the audience puzzled about the specifics of an event untaught in schools, the film moves on to vivid scenes in Japan showing the delight of the formerly segregated people at hearing of their victory in their legal battle against the government. These scenes establish Hansen's disease as a subject of great historical and political magnitude.

The film then inserts a brief interview with James L. Krahenbuhl, the director of the U.S. National Hansen's Disease Research Institute, who states that the sterilization of "lepers" is "barbaric" and has "no basis in modern thinking." Although the documentary touches on Nazi eugenics, Japanese colonial policy, and eugenic sterilization as the historical background of such violence, this interview sets modernity against that violence, erasing its systematic modern and scientific framing. This move raises critical questions. If the mistreatment of *Hansenin* is understood as barbaric and premodern, how then do we account for the ways in which the colonial authority and later the Korean government promoted its management and the institutionalization of *Hansenin* as the signs of status as a modern nation? The testimony of the American medical authority on the barbarism in Asian history exemplifies the West's erasure of its own violence, eugenic sterilization,[108] and segregation of people with Hansen's disease.

Part II of the documentary, "Beyond Prejudice and Segregation," continues to take the expert opinions of Western medical professionals, posing the question "Is leprosy hereditary or contagious?" By presenting a medical doctor who testifies that Hansen's disease is neither hereditary nor contagious, the documentary shifts the focus from the disease's sociohistorical dimension to its medical dimension. Inevitably, this move obscures the fact that prejudice and misinformation were not the only factors driving segregation and sterilization, which continued after the disease was made curable and shown not to be inherited or readily transmissible. In the documentary, Hansen's disease is positioned within binaries—ignorance versus enlightenment, premodern versus modern, and culture versus science—in which the latter solves the problems caused by the former. Its rhetoric prevents the documentary from exposing various ways in which the management of Hansen's disease was tied to the expansion of modernization and Christianity in Korean history, as well as to international propaganda in the name of public health and science. Because the voices of *Hansenin* in the United States and its former colonies are not represented, the documentary presents the United States as the ideal of an advanced society, much as *The Litany of Hope* does. Building on its description of the disease as curable and nonhereditary, *Ah! Sorokto* moves into a section titled "People Dreaming Reconciliation with the World," tracing the budding social changes that connect the divided worlds of *Hansenin* and the "healthy" for a hopeful future and for "reconciliation." Inclusion here is demonstrated by two marriages between disabled men and nondisabled women. In the documentary, as in *Your Paradise* and *The Litany of Hope*, the union between a disabled man cured of the disease and a nondisabled woman is depicted as a solution, effectively privatizing the remedies to the historical and social violence.

One couple introduced in the documentary is made up of Pyŏn Hye-min, a female nurse, and Yi Se-yong, a man who had been institutionalized in Sorokto. The woman's position as a nurse is emphasized as proof of his status as cured and posing no risk of transmitting the disease to her, as well as proof of her qualifications to care for and be devoted to him, a former patient. The scientific discourse is translated into the social arrangement of marriage and the cultural image created around it. It is assumed that marriage is possible when the threats of the disease's being contagious and hereditary are proven to be unfounded. According to this logic, marriage is exclusively located in the able-bodied world because it achieves symbolic value through the absence of disease. The existence of marriage proves Hansen's disease to be curable, noncontagious, and nonhereditary—all characteristics that function as preconditions for livable and valued life. The contemporary strategy of raising the awareness about stigmatized populations illustrates the tendency to seek cultural rehabilitation through the normalizing practices of gender roles, sanctioned marriage, and reproduction in the private realm, although *Hansenin* have reported many occasions on which they were not allowed either to enter restaurants or hospitals or to use public transportation.

Representations of marriage between men who are former patients and nondisabled women cast their unions as a symbolic bridge between the segregated space of "lepers" and the "healthy," though the unions' ability to reunite the nation is more apparent than real. The political formulation of marriage between disabled men and nondisabled women in efforts to eliminate the stigma exemplified by *Ah! Sorokto* affirms the gendered social order as a way to compensate for segregation. This becomes problematic when it reinforces the view that the nondisabled women is the only symbolic gateway to disabled men's integration.

In this privatized political partnership between marriage and human rights, disabled women—as well as the kinship and intimacy formed within the sanitaria and settlement villages—are rendered invisible. This move is geared toward domesticating people with Hansen's disease while ignoring the problems they face in public life, including education and employment. In 2012, out of the 12,488 *Hansenin* living in South Korea, 42 percent lived in 91 settlement villages and 7 residential institutions.[109] To date, inclusion remains largely rhetorical, suspended in the hope for the future, while stigma and patterns of segregation persist. The history and narratives of Hansen's disease dramatically reveal the making of family that should be uninhabited by disabled people and become a nondisabled unit during eugenic modernization. The familial space is constructed as incompatible with disabled bodies. In this process, public policy reconstructed the family, while problematizing the presence of disabled bodies and putting forward institutionalization as a solution that was inevitable and that naturalized the erasure from the public sphere of people with disabilities. This erasure effectively ignores the necessity of their public participation, including the necessity of making decisions about the future of the spaces used for segregation and policies for people with infectious diseases and their human rights protection.

Whereas narrative analyses show how the family was gradually constructed as an uninhabitable space as segregated medical treatments and institutionalization were enforced, contemporary activism resorts to moving people—who have been deprived of family and the ability to reproduce—into heterosexual families. The political formulation of marriage between disabled men and nondisabled women seen in works such as *Ah! Sorokto* shows a different affirmation of the cultural order. However, these alternative relations also depend on affirming a gendered configuration as a way to compensate for continued segregation and to culturally rehabilitate stigmatized men while making disabled women invisible.

The analyses speak to broader concerns about the limits of scientific and biomedical discourses in challenging social alienation and historically constructed stigma, as those discourses embedded in cultural, social, and political dynamics around diseases are employed to justify discriminatory policies. What would disability studies approaches to infectious diseases and public health look like? Without separating the physical disabilities that Hansen's disease can create and the disease itself as disability, what can the logic of inclusion based on curability tell us about incurable and infectious diseases and the ethical limits of public health measures? Based on the fact that people with Hansen's disease are entitled to human rights on the condition of complete curability and low to nontransmissibility, it follows that the human rights of people whose illness and disability are not curable and possibly infectious—including those with HIV and tuberculosis—become separate issues. HIV researchers, professionals, policy makers, and historians have drawn parallels between the stigmas of HIV and leprosy and have tried to learn from "the lessons of leprosy," but they have found that the parallels produce more questions than answers.[110] Perceived similarity between HIV and leprosy was used to make a case for isolating HIV-positive individuals on a Pacific island, evoking outrage from the community.[111]

If quarantining exposed persons and isolating infected persons are actions believed to be necessary to prevent an infectious disease's spread, without medical evidence, what can disability studies of infectious diseases say about human rights, public health, ethics, accessibility, vulnerability, survival, and lived experiences? Catherine Kudlick writes about smallpox epidemics in nineteenth-century France and points out that "epidemics have a hidden history that is deeply interwoven with disability and survival. Because of this, disability history has the potential to transform how we understand the impact of epidemic disease, not just at the level of individual reactions but also at the level of social and political responses." Kudlick continues, epidemics "provide the all-important stage for re-presenting disability and disabled people in history."[112] In addition, it provides the opportunity to reimagine the representation of cure that coexists with disability and with the desire for communities formed around the epidemics.

Regarding sexual desire and the individual's responsibility to disclose their HIV status, a disability studies scholar in the United States, Christopher Bell, calls for valuing sexual pleasure above safety and protection from infection and reinfection. Bell argues that denying HIV-positive subjects access to sexual experiences forecloses possibilities of pleasure: "The aims to legislate codes of conduct of HIV-positive individuals under an ideology of 'responsibility' may have been effective when modes of transmission were still unknown, but the time has long since passed." Now that the risk of transmission is at measurable levels, we are in what Bell calls "the HIV age of reason."[113] Bell's provocative initiation of a queer disability studies approach to infectious diseases from the point of pleasure and desire of infected persons should inform how to empower ethical readings of the cultural images of infectious diseases from the perspectives of lived experiences and social relations.

Nancy Waxler wrote in 1981 that fear and stigma of patients with Hansen's disease remain because "the organizations whose goals are 'to assist in [leprosy patients'] rehabilitation and to work toward the eradication of leprosy' at the same time perpetuate, through their actions (building inpatient hospitals and providing long-term care) and words (public education programs and fundraising brochures) the community's ideas of stigma."[114] The very act of care and specialized treatment that justify the removal of the patients from the communities continue their work by sustaining the stigma of leprosy.

In 2003, a qualitative research project by Eriko Sase, Masamine Jimba, and Susumu Wakai investigated why disabled Koreans still stay in leprosaria and found that "most people diagnosed with leprosy are still disconnected from their families and society even after being cured and abolishment of the isolation policy in 1963."[115] Their account makes clear that a long history of segregation cannot be remedied by a short-term intervention. The current lives of people—whether in institutions, settlement villages, or the community—and their diverse familial relations should not be discounted. In fact, some *Hansenin* decide to move back to Sorokto after initially leaving. The *Associated Press News* reported, "Starting about a decade ago, the number of returning former patients began gradually increasing. Over the past few years, about 70 people, mostly former residents, have resettled here each year," as they find the life outside unlivable due to stigma and economic hardship.[116] The return to the land of the history of segregation is not simply an exile but also a kind of coming home based on their connection to the space.

A more comprehensive coalitional understanding of the cultural and social elements of *Hansenin*'s experiences and their inseparability from those of other disabilities and other epidemics is required to further develop disability studies approaches to infectious disease. The image of Hansen's disease as a disease of the past is contradicted by the assumed need to isolate people now being treated until they are cured and even after their cure, and by the assumption that locates inclusion always in the future—despite our having reached "the Hansen's disease age of reason" half a century ago. Curability, rationality, universal access to treatment, and global elimination of the disease have not signaled the end of stigma: inclusion largely functions as a specter beheld in hope, while stigma and patterns of segregation persist. Apart from the inclusion-focused antistigma work, the communities that the experiences of disease created and the intimate relationships and kinship, as well as people's deep connection to the inhabited land, bring forth their sovereignty over the space demarcated by segregation and lived time.

CHAPTER 5

Curing Virginity

In a graphic short story titled "Big Event" ("Kŏsa" [1996]), a man with cerebral palsy asks his nondisabled male friend to take him to a place where he can have sex for the first time.[1] The disabled man worries aloud that he may not be allowed in because of his appearance, but his friend responds confidently: "Korea is a capitalist society. With money, nothing is impossible." When they arrive in what seems to be a hostess club, they are partnered with women who sit next to them and pour their drinks in a private room. While the non-disabled man touches and hugs his partner, displaying his familiarity with the space and the intimate service, the disabled man drinks alone, sitting far away from his partner. She becomes sympathetic toward him, comes near, and infantilizes him by calling him "my poor baby." She then appears to identify with him, as she tells him that they share an unfortunate fate and that God is unfair. But her sense that they are fellow members of outcast groups—namely, disabled persons and sex workers—is short-lived, as he suddenly says that he wants to have sex with her and forces his upper body onto hers. She screams, "I am not so debased as to sell my body to people like you!" He returns the insult by throwing cash in her face, saying, "I am a man too"—revealing his sense that his manhood, with the accompanying privilege that nondisabled men enjoy in the sexually saturated commercial space, has been unfairly denied.

This mutual exchange of humiliations does not seem evenly framed, given that the story was published in a disability rights magazine, *Hamkke kŏrŭm* (Walking together), to reflect the perspective of disabled men, whose sexuality is so thoroughly denied that "even" a sex worker will reject them, leaving them without options to have sex. This rejection invokes a melodramatic reaction to denied masculinity and the failure of capitalist logic and male access to women's sexual labor when confronted with disability oppression.

This story is one example of how the representation of sexuality and disability in South Korean media generates emotional reactions, consisting of shock at disabled persons' expression of sexual desire, of pity, and of the desire to help. The melodrama of a disabled man's virginity[2] is a popular motif in the cultural and political production of the sexuality of disabled people in South Korean society. Traditional belief that it is tragic and unfortunate for men and women to die a virgin combines with pity for a virginal life with disability.

Unlike the other chapters that address historical developments of the themes involved in curative violence, this chapter examines a relatively new discourse that emerged in late 1980s South Korea, which constructed disabled people's sexuality as a social problem in the mainstream media. I focus on how heterosexual experience became an apparatus to "cure" the assumed lack of sexual experience of people with disabilities, and how sexual experience is considered necessary for them to be recognized as human beings. This curative process simultaneously locates the humanity dependent on the making of heteronormative subjects simplifying this history of sexual oppression, othering disabled people further by exceptionalizing disabled sexuality and by disciplining asexual and nonheterosexual persons with disabilities. I analyze a feature-length documentary film, *Pink Palace* (dir. Seo Dong-il [2005]), which details the story of a disabled man as he attempts to "lose his virginity" in a brothel in Seoul. Another text I explore is the Korean translation of Kawai Kaori's book *Sex Volunteers* (2005), which introduced the notion of sex volunteers for disabled people. I then analyze the multilayered narratives of sex workers, sex volunteers, and disabled men in *Sex Volunteer: Open Secret, the First Story* (dir. Cho Kyeong-duk [2009]). In the last section, I explore the award-winning independently produced short film *Papa* (dir. Yi Su-jin [2004]), which depicts a father's search for the cure for a behavioral problem of his disabled daughter, supposedly caused by her sexual frustration. *Papa* presents incestuous rape as inevitable violence to address sexual needs.

The materials and discourses discussed in this chapter illustrate the major debates around disability and sexuality in South Korean contemporary politics and culture. By illuminating the narrow emphasis on the "sex drive" of physically disabled men and proposed solutions such as legalized and subsidized sexual services provided by a "sex surrogate," a person who acts as a sexual partner as part of "sexual therapy," or a "sex volunteer," who willingly engages in sexual acts with a disabled person without compensation but with a humanitarian motivation, I argue that these representations of sexuality of disabled people naturalize nondisabled phallocentric, biologically driven heteronormative sexuality as a goal to be reached by various means, including humanitarian action and violence. The representations of sexuality and disability strongly marked with emotional sentimentalism to a different degree appeal to neoliberal benevolence that hides embodied experiences, socioeconomic and physical violence, political marginalization, the reduction of welfare, and institutionalized ableism. The chapter addresses how disabled people, who are historically cast outside the binary gender system and sexual realms, become incorporated into sexual normativity by putatively humanitarian service inventions in a gendered way, while securing heterosexual marriage and the nuclear family as largely practices for nondisabled people.

The "Sexuality Problem" and Othering

Most of the Korean news reports and articles on disability and sexuality begin by stating that disabled men and women have been considered genderless or asexual (*musŏngjŏk*), but that their sex drive is the same as that of nondisabled people.[3] Similar claims are common in Western societies, and the belief that disability and sexuality are viewed as incompatible has been well documented.[4] Historically, sex, friendship, intimacy, marriage, family, and reproduction have been reserved in the West for heterosexual and nondisabled citizens.[5] Margrit Shildrick has succinctly argued that the incompatibility of disability and sexuality "plays a part in the maintenance of the normative attitudes that shore up the supposed stability of a social order founded on heterosexuality and nuclear family life."[6]

To correct this assumption of asexuality, an online newspaper article made a claim, "Disabled People Have Sex Drive Too" (*Changaein to sŏngyok i itta*) without addressing the sexual diversity of disabled people, including asexuality.[7] Various versions of this slogan encapsulate the topic of the sexuality of disabled people, who are presented as having the same sex drive as nondisabled people but not having an outlet due to social isolation. As the rhetoric of a universal and natural sex drive has focused on men with physical or intellectual disabilities, men with other kinds of disabilities and disabled women have been marginalized. For example, at a Pusan symposium on what should be done regarding the sexuality of "severely" disabled people, a speaker set aside disabled women, because, for them, sexuality is "a matter that needs to be dealt with caution." He then described a successful collaboration between a brothel owner and the director of an institution for intellectually disabled men to meet the needs of the residents. The sexuality of disabled women is treated at best as an afterthought, and the prevalence of sexual exploitation of and violence against women leads to more caution. But whereas women with physical disabilities are viewed as vulnerable, disabled women with intellectual disabilities are often understood as having uncontrollable urges once their sexuality is "awakened." Because of this perceived hypersexuality and the disavowal of reproduction of disabled women that I discussed in chapter 1, many such women have been involuntarily sterilized; others are forcibly given contraceptives, including Depo-Provera, to prevent pregnancy and to effect an absence of menstruation.[8] Moreover, women and men with sensory or mental disabilities, as well as women who are physically disabled or chronically ill, are often excluded from discussions and policy making about disability and sexuality. The paradigmatic figure in this discussion is a man with intellectual disabilities with strong sexual desire or a man with spinal cord injuries in his twenties to fifties who uses a wheelchair and has limited use of his upper body (with the emphasized difficulty of masturbation).[9]

The "sex drive" of disabled people came to public attention in South Korea rather suddenly as a result of the national and international media's coverage on the topic, as if their sexuality had just been discovered.[10] Sex drive and humanitarian sentiments also dominate the discussion of the sexuality of other minority populations, including older people and migrant laborers.[11] The attention paid in the 1980s to older bachelors in rural areas, which resulted in the policy of promoting their marriages to women who were recruited from China and South East Asia, has resonance here. Other rhetoric invokes not the intrinsic sex drive of disabled men but the sexual rights of disabled people, including the right to sexual self-determination, the right to enjoy sexuality (sŏng hyangyukwŏn), and the right to have their sexual agency and subjectivity respected. However, these claims themselves have been underdeveloped and used interchangeably with arguments about sex drive and the simplified need for sexual outlets.[12] The equation of sexuality with a biological sex drive, combined with the supposed lack of outlets, encouraged writers and filmmakers to construct sexuality as a problem that requires an immediate prescription and to disregard the historical, cultural, and social contexts of sexuality and disability.

Proposals outside South Korea for addressing the sexuality of disabled people, often involving strategies other than the traditional sex trade, have entered into this discussion. Among the disability-specific services are assistance to a couple for negotiating and engaging sexual activities; for accessing the venues, such as motels, for purchasing sexual materials and devices; and for masturbating as well as the services of direct touching and intercourse. The global circulation of information about specialized services helped South Korean advocates construct disabled men's sex drive as something that, like other aspects of their lives affected by their disability, must be addressed with formal services managed by various institutions in the name of therapies. According to media reports, specialized programs were in place for years in Denmark, Germany, Switzerland, and the Netherlands, but few details were given. A Swiss organization, Pro Infirmis, launched the Touchers Project for disabled people in Zurich in June 2003, attracting media attention.[13] The proposed services, which were later withdrawn due to funding shortages, ranged from massage, stroking, holding, and body contact to bringing people to orgasm. Korean media often discuss these programs with little consideration for their cultural specificity or disabled people's perspectives.

Such programs advocate practices intended to immediately address the sexual needs of disabled people; social changes to ensure their equality are perceived to be harder to achieve. Shildrick cautions against being too quick to see these new practices and policies, including what is called "facilitated sex" implemented by organizations and states, as real progress: the naming of such changes in public policy as simply "progress" is to overlook the considerable risks of attaining social recognition for sexual subjectivity at the cost of a certain normalization, even if individuals may find that the policies provide pleasure and meaningful experiences.[14] Shildrick suggests that "even the most seemingly benign developments arising from policies of liberalization with regard to sexual matters may merely mask a persistent and underlying failure to make space for that which resists the closure of final classification."[15]

In addition to drawing on the rhetoric of sexual liberalism, Korean discursive practices also reflect a kind of rhetorical dependency, as writers tend to view Western and Japanese practices as automatically progressive and to repeatedly use such information from abroad to justify their proposed domestic policy, such as legalizing the provision of sexual services. There are few nuanced narratives about the actual experiences and perspectives of those who in fact use and provide sexual services; instead, the information used is fragmentary and abstract. These references to other countries also lack any specifics about gender and disability relations and legal, historical, and cultural contexts. That special services are employed in a progressive atmosphere is almost always mentioned, but the experiences of disabled people and their diversity are not addressed. Some local programs, such as the Netherlands' Fleks Zorg (a for-profit business employing men and women who provide sexual services to disabled men in Amstelveen), are inaccurately presented as national phenomena, as politics and regional differences are ignored. By referring to these practices as widely available, the discourses on disabled men's sex drives seek to break sexual taboos and erotophobia and to remove the moral stigma of purchased sexual services. Advocates for specialized practices distinguish them from the sex trade, heavily associated with legal restrictions and women's commodification, in placing them in the vanguard of ideas for policy intervention.

The construction of the sexuality of physically or intellectually disabled men and women as a problem reflects a complicated mixture of prejudice based on the assumption that normative sexuality is practiced within married, loving, and private relationships. Sympathy for those whose sexual access in society is systematically denied is more easily generated in the case of disabled men than in other populations, such as soldiers and prisoners, as well as other sexually marginalized people, such as immigrants and older people. Thus the logic of the sex drive is applied selectively to morally justify inventive exceptional provisions, which solidifies normative sexuality as inaccessible for disabled people. Not only is heterosexual desire constructed as normative in these solutions, but the idea that everyone is sexual in general is emphasized as a counternarrative to the assumed asexuality of *all* disabled people, constructing prescribed sexuality as a new norm. Asexuality as a possibility for disabled people is not being considered, only being perceived as an oppressive misperception. Moreover, the othering and distancing that occur when individuals imagine those who have never had sex are grounded on an assumed heteronormative sexuality and the cultural atmosphere that naturalizes and confirms it.

Still a Virgin: *Pink Palace* and the Red-Light District

The documentary *Pink Palace* (2005) presents rich material for investigating how disability, gender, global rhetoric, and the sex trade shape the moral hierarchy among the kinds of sexual experiences. After the Touchers Project first became known, the South Korean disability rights magazine *Hamkke kŏrŭm* featured a series of essays on the sexuality of disabled people under the notion of "sexual rights" and discussed European practices, the sex trade, sexual normalization, and the oppression of women within the sex industry. Seo Dong-il, who directed *Pink Palace*, read an article titled "Disabled Friends, Claim Your Sexual Rights," containing a story similar to that told in the graphic short story discussed in the beginning of the chapter.[16] Seo starts the film with this story he read.

A man with severe cerebral palsy in his 40s, living in a rural town, went to Chŏngnyangni district with 300,000 won. Leaning his tense body against his scooter, he kept glancing at the women inside the window under the red lights and finally went into one brothel. But he had to turn around in tearful silence when the sex workers ruthlessly rejected him, saying, "We don't like a person like you, even with a lot of money. Go away." Because he cannot even dream of marriage owing to his severe disability, his only wish is to have sex once.

Seo confesses, "When I read this article, I was surprised that disabled people, too, have sexuality," indicating that he, like most of the public, held ableist views about who can be sexual.[17] Six months later, he quit his job so that he might make a documentary about the sexuality of disabled people and, more specifically, about the man featured in the article. *Pink Palace* marked his debut as a filmmaker.

What makes the story of a disabled male virgin rejected by a sex worker so compelling that it is repeatedly told, and why does this story generate strong reactions? The combination of disability and sex trade marks the intersection of two socially marginalized groups: disabled men and female sex workers. Re-envisioned as the last resort for sexually "undesirable" men in *Pink Palace* and the graphic short story "Big Event" alike, sex workers are portrayed as prejudiced against disabled men. The social alienation experienced by a disabled man apparently heightens when he is rejected and mistreated by a stigmatized and commercially available woman—someone who is not expected to be selective. Here, the rights of disabled customers to access sexual services and the rights of sexual workers to choose their own customers come into conflict outside the legal bounds of sexuality. The sex trade, though illegal, was long condoned in certain areas and regulated by local police and the government, whose crackdowns were high-profile but sporadic until international scrutiny about "sex trafficking" and the attendant national shame, especially about the red-light districts, began to influence the government in the early 2000s and culminated in the 2004 Act on the Prevention of the Sex Trade and Protection of Its Victims.

The fact that the men customers' social status determines the hierarchy of sex-selling women within the red-light districts might provide some background as to why sex workers discriminatorily choose certain kinds of customers. According to Won Mi-hye, interviewing a woman who worked in a red-light district, sex workers hesitated to serve disabled men "not because of their prejudice but because of the limited time per sexual transaction. It takes more time and [disabled men] are not easy to serve because they are sensitive, thinking that they are looked down upon. Sometimes they show a more authoritative attitude than 'regular' men."[18] Won explains that the refusal to serve certain customers is a way for sex workers to enforce their own boundary in order to control their labor conditions and avoid practical disadvantages imposed by the brothel owners and pimps.[19] However, the testimony does reflect generalized prejudices against disabled men that exist within society, at the same time that it acknowledges the difficulty sex workers face in accommodating disabled men within the rules and inaccessibly built environments. Outside the rigid brothel space, Won adds, there are women who specialize in serving disabled men in more flexible circumstances such as in-home service.[20]

The documentary's title, *Pink Palace*, is a reference to a brothel in Melbourne, Victoria, where brothels and escort services are legal. The brothel Pink Palace received widespread media coverage for its progressive efforts to help disabled people seeking sexual partners, as it boosted its business by installing doors large enough for wheelchair access and a sit-down shower for disabled male customers.[21] It created a niche market within the sex industry for disabled tourists and locals alike. By using its name, Seo makes the point that the sexuality of disabled people is recognized in Australia in contrast to the apparent moral repression of sexuality in South Korea.

The film is divided into two unequal parts. In the first, disabled men and women are interviewed about their sexual lives, marriage, dating, masturbation, and unusual erogenous zones. Although it is treated as a prelude to the longer second part, which features Ch'oe Tong-su, whose story was told in *Hamkke kŏrŭm*, the interviews introduce a wide variety of important narratives of men and women with visual, hearing, facial, cognitive, or physical disabilities, providing different perspectives that were previously unknown to the nondisabled public. For a man whose face was changed by burns, it is hard to find potential partners or even to make friends. A deaf couple is concerned about the possibility of engaging in sex and not noticing the presence of other family members in their home. A woman with a physical disability worries that she might involuntarily urinate during intercourse. One woman who uses a wheelchair explains that at her mother's suggestion—and largely for her mother's convenience—she underwent hormonal therapy to stop her menstrual periods. But it caused her to bleed for a month, so she stopped her hormonal therapy. Her mother is now talking about her getting a hysterectomy. Her experience is shared by many other women with intellectual or physical disabilities[22] and also featured in a film, *Sex Volunteer*, discussed later in this chapter, which also tells the story of a woman who is believed to have no right to reproduce and whose menstruation is viewed as an unnecessary nuisance for her caregivers and a source of indignity for them.

In these interviews, the sexualities of women and men receive different, unbalanced treatments, drawing the criticism that the film is male-focused and dominated by penetrative sex as the norm.[23] In the film, the sex and sexuality of disabled people are constructed in an essentialist manner and are frequently equated with the desire for food, water, and sleep. One disabled man compares himself to a dog to explain that his basic needs are ignored rather than to frame the problem as connected to a socially and physically inaccessible environment: "If a dog is in heat, people know it should be mating. But God! People don't care about our sexuality at all. I realized at that moment I am treated worse than a dog." The film in fact includes a scene of two dogs mating, captured by chance in the yard of Ch'oe's house. By framing sex this way, the main narrative of the film signifies that the gap between disabled men's desire and their limited opportunity to directly fulfill the desire is so large that nondisabled people are motivated to provide them with sexual experience.

In the second part of the film, Seo and his crew visit Ch'oe in a rural town and bring up the narrative featured in the magazine. Ch'oe explains that he felt miserable when the sex workers rejected him. One of the voices off camera—supposedly that of a crew member or the director—responds, "I feel like we need to make your wish come true," signaling that their project will focus on his wish to lose his virginity. The film is dominated by the story of Ch'oe's rejection and his status as a virgin at age forty-eight, despite the many interviews about disabled individuals' active sex lives that precede it. Thus, the emphasis remains on the "sexlessness" of disabled people, and the melodramatic focus on Ch'oe's virginity gives the film a sense of urgency and the pursuit of an immediate solution against legal, moral, and social disapproval.

After the initial interview at Ch'oe's house, *Pink Palace* captures Ch'oe's outing to Seoul to meet one of his friends. At first, to faithfully capture the reality of his journey, including a near traffic accident, the film crew simply follows him from a distance. It takes him three hours to reach the train station by scooter, and the buses and taxis are not accessible. Ch'oe's usual travel routine includes spending a night in the station's public bathroom to recharge the battery of his scooter; when Seo Dong-il asks why he does not go to a motel, Ch'oe takes the question as a suggestion and responds, "Shall we do that?" The director then participates in the journey, thereby undercutting his own claim of objective documentary representation. Later, as pornography plays on a television in the motel room, they continue to discuss Ch'oe's sexual desire. His embarrassment at the scenes on the television reveals his lack of familiarity with pornographic materials, an ignorance that the film portrays as a sign of tragic naïveté in someone of his age and gender. The hardships that accompany Ch'oe's outing hint that the problem of access to sex is inseparable from the issue of access to urban social spaces. Perhaps Ch'oe's experience would have been different if he had owned a scooter in his youth (the filmmaker recalls a young man interviewed earlier who is actively social, because his motorized chair and urban space give him mobility). But because Ch'oe lives in a rural area without accessible infrastructure and transportation, his social experience has remained quite limited even after his acquisition of a scooter. His trip to Seoul to meet his friends provides a glimpse of the enormous difficulty for his social interactions in general, let alone any interaction that might yield sexual activities.

After his initial edits were finished, the director decided to visit Ch'oe one last time. Text on the screen informs viewers that the 2004 Act on the Prevention of the Sex Trade and Protection of Its Victims was enacted, strengthening the law banning the sex trade and prosecuting those who engage in the sex trade, and the conversation starts with Ch'oe's response to the law, which came into force since their previous meeting: "We, disabled people like us, aren't human then?" Ch'oe thus gives voice to the humanist reaction to the news, and the director continues, "Well, Ajŏssi [a term used in addressing an older man], last time in my house, you mentioned that you would like to lose your virginity as your wish but that you had given up." Ch'oe answers, "Yes, I was passionate in the past. But now all the curiosity is gone, 'cause I watch this stuff"—with a glance at his television.

> SEO: You are saying, you lost curiosity and you don't want to do it?
> CH'OE: Yeah.
> SEO: But . . . if there is another opportunity one more time . . .
> CH'OE: I want to do it if there is another opportunity. It is different from those pictures, isn't it?

Following this suggestive conversation, the director warns him of the possible legal ramifications for both of them, and Ch'oe becomes contemplative. In the next sequence, Ch'oe is sitting in the back of a car at the entrance to a red-light district, and the two men engage in what seems to be a staged discussion to confirm his determination. Seo asks Ch'oe if he wants to wait until he finds a woman he loves. Ch'oe adamantly declares, "A woman I love won't appear. It is over for me. It's over, of course. I feel like I'm wasting my virginity on the woman over there, but I can't help it. Once born and dead, one never knows when he will be born again. If I die a virgin, it is so unfair, unfair!" The dialogue makes it clear that what Ch'oe is about to undertake is considered a "lesser" form of sexual experience, signaling a shift in perspective from focusing on the sex drive as a basic instinct to framing sexual experience within a norma-tive value-laden hierarchy. The sexual experience with a "woman over there," whose femininity is seen as degraded, in the red-light district is thus under-stood as inferior to that with a loved one, which is assumed to have social and cultural value beyond an "instinctual" drive. The film figuratively and literally returns to the moment of its conception—the melodrama surrounding Ch'oe's virginity and his rejection by a sex worker at the brothel. The film here provides another melodrama since, to accomplish his mission, Ch'oe must resort to a sex worker rather than a loving partner, who is putatively out of his reach. The presentation of this melodrama fails to address the systematic discrimination experienced by disabled people in their exclusion from intimate relationships and to highlight the sexual and asexual diversity of disabled people.

Once Ch'oe is on the street, leaving the filmmaker and the crew behind, the camera makes the viewer into a voyeur watching his brave yet somehow sad adventure as cued by the background music. He sits on a scooter alone in front of a brothel, framed in a long shot. A woman at the doorstep waves him away several times, but after some negotiation, facilitated by the note that the film crew wrote, he wheels through the brothel door, as the camera shows him finally allowed inside. Problematically, the film ends with Ch'oe wheeling into a brothel without conveying how Ch'oe would narrate his experience. The red-light district remains a taboo space, off-limits for the film crew and the audience alike. While this visit to the brothel has supposedly "cured" Ch'oe's virginity, the structural inaccessibility of his social environments and his iso-lation in his rural town remain.

Pink Palace was generally successful in getting the attention of mainstream media as well as coverage in disability newspapers. It was screened in theaters and other venues, such as on the cable television channel RTV. When RTV announced the plan to show the documentary again, several major women's organizations formed an alliance to oppose the rescreening of a film as they ar-gued that the film substantively endorses the illegal sex trade.[24] *Pink Palace* was caught in the heated debate between anti–sex trade activists and people who support legalizing the sex trade; among them were sex workers, who began to speak out in the face of more stringent anti–sex trade legislation. The director himself defended his film in a letter to the newspaper *Able News*, denying its endorsement of legalizing the sex trade.[25]

Advocates proclaimed June 29, 2005, as the first Sex Workers Day in South Korea, and the celebration was held in Seoul. The organizing committee scheduled a partial screening of *Pink Palace* (only Ch'oe's story), intending both to promote the legalization of the sex trade to meet disabled men's sexual needs and to educate sex workers, who might be less inclined to reject disabled men once they had come to sympathize with Ch'oe.[26] This emphasis on the need for the public sex trade echoes the rhetoric used by nondisabled activists seeking to garner support for legalization before the enactment of the new law.[27] Even though the sex trade is frequently discussed in relation to disabled men's sexuality, there is a gap between exploring it as a matter of equal access (and discrimination against disabled men)—only insofar as it is available to nondisabled men—and participating in the movement advocating for sex workers' rights and for legalization.

There is significant market interest in establishing disabled men as a target group of the sex trade, regardless of its illegality. In the rhetoric that ties disabled men to an industry tailored to masculine desire, there is little room for considering the disabled women who are often laborers in that industry. Because the discourses of sexuality are often based on stereotyped perceptions of the women's bodies as objects of consumption, women's perspectives are crucial in legal analyses of the individual's sexual rights. In January 2003, police found two nineteen-year-old women with intellectual disabilities in a brothel. According to the testimony of a nondisabled coworker, who had escaped and reported their presence in the brothel, for several months both had been brutally tortured and denied medical treatment by the brothel owner.[28] The brothel space to which disabled men wish to gain access becomes a more complicated and ambiguous space, given the presence of disabled women as sex workers, who in many cases are exploited. This is not to say that disabled women in the sex industry are always victimized; some disabled women find their place and a sense of belonging to the community of sex workers.[29] But ignoring disabled women's positions and experiences in the sex industry simply adds to the male-focused nature of this debate.

The gendered landscape of discourse regarding disability and sexuality demands a more careful examination of social dynamics and the operations of power across multiple marginalized groups including disabled and non-

disabled transgender workers in the sex industry. Furthermore, the dichotomous gendered emphases on "men's sex drive" and "women's vulnerability" do
not either adequately account for the diverse sexual lives of disabled people
or address their invisibility. In turn, disabled people's sexuality is prescribed
by—and at the same time significantly thwarted by—the social, cultural, and
historical instrumentalization of the sex trade, without deeply engaging with
the experiences of both groups and structural violence.

Sexual Humanitarianism and the Politics of Help

The publication of *Sex Volunteers* (*Seksŭ chawŏn pongsa*) in 2005 introduced
a key new concept into the discussion of sexuality and disability in South
Korea.[30] "Sex volunteers" are those who offer to provide sexual services to
disabled people without compensation, and the Sino-Korean word *pongsa*
(serving) implies sacrifice and help.[31] Because "volunteering" connotes charity without monetary compensation, even in the sexual realm, the issues
of illegality and exploitation connected with the sex trade are potentially
avoided. Such rhetoric relies on many sociocultural assumptions that must
be examined. How does the fact that one person has a disability change the
construction of a consensual sexual exchange into a service voluntarily performed by one for the other's pleasure, and under what assumptions? What
does this switch from the sex trade to sex volunteerism indicate about the
making of an individual citizen who is actively called to action to relieve the
assumed suffering of others, while complementing the neoliberal capitalism
and the reduction of social assistance? What are the power and affective dynamics defined in the rhetoric of help? Given the long-standing expectation
that women provide care without pay, what are the gendered implications for
this type of sexual practice?

Although discussion of Kawai Kaori's work in the domestic media focused
on the feasibility of sex volunteering—its pros and cons,[32] the book is far from
simply advocating volunteer sexual service. Presenting diverse narratives from
the people involved, it covers a wide range of sexual services provided by individuals or through organizations. These services include the typical sex trade,
male escort services, the sexual activities provided by personal assistants, and
surrogate therapy in the Netherlands. Kawai delivers diverse stories of men
and women with disabilities who hire sex workers for a fee or have engaged in
sexual activities with volunteers and "semi-volunteers" (who receive expenses
or nominal compensation). The book's suggestion that disabled people need

to be helped in order to have sexually active lives generated controversy within disabled communities.

Kawai also interviewed people who provide commercial sexual services to disabled people. In one case, Kawai follows Yurina, a deaf woman, on her first day as an escort for the Enjoy Club, an escort service for only disabled customers. She used to work as a paid dating partner for older men—a practice called *enjo kosai*—as a way to deal with her loneliness after becoming deaf as a high school student. She also worked in another sex business in which she was paid less than nondisabled colleagues and sometimes had her tips taken away. Yurina's story exemplifies how disabled women and girls enter into the sex trade because of their lack of resources and social isolation, and how even in that industry they are at a disadvantage in competing with those who are not disabled. Moreover, it shows how disabled women seek out intimacy and income through the sex trade, challenging the narrow focus on disabled men consumers that has characterized policy debates. Kawai writes that Yurina enjoyed her first day serving a physically disabled man and wants to continue working for the agency so that she can save enough money for a surgery to recover her hearing. This story of a deaf woman working for a commercial escort service for disabled men in order to earn money for her cure draws attention to an important intersection of the sex trade, disability, gender, and medical costs. The market for disabled men's sexual needs provides her with viable work in which she does not feel stigmatized, although she has to hide her job from her boyfriend. Her story poses a challenge to the simplistic kind of a feminist view that the sex trade is by definition a type of violence that victimizes women.

Kawai also introduces Natsuko, a physically disabled woman who hires a male escort at a host club. The host club offers a discount and waives the fee for disabled customers. Natsuko calls the man her "prince"; she had come to love him but could not tell him so, because he would stop providing his service to her. Natsuko thus experiences on a personal level the blurring between intimate relationships and purchased intimate services. Sato, a heterosexual male volunteer who has sex with disabled women, thinks that such distinctions are even harder for the male volunteer to draw: "When there is a [business] agency, the distinction between service provider and receiver is clear because there is money involved. But in sex volunteering it becomes ambiguous, especially when I ejaculate. When I helped disabled men to masturbate, my hand felt like a tool, but when I had sex with a disabled woman, it didn't feel like that."[33] He continues, "Perhaps I was interested in having sex with a disabled woman. I thought I needed to have a firsthand experience in order to [promote] the practice of sex volunteering, but in fact, the term 'volunteering' was giving me impunity. I think the sexual relationship with money is so much more convenient."[34] His feeling of sexual gratification invokes guilt and confuses the arrangement of volunteering that assumes a sacrifice of time and labor without any compensation or benefit to the volunteer.

Because of the power dynamics of volunteering, the sex services provided by a "sex volunteer," "sex carer," or "sex helper" do not meaningfully further sexual rights, but they may provide sexual experiences and pleasure that individuals find meaningful and life changing. These narratives also suggest that sexual services are not always connected to the commodification of women's bodies; nondisabled women may see themselves as helping and assisting disabled men. However, the logic of volunteering entails a different hierarchy—one based on disability status and on the politics of helping at an individual level without calling for systematic changes. Volunteering and charity privatize "problems" as difficulties to be solved by individual intervention.[35] Tom Shakespeare points out that "when a particular group of people is strongly associated with charitable provision, the result is to demean that group. . . . People with power or resources volunteer to help those without power or resources, but the consequence is to make the latter feel dependent and incapable of surviving independently. The charitable relationship is an unequal one."[36]

The idea of sex volunteering assumes that a disabled person would wish to have sex with anyone willing to provide sexual services in the absence of gratification, monetary compensation, or any sense of physical attraction, which all condition the activity as volunteering. It also assumes that a disabled person cannot find anyone who is mutually desirous of engaging in sex. Sex volunteering is an individual "humanitarian" solution to social and structural problems, aiming to alleviate perceived suffering. The attempt to distinguish sex volunteers from sex workers also seems problematic, because it leaves unquestioned the stigma attached to the latter. Thus the advocacy of sex volunteering/care/help for disabled people defines the boundaries of their potential sexual experiences in problematic ways.

Sexual Outcasts on the Edges of Morality

In the 2009 film *Sex Volunteer: Open Secret, the First Story*, which received quite a lot of attention in international film circles and from its domestic audience, sex volunteering is imagined as a temporary solution to the "problems" of disabled people's sexuality before their death, which requires rethinking the boundary of what is viewed as socially acceptable heterosexuality. Like the director of *Pink Palace*, Cho Kyeong-duk conceived of the film after reading about the sexuality of disabled people—in his case, Kawai's book, *Sex Volunteers*. He said that he was shocked that people born with severe disabilities have a sex drive.[37] This fiction film follows the making of two films: an investigative documentary on the practice of sex volunteering for disabled men featuring a reporter, and a short film directed by a college student about a sexual encounter between a sex worker and a disabled man. This way *Sex Volunteer* creates the distance from the sensational idea of sex volunteering and, at the same time, from the curious yet skeptical gaze of the audience taken up by the reporter. Through the inquisitive reporter's interviews and intrusive cameras, the film introduces the topic of tabooed sexuality with a reflective awareness of ableist moral prejudice and sexual privilege, while taking advantage of the sensationalized nature of the topic via its title.

Yeri, a nondisabled college student, is arrested in a motel room after having sex with Chŏngil, who has a physical disability, on the charge of engaging in the sex trade. A Catholic priest, who was also in the motel room assisting Chŏngil after sex, accompanies them to the police station. The interrogating detective asks Yeri if she received money for sex, to which she answers "no." He asks then if she loves Chŏngil. As she also answers negatively, the detective then asks, "Why did you have sex with him"? She asks back, "Do you masturbate because you love your fingers?," framing her body as a prosthesis for the disabled man's masturbation. She tells him that it was humanitarian help, highlighting her altruistic intention. The disgusted and perplexed detectives cannot understand how one has sex without having any of the three motivations for sexual activity known to them—"money," "love," or "enjoy"—revealing that her experience lies outside the boundary of legible sexual relations.

Opening with the startling police raid, documented with the handheld camera, the film sets out, through the character of the reporter, to explain the circumstances leading to the arrests. The disabled man in the motel room, Chŏngil, is a wheelchair user and a poet who was in love with a disabled woman. His marriage proposal was rejected not by his lover but by her father who cusses him out of their home, disallowing Chŏngil to see his daughter. His lover is a quadriplegic woman who lives with her parents and spends most of her days in bed. For her family's convenience of care, she received a hysterectomy. She says to the reporter, "I feel miserable when I think that I am finished as a woman. . . . I want to have menstruation again, if I could." Beyond the main topic of sex volunteering, the film is invested in telling the narratives of disabled people in relation to their sexuality and daily struggles while living in an ableist society that alienates them and denies their sexual and reproductive rights.

Chŏngil's aging mother tried to arrange his marriage with a woman whom she recruited via a newspaper advertisement, but the woman took his savings and ran away. Chŏngil's past, it seems, convinces the reporter that having sex for once with the volunteer Yeri was his last resort, especially when he is presented as having no future left for another relationship at his age. His full name is a homograph with the word hwangch'ŏnkil, "the path to the other side" by death. The name illustrates the unavailability of a future for him to wait for his circumstances to change.

The reporter initially sees Yeri and Chŏngil's sexual relation in the motel room with skepticism and features the perspectives of the public through street interviews. When introduced to the idea, everyone speaks against "sex volunteering" with various rationales, such as that "many disabled people love and do get married," that "it is an animal-like practice," or that "it is only for the volunteer's self-satisfaction." One Buddhist monk interviewed on the street brings up the traditional term "body offering" (yukposi) as conceptually connected to volunteering. "Body offering" refers to an act of physical labor for charitable causes. It also refers to a sexual offering, such as of a Buddhist monk, who would help women who are praying for fertility at a temple by offering them sexual intercourse to increase their chance of conception (connected with the discussion of infertility in chapter 1). The monk condemns sex volunteering and body offering, both disguised as doing good when they are actually self-rationalizing rhetoric. These religious and moral condemnations of sex volunteering, laid out in the beginning of the film, corner Yeri into displaying a hostile attitude to the reporter. By laying out several possible criticisms through the journalist's simplistic reporting and Yeri's resistance to the reporter, Sex Volunteer creates the audience's awareness of the layers of representations and guides them to look past their knee-jerk repulsion and rather to see it as a last resort of a disabled person, whose life is oppressed under broader systemic and social isolation. The film also defamiliarizes ordinary activities that are taken for granted to able-bodied viewers and shows how experiencing them becomes a lifetime struggle for people with disabilities and how some activities, such as retaining reproductive functions, using a public restroom, and starting a family, are denied to them.

Yeri majors in film directing and got to know Chŏngil at first as a subject of her film, which was to capture his everyday life. She wears a cross on her neck and volunteers at an orphanage and at a center for people with disabilities where the Catholic priest works, delivering a sense of the moral and religious sincerity that frames her decision to have sex with Chŏngil. As Chŏngil's health deteriorates at the end of the film, she decides to make another short film titled *Flag Stop* (*Kaniyŏk*) featuring a sex worker and a disabled man, based on her experience of sex volunteering for Chŏngil that led to her arrest. The title indicates that sex volunteering is not a final destination that she advocates but only a provisional measure. In her film, Yeri portrays a character of a sex worker who, after being convicted of the sex trade, is doing community service at the center for people with disabilities. But the actress who would play the role of the sex worker/volunteer bails, disgusted by the fact that she has to act with a disabled man; Yeri decides to play the sex worker herself. Through her previous filming, Yeri has become familiar with the life of the sex worker Minju working in a brothel. Yeri makes a crucial connection between two groups: women who sell sex and disabled men. The attention paid to the alienation both of sex workers and of disabled people distinguishes the film from the mutual othering we see in the framework that sets sex workers against disabled men and vice versa. This connection does not resemble the antagonistic, mutually othering relationship depicted in the graphic short story "Big Event," which I introduced at the beginning of this chapter. Yeri remarks on the inaccessibility of the world both to sex-selling women sitting inside the show window at the red-light district and to disabled people using wheelchairs: "Sex-selling women and disabled people, aren't they similar? The threshold is only ten centimeters high, but they can't step outside. Wearing extremely tall wedge shoes, the women cannot move freely. They bear the label in their entire life and everyone points fingers at them saying, 'Why are they living like that?'"

In this film-within-the-film *Flag Stop*, the experiences of Yeri, the sex volunteer, and of Minju, the sex worker, merge into the character of a sex worker who volunteers to provide sexual service to a disabled man. As they prepare to have sexual intercourse in the motel with the assistance of a priest of bathing and transferring him to the bed, the woman has a flashback to her traumatic memory in her brothel. When raided by the police, she swallows a used condom to hide the evidence of the sex trade, but throws it up in front of the police. Then the film shows the sexual activity with no music. When he thanks her at the end, she says, "No, I thank you more." The scene transitions to the red-light district, where the woman is shown walking out of the brothel display window with a suitcase and away from the camera in an empty street, implying that the volunteering experience has healed her and that she had been empowered to step over the threshold of the show window, so that she could leave her life in the brothel behind.

After the screening of *Flag Stop* in front of a small group of people who have inspired or helped her filming, including her mother who is an anti-sex trade feminist activist, Yeri says in front of the reporter's camera, "Something that is trivial to someone can be the life itself to others." Soon after, Chŏngil dies at the hospital. As the last word to the reporter, who asks him whether he would have sex with a volunteer again, if he were to have the same chance, Chŏngil says through the communication board, "I am not hungry for food. I am hungry for people." His last word resists the tired yet persistent equation between food and sex, but it delivers the sense of loneliness and the lack of sustainable social and sexual access as well as of intimate relations that sex volunteering cannot provide. The film ends with the text of Article 29 of the Anti-discrimination against and Remedies for Persons with Disabilities Act, prohibiting discrimination in sexuality, pointing to the need for broader social change.

Chŏngil's deteriorating health and eventual death magnify the emotional response to his life marked by the social denial of meaningful heterosexual relationships. His critical health condition also produces the sense of urgency for Yeri to represent their experience of sex volunteering in her film to the outside audience in order to raise social awareness. She creates herself as a proxy for representing his experience and Minju's experience through the short film *Flag Stop*. In a way, Yeri's sense of duty to become a proxy coinciding with the deteriorating health of a disabled person is reminiscent of a film by Lars von Trier, *Breaking the Waves* (1996), in which a woman named Bess goes out to engage in sex trade with men, thinking that her sexual exploits can cure her disabled husband, who is in critical condition. After becoming quadriplegic, her husband believes that he cannot have any sexual relations with his wife and wants to provide her sexual pleasure by making other men his surrogates. By having Yeri, the filmmaker, represent both Minju and Chŏngil, the director Cho Kyeong-duk embeds his commitment to representing the sexual outcasts in South Korean society using a medium of film. His endeavor is aided by the celibate Catholic priest to preempt easy erotophobic judgment of the film's topic, in a similar way that the priest functions in the Hollywood film *The Sessions*. However, *Sex Volunteer* eventually avoids advocating for sex volunteering as the ultimate "solution" to the sexuality of people with disabilities constructed as "problems," as the priest says that "the solutions can be as many as the number of people in this world," framing everyone's own take on sexuality a matter of equally valuable diversity.

The diversity framing at the end somewhat weakens the film's critique of symbolic violence that one imposes on the other in the name of help by do-gooders. For example, Yeri's mother is a self-righteous director of the outreach center for sex workers. Her hypocritical attitude and the distance she feels from the sex workers behind her political condemnation of the sex industry as exploiting women and violating women's human rights are revealed when she perceives her daughter to be a different kind of woman from the women she helps. She becomes hateful toward Minju, who, according to Yeri's mother, lured Yeri into the brothel. Minju reveals to the reporter her conviction against do-gooders, whom she perceives as self-serving hypocrites. When she moved out of the brothel to a shelter, a humanitarian organization that agreed to renovate the shelter did so by publicizing their charity work with a large placard and photo shoot. Disgusted by the helping organizations who stigmatize and alienate their constituencies by focusing on promoting their images, Minju left the shelter and returned to the brothel.

Defying a monolithic message, *Sex Volunteer* takes the "solution"-focused representations of the "problem" of sexual needs of people with disabilities to a space where the stories of sex workers, antiprostitution feminists, humanitarian volunteers, and disabled men and women are told in proximity to each other and in conflicting relationships. However, this multiplicity of voices avoids tackling the power dynamics between individuals negotiating sex, as it resorts to a melodramatic ending with the death of Chŏngil and with the transformation of the sex worker who can walk out of the brothel in Yeri's film. In the end Yeri does not screen her class project *Flag Stop* in front of her classmates, but she only shows it to those who are involved in the stories in the film and whose experiences are represented, signaling two points. First the director does not see the practice of sex volunteering gaining the understanding of the larger public, and, second, the fair representation without being reduced to a stereotype of one group to create a transformation story of another, often at the expense of another marginalized group, involves accountability and negotiating processes that take those who are represented as the primary audience. Yeri and the audience's ambivalent faces after the screening express the director's ambivalence about an individual solution to social and structural marginalization and the difficulties of representation. However, this argument for representational ethics is fraught with its gender and disability dynamics, in which a nondisabled Yeri's good intention becomes the most important mission, being above the voices of the disabled men and women. *Sex Volunteer* only features one woman with disability who does not talk about her sexual desire or absence thereof, instead only focusing on her forbidden marriage and obligatory sterilization for her family. The power dynamics within the sex industry and the police violence are simplified in the film's easy solution of a sex worker leaving the brothel, transformed after the sex volunteering for a disabled man, a transformation that ignores the complex reality of sex workers in their economic entanglement with their employers and their stigma as well as enduring isolation of the disabled man.

Curative Rape

Several documentaries on disabled women that deal with their sexuality focus primarily on marriage and the desire of intimate relationships (e.g., *The Story of the Marriage of a Disabled Woman* and the MBC television documentary *The Sexuality and Love of Disabled Women*),[38] but one exception is the independent film *Papa* (*Appa*), a short drama. *Papa* features a "caring" father living with Minju, a nonverbal daughter with a disability. When he notices her bloody fingers, he seems to think that her sex drive is causing her to scratch and to hurt her genitalia; he then consults with a doctor several times about possible solutions. On the street, he searches for a man who will satisfy Minju sexually, even offering money to likely candidates. At the end of the film, with no other way to provide her with sexual satisfaction, he rapes her. Interestingly, the film has been perceived not as representing rape but as breaking the taboos regarding incest and the sexual desires of "severely" disabled women. In a familiar rhetorical turn, the film critic Kim Hwa-bŏm holds up Europe as a model where disabled people's "sexual welfare" is taken seriously. Kim states the need to transcend the familiar and easy criticism about father-daughter incest in order to rethink the sexual needs of disabled people depicted in the film.[39] Through society's fixation with the sex drive and the framing of injuries self-inflicted by an isolated and deprived woman as a sexuality problem, the incestuous rape is presented as challenging moral repression and revealing the denial of disabled people's sexuality.

The film takes on an entirely different meaning if it is read as a depiction of the father's desire to control his daughter's behavior. For instance, he is shown trying to organize and control his environment, a different, perhaps subtler, depiction of his mental fixation (which also signals disability) on her cure.

When he visits the doctor to talk about Minju's behavior, he lines up the cigarette butts in the ashtray on the doctor's desk. He is portrayed as methodical in his attempts to stop Minju from touching her genital area, first taping gloves onto her wrists and later tying her hands to the furniture with fabric. He carefully shaves Minju's pubic hair from the scratched area and uses a vibrator to treat her "problem." In doing so, he kneels down and turns on a Beatles song, as if he were carrying out a ritual. As the sensation from the vibrator gives Minju pleasure, he bursts into tears. That he goes on to rape her later reveals his belief that penetrative sex, not sexual pleasure, is the only way to eliminate her self-injurious behavior. In a scene preceding the rape, the father undertakes another ritualistic activity. When he cooks dinner for himself, he cuts the claws off chicken feet, an act that symbolizes his desire to mutilate Minju's fingers because they caused her wounds. In the room where he is eating and Minju is sitting on a toy horse while touching her genitalia, the camera shows a wall tapestry of galloping horses. In order for her sexuality to be as free as the running horses and for her to reach an orgasm, he believes "having sex" with her is the only cure. As he rapes Minju, weeping, she screams in pain and hits his back repeatedly. His despair indicates that the act for him is tragic and yet he is forced to it by society's denial of disabled people's sexuality.

The context of the father's misguided and violent commitment to his daughter is the medicalized curative rhetoric of sexual needs, as he asks the doctor to perform sexual intercourse. The doctor explains that such European sexual services are not appropriate in Korean culture. All approaches to gain Minju's sexual "release" are seemingly blocked by social taboos and ableist disgust at the sexuality of disabled people. The father's fixation on finding Minju a sex partner is presented as caring and desperate. In one important scene, he visits an institution in an attempt to find her a partner after an able-bodied man has volunteered but failed to have sex with her.[40] The father looks into a room full of idly sitting young men with various disabilities and sees two men being physically intimate; one is pressing the other man's neck with his fingers in order to stimulate him. To the father, thus framed as a voyeur, apparently none of the men seem suitable because of the connotation of the nonnormative sexualities of disabled men. This scene in the institution is set up to rule out the possibility that Minju might have a relationship with any of the disabled men—as if it is a natural course of action—by visually disqualifying them as deviant. This leaves the father himself as the only sexual partner of Minju who can cure her self-wounding behaviors. Sin Mi-hye explains that the film attempts to expand our thinking: "If one gets rid of the stereotype [about the incest], the film opens itself unexpectedly easily. Although the film takes the theme to the extreme, it doesn't erase the father's original intention. The father loved Minju."[41]

How does Minju's wounding of her genitals make incestuous rape necessary? And what "problem" does the rape solve? Like *Pink Palace*, which ends with Ch'oe entering the brothel, *Papa* ends with the rape scene, leaving unexplored how such a "solution" causes trauma or the possibility that new narratives different from the sex drive/release formula might arise. In the closed binary framework of moral repression and the sexual crusade against it, the recognition of sexual agency to find pleasure and to problematize violence becomes difficult. In this film, as in *Oasis*, which shows a disabled woman falling in love with a man who had assaulted her (explored in chapter 3), to "free" disabled women sexually seems to require the intervention of violence against their will. This link for disabled women between sexual desire and violence evidences a gendered representation of how sexual desire is acted on. As subjects, men express their sexual desire and initiate sexual experiences; as objects, women have sexual desire that is recognized by others and curative rape is enacted against their bodies. By presenting the logic that the rape scene is inevitable, *Papa* makes violence invisible and promotes another melodrama of the "forced-to-rape" father.

Intimacy, Space, and Sexual Pleasure

Although the binary rhetorics of moral repression and sexual crusade broadly characterize the discursive landscape of disabled people's sexuality, voices have also emerged that carefully articulate the position that disabled people's sexuality is not an exceptional "problem" and that the sex trade and recruiting volunteers impose significant limitations to challenge sexual oppression of disabled people. Activists in the disabled women's movement lament their difficulty in being heard, as the debate has centered on disabled men. The sexuality of disabled women is discussed mainly in the contexts of sexual violence and reproductive control, including sterilization abuse. It is also framed in relation to interpersonal intimacy and marital relationships to deemphasize sexual pleasure. Activists experience these frameworks as limiting their ability to express their perspectives on sexual pleasure and the diversity of sexual desire. Park Young-hee argues against using the reductive framework of the sex drive to construct disabled people as recipients of another kind of service from the state or institutions.[42] She is wary of this process of institutionalizing (*chedohwa*) their sexuality, disciplining disabled people and their sexual and asexual practices, because the immediate remedies are often controlled by gendered and institutionalized settings. Corrective policies intended to encourage sexual experiences can turn into the pressure to manage sexuality when diversity and different desires, including the desire not to engage in sexual activities, are not accorded equal respect. Tari Youngjung Na argues that a safer space, the exploration of sexual pleasure, and the power to produce narratives will lead to alternative discourses about the sexuality of disabled people.[43] For example, Cho Mi-kyŏng describes her experience in the alternative space of a two-day workshop hosted by a disabled women's organization.[44] In the workshop, women shared their pleasurable imaginings about being liberated from norms and morality and considered how they could critically rethink social norms associated with sexuality, which often ignore certain groups.[45] The disabled feminist activists emphasize that societal barriers and inaccessible social and physical environments suppress their sexual and asexual expressions, pleasures, intimate lives, and relationships.

The gendered discourses of sexual oppression—casting disabled women as victims of sexual exploitation or as needing violent intervention to be satisfied and disabled men as denied access to sexual services—significantly limit a deeper understanding of disabled people's experiences of desexualization and denial of their sexualities and asexualities. The suggested ways of "dealing with" the sex drive of disabled people paradoxically discipline disabled people and their sexual and asexual practices, in that the immediate remedies are often controlled by gendered and institutionalized settings. Simple solutions remove any possibility that disabled people may be recognized as sexual and asexual beings with diversities and orientations. Further, reducing sexuality merely to the sex drive separates it from broader issues of political and civil rights and the continuing history of isolation and desexualization based on disability and health status. At the same time, the predominance of the sex drive discourse obscures the differences between violence and sexual pleasure and masks how the rights of disabled people to live in a community, to have access to intimate social spaces, and to have adequate assistance are interconnected with the rights of other sexual minorities. The shift from viewing the sex drive as a biological necessity and sexual charity as an immediate solution to recognizing diverse ways of pursuing pleasure in disabled people's lives is paramount, while ensuring access to and transforming all aspects of social spaces and to political, economic, and cultural dimensions.

Discussions of sexuality that insist on "problems" and "solutions" allow no room for disabled individuals to explore the complicated meanings and uncertain interpretations of a particular sexual encounter. *Pink Palace* does not reveal what Ch'oe experienced inside the brothel and how he interprets that experience. *Papa* clearly fails to imagine the disabled woman as obtaining sexual pleasure in a way that does, or does not, involve trauma, before jumping into a cure of an injurious behavior that occurs in the context of her isolation in her room with no other social contact.

The efforts to "help" disabled people enter the sexual realm have focused on immediate solutions; on limited information about other countries' practices, held up as the ideal; and on the politics surrounding the sex trade and charity that empower the providers of help than those who receive it. These approaches discipline the sexuality of disabled people in much the same way as the processes that relegate them to being outside the sexual realm. The notions of a necessary "release" (*haeso*) and of altruistic "volunteering" emerged as a way to solve the "sexuality problem" of disabled people in proximity to sexual violence simplistically equating sexual oppression with lack of a sexual outlet. The sexual oppression of disabled people cannot be separated from the politics of sexual shame and stigma in South Korean culture, and the search for institutional and policy solutions for the sex drive of disabled people constructs their sexuality as a special entity to be managed without bringing meaningful changes to the general practices that desexualize them.

Through these voices of disabled women living in institutions, disabled feminists, sex workers, and sexual minorities with disabilities challenging erotophobia, desexualization, and hypersexualization,[46] the sensational depictions of providing immediate solutions to eliminate "suffering" may be shifted to the focus on the historical, social, and cultural dimensions of disabled individuals' sexualities, while recognizing their multiplicity and fluidity and the crucial need for expanding public assistance that sustains the everyday life of disabled people. In addition to creating ways to express sexual pleasure and to promote social networks and friendship, it is also important to affirm (a) sexual subjectivity of disabled women without ignoring sexual victimization and impunity. The sex drive and virgin status of disabled men are used rhetorically to argue for their access to sexual services (presented as a solution). Although sexual services—for profit and not for profit alike—for people with disabilities can provide an important sexual opportunity and choice, they have appeared as a simplified, monolithic solution that does not open up spaces for sexual subjectivity and expressions, including disabled people's experiences within the sex industry. The cure for virginity by a one-time "volunteer" does not adequately question the current privileging in South Korean society of certain kinds of sexual experiences and the systematic discrimination that disabled people face. Future discussions and spaces that support the sexual rights of disabled people need to first engage with a wide range of groups, including disabled women, sexual and gender minorities, activists with diverse disabilities, and sexual laborers instead of rushing to institutionalize a single "solution" that necessarily limits diverse sexualities and shuts down possibilities and calls for social change.

Conclusion

How to Inhabit the Time Machine with Disability

In 2014 I arrived in Aeyang Pyŏngwŏn (the Wilson Leprosy Center and Rehabilitation Hospital, usually called Aeyangwŏn) in the southern coastal city of
Yŏsu. The biographical film *The Litany of Hope* (discussed in chapter 4) falsely
depicted the poet Han Ha-un, who had Hansen's disease, undergoing eyebrow
transplants and hand surgery here from an American doctor and then rejoining his love, thereby completing the cure narrative. I spend the night in the
house in which women with Hansen's disease lived in isolation during and
after their treatment. The renovated homes and gardens on the coast, now
named the Forest of Cure, are open for tourists. The house's interior, fully
equipped with contemporary amenities, probably bears little resemblance to
how it was as the women's residence. The two photos hanging on the wall offer
the only glimpse of the past (see figure c.1). The one on top is a black-and-
white shot of the building before its renovation. Gnarled tree branches, bare in
the wintertime, reach over the decrepit house. Taken from slightly above, the
photo shows the large roof surface that weighs down the house, as if it were
suppressing imaginings about the life inside. The house's slanted angle does
not invite viewers in. The other picture, in color, shows the house I am occupying after its reconstruction. The leafy trees in varied autumn colors frame the
house warmly, with the bright open sky in the middle of the photo. Only part
of the original stone outer wall remains, as a façade without a roof. What was
formerly a closed window is now an entryway under an arch. Next to it stands
a house in the form of a steel box, directly facing the camera.

How does time appear on this wall where the two photos are hanging in
front of me? The black-and-white photo reminds me of the notion of "an
anachronistic space . . . out of place in the historical time of modernity,"[1] even
though the homes were created in the midst of an international flow of co-

C.1 Two frames of photographs of the old (above) and new (below) houses hanging inside the residence at the Forest of Cure in Aeyangwŏn, Yŏsu (2014). Photograph by the author.

lonial modernity in the form of Christian medical humanitarianism. Rather than inviting the viewers to imagine those who lived there, the house of the past stands in contrast to the present as a condition of life that is wounded and as an encapsulation of the history of stigma and isolation. Yet I resist reading the steel-box house, with the stone wall that is now decorative, as the image of the cured present. Before-and-after pictures of bodies are commonly used to depict cure and bodily "betterment" through medical technology and consumption.[2] Moreover, the time-lapse photos are designed to erase the time in between, the presence of ephemeral bodies, and their lived time. Haunted by the absence of the people who once inhabited the place, I take a picture of the photos. In this Forest of Cure, how are tourists guided to feel about the lived time of the people who had the feared disease? Is this cure aimed at the history of prejudice that led to isolation or at the spiritual healing of the visitors who take refuge from their busy lives? How does one who used to live here remember this space in the present? Who has a right to name this space and occupy it?

In front of the hospital building stand two new bronze statues of American Presbyterian doctors. The statues were erected a few years ago as part of the celebration of the hospital's centennial anniversary to honor their dedication to the mission of helping people with Hansen's disease. In *The Litany of Hope*, one of the doctors appears and promises the poet that he can fix the poet's hands and eyebrows and erase visible signs of the disease. I meet with the director of the Aeyangwŏn History Museum, who has worked with the doctors since the 1970s, to ask if he knows something about the 1962 film about the poet's cure. He says the poet didn't receive treatments in Aeyangwŏn. Unexpectedly, he also tells me that besides those with Hansen's disease many Koreans who were affected by polio have had corrective orthopedic surgery there since the late 1960s.

Back in Seoul, in a gathering of activists and scholars discussing disability history and coalitions, Bae Bogjoo, a longtime leader in the disabled women's movement, recounts that when she was young, her mother took her to Aeyangwŏn to consult about the possibility of surgery on her leg. But for some reason she did not receive the surgery. Caressing her leg, she says she feels so lucky and proud that her leg was left untouched by the doctor. She shares that many of her friends had their legs straightened when they were young but now have regrets because of chronic pain that is worsening with age, which they believe to have been caused by the surgery. In contrast, Bae's coworker, who had undergone the surgery at Aeyangwŏn, tells her a different story—that the surgery enabled her to walk with minimal difficulty and without any prosthesis, which leaves her with no regrets.

The bodiless photos in the Forest of Cure, the statues of the celebrated doctors, the successful cure drama in the film, and the stories of those who had surgery make me consider the various meanings of cure in the time and space of Aeyangwŏn. I wonder how the ways we think about the benefits and costs of approximating normality might change if the narratives of various experiences and the life of the present were widely known and thus could shed light on biomedical and humanitarian promises. Throughout this book, I have explored how the images of cure often feature intended and unintended violence that disfigures disability or further destroys disabled subjects. "To disfigure," according to the *Oxford English Dictionary*, means "to mar the figure or appearance of, destroy the beauty of; to deform, deface; . . . to destroy the beauty or natural form of (something immaterial); . . . to alter the figure or appearance of." To disfigure disability, then, is to deny its aesthetic and ethical presence and representations. Often disability is disfigured by cure when the disabled body is forced at all costs to approximate the normal body.

Bae Bogjoo finds that she has been spared from such disfiguration: she views her leg as keeping its original shape and beauty with changing functionality as she ages, rather than having been damaged by the polio virus and needing to be fixed. The attribution of their pain and discomfort to the corrective surgery illustrates how individuals recognize the political nature of the exaggerated expectations and promises attached to curative treatment. But I don't think of the people who went through the surgery as simply misled, victimized, and damaged, no matter what resulted. They now embody another kind of disability created by the intervention and by time, which demands recognition of its presence. Even as I insist on the ideology of cure used in an act of violence or point out that cure itself has violent effects that are often rendered unrecognizable, in some narratives curative practices create changes that are considered benefits. Theorizing cure thus requires me to explore these multiple narratives and meanings of disability and illness without diluting their political, ethical, and aesthetic significance. I cannot simply reject cure as antagonistic to the presence of disability, discounting the individuals' desire for transformation and perceived benefits. At the same time, approximating normality or even being completely cured of disability may create new kinds of disability and coexist with a history of disability that cannot be undone.

Can one ever see a disabled body as it is, not as it was or as it should become?[3] What makes the present with disability livable, unlivable, or something in between? The struggle to inhabit the present both with the body's history and with its future, after aging, characterizes life in folded time, as attention is exclusively paid to the past and future, projecting nostalgia about the "better" past and hopes for a "better" future on the disabled body. I might call folded time a time machine, whose purpose is to enable one to leave the present. Rather than simply arguing for presentism and dismissing the importance of the past and the future, or suggesting that we all need to live in the moment or do nothing, I am making the case for exploring how the registers of betterment and deterioration are configured. I am also making the case for imagining a future outside the binary of grandiose hope and despair, a future that is livable without violence.

Cure and death are not opposites but inseparable complements in approaching problematized bodies. Risking death for a chance to be cured can be considered a rational choice and the expected course of action, when living with a chronic illness or disability is inconceivable—and when such a life is viewed as an unlived one. The conceptual model behind the World Health Organization's metrics called the Disability-Adjusted Life Year (DALY) captures this logic: "One DALY can be thought of as one lost year of 'healthy' life. The sum of these DALYs across the population, or the burden of disease, can be thought of as a measurement of the gap between current health status and an ideal health situation *where the entire population lives to an advanced age, free of disease and disability.*"[4] DALY is calculated by combining "the Years of Life Lost (YLL) due to premature mortality in the population and the Years Lost due to Disability (YLD) for people living with the health condition or its consequences." This assumption that years lived with disability and illness are lost time illustrates the difficulty of inhabiting the present with disability and illness. The meaningfulness of that lived time is disfigured when it is measured only against the nonexistent time and place "where the entire population lives to an advanced age, free of disease and disability."

In that time "lost" with disability and illness, the imperative toward an "improved" future and inclusion requires maximizing one's abilities. The World Health Organization defines rehabilitation as "a set of measures that assist individuals, who experience or are likely to experience disability, to achieve and maintain *optimum* functioning in interaction with their environments"; it is "instrumental in enabling people with limitations in functioning to *remain in* or *return* to their home or community, live independently, and participate in education, the labour market and civic life."[5] According to this international guideline for rehabilitation, "optimum functioning" is a condition for remaining in or returning to homes or communities.

The United Nations Convention on the Rights of Persons with Disabilities (CRPD) distinguishes between habilitation and rehabilitation. Habilitation is "a process aimed at helping people gain certain new skills, abilities, and knowledge," encompassing services for people born with disabilities. This special label is given to what for nondisabled people entails learning and education. Rehabilitation "refers to regaining skills, abilities, or knowledge that may have been lost or compromised as a result of acquiring a disability or due to a change in one's disability or circumstances." The CRPD obligates state parties, through habilitation and rehabilitation, "to enable persons with disabilities to attain and maintain *maximum* independence, full physical, mental, social and vocational ability, and full inclusion and participation in all aspects of life."[6] While the parallel listing of independence, ability, and inclusion suggests that independence and ability are not preconditions for inclusion, the emphasis is still on coming as close as possible to normality rather than on guaranteeing full inclusion and participation, regardless of level of ability. A publication intended to provide information on CRPD enforcement explains, "Unlike reasonable accommodation, habilitation and rehabilitation focus on equipping the individual with the specific knowledge, tools, or resources that he or she requires rather than ensuring that the general environment, program, practice, or job includes the features needed for an individual with a disability to succeed on an equal basis with others."[7] This statement reveals the tension about where the main site of intervention should be: at the level of the individual, or in the environment. Should adjusting social and physical environments start only after the "maximum" or "optimum" level of functioning and independence has been reached? These ideas that individuals should be equipped to have abilities through habilitation, that their previous and "proper" embodiment should be restored through *re*habilitation,[8] and that disability and chronic illness should be cured through spiritual, familial, or medical interventions can dislocate disabled individuals not only from their families and communities but also from the present, as for them life is suspended.

Coexisting in Time

The virtual and real violence embedded in the imperative of cure accumulates in the gap created by the everyday failure to imagine the uncured body as a mode of being. The archive of curative violence I examined may seem exceptional, extraordinary, and overdetermined by cultural differences. The impression that this violence is exceptional or explainable within Korean cultural traditions is possible only if one ignores how transnational flows of knowledge about systemic disability management and historical relations contribute to such violence. Those who write for a Western audience about disability and disabled people in non-Western cultures often find the status of people with disability being interpreted as a sign of cultural backwardness. When I came to the United States for the first time to attend graduate school, a person I met on the Chancellor's Committee on the Status of Persons with Disabilities asked me about the status of people with disabilities in South Korea. I explained that the overall environment is very inaccessible and that severe discrimination against people with disabilities exists. The person quickly responded, "It sounds the same as the situation in the U.S. twenty years ago." Our fleeting conversation ended there but left me with many questions. For example, how do we account for the fact that advanced technologies that can accommodate disability that were not available twenty years ago in the United States are available today in South Korea but are not affordable for most disabled people? How do the decisions made in Washington, D.C., connect people with disabilities in South Korea and in the United States? How can discrimination based on disability status in the United States be redressed, if the country is seen as having moved past such discrimination? More than a decade later, I still wonder, How do we build anti-ableist and decolonial transnational coalitions across distance, culture, and the perceived developmental gap of twenty years?

In the end, the person's response voiced imperialist logic, casting a nation-state as "behind" in the trajectory of the progress plotted by Western civilization. Johannes Fabian calls this the "denial of coevalness": "a persistent and systematic tendency to place the referent(s) of anthropology in a Time other than the present of the producer of anthropological discourse."[9] Much as the disabled singer Kang Won Rae at the concert (discussed in the introduction) couldn't coexist with the nondisabled Korean viewers who think that his disabled body should exist only in the past seen from the future, so in this temporal dislocation disabled people in non-Western cultures are denied coevalness with disabled people in Western cultures. The expectation that the United States is a better place for living with disability continues to betray many marginalized populations in the United States and many visitors with disabilities. It also continues to impede the communication between disabled people in different societies. If making an acquired disability disappear by conjuring up the nondisabled body in the past and the cured body in the future is one way of folding time, another kind of folding temporalities occurs in this Western identification of a non-Western present with its past.

This denial of coevalness is accompanied by the exoticization of another's culture as having no similarity with one's own, ignoring historical and social forces that connect here and there in shared time. Homi Bhabha warns, "The representation of difference must not be hastily read as the reflection of *pregiven* ethnic or cultural traits set in the fixed tablet of tradition. The social articulation of difference, from the minority perspective, is a complex, ongoing negotiation that seeks to authorize cultural hybridities that emerge in moments of historical transformation."[10] It is too easy to imagine the Korean culture of disability as different from that of the West, owing to stereotypical generalizations about East Asian culture, or to attribute gendered violence against disabled persons to some preconceived notions of Korean cultural difference. Instead, Bhabha asks us to focus on what is produced at the moment of the articulation of cultural differences. Who speaks of these differences to whom, for what purpose, and in what location? Contextualizing the discourses of differences is vital to understanding overlapping power relations and the interconnectedness of different locations. Donna Haraway also points out that Western logic constructs other cultural possibilities as resources for Western needs and actions.[11] It is important to refuse the positioning of non-Western representations of disability as exotic Other in that sense, so that "important differences can be appreciated, rather than mystified."[12] This appreciation of difference is required to avoid another trap: that of assuming the universal characteristics of disability insofar as everyone with a disability is believed to go through the same experiences wherever they are located.

Postcolonial feminist scholars have criticized the similar logic of viewing non-Western cultures as "behind" in dealing with the oppression of women, a stance that fails to allow for alliances between Western and non-Western women whose lives are interconnected. The situations of people with disabilities outside and within the Global North are circumscribed by the decisions made by supranational institutions and national politics. Meanwhile, technologies to accommodate daily challenges exist for those who can afford them: the difficulties experienced by disabled people are never simply an indication of being twenty years behind but are related closely to the conditions that enable affluent lives elsewhere. Coevalness, the "sharing of present Time, is a condition of communication" that enables ethnographic knowledge and unfolds temporalities to allow copresence.[13] The synchronicity of disability—the sharing of time inhabited by disability—across different cultures and across scientific, rhetorical, visual, and spiritual paradigms provides another important strategy of unfolding time to counter the erasure of the disabled present.

Veena Das explains, "Time is not purely something represented, but is an agent which 'works' on relationships, allowing them to be interpreted, rewritten, scratched over, as different social actors struggle to author stories in which collectivities are created or re-created."[14] This work of time as an agent can have a violent effect not just in erasing the present of the disabled body in the pursuit of "betterment" but also in freezing the present disabled body to prevent its "worsening." Alison Kafer gives a poignant example of such freezing in discussing the well-known Ashley X case in the United States. The growth attenuation treatment, hysterectomy, and double mastectomy were performed on seven-year-old Ashley X in the name of preserving her present body, given the prognosis of pain and discomfort and given the possibility of violence she might experience if she became a fully grown adult woman without the intellectual development expected to correspond to her level of physical maturity. Kafer explains,

> By arresting the growth of Ashley's body, the Treatment could stop this gap between mind and body from growing any wider. In order to make this argument, Ashley's parents and doctors had to hold her future body—her *imagined* future body—against her, using it as a justification for the Treatment. Without intervention, the asynchrony between mind and body would only grow wider; Ashley's body would become more and more unbearable to her, to her parents, and to those encountering her in public. This future burden, brought on by the future Ashley, could only be avoided by arresting the present Ashley in time.

Through this Treatment, Kafer argues, Ashley is "cast . . . out of time" as "an eternal child."[15] In contrast to the various kinds of cure to bring about putative "betterment" that I have elaborated in this book, Kafer's emphasis here is on another important practice: changing the body to prevent its putative "worsening." Whereas cure is performed by folding time to take us to the nondisabled past or to the nondisabled future, the Treatment that Ashley received to prevent her "worsening" gestures toward a different meaning of cure, which is to preserve and to harden—freezing time to prevent the future of further disability. In both cases, the opportunity to live in time is denied. However, embodied disabilities, whether disfigured by cure or not, undeniably inhabit space even as the curative time machine continues to move toward a "better" or "not worse" future. That is, disabilities remain animate even in frozen time. How then can we imagine the work of time in allowing relationships around cure and disability "to be interpreted, rewritten, scratched over," beyond the rigid ableist configuration of what is better and what is worse?

Just as the meanings of disability are diverse and fluid, so too what constitutes cure, the category crossing from disability to normality, varies. Examining cases that involve uncertain normality and disability, I have tried to describe the liminal and overlapping spaces among disability, curedness, and the conditions of normality. Hegemonic ideas about gender, sexuality, family, and nation play a crucial role in curative and re/habilitative interventions. Such interventions reveal that normality is constituted with many markers, such as gender recognition and reproduction (chapter 1); spiritual morality and the nondisabled family (chapter 2); class, race, and nations (chapter 3); marriage and curability (chapter 4); and heterosexuality (chapter 5).

The power associated with cure has had broader effects on disabled people and Korean society. Curative practices deployed to govern populations, through the ideology of filial piety and familial sacrifice and through institutional segregation of people with Hansen's disease, produced a national and transnational hierarchy based on humanitarianism. Curative humanitarianism put South Korean nationalists on the defensive to prove and improve its capacity. In the midst of these curative power dynamics, cure has also appeared as a rhetorical tool that justifies everyday violence against disabled people as beneficial and necessary. The imperative of cure makes it difficult to acknowledge that violence *as* violence.

Throughout the chapters, family has been the most prominent site constructed to enforce normality, while being denied to disabled people or forced on them with the demand that they approximate normative gender roles, heterosexuality, and reproduction. "To mother" has itself come to mean becoming a mother of a nondisabled child. The melodrama formed around women with hereditary disability, which I call the "heredity drama" in literary and filmic representations, exploits emotional reactions to the revelation of the disability and racial status of a newborn child. Tracing the national and transnational politics around the reproduction of disabled people and the births of disabled or biracial children, I argued that the presumed desire for disability's absence cannot be articulated without disability's persistent presence and without disfiguring it. Homing in on the presence of disability in these representations that aim to erase disability is therefore an ethical and political project that does not condemn individuals' negotiations with their circumstances by taking speculative risks within ableist society. For example, the documentary *Thumbelina Wants to Be a Mother*, which depicts Yun Sŏn-a's extraordinary and painful efforts to bear a nondisabled child (the only way of her becoming a mother) through reproductive technology, can be interpreted as antidisability and has led to blaming those disabled mothers who do not choose to go through the same process. At the same time, however, the representation of her disabled motherhood poses a significant challenge to normative motherhood and family reserved for able-bodied women.

In the texts I examined, family also appears as a deadly bond that demands sacrifice, when cure is required at all costs. Less often, family appears as a space that allows the presence of disability as it is. In articulating how the broad rhetoric of the "burden" of care for disabled family members is intertwined with the specific imperative to get better, I used the notion of proxyhood as a way to reveal the intercorporeal effects of the moral transformation of family through cure. Proxies for a disabled person have the responsibility of working toward cure within and beyond the boundary of a family; at the same time, they make disabled persons into receptacles for the rewards of their efforts. The logic of the proxy exploits disability as an interactive site of negotiations for collective survival, thereby challenging the individualist assumption of moral agency and normality. Proxies take up their role within heterosexual marriages and also in intergenerational relations between children and parents, reinforcing women's dedication to the heterosexual patriarchal family. Curative violence hinges not on coercion but on the assumption that an uncured status is unacceptable, because cure is based on complicated social and familial negotiations that occur beyond an individual's desire and volition. Furthermore, when located outside the livable boundary of family, disabled people are subject to sexual and physical violence exacted in the name of cure. Complicated social scripts of violence assume that disabled bodies are undesirable and demand that they be made to conform to the specific kinds of femininity and masculinity that undergird patriarchy and the modern capitalist state.

To conclude this book about the violence that is made unrecognizable in the name of cure, I will offer a reading of an image that illustrates the vision of the Korean disabled women's organization Changae Yŏsŏng Konggam (WDE), a vision that makes the need for cure irrelevant and decenters family as a main site of care and "betterment." An issue of *Konggam* (Empathy), a magazine for disabled women published by WDE, featured a map of a Disabled Women's Village on the land of Yongsan Garrison,[16] the headquarters of the U.S. military bases. It is located in a space originally created and occupied by the Imperial Japanese Army during the colonial era. By 2017 the U.S. military will move out of Yongsan and relocate outside Seoul, returning the territory to the Korean government. A plan has been drawn up to create a national ecological park with historical monuments. This park, named in the plan "Healing, the Future Park," is intended "to cure nature, history, and culture."[17] Toxic wastes around the base and lack of accountability for pollution are made invisible in this attempt to re-create the space as a national symbol of depoliticized healing, as if the label "healing" could suture the historical trauma of domination.

The imagined Disabled Women's Village comprises a school for feminist education, a wheelchair-accessible organic farm, and an outdoor moving walkway as well as social infrastructure, including banks, hospitals, and entertainment facilities. Unlike inclusion-focused disability activism, the map features the space centered on disabled women's bodies and desires. Moving away from focusing on buildings, the map makes visible disability-centered public place. Tari Youngjung Na explained to me that the map started with a naïve vision after the activists heard that Yongsan would be returned, rather than with a realistic plan. Instead of illustrating the desire for a future separatist utopia, the map communicates the desire for transformed public space for people with disabilities to inhabit and to traverse without the pressure of being altered through cure or re/habilitation.

Unlike the proposed Healing Park, this imaginative and playful appropriation of the space showcases the ambition of the disabled women's movement not only to eliminate disability oppression but also to transform communal, environmental, and spatial arrangements of society. A unique possibility for transnational feminist disability scholarship opens up in this representation of disability activism combined with antimilitarization and environmental consciousness, turning the simplistic demand for "healing" into a political and ethical discussion from the disabled women's perspective by unfolding time and asserting the presence of disability. The nonfamilial kinship and the chosen community in land previously occupied by the U.S. military-industrial complex defy the call for a nation-state healed and enabled through proxy protection that constantly feeds the need for more violence as a condition of peace. The possibility of life with disability without violence depends on such reimaginations of space and time that recognize and challenge the power relations that govern our bodies.

Introduction

1 Woo Suk Hwang, Sung Il Roh, et al., "Patient-Specific Embryonic Stem Cells Derived from Human SCNT Blastocysts," *Science* 308 (June 17, 2005): 1777–1783; Woo Suk Hwang, Young June Ryu, et al., "Evidence of a Pluripotent Human Embryonic Stem Cell Line Derived from a Cloned Blastocyst," *Science* 303 (March 12, 2004): 1669–1674. *Science* retracted both articles in 2006 after a report from the investigation committee of Seoul National University revealed that the authors "engaged in research misconduct and the papers contain fabricated data"; Donald Kennedy, "Editorial Retraction," *Science* 311 (January 20, 2006): 335.

2 Although Kang told the young future scientists in the audience that his big dream had been realized when he became a successful singer and when he could perform again on the big stage even after his accident, his disabled performance was not perceived as a sign of success. In fact, after his remark, Kang had to ask the hesitating audience for applause.

3 "Hwang U-sŏk, Kang Wŏl-lae ŭi hwilch'eŏ nŭn tŏ isang ŏpta" [Hwang Woo Suk, no more wheelchair for Kang Won Rae], *Chungang ilbo*, July 27, 2005.

4 McClintock, *Imperial Leather*, 37.

5 DiMoia explains that the aid organizations in South Korea claim that the nation "successfully completed the transformation, going from an aid recipient in the 1950s to an aid giver in the 1990s." DiMoia, *Reconstructing Bodies*, 216.

6 McRuer, "Critical Investments," 228.

7 David Cyranoski, "Cloning Comeback," *Nature* 505 (January 23, 2014): 468.

8 Donald Kennedy, in Andrew Pollack, "Cloning and Stem Cells: The Research; Medical and Ethical Issues Cloud Cloning for Therapy," *New York Times*, February 13, 2004.

9 Kang Yang-gu, "Hwang U-sŏk, nanch'ipyŏng hwanja changaein e taehan iyagi" [Hwang Woo Suk and the stories of patients with incurable illnesses and people with disabilities], *Science Times*, June 2, 2005.

10 Tari Youngjung Na (T'ari Yŏng-jŏng Na), "Independence of Women with Disabilities," in the booklet *Women with Disabilities Empathy Nanjang 2005* (2005), 2.

11 "Kang Wŏl-lae, 'Hwang U-sŏk yŏn'gu silyonghwa tŏegil'" [Kang Won Rae wishes Hwang Woo Suk's research becomes reality], *Han'gyŏre sinmun*, May

20, 2005. A blogger named Lai writes in "Changaein Kang Wŏl-lae ŭi iyu innŭn hangbyŏn" [Rebuttal of disabled Kang Won Rae, with a good reason] (*Han'gyŏre sinmun*, March 21, 2008) that an article in *Kyŏnghyang sinmun* (March 19, 2008) featuring an interview with Kang omitted Kang's pessimism about Hwang Woo Suk's research and featured only his hope for Hwang's success, citing Kang's response to the article.

12   Kang Won Rae (Kang Wŏl-lae), "Ch'obo changaein 12-nyŏn, pulp'yŏnhan chinsil" [Newly disabled for 12 years, uncomfortable truth], *Sŭp'och'ŭ Han'guk*, August 7, 2012.

13   Chŏn Hyŏng-hwa, "Kang Wŏl-lae ka hwilch'ŏŏ esŏ irŏnatta" [Kang Wŏl-lae got up from his wheelchair], *Star News*, July 20, 2005, http://star.mt.co.kr.

14   See Wendell, *Rejected Body*.

15   Clare, *Exile and Pride*, 106.

16   McRuer, "Critical Investments," 230.

17   Kafer, *Feminist, Queer, Crip*, 27, 28.

18   See Sherry, "(Post)colonizing Disability," for the use of disability as a metaphor for colonization.

19   Kafer, *Feminist, Queer, Crip*, 28.

20   Ahmed, *Promise of Happiness*, 1.

21   Andersen, *Little Mermaid*, 46.

22   Andersen, *Little Mermaid*, 50.

23   Beauchamp-Pryor, "Impairment, Cure and Disability," 12.

24   Stevens, "Interrogating Transability."

25   Stevens, "Interrogating Transability," emphasis in the original.

26   Baril, "Needing to Acquire a Physical Impairment/Disability," 33.

27   Wasserman and Asch, "Understanding the Relationship between Disability and Well-Being," 142.

28   "The Road I Have Taken: Christopher Reeve and the Cure: An Interview with Christopher Reeve and Fred Fay," *Ability Magazine* (1998), http://abilitymagazine.com/reeve_interview.

29   See Dean, *Unlimited Intimacy*, for the discussion of individuals who practice unprotected sex.

30   See Stevenson's *Life Besides Itself* (51–61) about the colonial regimes of tuberculosis care through the evacuation of the Inuit of the Canadian Arctic with tuberculosis to the sanitaria in southern Canada during the tuberculosis epidemic (1940 to the early 1960s) and the Inuit understanding of life and death.

31   In *Dissemination* (95–116), Jacques Derrida discusses the word *pharmakon* as used in Plato's *Phaedrus*, in order to describe the effect of writing on forgetfulness and speech.

32   Butler, *Gender Trouble*, xx. For more discussion of Butler's notion of normative violence, see Chambers and Carver, *Judith Butler and Political Theory*.

33   In the name of cure, Foucault's biopower manifests itself as "what brought life and its mechanisms into the realm of explicit calculations and made

knowledge-power an agent of transformation of human life," responsible for the "political technologies that ensued, investing the body, health, modes of subsistence and habitation, living conditions, the whole space of existence." Foucault, *History of Sexuality, Vol. 1*, 143–144.

34 *Inŏ kongju* [Mermaid], dir. Kim Chi-hyŏn (2013), http://csd.khcu.ac.kr/kh /site/Board?kind=movie&pageNo=&b_seq=630.

35 The 2002 film *Huayu* [Who are you], directed by Chʾoe Ho, also features a deaf woman who is a diver and performs as a mermaid in an aquarium show.

36 In a 1983 musical documentary produced for television in the United States, *Tell Them I'm a Mermaid*, seven women with disabilities provide their own narratives of living with a disability that requires ingenious ways of thinking and reframing. In a monologue at the ending credit, a voice-over narrates, "The children in the shopping center always ask, 'What's wrong with her legs?' Do you know what I say to them? I tell them, 'I'm a mermaid.'" Nancy Becker Kennedy in Lewis and Kennedy, *Tell Them I'm a Mermaid*.

37 Das, "Violence, Gender, and Subjectivity," 284.

38 Das, "Violence, Gender, and Subjectivity," 295.

39 See chapter 3 for specific cases.

40 "South Africa: Four Teens Get Bail over Gang Rape of Mentally Disabled Girl," *Global Post*, May 3, 2012, http://www.globalpost.com.

41 "Women with Disabilities at Risk of Rape," *Global Post*, May 21, 2012, http:// www.globalpost.com.

42 Dominique Mosbergen, "Battling Asexual Discrimination, Sexual Violence and 'Corrective' Rape," *Huffington Post*, June 20, 2013, http://www.huffingtonpost.com.

43 In "Exploring Homophobic Victimisation in Gauteng, South Africa" (24n2), Nel and Judge define "corrective rape" as "the prejudiced notion that a lesbian woman can be raped to 'make her straight': i.e., to 'correct' her lesbian sexuality. 'Corrective rape' seeks to justify the rape of those people who are perceived to not conform—or to disrupt—expected gender roles, behaviour and/or presentation. Misogyny and homophobia underpin the prejudice associated with 'corrective rape,' " citing unpublished 2008 fact sheets on "corrective rape" by Out LGBT Well-being.

44 Piepzna-Samarasinha, "Letter from Leah Lakshmi Piepzna-Samarasinha," 92.

45 Anzaldúa, "La Conciencia de la Mestiza," 386.

46 Anzaldúa, "(Un)natural Bridges, (Un)safe Spaces," 1.

47 Erevelles, *Disability and Difference in Global Contexts*, 141.

48 See Erevelles, *Disability and Difference in Global Contexts*; Davidson, *Concerto for the Left Hand*.

49 Livingston, "Insights from an African History of Disability," 113.

50 Puar, "Coda," 153.

51 Puar, "Coda," 153, 154.

52 Song Ho-gyun, "Na nŭn Taehan Min'guk chusik hoesa ŭi ssiio" [I am a CEO of Korea, Inc.], *Pressian.com*, April 17, 2008.

53 Yu Kang-ha, "Togani sindǔrom ǔl t'onghae pon munhak ǔi ch'iyujǒk ǔimi e taehayǒ."

54 Yu Kang-ha, "Togani sindǔrom ǔl t'onghae pon munhak ǔi ch'iyujǒk ǔimi e taehayǒ," 147–148.

55 Kyeong-Hee Choi, "Impaired Body as Colonial Trope."

56 Quayson, *Aesthetic Nervousness*, 24.

57 Anderson, *Imagined Communities*, 7.

58 McClintock, "Family Feuds," 64.

59 McClintock, "Family Feuds," 62.

60 Yuval-Davis, "Gender and Nation," 403–407.

61 Hyo-Chae Lee, quoted in Connie Kang, "Bitter Page of History: Koreatown Library Opens to Serve as Memorial to 'Comfort Women' Taken by Japan in WWII," *Los Angeles Times*, November 23, 1994.

62 Katharine Moon, "South Korean Movements against Militarized Sexual Labor," 317.

63 Hyun Sook Kim, "*Yanggongju* as an Allegory of the Nation," 181.

64 Hyun Sook Kim, "*Yanggongju* as an Allegory of the Nation," 179.

65 Enloe, *Maneuvers*, 114.

66 McClintock, "Family Feuds," 63.

67 I have described this history of the disabled women's movement of the late 1990s. See Kim Eunjung, "Chǒngsangsǒng e tojǒn hanǔn yǒsǒngdǔl."

68 Grosz, *Volatile Bodies*, 145.

69 Mitchell and Snyder discuss the limits of determining if a text is a positive or negative image of disability in *Narrative Prosthesis*, 18–24.

70 Henri-Jacques Stiker points out the "false opposition between discourse and the real": "Representations of a phenomenon are just as much part of reality as 'what happens.' Even if what happens is not discourse, how we talk about things, discourse is just as important for social reality." Stiker, *History of Disability*, 72.

71 Minh-ha, *Woman, Native, Other*, 120.

72 Park Hee Byoung, "Pyǒngsin eǔi sisǒn," 310, 353.

73 See Kafer's discussion of the need to pay more attention to able-mindedness and mental disabilities in *Feminist, Queer, Crip*, 16.

74 Sim Sǔng-gu, "Changae rǔl t'onghae pon Han'gugin ǔi mom insik," 23.

75 Kyeong-Hee Choi, "Impaired Body as Colonial Trope," 435.

76 Park Hee Byoung, "Pyǒngsin eǔi sisǒn," 348.

77 Sim Sǔng-gu, "Changae rǔl t'onghae pon Han'gugin ǔi mom insik," 26–27; Chǒng Ch'ang-gwǒn, "Chosǒn esǒǔi changaein ǔi insik," 46–49.

78 Sejo Year 8, *Chosǒn wangjo sillok* [The annals of the Chosǒn dynasty], April 29, 1462.

79 Sejo Year 13, *Chosǒn wangjo sillok* [The annals of the Chosǒn dynasty], April 5, 1467.

80 Chǒng Ch'ang-gwǒn, "Chosǒn esǒǔi changaein ǔi insik," 47.

81 Park Hee Byoung, "Pyŏngsin eŭi sisŏn," 353–354.

82 "Nochŏnyŏga" (1848), 109.

83 "Nochŏnyŏga" (1848), 109.

84 Cumings, *Korea's Place in the Sun*, 140.

85 Cumings, *Korea's Place in the Sun*, 140.

86 Kyeong-Hee Choi, "Impaired Body as Colonial Trope," 438. Nearing Korea's full annexation to Japan, a 1905 newspaper serial consisting of a dialogue between two disabled characters, "Questions and Answers between a Blind and a Paraplegic," was published in *Taehan maeil sinbo* in twenty-one installments (November 17–December 13) during the Patriotic Enlightenment Period (1905–1910). The serial engages in a social critique from the perspectives of a blind man and a paraplegic man in their traditional occupations—fortune-telling and traditional headband weaving, respectively—positioning them as targets of modern reform. Cho Nak-hyŏn interprets the two characters as an allegory for the abysmal situation of the nation at the time and suggests that newspaper editors invented the characters to address the importance of national autonomy during the crisis. Cho Nak-hyŏn, "'Sogyŏng kwa anjŭmbangi mundap' ŭi sisa pip'yŏng kwa allegori e taehayŏ," 297.

87 According to one report, labor conscription by the colonial government alone led up to 2,217 people becoming disabled. Yi Yun-sŏng, "Ilche kangje tongwŏn pusang changhae tŭnggŭp pullyu e kwanhan yŏn'gu" [Research on impairment classification and rating of people who were conscripted during Japanese rule] (research report, Prime Minister's Office, 2007).

88 "Chobak aptugo kŏrin tae chŏnggyŏl" [Nearing Chosŏn Exposition, cleaning up beggars], *Tonga ilbo*, June 19, 1929.

89 Han Man-Soo, "Singminji sigi kŏmyŏl kwa 1930-yŏndae changaeu inmul sosŏl," 8.

90 Han Man-Soo, "Singminji sigi kŏmyŏl kwa 1930-yŏndae changaeu inmul sosŏl," 19–24.

91 Jung-ho Yoon, "Disability as a Metaphor of Social Transformation in Korean Literature," 5.

92 Kyeong-Hee Choi, "Impaired Body as Colonial Trope."

93 Lee Bang Hyun, "Singminji Chosŏn esŏŭi chŏngsin pyŏngja e taehan kŭndaejŏk chŏpkŭn," 529–530.

94 Lee Bang Hyun, "Singminji Chosŏn esŏŭi chŏngsin pyŏngja e taehan kŭndaejŏk chŏpkŭn," 533.

95 Lee Bang Hyun, "Singminji Chosŏn esŏŭi chŏngsin pyŏngja e taehan kŭndaejŏk chŏpkŭn," 536.

96 Lee Bang Hyun, "Singminji Chosŏn esŏŭi chŏngsin pyŏngja e taehan kŭndaejŏk chŏpkŭn," 547.

97 Lee Bang Hyun, "Singminji Chosŏn esŏŭi chŏngsin pyŏngja e taehan kŭndaejŏk chŏpkŭn," 551.

98 Lee Bang Hyun, "Singminji Chosŏn esŏŭi chŏngsin pyŏngja e taehan kŭndae-jŏk chŏpkŭn," 553–554.

99 For more discussion of biracial children as being considered "disabled," see chapter 3.

100 Korea Child Welfare Committee, *Handicapped Children's Survey Report* (1962), 101.

101 "Flashback: The Kwangju Massacre," *BBC News*, May 17, 2000, http://news.bbc .co.uk/.

102 See the website for the May 18 Memorial Foundation for detailed statistics on compensation and officially confirmed cases, www.518.org.

103 For the detailed history of the disability movement in South Korea from 1987 to 2006, see Kim Do Hyun, *Ch'abyŏl e chŏhang hara.*

104 Committee on the Rights of Persons with Disabilities, "Convention on the Rights of the Persons with Disabilities: Concluding Observations on the Initial Report of the Republic of Korea" (United Nations 2014), CRPD/C/KOR/CO/1.

105 Ministry of Health and Welfare, *Changaein silt'ae chosa* [Census of people with disabilities], 4.

106 Statistics Korea, *2014 Han'guk ŭi sahoe chip'yo* [Social index of Korea], www .kostat.go.kr.

107 "Changae tŭnggŭp p'ihaeja kin'gŭp taech'aek maryŏn hara" [Create a solution immediately for disability rating recertification victims], *Ablenews*, June 18, 2014, http://www.ablenews.co.kr.

108 For more analysis of the film, see Eunjung Kim, "The Specter of Vulnerability and Bodies in Protest."

109 Kyung Hyun Kim, *Virtual Hallyu*, 5.

110 Kyung Hyun Kim, *Virtual Hallyu*, 19, 152.

Chapter 1. Unmothering Disability

1 "Ilsijŏk kamjŏng ŭi chibae ro paeuja sŏnt'aek ŭn malja" [Let's not choose a spouse under the dominance of temporary emotion], *Tonga ilbo*, October 8, 1937.

2 Robertson, "Blood Talks," 196. Robertson explains eugenic modernity as "the application of scientific concepts and methods as the primary means to constitute both the nation and its constituent subjects" (192). The rationalization of marriage is also in line with Max Weber's theory on rationalization as a key feature of modernity and capitalism.

3 Kafer, *Feminist, Queer, Crip*, 82.

4 Shin and Robinson, "Introduction," 11.

5 The chairman of the Chosŏn Eugenics Association, Yun Ch'i-ho, was a Christian who graduated from Vanderbilt University and later from Emory University in 1893. He was a leader of the Independence Association. Because of the 105 People Incident, known as the Korean Conspiracy Trial of 1912 in

which 105 people were accused of plotting to kill the governor general, he was imprisoned in 1912; his three-year incarceration made him pessimistic about winning independence by revolution, and he controversially became a "pro-Japanese" conformist.

6 Yi Myŏng-hyŏk, "Saengmurhak sang ŭro pon usaenghak" [Eugenics from a biological perspective], *Usaeng* [Eugenics] 1 (1934): 2–4.

7 "Tanjong iran muŏt?" [What is sterilization?], *Usaeng* [Eugenics] 3 (1936): 20–21.

8 Yi Myŏng-hyŏk, "Saengmurhak sang ŭro pon usaenghak"; Yi Kap-su, "Segyejŏk usaeng undong" [Eugenics movement worldwide], *Usaeng* [Eugenics] 1 (1934): 7.

9 Yi Myŏng-hyŏk, "Saengmurhak sang ŭro pon usaenghak," 4.

10 Yi Yŏng-jun discusses venereal diseases, tuberculosis, leprosy, pathological mental illness, idiocy, and epilepsy. He introduces the example of the Kallikak family written by Henry Goddard in the early twentieth century and the works of Darwin, Mendel, and Galton. "Usaenghak sang ŭro pon kyŏrhon ŭi yoso" [Elements of marriage from the perspective of eugenics], *Usaeng* [Eugenics] 3 (1936): 2–7.

11 "Isŏng ŭi todŏk ŭl nonhaya namnyŏ ŭi pansŏng ŭl yoguham" [Discussing morality of both sexes and requiring reflections of men and women], *Tonga ilbo*, August 15, 1920.

12 "Ilsijŏk kamjŏng ŭi chibae ro paeuja sŏnt'aek ŭn malja."

13 Yi Kap-su, "Segyejŏk usaeng undong" [Eugenics movement worldwide], *Usaeng* [Eugenics] 1 (1934): 6.

14 "Kŏn'gangch'e ŭi ssikssikhan t'usajŏk kibun i tonŭn chŏnyŏ" [A virgin with a healthy body and the spirit of a warrior], *Sinyŏsŏng* [New woman], March 1932.

15 "Sana chojŏlso" [Birth control office], *Samch'ŏlli* 13 (March 1931). The article introduced the same argument made by Margaret Sanger when she briefly stayed in Seoul on her way from Japan to China on April 7, 1922. The Japanese authorities did not allow her to speak publicly on the birth control issue at that time. "Kusok mandŭn Ilbon ŭl i haya" [Leaving Japan, which imposed constraint], *Tonga ilbo*, April 7, 1922.

16 Yi Kwang-su's "Minjok kaejoron" [frequently translated as "Treatise on the Reconstruction of the Korean Nation"] is often associated with Social Darwinism and eugenics. Yi's argument for reforming the Chosŏn ethno-nation stresses a cultural movement instead of controlling reproduction. He argued that although the Chosŏn minjok is regressive and corrupt in its moral characteristics, the Chosŏn people can be improved and civilized through the emphasis on enlightenment and education. He internalized the racialized thinking, as he praised British and American people and their superiority and sought to improve the "national character" of the Chosŏn ethno-nation in ways based on Western values and culture. Yi Kwang-su, *Minjok kaejoron*. Translating *minjok kaejo* as "racial rehabilitation," Jin-kyung Lee argues that Yi's "program

of 'racial rehabilitation' represents, on the one hand, his acceptance of the global hierarchy of race. It bases itself on racial self-degradation or what may be called auto-racialization." Jin-Kyung Lee, "Sovereign Aesthetics," 96. On the contrary, Choi Ju-han argues that even though Yi Kwang-su was influenced by racial psychology, especially the writings of Le Bon, he moved away from racial discrimination and segregation and toward mutual care and love for humanity. Choi Ju-han, "Minjok kaejoron kwa sangae ŭi yullihak."

17 Hyŏn Sang-yun, "Usimhakchŏk chongjok kaeryangron" [Eugenic mind theory of racial reform], *Tonggwang* 32 (April 1932): 17–19.

18 Ch'oe Hyŏn-bae, "Chosŏn minjok ŭi kaengsaeng ŭi to (1)" [The way toward the rehabilitation of the Chosŏn nation (1)], *Tonga ilbo*, September 25, 1926. The twenty-sixth column suggested reforming marriage for better reproduction, advocated abolishing early marriage for eugenic reasons, and set the appropriate age for marrying at twenty-five for men and twenty-one for women. Ch'oe Hyŏn-bae, "Chosŏn minjok ŭi kaengsaeng ŭi to (26)," *Tonga ilbo*, October 24, 1926.

19 Snyder and Mitchell, *Cultural Locations of Disability*, 103.

20 Snyder and Mitchell, *Cultural Locations of Disability*, 120.

21 Ch'oe Hyŏn-bae, "Chosŏn minjok ŭi kaengsaeng ŭi to (1)," *Tonga ilbo*, September 25, 1926.

22 Yun Ch'i-ho, "Kwŏndusa" [Preface], *Usaeng* [Eugenics] 1 (1934): 1.

23 Pak Sŏng-jin, "Ilcheha injong chuŭi t'ŭksŏng kwa chŏkyong hyŏngt'ae."

24 Jin-Kyung Lee, "Sovereign Aesthetics," 80.

25 So Hyŏn-suk argues that the goal of population increase in the early colonial period changed in the early 1930s to Chosŏn intellectuals' discourse of population control through eugenics with concerned poverty relief and maternal health protection through limiting reproduction. In the wartime ideology of population increase after 1937, the only birth control permitted was sterilization to prevent the birth of "undesirables." So Hyŏn-suk, "Ilche sigi ch'ulsan t'ongje tamron yŏn'gu," 223.

26 "Kat'ŭn kil ŭl kŏnnŭn pubu: Yi Kap-su, Yu Sŏng-sun pubu" [A couple who walk on the same path: Yi Kap-su and Yu Sŏng-sun], *Tonga ilbo*, April 8, 1957.

27 The name change was reported in the newspaper *Taedong sinmun* on October 20, 1946.

28 Kim Ye-rim, "Chŏnsigi orak chŏngch'aek kwa 'munhwa' rosŏ ŭi usaenghak."

29 Kim Ye-rim, "Chŏnsigi orak chŏngch'aek kwa 'munhwa' rosŏ ŭi usaenghak."

30 "Ch'anggansa" [Inaugural preface], *Pogŏn undong* [Public health movement] (January 1932): 1.

31 Shin Young-Jeon, "Singminji Chosŏn esŏ usaeng undong ŭi chŏn'gae wa sŏngkyŏk," 151.

32 Kyŏngsŏng Cheguk Taehak Wisaeng Chosabu, *T'omangmin ŭi saenghwal kwa wisaeng*.

33 "Pangnamhoe kyŏnggye che ilbo ro paegyŏ kŏrin ŭl inch'i, kŭmhu ronŭn

sinae kŏrin ch'ubang" [Approximately 100 beggars are arrested as a first stop for security during the expo, beggars inside the city will be expelled from now on], *Chosŏn ilbo*, August 20, 1929.

34 "Ponjŏng sŏ ilya e ch'ilsip myŏng ŭl kŏmgŏ" [Honmachi office arrested 70 people in one night], *Chungoe ilbo*, February 11, 1929.

35 "Pangnamhoe ki kkaji nobang sosang ŭl sot'ang" [Street vendors will be rounded up until the exhibit], *Chungoe ilbo*, February 22, 1929.

36 "Mundungi chaktae haya Chongno sŏ ch'ultu chinjŏng" [Lepers appeared into Chongno police to petition], *Tonga ilbo*, June 15, 1936.

37 Kang Sŏng-bo, "Ilche, Chosŏnin kangje purim susul, Sorokto namsŏng nahwanja 840-myŏng e" [Japanese performed forced sterilization on 840 male leprosy patients in Sorokto]," *Kyŏnghyang sinmun*, November 8, 1997.

38 Durow, "South Africa," 275.

39 Robertson, "Eugenics in Japan," 430–448.

40 Sin Tong-il thoroughly reviews the global history of eugenics in *Usaenghak kwa hyŏngsa chŏngch'aek* [Eugenics and criminology] and argues that abortion based on eugenics now allowed by the Mother and Child Health Act needs to be prohibited because it creates ethical problems and discrimination on the basis of disability and genetic status. What is missing in this problematization of eugenics as a justification for abortion is the consideration of legalizing abortion and any discussion of how criminalizing abortion limits women's reproductive rights. Feminist disability studies scholars argue that using the claim of discrimination against a potentially disabled fetus to totally ban abortion does not serve women overall, because the consideration of disability-based discrimination can be used in a way that limits disabled and nondisabled women's reproductive rights. However, sex-selective abortion and race-based abortion along with disability-based abortion need to be considered within the historical contexts in which sexism, racism, and ableism exist: a woman's right to choose abortion does not exist in a vacuum.

41 The magazine was quite successful, with sales ranging around ten thousand to twenty thousand during the colonial era. Chŏng Chin-sŏk, "Minjok ŭi chisŏng *Sindonga* 600-ho ŭi yŏksajŏk ŭimi" [Nation's intelligence New East Asia and the historical meaning of its six hundredth issue], *Sindonga* [New East Asia], September 2009, 650–664.

42 Kim Hye-wŏn, "1930-yŏndae tanp'yŏn sosŏl e nat'anan mom ŭi hyŏngsanghwa pangsik yŏn'gu" [A study on the modes of body configuration in 1930s short stories], master's thesis, Sogang University, 2002, 50.

43 "Changhwa Hongnyŏn chŏn," 15.

44 *P'alcha* indicates eight zodiac characters of the hour, date, and year of birth that determine one's fate and implies that the path of one's life is unchangeable unless one is reborn.

45 Chu Yo-sŏp, "Ch'umul," 295.

46 Chu Yo-sŏp, "Ch'umul," 303.

47 Chu Yo-sŏp, "Ch'umul," 305.

48 Chu Yo-sŏp, "Ch'umul," 304.

49 Quayson, *Aesthetic Nervousness*, 44.

50 Kye Yong-muk, "K'anggaru ŭi chosangi," 93.

51 "Chapnok: Ibaengnyŏn huenŭn chŏn segye illyu ka moda kwangin i toer-iranŭn haksŏl" [Miscellaneous records: A theory that humankind in the whole world will become mad after two hundred years], *Usaeng* [Eugenics] 1 (September 1934): 27.

52 Kye Yong-muk, "K'anggaru ŭi chosangi," 83, 94.

53 Kye Yong-muk, "K'anggaru ŭi chosangi," 93.

54 Čapek's play had considerable influence in Chosŏn's literary and performance communities beginning in the 1920s for a different reason. It stimulated the ideas about the role of science and technology as well as about human labor, gender, and proletarian liberation. Yŏdŏlmoe, "Karŏl Ch'ap'ek'ŭ ŭi injo nodongja" [Artificial humans by Karel Čapek], *Tonga ilbo*, February 9, 1925; "Ch'oe Sŭng-hŭi muyong ŭro kongyŏn" [Dance performance by Ch'oe Sŭng-hŭi], *Chosŏn ilbo*, August 28, 1931. Yi Kwang-su introduced *R. U. R.* in 1923 as a satirical portrayal of "the day of human extinction after humans become slaves to the technological civilization they created with their own hands." Yi Kwang-su, "Injoin" [Artificial humans], *Tongmyŏng* 31 (April 1923). Cited in Han Min Ju, "Injo in'gan ŭi ch'urhyŏn kwa kŭndae esŭep'u munhak ŭi t'ek'ŭnok'ŭrasi," 430.

55 Čapek, *R. U. R.*, 130–131.

56 Čapek, *R. U. R.*, 48.

57 Čapek, *R. U. R.*, 117.

58 Čapek, *R. U. R.*, 117–118.

59 Čapek, *R. U. R.*, 99.

60 Kye Yong-muk, "K'anggaru ŭi chosangi," 97.

61 Kye Yong-muk, "K'anggaru ŭi chosangi," 98.

62 Goffman, *Stigma*, 30.

63 Over seven months, from May to November 1938, *Tonga ilbo* published fourteen articles explaining why mandatory sterilization of disabled people and criminals is necessary.

64 "Pulguja egedo saeroun kwangmyŏng. Singi tae singi. Maengja ŭi nunttŭ nŭn pangbŏp" [New light to the disabled. Marvelous, really marvelous. The way for the blind to become sighted], *Pyŏlgŏn'gon* 20 (April 1, 1929): 77.

65 "Helen Kellŏ nŭn muŏt ŭl purŭjijŏnna" [What did Helen Keller call for?], *Tonga ilbo*, July 17, 1937.

66 Kim Hye-su, "Sinyŏsŏng to 'tal' ŭl mŏgŏyaman haessŭlkka?," 54.

67 Kim Hye-su, "Sinyŏsŏng to 'tal' ŭl mŏgŏyaman haessŭlkka?," 57.

68 Women's magazines began to publish articles related to birth control only after 1958. Bae Eun-kyoung, "Han'guk sahoe ch'ulsan chojŏl ŭi yŏksajŏk kwajŏng kwa chendŏ," 82.

69 Bae Eun-kyoung, "Han'guk sahoe ch'ulsan chojŏl ŭi yŏksajŏk kwajŏng kwa chendŏ," 115.

70 Han'guk Chŏngch'aek Pangsongwŏn [Korean policy broadcasting institute], "Che-51 hoe chŏn'guk ch'eyuk taehoe" [The 51st national sports competition], *Taehan nyusŭ* [Korean news] no. 797, televised by ROK Government on October 10, 1970, http://www.ehistory.go.kr.

71 "Kongju Yŏnga Taehoe" [Kongju baby contest], *Tonga ilbo*, May 29, 1925.

72 "T'aehwa yŏja chinch'also kŏn'gang adong chindan" [T'aehwa women's clinic examines children's health], *Tonga ilbo*, June 4, 1927.

73 The city of Seoul held the baby contest every year from 1957 until the 1970s.

74 "Uryanga sŏnbal kwa chaesusaeng kwa" [Better baby contest and a person who has been denied admission to a university], *Tonga ilbo*, February 12, 1976. Better baby contests ended around the mid-1980s, which coincides with the emergence of the shift in public opinion to favor breast milk.

75 "Kabu, imsin chungjŏl kungmin usaeng pŏban chisang kongch'ong" [Pros and cons, national discussion forum on abortion], *Tonga ilbo*, March 11, 1964; "Kajok kyehoek kwa sana chehan: Imsin chungjŏl ŭn sarin haengwi kat'ŭn kŏt" [Family planning and birth control: Abortion is the same as murder], *Kyŏnghyang sinmun*, March 23, 1964. Catholic priests expressed their opposition through advertisements in newspapers. "Kungmin usaeng pŏban e taehan uri ŭi kyŏnhae" [Our opinions on the national eugenics bill], *Kyŏnghyang sinmun*, May 14, 1965. In contrast, Protestant pastors tended to have more flexible attitudes, valuing the importance of the married couple's sexual life and intimacy and women's overall health. See "Kabu, imsin chungjŏl kungmin."

76 Abortion was defined as a crime in *Hyŏngpŏp taejŏn* [The great book of criminal law], written during the Taehan Empire (1905), and remained illegal during Japanese colonial rule. The Criminal Law of South Korea reaffirmed the same principle in 1953 without any exceptions. Yun Chŏng-wŏn, "Nakt'ae nonjaeng ŭi naeyong kwa ŭimi" [Abortion debates and their meanings], issue paper, Yŏn'gu Kongdongch'e Kŏngang kwa Taean [Center for Health and Social Change], May 2, 2010, http://www.chsc.or.kr/?post_type=paper&p=4771.

77 Subsequently the abortion rate increased tenfold. Cho Hong-sŏk, "Hyŏnhaeng Moja Pogŏnpŏp che 14-cho ŭi hŏnpop sang munjechŏm kwa kaesŏn pangan," 13, cited in Kim T'ae-gye, "Nakt'ae choe e kwanhan munjechŏm kwa ippŏmnon," 238.

78 Pak Tae-han, "Hŏnjae, nakt'ae sisul chŏbŏl haphŏn" [Constitutional Court rules punishing abortion provider constitutional], *Yŏnhap nyusŭ*, August 23, 2012.

79 The list of the parents' medical conditions that make abortion permissible was shortened to achondroplasia, cystic fibrosis, and "miscellaneous conditions that may be hereditary and have a high risk of affecting the fetus." Having an AIDS and HIV-positive status was included in the list in 1986 but removed in 2006. Infectious diseases currently listed are German measles, toxoplasmosis, and others that have a high risk of affecting fetuses.

80 Kim Hong-sin, "Changaein pulpŏp kangje purim susul silt'ae wa taech'aek e kwanhan chosa pogosŏ" [A research report on the status of illegal involuntary sterilization and solution], submitted to the National Assembly on August 19, 1999.

81 "Purim susul kkok haeya hana?" [Sterilization, is it really necessary?], *Chosŏn ilbo*, July 2, 1975.

82 "Chŏngbaga, chŏnhyŏng ŭi sach'un'gi purim susul sibi ŭi hyŏnjang" [Imbecile, adolescence of punishment in the debate for sterilization], *Chosŏn ilbo*, July 9, 1975.

83 "Ch'ungnam Chŏngsimwŏn sonyŏ 12-myŏng sangdae. Kangje purim susul wihan chŏkpu chosa silsi" [Ch'ungnam Chŏngsimwŏn, twelve girls tested for involuntary sterilization], *Chosŏn ilbo*, April 1, 1975.

84 "Kangje purim susul sinjung kŏnŭi" [Caution is requested for involuntary sterilization], *Chosŏn ilbo*, June 26, 1975.

85 Kim Hong-sin, "Changaein pulpŏp kangje purim susul silt'ae wa taech'aek e kwanhan chosa pogosŏ."

86 Zenderland, "Parable of *The Kallikak Family*."

87 Chi Kwang-jun, "Chŏngsin chich'e yujŏnsŏng nop'a huson to purhaeng soji" [Mental retardation has high possibility of inheritance, might cause misery for offspring too], *Sŏul sinmun*, September 6, 1999; Yi Tong-ik, "Chongjok pojon ponnŭng pakt'al ŭn chungdaehan inkwŏn ch'imhae" [Denying procreation instinct is grave human rights violation], *Sŏul sinmun*, September 6, 1999.

88 "Changaein kangje purim susul kwan i chudo" [Forced sterilization of disabled people, led by government agencies], *Yŏnhap nyusŭ*, August 22, 1999; Ch'oe Wŏn-gyu, "Saengmyŏng kwŏllyŏk ŭi chaktong kwa sahoe pokchi," 166.

89 Ch'oe Wŏn-gyu, "Saengmyŏng kwŏllyŏk ŭi chaktong kwa sahoe pokchi," 169–170.

90 Ch'oe Wŏn-gyu, "Saengmyŏng kwŏllyŏk ŭi chaktong kwa sahoe pokchi," 169–170.

91 Han'guk Yŏsŏng Tanch'e Yŏnhap [Korean Women's Association United], *Uri ka kkok araya hal imsin chungjŏl iyagi* [Stories that we must know about abortion] (Seoul: Korean Women's Association United, 2012).

92 Hwang Ji-sung (Hwang Chi-sŏng), "Imsin kwa nakt'ae e issŏ changae yŏsŏng ŭi sŏnt'aekkwŏn" [Disabled women's right to choose regarding pregnancy and abortion], on the official website of Han'guk Sŏngp'ongnyŏk Samdangso [Korea Sexual Violence Relief Center], http://www.sisters.or.kr/load.asp?sub _p=boardboard&b_code=3&page=36&f_cate=&idx=2566&board_md=view.

93 Personal communication, October 26, 2014.

94 Ch'oe Po-sik, "Na nŭn p'eminisŭtŭ, kŭrŏna chŏngch'ip'an esŏnŭn yŏsŏng to kyŏngjaeng sangdae" [I am a feminist, but in politics women are my competitors], *Chosŏn ilbo*, May 12, 2007.

95 Ku Pon-gwŏn, "Lee Myung Bak 'changaein nakt'ae, tongsŏngae pijŏngsang' palŏn p'amun" [Controversy arose about the statement by Lee Myung Bak,

"abortion of disabled fetus; abnormal homosexuality"], *Han'gyŏre sinmun*, June 14, 2007.

96 Ku Pon-gwŏn, "Lee Myung Bak 'changaein nakt'ae, tongsŏngae pijŏngsang' palŏn p'amun."

97 Yi Sŏng-gak and An T'ae-sŏng, "Changaeu inkwŏn pogosŏ: Sigak changaein ŭi ch'unggyŏkchŏgin sam" [Disabled women's human rights report: Shocking lives of visually impaired people], *Chŏnbuk ilbo*, July 22, 2002.

98 Hwang Sun-wŏn, "Maengawŏn esŏ," 305.

99 The episode was aired by Munhwa Broadcasting Company on August 8, 2002.

100 Vietnamese women also have been exploited for the purpose of reproductive surrogacy for childless couples. In 2007, there was a report on a Vietnamese woman who migrated to South Korea for marriage, but in fact the Korean couple wanted her as a surrogate. After she gave birth to two children, she was sent back to Vietnam after a divorce. In the early 2000s, marriage agencies started recruiting Vietnamese women as brides for Korean men with intellectual or physical disabilities, comprising a major consumer group in this market. Until they were banned, billboards and banners had been easily spotted with the phrases "Marry a Vietnamese virgin" and "They never run away." Most of the billboards said, "For older, disabled people, first-time or second-time marriage." The marriage rate between Korean men and Vietnamese women peaked around 2005 and 2006 and now shows a slight decrease. In these marginalized marriage arrangements, the stories of violent abuses and frauds experienced by both Korean men and Vietnamese women appear frequently.

101 Kang Yŏng-su, "Kkok yeppŭn ai rŭl katki rŭl: Ŏmji Kongju ŭi nunmulgyŏun tojŏn e sich'ŏngjadŭl kamgdong" [Wishing her a pretty baby: Viewers are moved by Thumbelina's difficult challenge], *Chosŏn ilbo*, May 16, 2007; Ch'oe Se-na, "Tak'yu *Ŏmji Kongju* kamdong chanjan. 2-bu kidae to nop'ajŏ" [Touching *Thumbelina* documentary. Expectation for its sequel is increasing], *Sŭp'och'ŭ Chosŏn*, May 16, 2007.

102 This exclusion of disabled people from the binary gender system provides grounds for convergence and divergence between women-centered anti-ableist activisms and transgender movements in South Korea. One such example is the coalition to create single occupancy restrooms, which are accessible and non–gender specific. The transgender rights activist scholar Ruin explains that they realized the similarity of the political agendas of the two camps— transgender rights and disabled women's movements—upon learning that the disabled women's movement criticized the gender-neutral accessible restroom as unrecognizing their gender and as considering them genderless. Ruin argues, "Disabled women are considered nongendered beings who cannot reach the hegemonic feminine norm. In terms of gender, transgendered people are discussed as having a chromosomal anomaly or in extremely negative ways, under the assumption of all people as nondisabled. Disability, body, and transgender inseparably infiltrate our lives. We need to explore how to develop

disability movement and transgender movement in different ways." Ruin, "T'ŭrensŭ chendŏ, sam ŭl chogakpo ro itta" [Transgender, connecting lives in quilts], *Han'gyŏre 21*, no. 989 (December 9, 2013).

103 "Sarang handamyŏn idŭl chŏrŏm" [If you are in love, love like them], *Yŏsŏng tonga* 501 (September 2005): 720–723.

104 Ch'oe Se-na, "Tak'yu *Ŏmji Kongju*."

105 "Ŏmji Kongju Yun Sŏn-a ŭi hŭimang iyagi" [Thumbelina Yun Sŏn-a's story of hope], *Kim Sŭng-hyŏn, Chŏng Ŭn-a ŭi choŭn ach'im* [Good Morning with Kim Sŭng-hyŏn, Chŏng Ŭn-a], televised by SBS on August 17, 2007.

106 *Yŏsŏng sinmun*, October 10, 2008.

107 Min T'ae-wŏn, "Yujŏnpyŏng toemullim pangji, kŏn'ganghan agi nannŭnda" [Preventing genetic illness from being passed down, giving birth to a healthy baby], *Kungmin ilbo*, March 31, 2008.

108 "Ch'aksang chŏn yujŏn chindanpŏp" [Preimplantation genetic diagnosis], *Chosŏn.com*, April 21, 2011.

109 Yi Ŭn-hŭi, "Yujŏn chindan, modŭn pyŏng ch'aja naelsu ŏpda" [Genetic diagnosis can't identify all diseases], *Tonga ilbo*, September 8, 2008.

110 Hwang Ji-sung (Hwang Chi-sŏng), "Changae yŏsŏng ŭi chaesaengsan kyŏng-hŏm: Chaesaengsan chŏngch'i ŭi kwanchŏm esŏ" [Reproduction experiences of disabled women: From the perspective of reproduction politics] (master's thesis, Seoul National University, 2011), 62.

111 Wendell, *Rejected Body*, 155–156.

112 Kim Sŏn-a, "Tak'yumentŏri ŭi hyŏnjae: Taehang yŏksa kisul, chŏnt'ongjŏk imiji ŭi p'agoe, kŭrigo hŏgu hŏnghwa ŭi chŏnyu" [The present of documentaries: Recording counter-history, destructing traditional images, and appropriating fiction films], *Tongnip yŏnghwa* [Independent films] 7 (2000), http://www.kifv .org/zine/number.html?quart_cd=3&quart_idx=53&quart_year=2000.

113 Ryu Mi-rye (Yu Mi-rye), "Oaesochŭng changaein Sujŏng, Yunjŏng chamae ŭi ilsanggi, *P'anji wa tamjaengi*" [The everyday life of the sisters Sujŏng and Yunjŏng who are disabled by dwarfism in *Pansy and Ivy*], *Widŭ nyusŭ* [With news], October 20, 2003.

Chapter 2. Cure by Proxy

1 Han'guk Yŏngsang Charyowŏn, *Singminji sidae ŭi yŏnghwa kŏmyŏl.*

2 "Hawai Liriha chwa esŏ yŏnghwa *Sim Ch'ŏng* sangyŏng" [The film *Sim Ch'ŏng* screened in Liliha Theater, Hawai'i], *Tonga ilbo*, February 16, 1938.

3 "Shim Chung," *Honolulu Advertiser*, February 7, 1938; "Shim Chung," *Kung-minbo*, February 16, 1938.

4 "Shim Chung," *Kungminbo*, February 2, 1938.

5 Four additional screenings were scheduled for people who wanted to watch it again or who had missed the first screening. "*Sim Ch'ŏng* hwaltong sajin" [Motion picture *Sim Ch'ŏng*], *Kungminbo*, February 16, 1938.

6 One of these origin stories is "The Dutiful Daughter Chiŭn," which was re-corded in *Samguk sagi* by Kim Pu-sik and in *Samguk yusa* by Iryŏn; both vol-umes record the history of the Three Kingdoms. The story was recorded as a *p'ansori* musical performance by Sin Chae-hyo in the nineteenth century.

7 Allen, "Sim Chung." Horace Newton Allen is an important figure in Korean medical history because he gained the full trust of King Kojong after success-fully curing a member of the royal family in 1884 and later was appointed as the head of the royal hospital Chejungwŏn. Allen's translation is a condensed version most similar to *Kyŏngp'anbon* (the twenty-four-chapter version printed in Seoul), which includes the story of Ch'ŏng's past life in heaven and her descent to the earth as a punishment for her love of a man who is sent as her father, Sim. Lee Moon-sung also points out that *Kyŏngp'anbon* has a conclu-sion similar to that of Allen's version in "P'ansorigye sosŏl ŭi haeoe yŏngmun pŏnyŏk hyŏnhwang kwa chŏnmang," 271. Lee hypothesizes that Allen's per-sonal preference might have influenced his choice of which version of the story to translate, pointing out that another translator, W. E. Skillend, noted that *Kyŏngp'anbon* is "extremely high in moral content" (272).

8 Allen, "Sim Chung," 156.

9 Allen, "Sim Chung," 169.

10 For example, Kim Yang-do is paralyzed after being possessed by ghosts, and the Buddhist monk Milbon deploys an army of spirits to expel them and bring a complete cure in Iryŏn's *Samguk yusa*. Kim Yang-do becomes a sincere Bud-dhist and offers his two daughters to be servants in the temple.

11 Titchkosky, "Ends of the Body as Pedagogic Possibility," 82–83, 92.

12 Roy Meadow, "Munchausen Syndrome by Proxy: The Hinterlands of Child Abuse," *Lancet* (August 13, 1977): 343–345.

13 American Psychiatric Association, *Diagnostic and Statistical Manual of Mental Disorders*, 5th ed.

14 Ingstad, *Community-based Rehabilitation in Botswana*, 328.

15 Grinker, *Unstrange Minds*.

16 In contrast, in a rural town in the film *Barefoot Kibong* (*Maenbal ŭi Kibongi* [2005]), a man with an intellectual disability, who enjoys running and loves his mother, decides to participate in a marathon to buy dentures for his aging mother, who has pain due to her inability to chew. Posing a stark contrast to *Marathon*, the elderly mother here does not engage in any curative attempt to change her son. Instead the village head takes the surrogate role by coaching the son in order for him to compete in the marathon for the promotion of the village name. On one level the son's efforts work as a well-worn metaphor uni-fying the town; he even reconnects the village head with his nondisabled son. Here the intense love between the mother and the son unites the village. The disabled son's love and effort illustrating his exemplary (and exceptionalized) morality, indeed his *hyo* to secure his mother's dentures, challenge the rest of the village to adopt filial piety as a goal.

17 Hwang Yŏng-ju, "*Sim Chŏng chŏn* ilkki ro pon Han'guk esŏŭi kukka wa yŏsŏng."

18 Yun In-sŏn, "Pŏrim padŭn ttal, Sim Chŏng."

19 Jung Ji Young, "P'allyŏgan ttal e taehan pulp'yŏnhan kiŏk."

20 Jung Ji Young, "P'allyŏgan ttal e taehan pulp'yŏnhan kiŏk," 179.

21 *Spring Fragrance* was a great hit, with 150,000 viewers. The Korean Movie Database lists *Sim Chŏng*'s audience size as 100,000, which reflects the popularity of the film. The metaphor of disability and cure has been applied to motion pictures, as sound film was called the "cured body" after the "muteness" of silent films. Pak Hye-suk, "Chŏt t'ok'i yŏnghwa" [The first sound film], *Tonga ilbo*, May 16, 1981.

22 "Hawai e sanŭn yukchŏn tongp'o ŭi sirhwang" [Status of 6,000 Koreans living in Hawai'i], *Kyebyŏk* [Genesis], no. 36 (June 1, 1923), records that 5,327 Koreans were living in Hawai'i.

23 Choy, *Koreans in America*, 74; Quoted in Cumings, *Korea's place in the Sun*, 437.

24 Korean women's immigration as picture-brides started in 1910 and stopped after Korean immigration into the U.S. territories was no longer allowed by the Immigration Act of 1924. Yi Kyŏng-min, "Sajin sinbu, kyŏrhon e olin hada 1," 411.

25 Yi Kyŏng-min, "Sajin sinbu, kyŏrhon e olin hada 2."

26 "*Sim Chŏng* wansŏng" [*Sim Chŏng* completed], *Tonga ilbo*, November 10, 1937.

27 Sŏ Kwang-je, "Yŏnghwa *Sim Ch'ŏng* simsap'yŏng" [Motion picture *Sim Ch'ŏng* review], *Tonga ilbo*, November 20, 1937.

28 "Shim Chung," *Kungminbo*, February 2, 1938.

29 Allen, "Sim Chung," 163–164.

30 A 2000 short film, *Sim Chŏng*, directed by Yu Chong-mi, plays off this love relationship, depicting the blind father's sexual desire toward the daughter as so intense that it rises to the level of incestuous violence.

31 Allen, "Sim Chung," 153–154.

32 Allen, "Sim Chung," 169.

33 Hubert and Mauss, *Sacrifice*, 9–10.

34 Jung Ji Young, "P'allyŏgan ttal e taehan pulp'yŏnhan kiŏk," 175; Ch'oe In-ho, "Nun ŭl ttŏra minjok iyŏ" [Open your eyes, our nation], *Han'guk ilbo*, August 15, 2000. The exclusively metaphorical reading of disabled bodies to symbolize national and colonial fates erases the everyday life of disabled bodies within the colonial spaces and makes it impossible to understand how disability is gendered and how the family is supposed to work collectively to remove disability by the processes that are often violent.

35 Hwang Sŏk-yŏng, *Sim Chŏng*; Ch'oe In-hun, "Tara tara palgŭn tara."

36 Jung Ji Young, "P'allyŏgan ttal e taehan pulp'yŏnhan kiŏk," 178.

37 Jung Ji Young, "P'allyŏgan ttal e taehan pulp'yŏnhan kiŏk," 179. For nuanced discussions of the experiences of former "comfort women," see Sarah Soh, *Comfort Women*, and Hyunah Yang, "Finding the Map of Memory."

38 When Ppaengdŏk hears that the soldiers are coming to take all blind men, she fears that she will be in trouble for running a fake fortune-telling business with Sim and abandons him.

39 Jung Ji Young noted that, in school textbooks, the father's confession to trafficking his own daughter appeared for the first time in 1983. Jung suspects that its appearance reflects the emergence of critical perspectives on the story among scholars of literature. Jung Ji Young, "P'allyŏgan ttal e taehan pulp'yŏnhan kiŏk," 175. However, the film predates this change in the textbooks.

40 In the *Wanp'anbon* version of Sim Chŏng's story, the expansion of the cure of disability is limited to blindness. At the moment of Sim's cure, all the blind men in the palace gain eyesight, as do all other blind people—including fetuses and babies—in their homes. Chŏng Ha-yŏng, ed., *Han'guk kojŏn munhak chŏnjip.*

41 Parsons, "Illness and the Role of the Physician," 104–105.

42 At least eleven films were produced based on the story over the course of the twentieth century: *Sim Chŏng chŏn* by Yi Kyŏng-son (1925), An Sŏk-yŏng (1937), Yi Kyu-hwan (1956), and Sin Sang-ok (North Korea, 1985); *Tae Sim Ch'ŏng chŏn* by Yi Hyŏng-p'yo (1962); *Hyonyŏ Sim Ch'ŏng* by Sin Sang-ok (1972); *Sim Chŏng* by Tongyang Tonghwa (1991, animated) and *Hwanghu Sim Ch'ŏng* by Nelson Shin (animated, North and South Koreas, 2005). The films that took the story of Sim Chŏng but set it in a contemporary time period with different details are *Hanŭl nara ŏmma pyŏl i* by Yi Yŏng-u (1981), discussed in this chapter, and the short films *Sim Ch'ŏng* by Yu Chong-mi (2000) and *Chŏnga* by Kim Chŏng-ho (2010).

43 "Hyŏndaep'an hyonyŏ Sim Chŏng, Kim Yang e taet'ongnyŏng p'yoch'ang" [Dutiful daughter Sim Chŏng of modern times, Miss Kim receives presidential award], *Maeil kyŏngje*, March 27, 1981.

44 "Hyŏndaep'an hyonyŏ Sim Chŏng Kim Min-sun Yang, kyaryŭkhan hyosim yŏnghwahwa hagiro" [The filial piety of Miss Kim Min-sun, modern-day dutiful daughter Sim Chŏng, planned to be made into a movie], *Tonga ilbo*, February 10, 1981.

45 "Hyŏndaep'an hyonyŏ Sim Chŏng Kim Min-sun Yang, kyaryŭkhan hyosim yŏnghwahwa hagiro."

46 Kim Mun-yŏp, "Hanŭl nara ŏmma pyŏl i" [Mother Star in Heaven], original screenplay (Tonghyŏp Sangsa, 1981).

47 Kim Mun-yŏp, "Hanŭl nara ŏmma pyŏl i."

48 *Pogŏn Pokchi T'onggye Yŏnbo* [Statistics on health and welfare], stat.mohw .go.kr.

49 Yi Myŏng-ja and Hwang Hye-jin, "70-yŏndae ch'eje ihaenggi ŭi Nambukhan pigyo yŏnghwasa," 26.

50 Yi Myŏng-ja and Hwang Hye-jin, "70-yŏndae ch'eje ihaenggi ŭi Nambukhan pigyo yŏnghwasa," 58.

51 Cumings, *Korea's Place in the Sun*, 358.

52 Yi Myŏng-ja and Hwang Hye-jin, "70-yŏndae ch'eje ihaenggi ŭi Nambukhan pigyo yŏnghwasa," 35–36.

53 Peterson, *Brief History of Korea*, 222.

54 Reynolds, *One World Divisible*, 286.

55 The three films are *Yŏngja ŭi chŏnsŏng sidae* (Kim Ho-sŏn [1975]), *Yŏngja ŭi chŏnsŏng sidae-sok* (Sim Chae-sŏk [1982]), and *'87 Yŏngja ŭi chŏnsŏng sidae* (Yu Chin-sŏn [1987]). In the 1982 film, Yŏngja is depicted as a nondisabled prostitute whose violent ex-husband is exploiting her. Ch'angsu stabs the ex-husband and flees with her to a seaside town, where they get married. In the 1987 version, a one-armed Yŏngja almost dies in a fire but recovers. She reunites with Ch'angsu, who becomes disabled during his attempt to rescue Yŏngja from the fire.

56 "Yŏngja ŭi chŏnsŏng sidae—Note," Korean Movie Database, http://www .kmdb.or.kr.

57 Mitchell and Snyder, *Narrative Prosthesis*, 47.

58 Mitchell and Snyder, *Narrative Prosthesis*, 57–58.

59 Cho Sŏn-jak, *Yŏngja ŭi chŏnsŏng sidae*, 59.

60 Molly Hyo Kim, "Genre Conventions of South Korean Hostess Films (1974–1982)," 464.

61 The film was remade in the United States as *The Uninvited*.

62 Like *Sim Ch'ŏng chŏn*, the folklore has been made into films multiple times in Korea since 1924.

63 "Changhwa Hongnyŏn chŏn," 15–16.

64 Hacking, *Rewriting the Soul*, 3, 13.

65 Hacking, *Rewriting the Soul*, 5.

66 Multiple personality disorder was renamed as dissociative identity disorder in 2000. See American Psychiatric Association, *Diagnostic and Statistical Manual of Mental Disorders, IV-TR.*, 543. Ian Hacking explains that this new name was based on the recognition that each personality that is manifested by an individual is incomplete. Hacking, *Rewriting the Soul*, 18.

67 The film defies a singular interpretation of the events, because many clues are embedded to produce multiple possibilities of what happened. The "clues" are often contradictory and thus deny any closure of the interpretation.

68 Ch'ae Man-sik, *Sim Pongsa*.

69 "'Changaein adŭl wihae,' 'Koa tŏemyŏn sudang padŭl kŏt,' saenghwalgo iryongjik 50-tae chasal" ["For the disabled son," "Will receive welfare when he becomes an orphan," daily worker in poverty commits suicide], *Kyŏnghyang sinmun*, October 8, 2010.

70 Mok Chŏng-min and Chŏng Yu-mi, "Changae adŭl wihae chasarhan iryongjik abŏji ŭi sayŏn" [Story of a father who was a daily worker and committed suicide for his disabled son], *Kyŏnghyang sinmun*, October 11, 2010.

71 Another law that activists seek to eliminate requires certification of the ratings of disability, which determines eligibility for state-supported services based on

the degrees of functional limitations. Each individual has to be recertified after a certain period of time.

72 Kungmin Kich'o Saenghwal Pojang Pŏp (the National Basic Living Security Law) was enacted in August 2012.

73 National Basic Living Security Law, Article 5 (3) and National Basic Living Security Law Regulations, Article 5 (4).

74 Civil Law Article 979.

75 "Kich'o sugŭpcha t'allak t'ongbo e noindŭl ittan chasal" [Frequent suicide of elderly upon notification of the loss of basic welfare], *Han'guk ilbo*, July 19, 2011.

76 "'Tandon 7000-wŏn ttaemune . . .' Sich'ŏng hwadan sŏ chasarhan halmŏni" [An old woman who killed herself in front of the city hall garden for only $7], *Han'gyŏre sinmun*, August 9, 2012.

77 World Health Organization, "Preventing Suicide: A Global Imperative" (2014), http://apps.who.int/iris/bitstream/10665/131056/1/9789241564779_eng.pdf ?ua=1. Despite the persistent disability activism and the growing scholarship promoting disability rights, the statistics from the Organisation for Economic Co-operation and Development (OECD), an international economic organization of thirty-four relatively higher income countries—often cited by the Korean media to measure the degree of its development and advancement—does not show an improving trend. In 2014, South Korean public spending on social services was 10.4 percent of the GDP, marking the lowest among the OECD countries (their average was 21.6 percent). In 2011 Korea's specific spending on "incapacity," which includes social service spending for disability, illness, and occupational injury was only 0.5 percent of the GDP (the OECD average was 2.2 percent). As one measure, these numbers describe the limited portions of government budget expenditures on overall social services, including specific disability welfare and provisions. Public spending percentages in Korea are a significantly small portion of overall government spending, indicating the severity of its neoliberalization.

78 Stevenson, *Life beside Itself*, 178.

Chapter 3. Violence as a Way of Loving

1 The Korean banner reads "Changae yŏsŏng ŭn sŏngp'ongnyŏk ŭi taesang i toego sipchi ant'a."

2 Yi Su-hyŏng, "Oasisŭ" [Oasis], *Tonga ilbo*, November 30, 2005.

3 The columnist describes this as an interview, but, according to another justice, it was M's official testimony that was not available to the public. Hwang Chin-gu, "Han Ki-t'aek Pujangnim ŭl kiŏk hamyŏ" [Remembering Chief Han Ki T'aek], in *P'ansa Han Ki-t'aek* [Justice Han Ki T'aek], ed. People Who Remember Han Ki-t'aek (Seoul: Kungni, 2006), 225.

4 Yi Su-hyŏng, "Oasisŭ."

5 Hwang Chin-gu, "Han Ki-t'aek Pujangnim ŭl kiŏk hamyŏ," 226.

6 McRuer, *Crip Theory*, 92; Kafer, *Feminist, Queer, Crip*, 17.

7 In 2010, a female middle-school student with intellectual disability was raped and then gang-raped by sixteen young men in high schools in Taejŏn. All of the offenders were put on probation.

8 Yi Mun-yol, *Aga*.

9 Kwon Seong-woo, "Rediscovering Korea's Literary Giant," *List Magazine* 14 (Winter 2011).

10 Suh Ji-moon, "Yi Munyŏl," 729.

11 Park Young-hee [Pak Yŏng-hŭi], "Na nun sŏngp'ongnyŏk ŭi taesang i toegil wŏnhaji annŭnda" [I do not want to become a victim of sexual violence], *Konggam* [Empathy] 4 (2001): 32–35.

12 Yi Mun-yol, *Aga*, 30.

13 Yi Mun-yol, *Aga*, 17.

14 Yi Mun-yol, *Aga*, 18.

15 Yi Mun-yol, *Aga*, 55.

16 Yi Mun-yol, *Aga*, 60.

17 Yi Mun-yol, *Aga*, 61.

18 Yi Mun-yol, *Aga*, 61–62.

19 Yi Mun-yol, *Aga*, 62.

20 Yi Mun-yol, *Aga*, 75–76.

21 Yi Mun-yol, *Aga*, 31.

22 Yi Mun-yol, *Aga*, 31.

23 Yi Mun-yol, *Aga*, 8.

24 Yi Mun-yol, "*Aga* e taehan nonŭi rŭl pomyŏ" [Looking at the discussion about *Song of Songs*], *Chosŏn ilbo*, March 27, 2000.

25 Kim Chŏng-ran, "Uahan sarang norae? *Aga*?," 226–227.

26 Miles, "Blindness in South and East Asia," 88, emphasis in the original.

27 Miles, "Blindness in South and East Asia," 88.

28 Yi Mun-yol, "Anonymous Island," 73.

29 Yi Mun-yol, "Anonymous Island," 73.

30 Yi Mun-yol, "Anonymous Island," 75.

31 Yi Mun-yol, "Anonymous Island," 76.

32 Yi Mun-yol, "Anonymous Island," 76.

33 Yi Mun-yol, "Anonymous Island," 74.

34 Kim Chŏng-ran, "Uahan sarang norae? *Aga*?," 226, 227.

35 Kim Chŏng-ran, "Uahan sarang norae? *Aga*?," 234.

36 See Wendell, *The Rejected Body*, 143–144.

37 Yi Mun-yol, *Aga*, 214.

38 Pak Chu-hŭi, Yi Chŏng-min, and Chŏng Yŏng-ran, "Yi Mun-yŏl ŭi changaein e taehan chalmottoen sigak" [Yi Mun-yol's misperception about disabled people], *Konggam* [Empathy], no. 4 (2001): 38.

39 O Hwa-Su, narrator, "The Bride Who Would Not Speak," 1920, in *Folk Tales from Korea*, compiled by Zong In-Sob (New York: Greenwood, 1969), 189.

40 Zong In-Sob, *Folk Tales from Korea*, 189.

41 Kye Yong-muk, "Paekch'i Adada," 47.

42 Kye Yong-muk, "Paekch'i Adada," 47.

43 Kye Yong-muk, "Paekch'i Adada," 48.

44 Kye Yong-muk, "Paekch'i Adada," 48.

45 Kye Yong-muk, "Paekch'i Adada," 49.

46 Chŏng Ch'ang-bŏm, "Kye Yong-muk ron," 34.

47 Chŏng Ch'ang-bŏm, "Kye Yong-muk ron," 34.

48 Kyung Hyun Kim, "Korean Cinema and Im Kwon-Taek," 37. "Adada, the Idiot" was first made into a film with the same title in 1956 by Yi Kang Chŏn.

49 James and Kim, "An Interview with Im Kwon-Taek," 250.

50 Eunsun Cho notes that the deletions of the word "idiot" and the idiocy from Adada's characterization reflect the film's "aestheticized image of her," illustrating that conventional beauty and idiocy are made incompatible. Eunsun Cho, "The Female Body and Enunciation in *Adada* and *Surrogate Mother*," 105n3.

51 Pyŏn In-sik, "Im Kwŏn-t'aek ŭi yŏnghwa e nat'anan in'gan hoebok ŭi t'emaron: *T'ik'et*, *Ssibaji*, *Adada* ŭi kyŏngu," 51.

52 Pyŏn In-sik, "Im Kwŏn-t'aek ŭi yŏnghwa e nat'anan in'gan hoebok ŭi t'emaron," 51.

53 Hyaeweol Choi, *New Women in Colonial Korea*, 26.

54 Hyaeweol Choi, *New Women in Colonial Korea*, 72.

55 When Adada returns to her own family, although they are not portrayed as physically violent toward her as in the original story, her father does not accept her, owing to his Confucian belief that married women belong to their marital family. Falling in between the modernized marital family and the traditional birth family, she becomes homeless.

56 Eunsun Cho, "The Female Body and Enunciation in *Adada* and *Surrogate Mother*," 95.

57 Eunsun Cho, "The Female Body and Enunciation in *Adada* and *Surrogate Mother*."

58 Koh Dong-Yeon, "Chŏnhu Han'guk yŏnghwa e tŭngjang hanŭn chuhan Migun ŭi imiji: *Chiokhwa* (1958) esŏ *Such'wiin pulmyŏng* (2001) kkaji."

59 Ministry of Health and Social Affairs, *Pogŏn Sahoe T'onggye Yŏnbo* [Annual statistics on public health and social affairs] (Seoul: Ministry of Health and Social Affairs, 1954, 1955).

60 Korea Child Welfare Committee, *Handicapped Children's Survey Report*.

61 Korea Child Welfare Committee, *Handicapped Children's Survey Report*, 91.

62 Korea Child Welfare Committee, *Handicapped Children's Survey Report*, 71.

63 The actor's labor of simulated violence—including the injuries that actors endure in their physical bodies, often illustrates how a seemingly neat divide between the real and simulated violence in film does not always persist. In addition, a stunt double is employed selectively as a proxy as the action can harm the bodies. This further blurs the division between representational and experienced violence.

64 Groeneveld, "Animal Endings," 39.

65 McRuer, *Crip Theory*; Kafer, *Feminist, Queer, Crip*.

66 In this chapter I use "mental disability," rather than "mental illness" or "mental disorder," following the discussion of these terms by Margaret Price. Citing Cynthia Lewiecki-Wilson, Price explains that mental disability includes not only madness but also cognitive and intellectual disabilities of various kinds, as well as the physical differences that accompany mental illnesses. Price, *Mad at School*, 19; Lewiecki-Wilson, "Rethinking Rhetoric through Mental Disabilities," 156–167.

67 *Welcome to Dongmakgol* (*Welk'ŏm t'u Tongmakkol*, dir. Pak Kwang-hyŏn [2005]) features a girl with mental disability with a flower in her hair, who represents traditional apolitical innocence in an isolated mountain village during the Korean War.

68 Ch'oe Yun, "Chŏgi hanjŏm sori ŏpsi kkonnip i chigo."

69 Gi-Wook Shin, "Introduction," xvii. The May 18 Memorial Foundation currently lists 4,362 cases of compensation for death, disappearance, or disablement; "Kwallyŏn t'onggye" [Relevant statistics], www.518.org.

70 Keun-sik Jung, "Has Kwangju Been Realized?"

71 Gi-Wook Shin, "Introduction," xxv.

72 The television dramas *Hourglass* (*Morae sigye* [1995]) and *Peppermint Candy* (*Pakha sat'ang* [2000]) are other popular depictions of the Kwangju uprising. Two former presidents, Chun Doo Hwan and Roh Tae Woo, were convicted in 1996 and sentenced to death and to life in prison, respectively; in 1997 both were pardoned by President Kim Young Sam. Scholars have paid significant attention to the film *A Petal*, and my reading of the film owes a great deal to their detailed analyses. See *Han'guk nyu weibŭ ŭi chŏngch'ijŏk kiŏk* by Yŏnsedae Midiŏ Atŭ Yŏn'guso.

73 Koh Boo Eung, "Munhwa wa minjok chŏngch'esŏng."

74 Kim Hyŏn-sŏng, "*Kkonnip* enŭn Kwangju ka ŏpda: *Kkonnip* ŭl pogo" [There is no Kwangju in *A Petal*: After watching *A Petal*], *Ssine 21* [Cine 21] 50 (April 30, 1996): 95.

75 Ch'oe Yun, "There a Petal Silently Falls," in Ch'oe Yun, *There a Petal Silently Falls*, 15.

76 Ch'oe Yun, "There a Petal Silently Falls," 26.

77 Gilbert and Gubar, *Madwoman in the Attic*, 78, emphasis in the original.

78 Caminero-Santangelo, *Madwoman Can't Speak*, 4.

79 Caminero-Santangelo, *Madwoman Can't Speak*, 2, 3.

80 Caminero-Santangelo, *Madwoman Can't Speak*, 4.

81 Caminero-Santangelo, *Madwoman Can't Speak*, 9, 12.

82 Caminero-Santangelo, *Madwoman Can't Speak*, 11.

83 Felman, *What Does a Woman Want?*, 21–22.

84 Donaldson, "Corpus of the Madwoman," 14.

85 Donaldson, "Corpus of the Madwoman," 28. Donaldson recognizes the risk

of describing mental illness as a "neurobiological disorder," but she views it as necessary. Borrowing from Judith Butler's discussion of the notion of sex in the sex–gender system, Donaldson argues that we can "conceive of a more complex, nuanced, and politically effective notion of mental illness within the impairment-disability system" (30n21).

86 Caminero-Santangelo, *Madwoman Can't Speak*, 3.
87 Ch'oe Yun, "There a Petal Silently Falls," 74.
88 Ch'oe Yun, "There a Petal Silently Falls," 5.
89 Ch'oe Yun, "There a Petal Silently Falls," 30.
90 Chen, *Animacies*, 18.
91 Ch'oe Yun, "There a Petal Silently Falls," 24.
92 Ch'oe Yun, "There a Petal Silently Falls," 32.
93 Ch'oe Yun, "There a Petal Silently Falls," 31.
94 Ch'oe Yun, "There a Petal Silently Falls," 49.
95 Ch'oe Yun, "There a Petal Silently Falls," 32.
96 Ch'oe Yun, "There a Petal Silently Falls," 32–33.
97 Ch'oe Yun, "There a Petal Silently Falls," 33.
98 Ch'oe Yun, "There a Petal Silently Falls," 9.
99 Ch'oe Yun, "There a Petal Silently Falls," 34–35.
100 Ch'oe Yun, "There a Petal Silently Falls," 34.
101 Ch'oe Yun, "There a Petal Silently Falls," 6.
102 Ch'oe Yun, "There a Petal Silently Falls," 8.
103 Ch'oe Yun, "There a Petal Silently Falls," 35–36.
104 Ch'oe Yun, "There a Petal Silently Falls," 57.
105 Ch'oe Yun, "There a Petal Silently Falls," 72.
106 Ch'oe Yun, "There a Petal Silently Falls," 60.
107 Ch'oe Yun, "There a Petal Silently Falls," 61, 37.
108 Ch'oe Yun, "There a Petal Silently Falls," 42.
109 Ch'oe Yun, "There a Petal Silently Falls," 44.
110 Ch'oe Yun, "There a Petal Silently Falls," 44–45. I have corrected "four" in this translation to "three," as in the Korean original.
111 Ch'oe Yun, "There a Petal Silently Falls," 62.
112 Ch'oe Yun, "There a Petal Silently Falls," 74–75.
113 Ch'oe Yun, "There a Petal Silently Falls," 75.
114 Ch'oe Yun, "There a Petal Silently Falls," 76.
115 Ch'oe Yun, "There a Petal Silently Falls," 53.
116 Ch'oe Yun, "There a Petal Silently Falls," 51.
117 Kuppers, "Toward the Unknown Body," 137.
118 Ch'oe Yun, "There a Petal Silently Falls," 3–4.
119 Hesford, *Spectacular Rhetorics*, 214n1.
120 Disagreeing with feminists' criticism that the film employs the male voyeuristic gaze upon the girl's body and that national mourning takes place in the film at the expense of the woman's body and sanity, Rhee Suk Koo points out

that the mourning is never complete, never achieving peace and freedom from guilt. Rhee Suk Koo, "Yŏnghwa *Kkonnip* e nat'anan 'namsŏngjŏk sisŏn' kwa 'aedo' ŭi munje," 149.

121 Tabide K'asaro, "Ije kŏjitmal ŭl kŭman tuŏya," 390.

122 Saito Ayako, "Kkonnip ŭi muge," 298–299.

123 Saito Ayako, "Kkonnip ŭi muge," 295.

124 Nam Ta-ŭn, "Uri nŭn kŭnal ŭl nugu ŭi kiŏk ŭro sayu hanŭn'ga," 235.

125 Agamben, *Remnants of Auschwitz*, 69.

126 The film scholar Nam Ta-ŭn explains how the film's rescue fantasy distorts the source of the threat, which is her own self and guilt rather than the external force. In the novella, she fights off an insect herself and is worried that she might transform into a bug. Nam Ta-ŭn, "Uri nŭn kŭnal ŭl nugu ŭi kiŏk ŭro sayu hanŭn'ga," 234–235.

127 To the contrary, Aida Alayarian argues, "Usually, the intrusion of the past into the present is one of the main problems confronting the person who has endured trauma." Alayarian, *Consequences of Denial*, 36.

128 Tabide K'asaro, "Ije kŏjitmal ŭl kŭman tuŏya," 390.

129 Kim Ch'ang-hwan, "Mom ŭl t'onghan kiŏk kwa 'oppa' ŭi narŭsisijŭm," 196–197.

130 Kuppers, "Toward the Unknown Body," 130.

131 Grosz, *Volatile Bodies*, 159.

132 Park Young-Sook, *Mich'innyŏn p'ŭrojekt'ŭ 1999–2005*, 85.

133 Beck Jee-Sook, "Mad Women Project," 14.

134 Park Young-Sook, *Mich'innyŏn p'ŭrojekt'ŭ 1999–2005*, 84.

135 Park Young-Sook, *Mich'innyŏn p'ŭrojekt'ŭ 1999–2005*, 84.

136 Park Young-Sook, *Mich'innyŏn p'ŭrojekt'ŭ 1999–2005*, 84.

137 Kuppers, "Toward the Unknown Body," 139–140.

138 Changae Yŏsŏng Konggam [Women with Disabilities Empathy], "Op-Ed: *Togani*, punno hanŭn uridŭl i toraboaya hal kŏt" [Things we need to reflect on in the midst of our outrage], September 30, 2011, http://www.wde.or.kr /?hid=talk&ano=419.

Chapter 4. Uninhabiting Family

1 "The 57th International Day for Hansen's Disease" (2010), in Hansen's disease posters, Korean Hansen Welfare Association, http://www.khwa.or.kr.

2 In his memoir, *The Memories and Reflections of Dr. Gerhard Armauer Hansen*, Hansen claims credit for finding the origin of leprosy, which, "in medical literature . . . is now partly referred to as the Leprosy Bacillus, partly as Hansen's Disease" (99).

3 In 1954 a poet with Hansen's disease, Han Ha-un, launched Taehan Hansen Hyŏphoe (the Korean Hansen Association). Han Ha-un, *Han Ha-un chŏnjip*, 860; Chŏng Min, "Chŏnyŏmpyŏng kaenyŏm ŭi hondong" [Confusion about

the concept of infectious disease], *Tonga ilbo*, February 28, 1957; Yu Chun, "Nabyŏng ŭn naŭl su itta" [Leprosy is curable], *Tonga ilbo*, September 1, 1957.

4 The term "leper" was discontinued in the Eighth International Congress of Leprosy in 1963: "Timeline: Conferences/Congresses," International Leprosy Association, Global Project on the History of Leprosy, accessed October 2, 2013, http://www.leprosyhistory.org.

5 Edmond, *Leprosy and Empire*, 18.

6 Watt, "Preface."

7 "Elimination" is defined as a prevalence rate of 1 case or fewer per 10,000 inhabitants; it has to be distinguished from "eradication"—the complete absence throughout the world of the disease and the organism that causes it. World Health Organization, *The Final Push Strategy to Eliminate Leprosy as a Public Health Problem: Questions and Answers*, 2nd ed. (Geneva: WHO, 2003), 6.

8 Vicki Luker, "The Lessons of Leprosy? Reflections on Hansen's Disease in the Response to HIV and AIDS in the Pacific," unpublished manuscript, 2013.

9 Waxler, "Learning to Be a Leper," 170.

10 Niehaus, "Leprosy of a Deadlier Kind," 311–312; Edmond, *Leprosy and Empire*, 16.

11 Treichler, *How to Have Theory in an Epidemic*, 15.

12 "Pyŏng e kŏlligi shwiun t'yejil i ttaro itta" [There are traits that are susceptible to diseases], *Tonga ilbo*, October 27, 1928; "Kyŏrhon ŭihak ŭi chisik" [Knowledge of marriage medicine], *Tonga ilbo*, November 6, 1928.

13 Butler, *Gender Trouble*, xx.

14 Han Ha-un, "In'gan haengjin," 130.

15 Foucault, *Madness and Civilization*, 3.

16 By connecting leprosy to social Darwinism and the flourishing of eugenics in the United States, Gussow links the modern stigma of leprosy to racism. Gussow, *Leprosy, Racism and Public Health*, 19–20.

17 Hansen, *Memories and Reflections of Dr. Gerhard Armauer Hansen*, 108.

18 Hansen, *Memories and Reflections of Dr. Gerhard Armauer Hansen*, 99.

19 Hansen, *Memories and Reflections of Dr. Gerhard Armauer Hansen*, 99–100.

20 Hansen presented his method of using noninfected people as guards at the Berlin conference in 1897: "I travel all over the country, where lepers live. . . . Our lectures on the rules of cleanliness and isolation of lepers are not accepted. Lepers never accept that he can be dangerous for his fellow men, and naturally does not want his freedom to be restricted; hence I see to it that healthy persons attend our lectures. The healthy persons listen. . . . [It] is important that they do not want contact with the lepers. If I achieve that then my goal is reached. In Norway we have achieved that a leper who wants a servant does not find one." G. A. Hansen, "Optional and Obligatory Isolation of Lepers," *Mittheilungen und Verhandlugen der Internationaladen Wissenschaftlichen Lepra-Conferenz zu Berlin*, vol. 2, p. 165; quoted in Pandya, "First International Leprosy Conference, Berlin, 1897," 172.

21 Pandya, "First International Leprosy Conference, Berlin, 1897," 172.

22 Pandya, "First International Leprosy Conference, Berlin, 1897," 172, 174.

23 Pandya, "First International Leprosy Conference, Berlin, 1897," 174.

24 "Timeline: Conferences/Congresses."

25 Jung Keun-sik, "Han'guk esŏ ŭi kŭndaejŏk na kuryo ŭi hyŏngsŏng," 16.

26 Unlike the English translation Mr. or Mrs., "Ssi" is not a gendered term. Sorokto History Museum has a display of the unique terminologies that were used on the island.

27 Ministry of Education and Human Resources Development, *Kyoyuk kongmuwŏn posu ŏpmu p'yŏnram* [Public educators' complementary tasks list] (Seoul: Kyoyuk Inchŏk Chawŏnbu, 2001).

28 Korea Child Welfare Committee, *Handicapped Children's Survey Report*.

29 Bang, "Uninfected Children of Leper Parents," 75. The survey didn't officially count the "healthy children of leper parents" who "find themselves rejected by and ostracized from society, . . . because of technical difficulties in the method of the survey that was employed" (Korea Child Welfare Committee, *Handicapped Children's Survey Report*, 3).

30 Jung Keun-sik, "Han'guk esŏ ŭi kŭndaejŏk na kuryo ŭi hyŏngsŏng," 11–13.

31 "Ahae chugin wŏnsu rago nabyŏngja hamnyŏk nant'a" [Leprosy patients accused of murdering a child and beaten by a mob], *Tonga ilbo*, June 28, 1928; "Nabyŏng hwanja ch'ukch'ul" [Expelling leprosy patients], *Tonga ilbo*, March 24, 1931; "Saeng kan mŏgŭn nahwanja algo poni nŏnsenssŭ" [Leprosy patients eating a raw liver, turned out to be untrue], *Tonga ilbo*, August 25, 1935; "Yuŏnbiŏ nŭn ŏmjunghi ch'wich'ŏ" [Strict regulation for wild rumors], *Tonga ilbo*, June 21, 1936; "Wangsimni e sogul tun nahwanja ŭi pŏmhaeng" [A crime of leprosy patients based in Wangsimni], *Tonga ilbo*, June 14, 1936.

32 "Nabyŏngja ch'ong kŏmgŏ, ai ilhŭn kkadak" [Rounding up leprosy patients for a missing child], *Tonga ilbo*, May 24, 1931.

33 "Yua ŭi pup'aesi palgul cheju hae mŏgŭn nahwanja" [A leprosy patient exhumed a rotten baby corpse, distilled it into alcohol, and drank it], *Tonga ilbo*, July 1, 1934; "Misin i choeak! nahwanja ka sipse a rŭl sarhae sigyuk" [Superstition is to blame! A leprosy patient killed and ate a ten-year-old child], *Tonga ilbo*, April 24, 1934; "Saenggant mŏgŭn nabyŏngja kuhyŏng taero sahyŏng p'angyŏl" [A leprosy patient who ate raw liver sentenced to death as requested by prosecution], *Tonga ilbo*, July 23, 1936; "Ai chaba mŏgŭn mundungi sahyŏng" [A leper who ate a child sentenced to death], *Tonga ilbo*, June 20, 1937.

34 "Sorokto ŭi pyŏlch'ŏnji ro ch'ŏn yŏ nahwanja susong" [More than one thousand leprosy patients transported to Sorokto, a different world], *Tonga ilbo*, August 18, 1934; "Hwakchang toenŭn Sorok nagwŏn" [Expanding Sorok paradise], *Tonga ilbo*, February 20, 1936.

35 Sŏ Chŏng-ju, "The Leper," 23.

36 "Mundungi, saeng ui aech'ak sonyŏn sarhaebŏm kongp'an" [Out of an obsession for life, a leper is on trial for murdering a boy], *Tonga ilbo*, June 15, 1937.

37 Gale, *History of the Korean People*, 22–24, quoted in Cumings, *Korea's Place in the Sun*, 127.

38 Sherwood Hall reports that people feared the removal of blind children by Western doctors because Koreans believed that Westerners used children's organs to make medicine. He uses his mother's experience as an illustration: "Although Mrs. Hall had wanted to do something to help blind children, she had been cautioned that the Koreans might not understand her purpose. In time of any disturbances, they might point to the blind students as proof of the false tale that circulated during the Baby Riots of 1888 that doctors were taking out the children's eyes to make medicine." Hall, *With Stethoscope in Asia*, 144.

39 Robert D. Neff, "Bullied in Christmas," *Korea Times*, December 10, 2004.

40 There is a question whether in the Chosŏn period *nabyŏng* referred to leprosy or to a group of skin diseases.

41 Sŏngjong Year 3, *Chosŏn wangjo sillok* [The annals of the Chosŏn dynasty], February 29, 1472.

42 Sŏnjo Year 9, *Chosŏn wangjo sillok* [The annals of the Chosŏn dynasty], June 26, 1576.

43 *Tonga ilbo* includes the articles "Maedok ŭl koch'indago kongdong myoji esŏ sich'e rŭl p'anaeŏ inyuk ŭl sikhan yŏja, simnihan hu kongp'an" [A woman who dug up a grave and ate a human body to cure her syphilis was prosecuted and sent to a trial] (August 20, 1922) and "Haegol ŭl togul sosik, maedok ŭl koch'iryŏda kyŏngch'al sinse" [Dug up the grave and ate dead body, trying to cure syphilis, locked up in the cell] (September 23, 1925).

44 Chŏng Ch'ang-gwŏn argues that these plays, such as *T'ongyŏng ogwangdae* [T'ongyŏng five jesters] and *Kasan ogwangdae* [Kasan five jesters], realistically portray the *mundungi*'s marginalized lives. Chŏng Ch'ang-gwŏn, "Chosŏn esŏ ŭi changaein insik," 22–28.

45 Yi Hun-sang, *Kasan ogwangdae*, 15.

46 Pak Chin-t'ae, *T'ongyŏng ogwangdae*, 18–19.

47 Pak Chin-t'ae, *T'ongyŏng ogwangdae*, 122–124.

48 "Ch'ilgok nahwanjach'on kŏnmul chihasil e Sŏngsŏ Kukkyosaeng 5-myŏng ammaejang" [Five Sŏngsŏ Elementary School students buried in the basement of a building in Ch'ilgok Leprosy Patients Settlement Village], *Yŏngnam ilbo*, August 21, 1992; "Kaeguri Sonyŏn susaek kwallyŏn podo e pulman, chumin tŭl kija tŭng 25-myŏng kamgŭm p'okhaeng" [Dissatisfied with the reports on the search of Frog Boys, residents locked up and beat reporters and others], *Maeil sinmun*, August 22, 1992.

49 Another contemporary example involves a famous television series about a doctor during the Chosŏn period, *Hŏ Chun*. In one episode, a great physician's son was murdered by "lepers," who ate his organs so that they could be cured. *Hansenin* immediately and strongly protested, and at the end of the following episode the Munhwa Broadcasting Company aired an apology for misrepresenting *Hansenin*. Kim In-jŏng, "Tŭrama *Hŏ Chun* kwa tak'yument'ari A!

Sorokto" [Drama *Hŏ Chun* and documentary *Ah! Sorokto*], *Chŏlla-do tatkŏm*, December 19, 2001, http://www.jeonlado.com.

50 Cumings, *Korea's Place in the Sun*, 182.

51 Land-tenancy disputes accounted for 667 cases in 1931 and went up to 25,834 cases in 1935. Kim Chong-chŏl, "Chŏhang kwa in'gan haebang ŭi liŏllijŭm," 96.

52 Kim Chŏng-han, "Oksimi," 26.

53 Kim Chŏng-han, "Oksimi," 27.

54 Ch'oe Wŏn-sik, "Kusip-yŏndae e tasi ingnŭn Yosan," 45.

55 Kim Chŏng-han, "Oksimi," 27.

56 Kim Chŏng-han, "Oksimi," 34.

57 Kim Chŏng-han, "Oksimi," 31.

58 Cumings, *Korea's Place in the Sun*, 175.

59 Mun So-jŏng, "Sikminji sidae yŏsŏng nodong kwa mom ŭi ch'ehŏm," 120–132.

60 Kim Chŏng-han, "Oksimi," 33.

61 Kim Chŏng-han, *Naktonggang ŭi p'asukkun*, 76.

62 Kim Chŏng-han, "Oksimi," 38.

63 In the 1930s, as Cumings argues, land tenancy became increasingly exploitative, marked by insecure tenure, widespread debt and usury, uncompensated labor, and general penury; and landowners made little contribution to the production process. Cumings, *Korea's Place in the Sun*, 182.

64 Kim Chŏng-han, "Oksimi," 39.

65 Kim Chŏng-han, "Oksimi," 41.

66 Ch'oe Wŏn-sik, "Kusip-yŏndae e tasi ingnŭn Yosan," 45.

67 Ch'oe Wŏn-sik, "Kusip-yŏndae e tasi ingnŭn Yosan," 45.

68 Ch'oe Wŏn-sik, "Kusip-yŏndae e tasi ingnŭn Yosan," 45.

69 Kim Tong-ni, "Pawi" (1947), 68; Kim Tong-ni, "The Rock," 53.

70 Kim Tong-ni, "Pawi" (1936), 325.

71 Kim Tong-ni, "Pawi" (1936), 325.

72 Kim Tong-ni, "The Rock," 53.

73 Kim Tong-ni, "The Rock," 53.

74 Much as in this story, murdering a leprosy patient has been reported. "Pulch'i ŭi akchil kŏllin aenyŏ rŭl yanghoe ŭmdok sik'yŏ t'ugang kkaji" [Poisoned their beloved daughter with an incurable disease twice and dumped in the river], *Tonga ilbo*, May 5, 1933.

75 Kim Tong-ni, "The Rock," 54.

76 Kim Tong-ni, "The Rock," 54.

77 Kim Tong-ni, "The Rock," 55.

78 Kim Tong-ni, "The Rock," 55.

79 Kim Tong-ni, "The Rock," 56.

80 Han Hye-sŏn, *Han'guk sosŏl kwa kyŏlson inmul*, 109.

81 Jane Kim, "Leprosy in Korea," 112–113.

82 Saunders, *Cultural Cold War*.

83 Personal conversation, May 28, 2014.

84 Park Chung Hee repeated this slogan in many public addresses. For example, in his address at the 51st National Sports Games in 1970 he stated, "Physical strength is the foundation of the national power." See chapter 1 for a discussion of the eugenics written into the Mother and Child Health Act.

85 Until October 2002, Sorokto National Hospital maintained an internal policy of prohibiting marriage unless the patient was sterilized.

86 Han Ha-un, "K'ŭn k'o tach'inda," 730.

87 In "Ŏnŭ nal ŭi tansang," Han Ha-un writes that even if eyebrow transplants succeed and the thought of the procedure excites him, he doesn't want to have it (741); "Na ŭi ilgŭp pimil: Nunssŏp ŏpnŭn kyŏmson" [My top secret: Modesty without eyebrows], *Kyŏnghyang sinmun*, March 13, 1962.

88 Han Ha-un, "Na ŭi sŭlp'ŭn pansaenggi."

89 Kang Hong-kyu, "Kwanch'ŏl-dong sidae 70-yŏndae Han'guk mundan p'ung-sokhwa 41: Siin Han Ha-un ŭi piryŏn" [Korean literary scene in 1970s Kwanch'ŏltong 41: A tragic love of poet Han Ha-un], *Kyŏnghyang sinmun*, January 24, 1987.

90 Han Ha-un, "Ch'ŏnhyŏng siin ŭi piwŏn," 723. His notion of eugenics is vague and paradoxical. He argues for the freedom to marry with a strict birth control policy but condemns sterilizations. In his works he emphasizes human rights and responsibilities of people with disabilities.

91 Han Ha-un, "Ch'ŏnhyŏng siin ŭi piwŏn," 725.

92 Kim Hyŏn, "Chayu wa sarang ŭi silch'ŏnjŏk hwahae," 219.

93 Yi Chŏng-jun, "Tangsindŭl ŭi ch'ŏn'guk," 363. In an interview, Yi mentions that he thought of Park Chung Hee in creating the character of Director Cho. U Ch'an-je, "Uridŭl ŭi chŏnguk ŭl hyanghan tangsindŭl ŭi chŏnguk ŭi taehwa," 274.

94 Yi Kyu-t'ae, "Sorokto ŭi pallan."

95 Yi Chŏng-jun, *Your Paradise*, 502.

96 Yi Chŏng-jun, *Your Paradise*, 503.

97 Yi Chŏng-jun, *Your Paradise*, 508–509.

98 U Ch'an-je, "Uridŭl ŭi chŏnguk ŭl hyanghan tangsindŭl ŭi chŏnguk ŭi taehwa," 271.

99 U Ch'an-je, "Uridŭl ŭi chŏnguk ŭl hyanghan tangsindŭl ŭi chŏnguk ŭi taehwa," 271.

100 U Ch'an-je, "Uridŭl ŭi chŏnguk ŭl hyanghan tangsindŭl ŭi chŏnguk ŭi taehwa," 274.

101 Cho Su-jin, "Hansenpyŏng kukhoe muntŏk nŏmta" [Hansen's disease enters the congress], *Tonga ilbo*, October 12, 2004.

102 Jung Keun-Sik, "Il Hansenpyŏng inkwŏn undong ŭi kyohun" [Lessons from Japanese *Hansenin* human rights movements], *Kyŏnghang sinmun*, June 28, 2001.

103 No Sŏng-ryŏl, "Sorokto kyŏngni Hansenpyŏng hwanja Il sangdae sonbaeso" [Segregated patients in Sorokto filed a lawsuit against Japan for compensation], *Munhwa ilbo*, August 24, 2004.

104 Kim Tŏk-nyŏn, "Sosong chiji simin tŭl sŏmyŏng i Il chŏngbu hangso magŭl kŏt" [Citizens who signed to support the lawsuit will stop the Japanese government's appeal], *Oh My News*, May 2, 2005.

105 Taehan Min'guk Oegyobu [Korean Ministry of Foreign Affairs], "Ilbon chŏngbu ŭi uri Hansenin p'ihaeja 62-myŏng e taehan posanggŭm chigŭp kyŏlchŏng kwallyŏn oegyobu taebyŏnin nonp'yŏng" [Opinion of the ministry of foreign affairs on the Japanese government's decision to compensate 62 Hansen's disease victims], June 23, 2006, http://www.newswire.co.kr/.

106 Chŏng Ŭn-ju, "Sorokto nŭn tŏ isang oeropchi ant'a" [Sorokto is no longer lonely], *Sŏul sinmun*, December 16, 2004.

107 Kim Sŏn-sik, "Hansenin kangje tanjong nakt'ae pobwŏn 56-ŏk kukka paesang ŭl" [*Hansenin* forcible sterilization and abortion, court orders the government to pay 5.6 billion won], *Yonhap news*, February 12, 2015. However, the government most recently appealed to revoke these decisions.

108 See Davis, "Racism, Birth Control and Reproductive Rights," 202–271.

109 "Hansen saŏp taesangja punp'o [Distribution of Hansen business recipients], on the official website of Han'guk Hansen Pokjihyŏphoe [Korean Hansen Welfare Association], http://www.khwa.or.kr/business/distri.asp.

110 Luker, "Lessons of Leprosy?"

111 Dr. Sitaleki Finau of Niue commented, "The problem now is that there is no political will to debate these issues. We have tried successfully with other infectious diseases like leprosy, tuberculosis and dengue fever, why not HIV/AIDS?" Rietesh Kumar, "Isolate People Living with HIV/AIDS—Dr Finau," Pacific Islands News Association, August 19, 2008, http://www.pina.com.fj.

112 Kudlick, "Smallpox, Disability, and Survival in Nineteenth-Century France," 197.

113 Bell, "I Am Not the Man I Used to Be," 226.

114 Waxler, "Learning to Be a Leper," 189.

115 Sase, Jimba, and Wakai, "Scar of Japan's Leprosy Isolation Policy in Korea," 1396.

116 Hyung-Jin Kim, "Korean Ex-Leprosy Patients Return to Island Colony," AP *News*, November 24, 2013, http://news.yahoo.com/korean-ex-leprosy-patients -return-island-colony-093149755.html.

Chapter 5. Curing Virginity

1 Yi T'ae-gon (text) and Yi Sang-yun (illustration), "Kŏsa" [Big event], *Hamkke kŏrŭm* [Walking together] (November 1996): 58–65.

2 "Bachelor" is a more literal translation of the term *ch'onggak*, but the phrase *ch'onggak ttakchi* (bachelor label) emphasizes the lack of any sexual experience rather than an unmarried status. Thus, despite its gendered connotation and history in English, I find "virginity" more appropriate here.

3 Yŏ Chun-min, "Changaeu tŭriyŏ, ije sŏngchŏk kwŏlli rŭl chujang hara" [Disabled friends, claim your sexual rights], *Hamkke kŏrŭm*, June 1, 2003; Hŏ

Chŏng-hŏn, "Mainŏrit'i ŭi sŏng: Changaein" [The sexuality of minority: Disabled people], *Han'guk ilbo*, April 15, 2008.

4 O'Toole and Bregante, "Disabled Women."

5 Hahn, "Social Components of Sexuality and Disability"; Cole and Cole, "Sexuality, Disability, and Reproductive Issues through the Lifespan"; Shakespeare, Gillespie-Sells, and Davies, *Sexual Politics of Disability*; Gill, "Dating and Relationship Issues"; Garland-Thomson, *Extraordinary Bodies*.

6 Shildrick, *Dangerous Discourses of Disability, Subjectivity, and Sexuality*, 65.

7 Yi Myŏng-gu, "Changaein to sŏngyok i itta!" [Disabled people have sex drive too], *Sp'och'ŭ Ssŏndei*, May 1, 2009.

8 Ji-sung (Chisŏng), "Paltal changae yŏsŏng ŭi sam kwa seksyuŏllit'i" [Lives and sexuality of developmentally disabled women], *Alza.net*, December 9, 2009.

9 See Chŏn Hŭng-yun, "Changaein ŭi kyŏrhon wae ŏryŏ unga" [Why is marriage difficult for disabled people?], *Hamkke kŏrŭm*, September 1, 1989.

10 Tari Youngjung Na (T'ari Yŏng-jŏng Na), "Changaein ŭi seksyuŏllit'i: Ch'iryo, pongsa, maemae esŏ it'al hagi" [Disabled people's sexuality: Escaping from therapy, volunteer service, transaction], *Konggam* [Empathy] 8 (2005): 89–98; Sinu, "'Tadŭl hagu innyaguyo? *P'ingk'ŭ p'aellisŭ* rŭl t'onghae pon sŏng tamnon" [Are we all doing it? Sexuality discourse through *Pink Palace*], *Konggam* 8 (2005): 63–72.

11 Hŏ Chŏng-hŏn and Kim Sŏng-hwan, "Mainŏrit'i ŭi sŏng: Ŏegugin nodongja" [The sexuality of the minority: Migrant laborers], *Han'guk ilbo*, April 16, 2008; Kim Chŏng-hwan, "Mainŏrit'i ŭi sŏng: Noin" [The sexuality of the minority: Elderly people], *Han'guk ilbo*, April 14, 2008.

12 Kim Hyŏn-sŏn, "Changaein ŭi sŏngyok kwa sŏngmaemae" [Disabled people's sex drive and sex trade], *Hamkke kŏrŭm*, June 11, 2003.

13 "Zurich Disabled Get Sexual Relief," *Swissinfo*, April 8, 2003; "Disabled Organization Withdraws Sex Project," *Swissinfo*, September 11, 2003; "Disabled Sex 'Assistants' Tackle Taboo," *Swissinfo*, April 8, 2006.

14 Shildrick, *Dangerous Discourses of Disability, Subjectivity, and Sexuality*, 74.

15 Shildrick, *Dangerous Discourses of Disability, Subjectivity, and Sexuality*, 74.

16 Yŏ Chun-min, "Changaeu tŭriyŏ, ije sŏngchŏk kwŏlli rŭl chujang hara."

17 Song Chu-yŏn, "*P'ingk'ŭ p'aellisŭ* Sŏ Tong-il kamdok ŭi insaeng iyagi" [*Pink Palace*, the director Seo's life story], *Film 2*, November 7, 2005.

18 Won Mi-hye, *Sŏng p'anmae yŏsŏng ŭi saengae ch'ehŏm yŏn'gu*, 147.

19 Won Mi-hye, *Sŏng p'anmae yŏsŏng ŭi saengae ch'ehŏm yŏn'gu*, 147.

20 Personal communication (2010).

21 "Brothel Offers Easy Access for Disabled," *BBC News*, March 14, 2001.

22 Pak Sun-chŏn, "Ch'ukpok to chŏju to anin na ŭi wŏlgyŏng: Changae yŏsŏng ŭi wŏlgyŏng" [My menstruation, neither blessing nor a curse: Menstruation of disabled women], *Konggam* 6 (2003): 26–31; McCarthy, "Whose Body Is It Anyway?"

23 Pak Chi-ju, "Yŏnghwa *P'ingk'ŭ p'aellisŭ* ŭi han'gye wa kach'i" [Limits and values of the film *Pink palace*], *Able News*, June 30, 2005.

24 Kim Min-kyŏng, "Changaein ŭi sŏngyok ŭn yujoe in'ga?" [Is disabled people's sex drive at fault?] *Han'gyŏre 21*, April 18, 2006.

25 Yi Hun-hŭi, "Changaein ŭi sŏngmunje tarun *P'ingkŭ p'aellisŭ* yugam: Nuga i yŏnghwa rŭl changaein yŏnghwa rago marhanŭn'ga" [Regrets about *Pink Palace* on disabled people's sexuality problem: Who says it is a disability movie?], *With News*, June 29, 2005; Yi Hun-hŭi, "Chae panron: *P'ingkŭ p'aellisŭ* panron e taehan tŏ k'ŭn ant'akkaum" [Rebuttal: More regrets about the response to *Pink Palace*], *With News*, July 5, 2005; Seo Dong-il [Sŏ Tong-il], "*P'ingk'ŭ p'aellisŭ* ŭi ant'akkaum ŭl chŏnhamnida" [Sending *Pink Palace*'s regret], *With News*, July 4, 2005.

26 Pak Chi-ju, "Sŏng nodongja ŭi nal haengsa e changaein ŭi sŏngi iyongdanghal ppŏn" [Disabled people's sexuality has almost been taken advantage of at the event for sex workers' day], *Able News*, July 5, 2005. Because the members of the film's production group opposed the purpose of the event and objected to this partial screening, the film was not shown.

27 Kim Hyŏn-sŏn, "Changaein ŭi sŏngyok kwa sŏngmaemae."

28 Yŏ Chun-min, "Yullak ka ŭi tu changae yŏsŏng, idŭl ege musŭn iri irŏnanna" [Two disabled women in the red-light district, what happened to them?], *Hamkke kŏrŭm*, March 1, 2003.

29 Ŏm Sang-mi, "Hannat ttŏri ka toenŭn ch'am ch'ak'an yŏjadŭl" [Very good women, who are sold at clearance], *Konggam* 6 (2003): 44–50.

30 For the sexual services for people with disabilities and their politics in Japan and the impact of the book *Sex Volunteers*, see Nakamura, "Barrier-Free Brothels."

31 In Japan, "sex volunteers" is also used to refer to men who help women in sex-less marriages experience sex. Other related terms have emerged in Korean, such as *seksŭ tolbomi* and *sŏng toumi* (sex helper), which is ambiguous in its connotation regarding compensation but is distinguished from personal assistants for daily living activities (*hwaltong pojoin*).

32 Cho Ŭn-yŏng, "Changaeu seksŭ sŏbisŭ e taehan ch'anban" [Pros and cons of sex services for disabled people], *Hamkke kŏrŭm*, April 1, 2005.

33 Kawai Kaori, *Seksŭ chawŏn pongsa*.

34 Kawai Kaori, *Seksŭ chawŏn pongsa*, 101.

35 Shakespeare, *Disability Rights and Wrongs*.

36 Shakespeare, *Disability Rights and Wrongs*, 155.

37 Chang Kyŏng-min, "Seksŭ wa chawŏn pongsa, kŭrigo chungchŭng changaein" [Sex, volunteer service, and severely disabled people], *Able News*, January 26, 2010.

38 *Yŏsŏng changaein Kim Chin-ok Ssi ŭi kyŏrhon iyagi* [The story of the marriage of a disabled woman, Kim Chin-Ok], dir. Kim Chin-ok, 1999; *Changae yŏsŏng ŭi sŏng kwa sarang* [The sexuality and love of disabled women], MBC *Special*, dir. Kim Yŏng-ho (Seoul: Munhwa Broadcasting Company), aired on April 15, 2007.

39 Kim Hwa-bŏm, "Program Note: *Appa* [Papa]," *Susangjak soch'aekcha: Sŏul Tongnip Yŏnghwaje 2004* [Booklet for the Seoul Independent Film Festival award-winning film collection], 2004, 15.

40 According to Ryu Mi-rye (Yu Mi-rye), the sequence was filmed at a real institution and the disabled men were not actors. "Changaein ŭi sŏng ŭl sojae ro han tongnip yŏnghwa: *Appa*" [An independent film on the topic of disabled people's sexuality: *Papa*], *With News*, July 8, 2005.

41 Sin Mi-hye, "*Appa*: Insik ŭi hwakchang ŭl yogu hanŭn yŏnghwa" [Papa: A film that demands the expansion of our consciousness], *Tongnip Yŏnghwa* [Independent film] 24 (2005): 30–31.

42 Cho Ŭn-yŏng, "Changaeu seksŭ sŏbisŭ e taehan ch'anban."

43 Tari Youngjung Na, "Changaein ŭi seksyuŏllit'i," 89–98.

44 Yongrong, "Changaein ŭi seksyuŏllit'i nŭn palgyŏn toenŭn kŏsi anida" [Disabled people's sexuality is not a thing that can be discovered], *Hamkke kŏrŭm*, September 11, 2008.

45 Sinu also points out that the construction of "disabled people" as a group lacking sexual opportunity is false. Sinu, "Tadŭl hagu innyaguyo?"

46 Wilkerson, "Disability, Sex Radicalism, and Political Agency."

Conclusion

1 McClintock, *Imperial Leather*, 40.

2 The documentary *The Lazarus Effect* (dir. Lance Bangs [2010]) is a good example of using before-and-after images of HIV-positive South Africans to show the power of antiretroviral treatment and to solicit donations from the Western world.

3 Adam Frank describes the night sky as a "time machine": "We never see the sky as it is, but only as it was." "Where Is Now? The Paradox of the Present," July 26, 2011, www.npr.org/sections/13.7/2011/07/26/138695074/where-is-now-the-paradox-of-the-present.

4 World Health Organization, "Health Statistics and Information Systems," www.who.int/healthinfo/global_burden_disease/metrics_daly/en, emphasis added. For the critique of DALY, see Erevelles, *Disability and Difference in Global Contexts*, 139–141.

5 World Health Organization, "Concept Paper: WHO Guidelines on Health-related Rehabilitation (Rehabilitation Guidelines)," December 2012, www.who.int/entity/disabilities/care/concept_note.doc, emphases added.

6 University of Minnesota Human Rights Center, *Human Rights. Yes! Action and Advocacy on the Rights of Persons with Disabilities*, 2nd ed., http://www1.umn.edu/humanrts/edumat/hreduseries/HR-YES/chap-9.html, emphasis added.

7 University of Minnesota Human Rights Center, *Human Rights.*

8 In *The Mystery of the Eye and the Shadow of Blindness*, Michalko explains how disabilities are seen as "incomplete, distorted, and defective in relation to their

origin," and reveals the moral character of rehabilitation as restoring a "proper condition," rather than a "previous condition" (68).

9   Fabian, *Time and the Other*, 31.

10 Bhabha, *Location of Culture*, 2.

11 Haraway, *Primate Visions*, 247.

12 Haraway, *Primate Visions*, 247.

13 Fabian, *Time and the Other*, 32.

14 Das, "Violence and the Work of Time," 67.

15 Kafer, *Feminist, Queer, Crip*, 48–49.

16 Sinu, "Yongsan migun kiji e seun changae yŏsŏng maŭl" [The village of disabled women built on Yongsan US military base], *Konggam* [Empathy] 7 (2004), 17.

17 Pak Yŏng-yul, "Yongsan kongwŏn sŏlgye kongmo tangsŏnjak: 'Mirae chihyang hanŭn ch'iyu ŭi kongwŏn'" [Winning design for Yongsan park: Future-oriented "healing park"], *Han'gyŏre sinmun*, April 23, 2012.

BIBLIOGRAPHY

Adada. Directed by Im Kwon-Taek [Im Kwŏn-t'aek]. 1987. VHS.

Address Unknown [*Such'wiin pulmyŏng*]. Directed by Kim Ki Duk [Kim Ki-dŏk]. 2001. DVD.

Agamben, Giorgio. *Remnants of Auschwitz*. Translated by Daniel Heller-Roazen. New York: Zone, 1999.

Ah! Sorokto. Directed by Kim Hui and Kim Myŏng-gon. Munhwa Broadcasting Company. Aired on December 19 and December 20, 2001.

Ahmed, Sara. *The Promise of Happiness*. Durham: Duke University Press, 2010.

The Aimless Bullet [Obalt'an]. Directed by Yu Hyŏn-mok. 1961. DVD.

Alayarian, Aida. *Consequences of Denial: The Armenian Genocide*. London: Karnac, 2008.

Allen, Horace Newton. "Sim Chung: The Dutiful Daughter." In *Korean Tales: Being a Collection of Stories Translated from the Korean Folk Lore*, 152–169. Library of Alexandria, 1889.

American Psychiatric Association. *Diagnostic and Statistical Manual of Mental Disorders, IV-TR*. Arlington, VA: American Psychiatric Press, 2000.

American Psychiatric Association. *Diagnostic and Statistical Manual of Mental Disorders*. 5th ed. Arlington, VA: American Psychiatric Press, 2013.

Andersen, Hans Christian. *The Little Mermaid*. Translated by David Hohnen. Copenhagen: Høst and Søn, 1962.

Anderson, Benedict. *Imagined Communities: Reflections on the Origin and Spread of Nationalism*. Revised ed. London: Verso, 1991.

Anzaldúa, Gloria. "La Conciencia de la Mestiza: Toward a New Consciousness." In *The Essential Feminist Reader*, edited by Estelle B. Freedman, 385–390. New York: Modern Library, 2007.

———. "(Un)natural Bridges, (Un)safe Spaces." In *This Bridge We Call Home: Radical Visions for Transformation*, edited by Gloria E. Anzaldúa and AnaLouise Keating, 1–5. New York: Routledge 2002.

Bae Eun-kyoung [Pae Ŭn-gyŏng]. "Han'guk sahoe ch'ulsan chojŏl ŭi yoksajŏk kwajŏng kwa chendŏ" [Historical process of birth control and gender in Korean society]. PhD diss., Seoul National University, 2004.

Bang Sung Joon [Pang Sŏng-jun]. "Uninfected Children of Leper Parents." In *Handicapped Children's Survey Report*, edited by Korea Child Welfare Committee, 75–76. Seoul: Korea Child Welfare Committee, 1962.

Baril, Alexandre. "Needing to Acquire a Physical Impairment/Disability: (Re) Thinking the Connections between Trans and Disability Studies through Transability." Translated by Catriona Leblanc. *Hypatia* 30, no. 1 (2015): 3–48.

Beauchamp-Pryor, Karen. "Impairment, Cure and Disability: 'Where Do I Fit In?'" *Disability and Society* 26, no. 1 (2011): 5–17.

Beck Jee-Sook [Paek Chi-suk]. "Mad Women Project: A Feminist Perspective on Women's Reality." In *Mich'innyŏn p'ŭrojekt'ŭ 1999–2005: Pak Yŏng-suk sajinjip* [Mad women project 1999–2005: Photographs by Park Young-Sook]. Seoul: Nunpit, 2005.

Bell, Christopher. "I Am Not the Man I Used to Be." In *Sex and Disability*, edited by Robert McRuer and Anna Mollow, 208–230. Durham: Duke University Press, 2012.

Bhabha, Homi K. *The Location of Culture.* New York: Routledge, 1994.

Butler, Judith. *Gender Trouble.* New York: Routledge, 2007.

Caminero-Santangelo, Marta. *The Madwoman Can't Speak: Or, Why Insanity Is Not Subversive.* Ithaca, NY: Cornell University Press, 1998.

Čapek, Karel. *R. U. R. (Rossum's Universal Robots): A Fantastical Melodrama.* Translated by Paul Selver. Garden City, NY: Doubleday, 1923.

Ch'ae Man-sik. *Sim Pongsa* [Sim the blind] (1935). In *Ch'ae Man-sik chŏnjip* [The compilation of Ch'ae Man-sik's work] 9: 28–101. Seoul: Ch'angjaksa, 1989.

Chambers, Samuel A., and Terrell Carver. *Judith Butler and Political Theory: Troubling Politics.* New York: Routledge, 2008.

"Changhwa Hongnyŏn chŏn." In *Uri kojŏn tasi ilkki* [Rereading our traditional literature] 16, edited by Ku In-hwan, 13–43. Seoul: Sinwŏn Munhwasa, 2003.

Chen, Mel Y. *Animacies: Biopolitics, Racial Mattering, and Queer Affect.* Durham: Duke University Press, 2012.

Ch'oe In-hun. "Tara tara palgŭn tara" [Dear moon, moon, the bright moon]. In *Yetnal yetchŏk hwŏi hwŏi* [Once upon a time, whoosh whoosh]. Seoul: Munhak kwa Chisŏngsa, 1978.

Cho, Eunsun. "The Female Body and Enunciation in *Adada* and *Surrogate Mother*." In *Im Kwon-Taek: The Making of a Korean National Cinema*, edited by David E. James and Kyung Hyun Kim, 84–106. Detroit, MI: Wayne State University Press, 2002.

Ch'oe Wŏn-gyu. "Saengmyŏng kwŏllyŏk ŭi chaktong kwa sahoe pokchi: Kangje purim tamron ŭl chungsim ŭro" [Operation of biopower and social welfare: Focused on discourse of compulsory sterilization]. *Sanghwang kwa pokji* [Situation and welfare] 12 (2002): 143–181.

Ch'oe Wŏn-sik. "Kusip-yŏndae e tasi ingnŭn Yosan" [Re-reading Yosan in the 1990s]. In *Kim Chŏng-han: Taetchok katŭn sam kwa munhak* [Kim Chŏng-han: His upright life and literature], edited by Kang Chin-ho, 39–56. Seoul: Saemi, 2002.

Ch'oe Yun. "Chŏgi hanjŏm sori ŏpsi kkonnip i chigo" [There a petal silently falls]. *Munhak kwa sahoe* [Literature and society] 1, no. 2 (May 1988): 730–788.

———. *There a Petal Silently Falls: Three Stories by Ch'oe Yun*. Translated by Bruce and Ju-chan Fulton. New York: Columbia University Press, 2008.

Cho Hong-sŏk. "Hyŏnhaeng Moja Pogŏnpŏp che 14-cho ŭi hŏnpŏp sang munjechŏm kwa kaesŏn pangan" [The problems of current Mother and Child Health Act article 14 and suggestions for remedy]. *Pŏpche* [Legislation] no. 515 (2000): 12–26.

Cho Nak-hyŏn. "'Sogyŏng kwa anjŭmbangi mundap' ŭi sisa pip'yŏng kwa allegori e taehayŏ" [On social criticism and allegory in "questions and answers between a blind person and a paraplegic"]. *Kugŏ kyoyuk* [Korean education] 90 (1995): 283–297.

Choi, Hyaeweol. *New Women in Colonial Korea: A Sourcebook*. Hoboken, NJ: Taylor and Francis, 2012.

Choi Ju-han [Ch'oe Chu-han]. "Minjok kaejoron kwa sangae ŭi yullihak" [National reformation and ethics of mutual care]. *Sŏgang inmun nonch'ong* [Sŏgang humanities forum] 30 (2011): 295–335.

Choi, Kyeong-Hee. "Impaired Body as Colonial Trope: Kang Kyŏng'ae's 'Underground Village.'" *Public Culture* 13, no. 3 (2001): 431–458.

Chŏng Ch'ang-bŏm. "Kye Yong-muk ron: Chakp'um kyŏnghyang ŭi punsŏk" [Kye Yong-muk theory: An analysis of the tendency of his works]. *T'ongil inmunhak nonch'ong* [The humanities for unification forum] 8, no. 2 (1976): 27–42.

Chŏng Ch'ang-gwŏn. "Chosŏn esŏŭi changaein ŭi insik." In *Han'gugin, mom ŭi sahoesa* [Koreans, the sociological history of the body], 29–54. Seoul: Han'guk Sahoesa Hakhoe, 2004.

———. *Yŏksa sok changaein ŭn ŏttŏk'e sarassŭlkka* [How did the lives of people with disabilities appear in history?]. Seoul: Kŭl Hangari, 2011.

Chŏng Chin-sŏk. "Minjok ŭi chisŏng *Sindonga* 600-ho ŭi yŏksajŏk ŭimi" [Nation's intellect in *Sindonga* and the historical implication of its 600th issue]. *Sindonga* [New East Asia] (September 2009): 650–664.

Chŏng Ha-yŏng, ed. *Han'guk kojŏn munhak chŏnjip: Sim Chŏng chŏn* [Korean traditional literature compilation: Sim Chŏng chŏn]. Seoul: Koryŏ Taehakkyo Minjok Munhwa Yŏn'guso, 1995.

Cho Sŏn-jak. *Yŏngja ŭi chŏnsŏng sidae* [Yŏngja's heydays]. Seoul: Minŭmsa, 1974.

Chu Yo-sŏp. "Ch'umul" [The ugly creature]. *Sindonga* [New East Asia] (April 1936): 290–305.

Clare, Eli. *Exile and Pride: Disability, Queerness, and Liberation*. Cambridge, MA: South End, 1999.

Cole, Sandra S., and Theodore M. Cole. "Sexuality, Disability, and Reproductive Issues through the Lifespan." *Sexuality and Disability* 11, no. 3 (1993): 189–205.

The Crucible [*Togani*]. Directed by Hwang Tong-hyŏk. 2011. DVD.

Cumings, Bruce. *Korea's Place in the Sun: A Modern History*. New York: W. W. Norton, 1997.

Das, Veena. "Violence and the Work of Time." In *Signifying Identities*, edited by Anthony Cohen, 59–73. New York, Routledge, 2000.

———. "Violence, Gender, and Subjectivity." *Annual Review of Anthropology* 37 (2008): 283–299.

Davidson, Michael. *Concerto for the Left Hand: Disability and the Defamiliar Body.* Ann Arbor: University of Michigan Press, 2008.

Davis, Angela. "Racism, Birth Control and Reproductive Rights." In *Women, Race, & Class*, 202–271. New York: Random House, 1981.

Dean, Tim. *Unlimited Intimacy: Reflections on the Subculture of Barebacking.* Chicago: University of Chicago Press, 2009.

Derrida, Jacques. *Dissemination.* Translated by Barbara Johnson. Chicago: University of Chicago Press, 1981.

DiMoia, John. *Reconstructing Bodies: Biomedicine, Health, and Nation Building in South Korea since 1945.* Stanford, CA: Stanford University Press, 2013.

Donaldson, Elizabeth J. "The Corpus of the Madwoman: Toward a Feminist Disability Studies Theory of Embodiment and Mental Illness." In *The Madwoman and the Blindman: Jane Eyre, Discourse, Disability*, edited by David Bolt, Julia Miele Rodas, and Elizabeth J. Donaldson, 11–31. Columbus: Ohio State University Press, 2012.

Durow, Saul. "South Africa: Paradoxes in the Place of Race." In *The Oxford Handbook of the History of Eugenics*, edited by Alison Bashford and Philippa Levine, 274–288. New York: Oxford University Press, 2010.

Dutiful Daughter Chŏng [*Hyonyŏ Chŏngi*]. Directed by Sin Sang-ok. 1972. VHS.

Edmond, Rod. *Leprosy and Empire: A Medical and Cultural History.* Cambridge: Cambridge University Press, 2006.

Enloe, Cynthia. *Maneuvers: The International Politics of Militarizing Women's Lives.* Berkeley: University of California Press, 2000.

Erevelles, Nirmala. *Disability and Difference in Global Contexts: Enabling a Transformative Body Politic.* New York: Palgrave Macmillan, 2011.

The Evening Bell [*Manjong*]. Directed by Sin Sang-ok. 1970.

Fabian, Johannes. *Time and the Other: How Anthropology Makes Its Object.* New York: Columbia University Press, 2002.

Felman, Shoshana. *What Does a Woman Want? Reading and Sexual Difference.* Baltimore: Johns Hopkins University Press, 1993.

Foucault, Michel. *The History of Sexuality, Vol. 1, An Introduction.* Translated by Robert Hurley. New York: Random House, 1978.

———. *Madness and Civilization: A History of Insanity in the Age of Reason.* Translated by Richard Howard. New York: Vintage, 1973.

Gale, James Scarth. *History of the Korean People.* Seoul: Royal Asiatic Society, 1972.

Garland-Thomson, Rosemarie. *Extraordinary Bodies: Figuring Physical Disability in American Culture and Literature.* New York: Columbia University Press, 1997.

Gilbert, Sandra, and Susan Gubar. *The Madwoman in the Attic.* New Haven, CT: Yale University Press, 1979.

Gill, Carol J. "Dating and Relationship Issues." *Sexuality and Disability* 14, no. 3 (1996): 183–190.

Goffman, Erving. *Stigma: Notes on the Management of Spoiled Identity*. New York: Simon and Schuster, 1963.

Grinker, Roy. *Unstrange Minds: Remapping the World of Autism*. Philadelphia: Basic Books, 2007.

Groeneveld, Sarah. "Animal Endings: Species Necropolitics in Contemporary Transnational Literature." PhD diss., University of Wisconsin, Madison, 2014.

Grosz, Elizabeth. *Volatile Bodies: Toward a Corporeal Feminism*. Bloomington: Indiana University Press, 1994.

Gussow, Zachary. *Leprosy, Racism and Public Health: Social Policy in Chronic Disease Control*. Boulder, CO: Westview, 1989.

Hacking, Ian. *Rewriting the Soul: Multiple Personality and the Science of Memory*. Princeton, NJ: Princeton University Press, 1995.

Hahn, Harlan. "The Social Components of Sexuality and Disability: Some Problems and Proposals." *Sexuality and Disability* 4, no. 4 (1981): 220–233.

Hall, Sherwood. *With Stethoscope in Asia: Korea*. McLean, VA: MCL Associates, 1978.

Han Ha-un. "Chŏnhyŏng siin ŭi piwŏn" [An earnest prayer of a poet with divine punishment]. In *Han Ha-un chŏnjip* [Han Ha-un compilation], 716–729. Seoul: Munhak kwa Chisŏngsa, 2010.

———. *Han Ha-un chŏnjip* [Han Ha-un compilation]. Seoul: Munhak kwa Chisŏngsa, 2010.

———. "In'gan haengjin" [The march of human beings]. *Sae pit* [New light], January 1969. In *Han Ha-un chŏnjip* [Han Ha-un compilation], 130. Seoul: Munhak kwa Chisŏngsa, 2010.

———. "K'ŭn k'o tach'inda" [You will be hurt badly]. *Sinmunye* [New literature], July 1958. In *Han Ha-un chŏnjip* [Han Ha-un compilation], 730. Seoul: Munhak kwa Chisŏngsa, 2010.

———. "Na ŭi sŭlp'ŭn pansaenggi" [My sorrowful midlife memoir]. In *Han Ha-un chŏnjip* [Han Ha-un compilation], 219–495. Seoul: Munhak kwa Chisŏngsa, 2010.

———. "Ŏnŭ nal ŭi tansang" [Small thoughts of a day]. *Sinmunye* [New literature], December 1958. In *Han Ha-un chŏnjip* [Han Ha-un compilation], 738–742. Seoul: Munhak kwa Chisŏngsa, 2010.

Han Hye-sŏn. *Han'guk sosŏl kwa kyŏlson inmul* [Korean novels and impaired characters]. Seoul: Kukhak Charyowŏn, 2000.

Han Man-Soo [Han Man-su]. "Singminji sigi kŏmyŏl kwa 1930-yŏndae changaeu inmul sosŏl" [Censorship in Japanese colonial period and the impaired characters: Novels in 1930]. *Korean Literature Studies* 29 (2005): 7–33.

Han Min Ju [Han Min-ju]. "Injo in'gan ŭi ch'urhyŏn kwa kŭndae esŭep'u munhak ŭi t'ek'ŭnok'ŭrasi: Injo nodongja rŭl chungsimŭro" [A technocracy in the emergence of robots and modern science fiction literature: Focusing on artificial laborers]. *Han'guk munhak yŏn'gu* [Journal of modern Korean literature] 25 (2012): 417–449.

Han'guk Chŏngch'aek Pangsongwŏn [Korean Policy Broadcasting Institute]. "Che-51 hoe chŏn'guk ch'eyuk taehoe" [The 51st national sports competition]. *Taehan nyusŭ* [Korean News], no. 757, televised by ROK Government on October 10, 1970. http://www.ehistory.go.kr.

Han'guk Yŏngsang Charyowŏn [Korean Film Archive]. *Singminji sidae ŭi yŏnghwa kŏmyŏl, 1910–1934* [Film censorship during the colonial period, 1910–1934]. Seoul: KOFA, 2009.

Hansen, Gerhard A. *The Memories and Reflections of Dr. Gerhard Armauer Hansen.* Würzburg: German Leprosy Relief Association, 1976.

Haraway, Donna. *Primate Visions: Gender, Race, and Nature in the World of Modern Science.* New York: Routledge, 1989.

Hesford, Wendy. *Spectacular Rhetorics: Human Rights Visions, Recognitions, Feminisms.* Durham: Duke University Press, 2011.

Hubert, Henri, and Marcel Mauss. *Sacrifice: Its Nature and Function.* Chicago: University of Chicago Press, 1964.

Hwang Sŏk-yŏng. *Sim Chŏng.* Seoul: Munhak Tongne, 2003.

Hwang Sun-wŏn. "Maengawŏn esŏ" [In the institution for blind children]. In *Hwang Sun Wŏn chŏnjip* [Compilation of Hwang Sun Wŏn's work] 2: 297–308. Seoul: Ch'angusa, 1964.

Hwang Yŏng-ju. "*Sim Chŏng chŏn* ilkki ro pon Han'guk esŏŭi kukka wa yŏsŏng" [Nation-state and women through reading *Sim Chŏng chŏn* in Korea]. *Han'guk chŏngch'i hakhoebo* [Korean political science review] 34, no. 4 (2000): 77–92.

If You Were Me [*Yŏsŏtkae ŭi sisŏn*]. Directed by Park Chan-wook [Pak Ch'an-uk], Yim Soon-rye [Im Sun-rye], Yeo Gyun-Dong [Yŏ Kyun-dong], Park Jin-pyo [Pak Chin-p'yo], Jeong Jae-eun [Chŏng Chae-ŭn], and Park Kwang-su [Pak Kwang-su]. 2003. DVD.

Ingstad, Benedict. *Community-Based Rehabilitation in Botswana: The Myth of the Hidden Disabled.* Lewiston, NY: Edwin Mellen, 1997.

Iryŏn. *Samguk yusa* [The history of three kingdoms]. Translated by Kim Yŏng-sŏk. Seoul: Hakwŏnsa, 1994.

James, David E., and Kyung Hyun Kim. "An Interview with Im Kwon-Taek." In *Im Kwon-Taek: The Making of a Korean National Cinema*, edited by David E. James and Kyung Hyun Kim, 247–265. Detroit, MI: Wayne State University Press, 2002.

Jung Ji Young [Chŏng Chi-yŏng]. "P'allyŏgan ttal e taehan pulp'yŏnhan kiŏk" [Uncomfortable memories of Sim Chŏng, the "sold daughter"]. *Han'guk yŏsŏnghak* [Korean women's studies] 27, no. 1 (2011): 155–187.

Jung Keun-sik [Chŏng Kŭn-sik]. "Han'guk esŏ ŭi kŭndaejŏk na kuryo ŭi hyŏngsŏng" [The formation of modern leprosy control in colonial Korea]. *Pogŏn kwa sahoe kwahak* [Public health and social science] 1, no. 1 (1997): 1–30.

———. "Has Kwangju Been Realized?" In *Contentious Kwangju*, edited by Gi-Wook Shin and Kyung Moon Hwang, 43–50. Lanham, MD: Rowman and Littlefield, 2003.

Kafer, Alison. *Feminist, Queer, Crip*. Bloomington: Indiana University Press, 2013.

Kawai Kaori. *Seksŭ chawŏn pongsa: Ŏngnulin changaein ŭi sŏng* [Sex volunteers: Repressed sexuality of disabled people]. Translated by Yuk Min-hye. Seoul: Arom Media, 2005.

Kim Ch'ang-hwan. "Mom ŭl t'onghan kiŏk kwa 'oppa' ŭi narŭsisijŭm" [Memory through "the body" and the narcissism of "the brother"]. In *Han'guk nyu weibŭ ŭi chŏngch'ijŏk kiŏk* [The political memory of the Korean new wave], edited by Yŏnsedae Midiŏ Atŭ Yŏn'guso [Yonsei University Media Art Research Center], 195–218. Seoul: Yonsei University Press, 2007.

Kim Chong-chŏl. "Chŏhang kwa in'gan haebang ŭi liŏllijŭm" [Resistance and the realism of human liberation]. In *Kim Chŏng-han, taetchok katŭn sam kwa munhak* [Kim Chŏng-han: His upright life and literature], edited by Choe Wŏn-sik, 39–96. Seoul: Saemi, 2002.

Kim Chŏng-han. *Naktonggang ŭi p'asukkun* [The vigilant in the Naktong river]. Seoul: Han'gilsa, 1978.

———. "Oksimi" (1936). In *Sin Han'guk munhak chŏnjip* [The compilation of Korean literature] 17: 25–42. Seoul: Ŏmun'gak, 1975.

Kim Chŏng-ran. "Uahan sarang norae? *Aga*? Yi Mun-yŏl ŭi t'oehaengjŏk segyegwan" [A gracious love song? *Aga*? The degenerate worldview of Yi Mun-yŏl]. In *Yŏndusaek kŭlssŭgi* [Writing in light green], 217–237. Seoul: Saeum, 2001.

Kim Do Hyun [Kim To-hyŏn]. *Ch'abyŏl e chŏhang hara* [Fight discrimination]. Seoul: Pak Chong-chŏl Ch'ulp'ansa, 2007.

Kim Eunjung [Kim Ŭn-jŏng]. "Chŏngsangsŏng e tojŏn hanŭn yŏsŏngdŭl" [Women who challenge normality]. In *Han'guk yŏsŏng ingwŏn undongsa* [The history of the Korean women's rights movement], edited by Korean Association of Women's Hotline, 404–451. Seoul: Hanwool, 1999.

———. "Minority Politics in Korea." In *Intersectionality and Beyond: Law, Power, and the Politics of Location*, edited by Emily Grabham, Davina Cooper, Jane Krishnadas, and Didi Herman, 230–250. New York: Routledge-Cavendish, 2008.

———. "The Specter of Vulnerability and Bodies in Protest." *Disability, Human Rights, and The Limits of Humanitarianism*, edited by Michael Gill and Cathy Schlund-Vials, 137–154. Burlington, VT: Ashgate, 2014.

Kim Hye-su. "Sinyŏsŏng to 'tal' ŭl mŏgŏyaman haessŭlkka?" [Did the New Women also have to eat "the Moon"?] *Uri nara yŏsŏng ŭn ŏttŏke sarassŭlkka?* [How did Korean women live?] 1, edited by Yi Pae-yong, 50–72. Seoul: Chŏngnyŏnsa, 1999.

Kim Hyŏn. "Chayu wa sarang ŭi silch'ŏnjŏk hwahae" [Practical reconciliation of freedom and love]. In *Yi Chŏng-jun kip'i ilkki* [Reading Yi Chŏng-jun closely], edited by Kwŏn O-ryong, 218–233. Seoul: Munhak kwa Chisŏngsa, 1999.

Kim, Hyun Sook. "Yanggongju as an Allegory of the Nation: Images of Working-Class Women in Popular and Radical Texts." In *Dangerous Women: Gender and*

Korean Nationalism, edited by Elaine H. Kim and Chungmoo Choi, 175–202. New York: Routledge, 1998.

Kim, Jane Sung Hae. "Leprosy in Korea: A Global History." PhD diss., University of California, Los Angeles, 2012.

Kim, Kyung Hyun. "Korean Cinema and Im Kwon-Taek: An Overview." In *Im Kwon-Taek: The Making of a Korean National Cinema*, edited by David E. James and Kyung Hyun Kim, 19–46. Detroit, MI: Wayne State University Press, 2002.

———. *Virtual Hallyu: Korean Cinema of the Global Era*. Durham: Duke University Press, 2011.

Kim, Molly Hyo. "Genre Conventions of South Korean Hostess Films (1974–1982): Prostitutes and the Discourse of Female Sacrifice." *Acta Koreana* 17, no. 1 (2014): 455–477.

Kim T'ae-gye. "Nakt'ae choe e kwanhan munjechŏm kwa ippŏpnon" [Problems of abortion crime and legislation theory]. *Pŏphak yŏn'gu* [Legal studies] 18, no. 1 (2010): 233–261.

Kim Tong-ni. "Pawi" [The rock]. *Sindonga* [New East Asia] (May 1936): 322–335.

———. "Pawi" [The rock]. In *Munyŏdo* [The portrait of a shaman], 66–79. Seoul: Ŭlsŏ Munhwasa, 1947.

———. "The Rock." Translated by Kevin O'Rourke. *Korea Journal* 15, no. 11 (1975): 52–56.

Kim Ye-rim. "Chŏnsigi orak chŏngch'aek kwa 'munhwa' rosŏŭi usaenghak" [Entertainment policy and eugenics as a "culture" in wartime], *Yŏksa pip'yŏng* [Critical review of history] 73 (2005): 325–350.

Kim, Yoon-Shik. "Phases of Development of Proletarian Literature in Korea." *Korea Journal* 27, no. 1 (1987): 31–36.

Koh Boo Eung [Ko Pu-ŭng]. "Munhwa wa minjok chŏngch'esŏng" [Culture and ethno-national identity]. *Pip'yŏng kwa Iron* [Criticism and theory] 5, no. 2 (2000): 101–124.

Koh Dong-Yeon [Ko Tong-yŏn]. "Chŏnhu Han'guk yŏnghwa e tŭngjang hanŭn chuhan Migun ŭi imiji: *Chiokhwa* (1958) esŏ *Such'wiin pulmyŏng* (2001) kkaji" [Representing American GIs in postwar Korean cinema: From *The Flower in Hall* (1958) to *Address Unknown* (2001)]. *Miguksa Yŏngu* [Korean Journal of American History] 30 (2009): 147–172.

Korea Child Welfare Committee. *Handicapped Children's Survey Report*. Seoul: Korea Child Welfare Committee, 1962.

Kudlick, Catherine. "Smallpox, Disability, and Survival in Nineteenth-Century France: Rewriting Paradigms from a New Epidemic Script." In *Disability Histories*, edited by Susan Burch and Michael Rembis, 185–200. Champaign: University of Illinois Press, 2014.

Kuppers, Petra. "Toward the Unknown Body: Stillness, Silence and Space in Mental Health Settings." *Theater Topics* 10, no. 2 (2000): 129–143.

Kye Yong-muk. "Adada the Idiot." Translated by Morgan E. Clippinger. *Korea Journal* 14, no. 1 (1974): 45–52, 67.

————. "K'anggaru ŭi chosangi" [Kangaroo's ancestors]. In *Paekch'i Adada: Sin Han'guk munhak munjip 25* [Adada, the idiot: The compilation of new Korea literature], 82–100. Seoul: Ŏmungak, 1985.

————. "Paekch'i Adada" [Adada the idiot] (1935). In *Han'guk taep'yojak sŏnjip: Sosŏl* [Korean literature: Novels] 1: 194–205. Seoul: Myŏngmundang, 1994.

Kyŏngsŏng Cheguk Taehak Wisaeng Chosabu [Keijō imperial university hygiene inspection department]. *T'omangmin ŭi saenghwal kwa wisaeng* [1941] [Shanti dwellers' life and hygiene]. Translated by Pak Hyŏn-suk. Seoul: Minsokwŏn, 2010.

Lee Bang Hyun [Yi Pang-hyŏn]. "Singminji Chosŏn esŏŭi chŏngsin pyŏngja e taehan kŭndaejŏk chŏpkŭn" [A modern approach to treating mental patients in colonial Chosŏn]. *Korean Journal of Medical History* 22 (2013): 529–578.

Lee, Jin-Kyung. "Sovereign Aesthetics, Disciplining Emotion, and Racial Rehabilitation in Colonial Korea 1910–1922." *Acta Koreana* 8, no. 1 (2005): 77–107.

Lee Moon-sung [Yi Mun-sŏng]. "P'ansorigye sosŏl ŭi haeoe yŏngmun pŏnyŏk hyŏnhwang kwa chŏnmang" [A study on English publications of P'ansori's novels abroad]. *Han'gukhak yŏn'gu* [Korean studies research] 38 (2011): 259–285.

Lewiecki-Wilson, Cynthia. "Rethinking Rhetoric through Mental Disabilities." *Rhetoric Review* 22, no. 2 (2003): 156–167.

Lewis, Victoria Ann, and Nancy Becker Kennedy. *Tell Them I'm a Mermaid*. Embassy Television, Taper Media, Metromedia Television, 1984.

The Litany of Hope. Directed by Yang Sŭng-ryong. The Humphrey W. Leynse Collection, Films and Papers, 1916–1977. Manuscripts, Archives, and Special Collections, Cage 438, Washington State University Libraries, Pullman, Washington.

Livingston, Julie. "Insights from an African History of Disability." *Radical History Review*, no. 94 (2006): 111–126.

McCarthy, Michelle. "Whose Body Is It Anyway? Pressure and Control for Women with Learning Disabilities." *Disability and Society* 13, no. 4 (1998): 557–574.

McClintock, Anne. "Family Feuds: Gender, Nationalism and the Family." *Feminist Review* 44 (1993): 61–80.

————. *Imperial Leather: Race, Gender, and Sexuality in the Colonial Contest*. New York: Routledge, 1995.

McRuer, Robert. *Crip Theory: Cultural Signs of Queerness and Disability*. New York: New York University Press, 2006.

————. "Critical Investments: AIDS, Christopher Reeve, and Queer/Disability Studies." *Journal of Medical Humanities* 23, nos. 3–4 (2002): 221–237.

Michalko, Rod. *The Mystery of the Eye and the Shadow of Blindness*. Toronto: University of Toronto Press, 1998.

Miles, M. "Blindness in South and East Asia: Using History to Inform Development." In *Disability in Different Cultures: Reflections on Local Concepts*, edited by Brigitte Holzer, Arthur Vreede, and Gabrielle Weigt, 88–101. New Brunswick, NJ: Transaction, 1999.

Minh-ha, Trinh T. *Woman, Native, Other: Writing Postcoloniality and Feminism.* Bloomington: Indiana University Press, 1989.

Mitchell, David T., and Sharon S. Snyder. *Narrative Prosthesis: Disability and the Dependencies of Discourse.* Ann Arbor: University of Michigan Press, 2000.

Moon, Katharine H. S. "South Korean Movements against Militarized Sexual Labor." *Asian Survey* 39, no. 2 (1999): 310–327.

Mother Star in Heaven [*Hanŭl nara ŏmma pyŏl i*]. Directed by Yi Yŏng-u. 1981. VHS.

Mun So-jŏng. "Singminji sidae yŏsŏng nodong kwa mom ŭi ch'ehŏm" [Women's labor and bodily experiences during colonial period]. In *Han'guk sahoesa hakhoe haksul taehoe* [Conference of Korean scholarly association of social history], 120–132. Seoul: Han'guk Sahoesa Hakhoe, 2004.

Nakamura, Karen. "Barrier-Free Brothels: Sex Volunteers, Prostitutes, and People with Disabilities." In *Capturing Contemporary Japan: Differentiating and Uncertainty*, edited by Glenda Roberts, Satsuki Kawano, and Susan Orpett Long, 202–220. Honolulu: University of Hawai'i Press, 2014.

Nam Ta-ŭn. "Uri nŭn kŭnal ŭl nugu ŭi kiŏk ŭro sayu hanŭn'ga" [In whose memory do we think about that day]. In *Han'guk nyu weibŭ ŭi chŏngch'ijŏk kiŏk* [The political memory of the Korean new wave], edited by Yŏnsedae Midiŏ Atŭ Yŏn'guso [Yonsei University Media Art Research Center], 219–243. Seoul: Yonsei University Press, 2007.

Nel, Juan A., and Melanie Judge. "Exploring Homophobic Victimisation in Gauteng, South Africa: Issues, Impacts and Responses." *Acta Criminologica* 21, no. 3 (2008): 19–36.

Niehaus, Isak. "Leprosy of a Deadlier Kind: Christian Concepts of AIDS in the South African Lowveld." In *AIDS and Religious Practice in Africa*, edited by Felicitas Backer and Wentzel Geissler, 309–332. Leiden: Brill, 2009.

"Noch'ŏnyŏga" [A spinster's song] (1848). In *Uri kojŏn tasi ilkki: Samsŏlgi, Hwasa* [Rereading our traditional literature: *Samsŏlgi, Hwasa*], edited by Ku In-hwan, 108–115. Seoul: Sinwŏn Munhwasa, 2003.

Oasis [Oasisŭ]. Directed by Lee Chang-dong. 2000. DVD.

O'Toole, Corbett Joan, and Jennifer K. Bregante. "Disabled Women: The Myth of the Asexual Female." In *Sex Equity and Sexuality in Education*, edited by Susan S. Klein, 271–279. Albany: State University of New York Press, 1992.

Pak Chin-t'ae. *T'ongyŏng ogwangdae* [T'ongyŏng five jesters]. Seoul: Hwasan Munhwa, 1994.

Pak Sŏng-jin. "Ilcheha injong chuŭi t'ŭksŏng kwa chŏgyong hyŏngt'ae" [Characteristics and applications of racism during the Japanese colonial era]. *Han'guk kŭnhyŏndaesa yŏn'gu* [Korean modern and contemporary historical studies] no. 5 (1996): 89–113.

Pandya, Shubhada S. "The First International Leprosy Conference, Berlin, 1897: The Politics of Segregation." *História, Ciências, Saúde–Manguinhos* 10, suppl. 1 (2003): 161–177.

Pansy and Ivy [*Paenji wa tamjaengi*]. Directed by Kye Un-kyŏng. 2000. VHS.

Papa [*Appa*]. Directed by Yi Su-jin. 2004. DVD.

Park Hee Byoung [Pak Hŭi-byŏng]. "Pyŏngsin eŭi sisŏn: Chŏn'gŭndae t'aeksŭt'ŭ esŏŭi" [The gaze toward disabled people: In premodern texts]. *Kojŏn munkak yŏn'gu* [Traditional literature studies] 12 (2003): 309–361.

Park Young-Sook [Pak Yŏng-suk]. *Mich'innyŏn p'ŭrojekt'ŭ 1999–2005: Pak Yŏng-suk sajinjip* [Mad women project 1999–2005: Photographs by Park Young-Sook]. Seoul: Nunpit, 2005.

Parsons, Talcott. "Illness and the Role of the Physician." In *The Talcott Parsons Reader*, edited by Bryan S. Turner, 101–109. Malden, MA: Blackwell 1999.

A Petal [*Kkonnip*]. Directed by Chang Sŏn-u. 1996. DVD.

Peterson, Mark. *A Brief History of Korea*. New York: Infobase, 2010.

Piepzna-Samarasinha, Leah Lakshmi. "Letter from Leah Lakshmi Piepzna-Samarasinha." In *El Mundo Zurdo 2: Selected Works from the Meetings of the Society for the Study of Gloria Anzaldúa*, edited by Sonia Saldívar-Hull, Norma Alarcón, and Rita E. Urquijo-Ruiz, 91–97. San Francisco: Aunt Lute, 2012.

Pink Palace [*P'ingkŭ p'aelissŭ*]. Directed by Seo Dong-il [Sŏ Tong-il]. 2005. DVD.

Pyŏn In-sik. "Im Kwŏn-t'aek ŭi yŏnghwa e nat'anan in'gan hoebok ŭi t'emaron: *T'ik'et, Ssibaji, Adada* ŭi kyŏngu" [The study on the theme of the recovery of the human in Im Kwŏn-t'aek's films: The cases of *Ticket, Surrogate Mother, Adada*]. *Yŏnghwa yŏn'gu* [Film studies] 6 (October 1989): 39–54.

Price, Margaret. *Mad at School: Rhetorics of Mental Disability and Academic Life*. Ann Arbor: University of Michigan Press, 2011.

Puar, Jasbir. "Coda: The Cost of Getting Better: Suicide, Sensation, Switchpoints." GLQ: *A Journal of Lesbian and Gay Studies* 18, no. 1 (2012): 149–158.

Quayson, Ato. *Aesthetic Nervousness: Disability and the Crisis of Representation*. Toronto: University of Toronto Press, 2007.

Reynolds, David. *One World Divisible: A Global History since 1945*. New York: W. W. Norton, 2000.

Rhee Suk Koo [Yi Sŏk-gu]. "Yŏnghwa *Kkonnip* e nat'anan 'namsŏngjŏk sisŏn' kwa 'aedo' ŭi munje" ["Male gaze" and "mourning" in *A Petal*]. *Pigyo munhak* [Comparative literature] 47 (February 2009): 147–169.

Robertson, Jennifer. "Blood Talks: Eugenic Modernity and the Creation of New Japanese." *History and Anthropology* 13, no. 3 (2002): 191–216.

———. "Eugenics in Japan: Sanguinous Repair." In *The Oxford Handbook of the History of Eugenics*, edited by Alison Bashford and Philippa Levine, 430–448. New York: Oxford University Press, 2010.

Saito Ayako. "*Kkonnip* ŭi muge: Yŏksajŏk t'ŭrauma wa p'ongnyŏk ŭi chaehyŏn" [The weight of *A Petal*: Historical trauma and the representation of violence]. In *Han'guk nyu weibŭ ŭi chŏngch'ijŏk kiŏk* [The political memory of the Korean new wave], edited by Yŏnsedae Midiŏ Atŭ Yŏn'guso, 245–310. Seoul: Yonsei University Press, 2007.

Sase, E., M. Jimba, and S. Wakai. "Scar of Japan's Leprosy Isolation Policy in Korea," *Lancet* 363, no. 9418 (2004): 1396-1397.

Saunders, Frances Stonor. *The Cultural Cold War: The CIA and the World of Arts and Letters*. New York: W. W. Norton, 2001.

Sergeant Kim's Return from Vietnam [*Wŏlnam esŏ toraon Kim Sangsa*]. Directed by Yi Sŏng-gu. 1971. VOD.

Sex Volunteer: Open Secret, the First Story [*Seksŭ bolant'iŏ: Kongkongyŏnhan pimil, chŏt pŏnchae iyagi*]. Directed by Cho Kyeong-duk [Cho Kyŏng-dŏk]. 2009. DVD.

Shakespeare, Tom. *Disability Rights and Wrongs*. London: Routledge, 2006.

Shakespeare, Tom, Kath Gillespie-Sells, and Dominic Davies. *The Sexual Politics of Disability: Untold Desires*. London: Cassell, 1996.

Sherry, Mark. "(Post)colonizing Disability." *Wagadu: Journal of Transnational Women's and Gender Studies* 4 (2007): 10–22.

Shildrick, Margrit. *Dangerous Discourses of Disability, Subjectivity, and Sexuality*. New York: Palgrave Macmillan, 2009.

Shin, Gi-Wook. "Introduction." In *Contentious Kwangju*, edited by Gi-Wook Shin and Kyung Moon Hwang, xi–xxxi. Lanham, MD: Rowman and Littlefield, 2003.

Shin, Gi-Wook, and Michael Robinson. "Introduction: Rethinking Colonial Korea." In *Colonial Modernity in Korea*, edited by Gi-Wook Shin and Michael Robinson, 1–18. Cambridge, MA: Harvard University Asia Center, 1999.

Shin Young-Jeon [Sin Yŏng-jŏn]. "Singminji Chosŏn esŏ usaeng undong ŭi chŏn'gae wa sŏngkyŏk" [The characteristics of Korea's eugenic movement in the colonial period]. *Ŭisahak* [Korean Journal of Medical History] 15, no. 2 (2006): 133–155.

Sim Chŏng. Directed by An Sŏk-yŏng. 1937. VOD.

Sim Sŭng-gu. "Changae rŭl t'onghae pon Han'gugin ŭi mom insik: Chŏn'gŭndae rŭl chungsim ŭro." [Korean perception of body through disability: With a focus on the premodern period]. In *Han'gugin, mom ŭi sahoesa* [Koreans, the sociological history of the body], 22–28. Seoul: Han'guk Sahoesa Hakhoe 2004.

Sin Tong-il. *Usaenghak kwa hyŏngsa chŏngch'aek* [Eugenics and criminology]. Seoul: Han'guk Hyŏngsa Chŏngch'aek Yŏn'guwŏn [Korean Criminology Research Institute], 2007.

Snyder, Sharon L., and David T. Mitchell. *The Cultural Locations of Disability*. Chicago: University of Chicago Press, 2006.

Sŏ Chŏng-ju. "The Leper." Translated by In-soo Lee. *Korea Journal* 5, no. 10 (1965): 23.

So Hyŏn-suk. "Ilche sigi ch'ulsan t'ongje tamron yŏn'gu" [A study on discourses of birth control in colonial Korea]. *Yŏksa wa hyŏnsil* [History and reality] 38 (December 2000): 221–252.

Soh, Sarah. *The Comfort Women: Sexual Violence and Postcolonial Memory in Korea and Japan*. Chicago: University of Chicago Press, 2008.

Stevens, Bethany. "Interrogating Transability: A Catalyst to View Disability as Body Art." *Disability Studies Quarterly* 31, no. 4 (2011), n.p.

Stevenson, Lisa. *Life beside Itself: Imagining Care in the Canadian Arctic*. Berkeley: University of California Press, 2014.

Stiker, Henri-Jacques. *A History of Disability*. Ann Arbor: University of Michigan Press, 2000.

The Story of Ongnye [*Ongnye ki*]. Directed by Im Kwŏn-t'aek. 1977. VHS.

Suh, Ji-moon. "Yi Munyŏl." In *The Columbia Companion to Modern East Asian Literature*, edited by Joshua S. Mostow, 727–730. New York: Columbia University Press, 2003.

Tabide, K'asaro. "Ije kŏjitmal ŭl kŭman tuŏya: Chang Sŏn-u wa ŭi intŏbyu" [It's time to stop lying: Interview with Chang Sŏn-u]. In *Han'guk nyu weibŭ ŭi chŏngch'ijŏk kiŏk* [The political memory of the Korean new wave], edited by Yŏnsedae Midiŏ Atŭ Yŏn'guso, 363–407. Seoul: Yonsei University Press, 2007.

A Tale of Two Sisters [*Changhwa, Hongnyŏn*]. Directed by Kim Jee-woon [Kim Chi-un]. 2003. DVD.

Thumbelina Wants to Be a Mother [*Ŏmji Kongju, ŏmma ka toego sipŏyo*]. Directed by Yu Hae-jin. Munhwa Broadcasting Company, no. 1, May 15, 2007; no. 2, May 30, 2008; no. 3, May 29, 2009. VOD.

Titchkosky, Tanya. "The Ends of the Body as Pedagogic Possibility." *Review of Education, Pedagogy, and Cultural Studies* 34, nos. 3–4 (2012): 82–93.

Treichler, Paula. *How to Have Theory in an Epidemic: Cultural Chronicles of AIDS*. Durham: Duke University Press, 1999.

Turbayne, Colin Murray. *The Myth of Metaphor*. New Haven, CT: Yale University Press, 1962.

U Ch'an-je. "Uridŭl ŭi chŏn'guk ŭl hyanghan tangsindŭl ŭi chŏn'guk ŭi taehwa" [Dialogue of your paradise toward our paradise]. *Munhak kwa chisŏng* [Literature and intellectuality] (Spring 2003): 260–285.

Wasserman, David, and Adrienne Asch. "Understanding the Relationship between Disability and Well-Being." In *Disability and the Good Human Life*, edited by Jerome E. Bickenbach, Franziska Felder, and Barbara Schmitz, 141–167. New York: Cambridge University Press, 2015.

Watt, Frederick B. "Preface." In *The Memories and Reflections of Dr. Gerhard Armauer Hansen*, by Gerhard A. Hansen, 19–21. Würzburg: German Leprosy Relief Association, 1976.

Waxler, Nancy. "Learning to Be a Leper: A Case Study in the Social Construction of Illness." In *Social Contexts of Health, Illness, and Patient Care*, 169–194. New York: Cambridge University Press, 1981.

Wendell, Susan. *The Rejected Body: Feminist Reflections on Disability*. New York: Routledge, 1996.

Wilkerson, Abby. "Disability, Sex Radicalism, and Political Agency." *NWSA Journal* 14, no. 3 (2002): 33–57.

Won Mi-hye [Wŏn Mi-hye]. "Sŏng p'anmae yŏsŏng ŭi saengae ch'ehŏm yŏn'gu:

Kyoch'ajŏk sŏng wigye ŭi sigongganjŏk chagyong ŭl chungsim ŭro" [A life
history research of women who sell sex: The temporal and spatial operations of
intersectional sex hierarchy]. PhD diss., Ewha Womans University, 2010.

Yang, Hyunah. "Finding the Map of Memory: Testimony of the Japanese Military
Sexual Slavery Survivors." *positions* 16, no. 1 (2008): 79–107.

———. "Re-membering the Korean Military Comfort Women: Nationalism,
Sexuality, and Silencing." In *Dangerous Women: Gender and Korean
Nationalism*, edited by Elaine H. Kim and Chungmoo Choi, 123–149. New
York: Routledge, 1998.

Yi Chŏng-jun. *Tangsindŭl ŭi chŏn'guk* [Your paradise] (1976). Seoul: Munhak kwa
Chisŏngsa, 1996.

———. "*Tangsindŭl ŭi chŏn'guk*: Sara innŭn chuin'gong Cho Ch'ang-wŏn
Wŏnjangnim kke" [*Your Paradise*: Dear director Cho Ch'ang-wŏn, the living
protagonist]." In *Yi Chŏng-jun kip'i ilkki* [Reading Yi Chŏng-jun closely], edited
by O Ryong Kwŏn, 361–369. Seoul: Munhak kwa Chisŏngsa, 1999.

———. *Your Paradise*. Translated by Jennifer M. Lee and Timothy R. Tangherlini.
Los Angeles: Green Integer, 2004.

Yi Hun-sang. *Kasan ogwangdae* [Kasan five jesters]. Seoul: Kungnip Munhwajae
Yŏn'guso, 2004.

Yi Hyo-sŏk. "Sanhyŏp" [A mountain valley] (1941). In *Han'guk hyŏndae taep'yo
sosŏlsŏn* [Korean modern novel selection], vol. 4: 339–365. Seoul: Ch'angjak
kwa Pip'yŏngsa, 1996.

Yi Kwang-su. *Minjok kaejoron* [The ethnicity reform theory] (1922). Seoul: Unsinsa,
1979.

Yi Kyŏng-min. "Sajin sinbu, kyorhon e olin hada: Hawai imin kwa sajin kyŏrhon ŭi
t'ansaeng 1" [Picture-brides, gamble in Marriage: Emigration to Hawai'i and the
birth of picture-marriage 1]. *Hwanghae Munhwa* [Yellow Sea culture] 56 (fall
2007): 402–411.

———. "Sajin sinbu, kyorhon e olin hada: Hawai imin kwa sajin kyŏrhon ŭi
t'ansaeng 2" [Picture-brides, gamble in marriage: Emigration to Hawai'i and
the birth of picture-marriage 2]. *Hwanghae Munhwa* [Yellow Sea culture] 57
(winter 2007): 406–414.

Yi Kyu-t'ae. "Sorokto ŭi pallan [Rebellion of Sorokto]." *Sasanggye* (October 1966):
334–361.

Yi Mun-yol [Yi Mun-yŏl]. *Aga: Hŭimihan yetsarang ŭi kŭrimja* [The song of songs:
Faint shadow of old love]. Seoul: Minŭmsa, 2000.

———. "An Anonymous Island." Translated by Heinz Insu Fenkl. *New Yorker*,
September 12, 2011, 72–77.

Yi Myŏng-ja, and Hwang Hye-jin. "70-yŏndae ch'eje ihaenggi ŭi Nambukhan pigyo
yŏnghwasa: Chibae ideollogi wa yŏnghwajŏk chaehyŏn sai ŭi panyŏng kwa
ch'ungdol" [North and South Korean comparative film history of the 1970s:
Projections and crashes between dominant ideology and filmic representation].

Report submitted to the Korean Film Council. Seoul: Yŏnghwa Chinhŭng Wiwŏnhoe, 2004.

Yŏngja's Heydays [*Yŏngja ŭi chŏnsŏng sidae*]. Directed by Kim Ho-sŏn. 1975. DVD.

Yŏnsedae Midiŏ Atŭ Yŏn'guso [Yonsei University Media Art Research Center], ed. *Han'guk nyu weibŭ ŭi chŏngch'ijŏk kiŏk* [The political memory of the Korean new wave]. Seoul: Yonsei University Press, 2007.

Yoon, Jung-ho. "Disability as a Metaphor of Social Transformation in Korean Literature." *Journal of the Southwest Conference on Asian Studies* 4 (2003): 1–29.

Yu Chu-hyŏn. "T'aeyang ŭi yusan" [Inheritance of the Sun] *Han'guk munhak tae chŏnjip* 26 [Korean literature compilation 26], 270–280. Seoul: Hagwŏn Ch'ulp'an Kongsa, 1996.

Yu Kang-ha. "Togani sindŭrom ŭl t'onghae pon munhak ŭi ch'iyujŏk ŭimi e taehayŏ" [A study of healing power of literature through Togani syndrome]. *Asia munhwa yŏn'gu* [Asian culture studies] 27 (2012): 147–171.

Yun In-sŏn. "Pŏrim padŭn ttal, Sim Chŏng" [Abandoned daughter Sim Chŏng]. *Han'guk ŏnŏ munhak* [Korean language literature] 49 (2002): 113–139.

Yuval-Davis, Nira. "Gender and Nation." In *Space, Gender, Knowledge: Feminist Readings*, edited by Linda McDowell and Joanne P. Sharp, 403–407. New York: Arnold, 1997.

Zenderland, Leila. "The Parable of *The Kallikak Family*: Explaining the Meaning of Heredity in 1912." In *Mental Retardation in America: A Historical Reader*, edited by Steven Noll and James W. Trent Jr., 165–185. New York: New York University Press, 2004.

nition of, 6; environmental, 4, 95; and epidemics, 195; family and, 13, 82, 90, 98, 105, 233 (*see also* piety, filial); beyond family, 92, 107; gender and, 71, 131; gender conformity and, 10; of Hansen's disease, 166, 170, 172–76, 182–85, 190–91, 196; Hansen's disease, plastic surgery and, 185–86; harms of, 143; and heredity, 54; heterosexuality and, 169, 188, 198, 207, 215; of illness, 13–14; imperative of, 8, 21, 25, 84, 86, 120, 176, 228, 232; killing as, 53; Korean definition of, 3; marriage as a symbol of, 188, 192–93; medical, 9, 18, 79, 96, 98, 117, 124, 137; of mental disability, 106, 107, 147; of mental illness, 33; metaphor of, 92, 250n21; multiple meanings of, 17; nation-state and, 4; nonmedical, 9; objection to sterilization and, 66; obligation of, 38; politics of, 168; presence of disability before and after, 9; process, 9; by proxy, 39, 83, 104, 105, 113; rehabilitation, 8, 99–100, 106, 109, 113, 168; reproduction, 57, 72; as reward, 99, 101; sacrifice for, 82, 91, 94, 118; vs. self-injury, 118, 142; sexuality and, 10; of sexually transmitted disease, 110, 261n43; spectacles of, 1–4; suicide and, 120, 159; time and, 8, 229, 231; as transability, 12–13; as transaction, 139; as transformation, 8; transnational politics of, 184, 187; trauma and, 114, 117, 148; violence as, 15, 110, 131, 138, 142, 165, 182–83, 186, 218
curedness, 84, 169, 232

Darwin, 46, 241n10; social Darwinism, 259n16
Das, Veena, 231
deafness, 25, 26, 29–30, 35, 38, 39, 127, 132, 134–35, 210, 237n35; colonial education for, 34, 58; and heritability, 63; heritage, 62; Korean term for, 27; residential school, 163–65; sexuality and, 204; shame and, 16
death drive, 84, 118–20
debility, 18–19, 47
decolonial feminism, 18

dehumanization, 140, 141, 156
deinstitutionalization movement, 36, 125, 130–31
dependency: curative, 39, 114, 118; rhetorical, 201
desexualization, 57, 220
Diagnostic and Statistical Manual of Mental Disorders, 84, 252n66
diagnostic gaze, 154
disability, 12, 39, 41, 57, 60, 66–67, 76, 83, 91, 97, 100–101, 103, 104, 110–13, 118, 125, 132, 133, 158, 165, 202, 217, 220, 228; abortion based on, 65, 68, 69, 74, 243n40; acquired, 25, 77, 229; vs. antidisability ideology, 62, 233; and binary genders, 78, 247n102; biracial status as, 139; as burden, 26, 47, 55, 84, 102, 120, 227, 231, 233; categories of, 25, 27, 36; cause of, 90, 94; and charity, 128; as colonial body politic, 3, 32–33; and cultural difference, 228–30; as culture, 24; curedness as, 169; definitions of, 26, 140; desire for, 12–13; as difference, 29; disappearance of, 2; discrimination based on, 37, 190, 207, 208, 222, 229, 243n40; disfiguring of, 9, 96, 137, 226; documentaries on, 70–71, 77, 217; elimination of, 80; and eugenics, 45, 46, 48, 50, 64; experiences of, 21, 24; exploitation of, 106, 233; gender and, 113, 201, 208, 216, 250n34; genetic, 12, 72; and Hansen's disease, 173, 194; hereditary, 55–56, 58, 70; hierarchy of, 77, 127, 135, 211; history of, 9, 11, 225, 226; and humanity, 27; identity, 3, 18, 20; vs. illness, 13–14; and infertility, 129; intellectual, 126, 134–35, 164, 249, 254n7; Korean terms for, 26; management, 229; meanings of, 17, 232; medical model of, 6; mental, 34, 35, 38, 87, 107, 115, 123, 134, 143, 146–48, 152–53, 159, 162–63; 256n66, 256n67, 256–57n85; metaphor, 20, 32, 109, 236n18; and miracle, 39, 53, 87, 111, 186; as moral signifier, 113, 136; as moral test, 102; muteness, 10, 25, 132, 134–35, 148–49; physical, 75, 122, 204, 212; as political, 38, 155; oppression, 197, 234;

disability (*continued*)

overcoming, 73, 99; premodern perception of, 29–31; presence of, 7, 9, 59, 79, 95, 117, 226; and present, 227; privatized narratives of, 38; registration and rating system of, 36–37, 252n71; representations of, 24, 197; reproduction of, 44, 51, 54, 70, 74; restoration of, 118, 137, 142, 143; as risk, 72; sex trade and, 203, 210; sexuality, 198–200, 209; simulation of, 163; as social and economic product, 33; social rejection of, 53, 58, 63, 71; as species diversity, 16; speech, 93; status, 22, 27, 57, 72, 87, 113, 138, 142, 211; and survival, 195; as symbol, 20, 250n34; synchronicity of, 230; as tragedy, 160; transference of, 86, 88, 89; uncured, 97; unmothering, 75, 85; and welfare spending, 253n77

Disability–Adjusted Life Year (DALY), 227

disability rights movement, 6, 8, 18, 35–36, 68, 69, 130, 119; 130; activism, 5, 21, 119, 125, 222, 253n77; on cure, 13, 234; history of, 35–36, 240n104; Seoul Paralympics, 35

disability studies, 38, 86; feminist, 74, 146, 243n40; on infectious disease, 194–95; on medical cure, 6–7; queer, 195; transnational feminist, 17–18; Western, 6, 18, 50

disabled bodies, 9, 19, 126, 169; and capitalism, 36; and cure, 25; cured bodies as, 12; and despair, 137; difference of, 18; disruptive potential of, 79; and future, 8; and humanity, 83; as national body, 33, 92; performed by nondisabled women, 159; as prehuman, 124; presence of, 3, 95, 194; removal of, 120; as undesirable, 233; violence against, 32, 165

disabled embodiment, 3, 14, 84, 142; and cure, 84; metaphorization of, 138; of personhood, 31

disabled veterans, 34, 35, 39, 105–8, 139

disabled women's movement, 9, 12, 21–24; and reproduction, 68; against sexual violence, 122, 124; and transgender movement, 247–48n102. *See also* Changae Yŏsŏng Konggam

Disabled Women's Sexual Violence Counseling Center, 122

Disabled Women's Village, 233–34

dissociative identity disorder, 114, 252n66

Donaldson, Elizabeth J., 146, 256–57n85

Dutiful Daughter Chŏng (Sin Sang-ok), 39, 86, 92–95

East Asia, 92; cultures of, 230; European expansion to, 31; idealization of, 128; leprosy in, 172

economy: as agrarian, 101; domestic, 102; 105; moral, 95; neoliberal, 18–19; shifting, 31; and survival, 110

Edmond, Rod, 167

education, 19, 23, 24, 55, 59, 99, 193, 227; and eugenics, 47–48; as habilitation, 228; about Hansen's disease, 195; and *hyo*, 87; as inaccessible, 22; segregated, 164–65; sex, 45, 46; special, 36, 58; Yi Kwang-su, 241n16

employment, 36, 51, 52, 96, 107, 193; lack of, 78, 165

English language, 82, 125, 166, 181, 184, 226, 260n26, 264; and adoption, 140; as dominant language, 138–39, 141–43; literature on madness, 146

enlightenment, 32, 44, 47, 92, 241n16; vs. ignorance, 192; as period, 239n86

epidemics, 171, 195–96

Erevelles, Nirmala, 17–18

erotophobia, 201, 215, 221

ethnicity, 9, 16, 18, 45, 46, 48, 50, 60; as disability, 37

ethno-nation, Chosŏn, 4, 47, 48, 155; as *minjok*, 46, 47, 49, 100, 241n16

Eugenic Atlantic, 47

eugenics, 25, 33, 79; as anticolonial, 48; colonial, 47–48, 50; cultural, 48, 63; cultural representation of, 38; as elimination of disability, 59; eugenic modernity, 43, 240n2; eugenic traits, 42; and family, 43–46, 64; Han Ha-un, 187; and Helen Keller, 58; as ideology, 44, 62; vs. infanticide, 45, 49; legalization of, 64, 186; and marriage, 54; and modernization,

Han Ha-un, 169–70, 184, 186–87, 223, 225, 258n3, 263n87, 263n90; "Barley Stem Flute," 186. See also *The Litany of Hope*

Han Hye-sŏn, 183

Handicapped Children's Survey Report, 34, 138, 173

Handmaid's Tale, The (Atwood), 71

Hansen, Gerhard Armauer, 166–68, 258n2, 259n20

Hansen's disease, 34, 40, 45, 69; Aeyangwŏn and, 223–25; antistigma campaign for, 166; cannibalism, 174–76; disability studies and, 196; and HIV/AIDS, 168, 194–95; institution for people with, 99; legal advocacy and, 190–91; medical vs. cultural cure for, 169–70; and organizations, 195; origin of the term, 167–68, 258n2; segregation of people with, 50, 166, 168, 170–73, 176, 183, 190, 192–94, 196, 232. See also *Ah! Sorokto*; *The Litany of Hope*; "Oksimi"; "The Rock"; *Your Paradise*

Hansenin: and *Ah! Sorokto*, 192–93; definition of, 172; and Han Ha-un, 187; human rights violations of, 183; and legal advocacy, 191; *The Litany of Hope*, 185; and marriage, 190; massacre of, 166, 172, 191; *migama* as, 173; and missing children, 176; protests of, 261n49; and Sorokto, 196

Hansenin Incidents Law, 191

Haraway, Donna, 230

health, 37, 84; and abortion, 65, 68, 245n75; and biopower, 236–37n33; and consumption, 19; and cure, 6, 9, 105; and deafness, 62; and eugenics, 45–47, 49, 61, 64–66, 242n25; of family, 46, 95, 169; as healthiness, 14, 26, 33, 127, 171, 189–190, 193, 227, 260n29; and humanity, 27; and marriage, 58; and morality, 28–29, 152; and reproduction, 59; and sexuality, 214–15, 220

health care, 7, 168; medical care, 6, 7, 32, 152

hegemony: American, 137, 143; of West, 104

heredity drama, 38, 44, 54, 72, 75, 79; and biraciality, 60; and deafness, 62; definition of, 51, 232; and infertility, 59

heteronormativity, 16, 55, 198, 202; and cure, 29, 30, 40, 132, 184, 198; and family,

194; and femininity, 16, 52; heterosexuality, 10–13, 17, 28, 71, 105, 112, 124, 212, 215, 232; and marriage, 29, 113, 169, 199, 233; presumptive heterosexuality, 15

Hinzpeter, Jurgen, 144

HIV/AIDS: and abortion, 245n79; coalitions, 24; and cure, 13; as disability, 36; and Hansen's disease, 168, 194–95

Hubert, Henri, 91

human, 59, 135, 171; and biopower, 237–38n33; categories of, 12, 16; eugenics, 46–51, 53, 55; extinction of, 56–57; as humanity, 26, 27, 40, 83, 124–25, 156, 169, 170, 185, 186, 198, 242–25n16; vs. non-human, 10, 11, 28, 132, 138, 140–41, 149, 150–51, 183, 206; normative criteria of, 83; as species, 55, 56, 58, 152

humanitarianism, 38, 98, 153, 166, 183, 187, 225–26; curative, 232; and eugenics, 45, 49, 67; sexual, 41, 198–99, 209, 211–12, 216, 225–26, 232

human rights, 134, 193–95; coalitions, 24; disability activism, 22, 23, 67; of disabled women, 126, 193; films, 37, 120, 164; Hansen's disease, 172, 183, 190–91, 263n90; National Human Rights Commission, 37; reproductive rights as, 66; and UN, 35, 99; violations of, 19, 37, 69, 216

Hwang Hye-jin, 100–101, 104

Hwang Ji-sung, 74

Hwang Sŏk-yŏng, 92

Hwang Sun-wŏn, 69

Hwang, Woo Suk: and cloning, 1, 4, 5; conviction of, 4; and Kang Won Rae, 235–36n11; and postage stamp, 2, 3; and Reeve, 2

hyo, 81, 86–87, 91, 97, 100, 105, 118. See also piety, filial

hysterectomy: of Ashley X, 231; and menstruation, 15, 204–5, 212–13

idiocy, 45, 128, 134–35, 241n10, 255n50

If You Were Me, 37, 120

Im Kwon-Taek, 100, 134. See also *Adada*; *The Story of Ongnye*

"Immoral Woman," The, 178. See also "Oksimi"

Leprosy Prevention Law (Japan), 191

leprosy, 27, 50, 64, 139, 170, 171, 192, 241n10; and cannibalism, 174–76; disappearance of, 170; vs. Hansen's disease, 167; and HIV, 194, 264n111; hostility toward, 178, 180, 182; isolation of affected people, 177; and kinship, 173; leper, 259n4; management of, 45, 172, 181, 183, 187, 195; vs. skin diseases, 261; usage of term, 168, 258n2. See also Hansen's disease; Han Ha-un

liminality, 11, 17, 62, 139, 232; nepantla, 17

Litany of Hope, The (Yang Sŭng-ryong), 40, 169, 184–87, 192, 223, 225

Little Mermaid, The (Andersen), 10–11

Livingston, Julie, 18

madness, 142, 145, 146, 154, 158, 159; and eugenics, 45, 55; madwoman, 143–46, 155, 158, 159, 160, 162–63; performance of, 160, 162, 163, 154, 256n66; qualification for, 57

Mad Women Project, The (Park Young-Sook), 159–63

Marathon, 39, 86

marriage, 52, 54, 71, 76, 93, 112, 129, 132, 203; and age, 45, 77, 127, 242n18; arranged, 30–31, 44, 45, 62–63, 103–4, 132, 133, 135, 136, 213; broker, 88, 100; coerced, 131; demystifying, 78; emotionalization of, 43; and eugenics, 42–43, 45, 48, 51, 242n18; extramarital reproduction, 139; fantasy of, 75; free, 45–46, 51; heterosexual, 29, 113, 169, 199, 233; modern, 42, 46, 51, 58, 59, 136; prohibition of, 263n85; and promotion of, 200, 247n100; proposal, 12; qualification for, 29, 30, 44, 57, 70, 101; rationalization of, 42–43, 50, 240n2; rehabilitation and, 168, 189, 194; rejection of, 39, 212; and sexuality, 217, 266n31; as symbol, 40, 187, 190, 192–93, 232

masculinity, 21, 27, 40, 105, 107, 125, 142, 197, 233

Mauss, Marcel, 91

McClintock, Anne, 2, 20–21

McRuer, Robert, 7, 124, 143

melodrama, 108, 197, 198, 205, 207, 216, 219, 232

menstruation, 127, 131, 200, 205, 212

mental disability. See disability: mental

mental health, 22, 134, 135, 163

mental illness, 31, 127, 143, 146, 159; colonial law, 32–33; and eugenics, 42, 64, 241n10; and family, 34; and religious cure, 33, 34; supernaturality, 117; and traditional Korean medicine, 33; usage of term, 256n66

Michel, Foucault, 170, 236–37n33

migama, 188, 189, 190; definition of, 173

Miles, M., 128

Minh-ha, Trinh T., 25

Ministry of Patriots and Veterans Affairs, 107

minjok, 46, 47, 49, 241n16

Minju (on Papa), 214–219

Minsun (on Mother Star in Heaven), 96–99

Mitchell, David, 47, 109, 238n69

Modern Girl, 135–36

modernity, 44, 128, 180, 185, 223; colonial, 26, 45, 47, 224–25; eugenic, 43, 240n2; vs. violence, 192

Moon, Katharine, 21

morality, 44, 220, 249n16; and cure, 14; disability and, 113; and eugenics, 46, 57; of masses, 29; 101; mental health as, 134; new, 46; reproduction and, 79, 80; sexual, 60, 105, 110, 129; spiritual, 232; traditional, 81, 179; women's, 101, 177

Mother and Child Health Act, 35, 50, 64–65, 68, 243n40, 263n84

Mother Star in Heaven (Yi Yŏng-u), 39, 86, 96–99

motherhood: biological, 70; and disability status of child, 71; of disabled women, 85, 233; naturalized, 180, 183; and risk of disability, 74

"Mountain Valley," A (Yi Hyo-sŏk), 39, 59

mourning, 141, 148; and Kwangju, 257–58n120

Munbo (on "The Kangaroo's Ancestor"), 54–62, 79

muteness, 10, 25, 132–35, 148, 149; of film, 250n21

Na, Tari Youngjung, 5, 220, 234

nation-state, 17, 18, 104, 234; as benefactor, 3; and benevolence, 113; branding of, 4; capitalist, 40, 50; and cure, 9; as defective, 29; and Eugenic Atlantic, 47; and family, 118; and Hansen's disease, 166; hierarchy of, 171; postcolonial, 121, 183; and rehabilitation, 87; sovereign, 16, 20, 61; spectacle of, 2; and violence, 155

National Basic Living Security Law, 119

National Human Rights Commission of Korea, 37

nationalism, 5, 9, 22, 91, 101, 105, 106, 138, 232; and anti-Americanism, 144; and biopolitics, 48; and eugenics, 50, 67; and gender, 21, and hyo, 86; maternal, 100, 142; metaphors of, 21; and rehabilitation, 98; spectacle of, 2

Nazism, 45, 50, 69, 192

nepantla: definition of, 17

neoliberalism, 18–19, 199, 209, 253n77

New Woman, 46, 55, 132, 241n14; vs. Old Woman, 135

nondisability, 11, 13, 26, 58, 72; engineering of, 80; mothering, 78–79

non-Western societies, 18, 41, 170; as backward, 229, 230

normalcy, 26, 33, 37, 84–86, 143, 150, 160, 185

normality, 4, 10, 40, 121, 185; approximation of, 8, 226, 228; compulsory, 83; and crossing, 11, 30–31, 137, 232; desirability of, 13, 19; as nondisability, 26; vs. otherness, 17, 24; and sacrifice, 95; sightedness as, 99; of society, 164

normativity, 18, 26, 142; and aesthetics, 138; of body, 11, 16, 113, 126; of family, 24, 50, 87; of femininity, 31, 131; of functioning, 2, 22; of gender roles, 232; and heterosexuality, 16, 199, 202, 207; and human, 83; and intimacy, 79; and moral status, 84; vs. nonnormative bodies, 143, 218; of past and future, 4; of personhood, 13; pressure of, 10; of reproductive prognosis, 63; of society, 3; of violence, 15, 236n32; and wholeness, 147

North Korea, 34, 35, 92, 95, 139, 143, 184, 187, 251n42

O'Connor, Sean, 12

Oasis (Lee Chang-dong), 38, 122, 124, 126, 157–58, 219

Oksim (on "Oksimi"), 176–80, 183

"Oksimi" (Kim Chŏng-han), 40, 169, 176–80, 183

Ongnye (on *The Story of Ongnye*), 100–105

Ŏnnyŏni (on "The Ugly Creature"), 51–54, 58, 80

oppression, 17; class-based, 22; disability, 38, 197, 219, 220, 234; and happiness, 9; and imperative of betterment, 118; and imperialism, 136–37; interlocking nature of, 7; patriarchal, 159; and sex industry, 202; sexual, 41, 198, 221; and social and material conditions, 23; systems of, 6; and violence, 20, 124, 162; of women, 230

osteogenesis imperfecta (OI), 70, 72, 74

otherness, 9, 11, 17, 24, 31, 38, 230

Pak Chi-won, 29

Pak Kyu-sang, 64

Pandya, Shubhada S., 171–72

panoptical time, 2

Pansy and Ivy (Kye Un-kyŏng), 39, 75–79

Papa (Yi Su-jin), 41, 198, 217–19, 221

Park Chung Hee, 34, 61, 104, 144, 186, 188, 263n84, 263n93; and Yushin system, 35, 64, 104

Park Hee Byoung, 28

Park Young-hee, 125–26, 219

Park Young-Sook: *Mad Women Project*, 159–63

Parsons, Talcott, 95

passivity, 5, 95

peasants: and factory labor, 178; exploitation of, 134, 176; uprising, 31, 177

Peppermint Candy, 158–59

Petal, A (Chang Sŏn-u), 40, 125, 144, 147, 149, 155–58, 159, 160, 162, 165, 256n72

pharmakon, 14, 148, 165, 236n31

phenomenology, 146, 149

picture-brides, 88, 93, 101, 250n24

Piepzna-Samarasinha, Leah Lakshmi, 17

piety, filial, 39, 81–82, 86, 89–90, 93, 98, 100, 101, 103, 232, 249n16; as ideology, 91; as national ethos, 96

piety, marital, 99

piety, religious, 84

Pink Palace (brothel), 204

Pink Palace (Seo Dong-il), 41, 198, 202–8, 212, 219, 221

polio, 225–26

preimplantation genetic diagnosis (PGD), 44, 71–74

Promotion of Employment of Disabled Persons Act, 36

proxy, 90, 93, 95, 99, 103, 107, 108, 113, 115, 119, 215, 255n63; curative, 86, 87, 89, 92, 104, 105; definitions of, 39, 83, 84–85; Münchausen syndrome by, 84; within oneself, 114, 116, 117–18; proxyhood, 83–86, 97, 98, 105, 108, 233

Puar, Jasbir, 18–19

public health, 33, 48, 49, 95, 181, 192, 194–95

pulguja, 25, 33

pyŏngsin, 25, 27–29, 110

Pyŏn In-sik, 135

Quayson, Ato, 20, 54

queer, 9, 143, 195

race, 9, 11, 16, 18, 57, 60, 138, 142, 232; abortion based on, 243n40; and eugenics, 44, 47, 48, 241–42n16

rape, 38, 109, 110, 122, 123, 127, 137, 142, 145, 146, 149–51, 155–57, 164; and abortion, 65, 68; corrective, 17, 237n43; as curative, 16, 219; as favor, 124–25; incestuous, 41, 198, 217–19; of sex workers, 21

rationality, 46, 51, 56, 57, 184, 196; of New Woman, 55; rationalization, 50, 213, 240n2; and violence, 137

red-light district, 92, 152, 203, 206–7, 214

Reeve, Christopher: on AIDS, 6, 13–14; and Nuveen Super Bowl commercial, 2–4, 7–8

rehabilitation, 5, 9, 41, 86, 98, 99, 101, 106, 108–9, 113, 117, 195, 232, 234; centers for, 127; of Chosŏn ethnicity, 50; as condition of charity, 97; cultural, 189, 193, 194; definitions of, 8, 227–28; drama, 105; family and, 78; and marriage, 168; of nation, 3–4, 8, 47, 87, 242n18; obligation of, 38; as power to govern, 19; racial, 241–42n16; services for, 37; of sex worker, 111, 112; Sorokto, 174; and UN, 228; and will to rehabilitate, 99

reincarnation, 39, 82, 93, 94, 114

relationality, 18, 85, 114, 118, 155

religion, 9, 18; abortion, 64, 66; and cure, 14, 30, 83, 89, 118; as differences, 175; and Hansen's disease, 166, 185; and mental illness, 33; and reward, 39; and sacrifice, 91, 94; and sex volunteering, 213; symbol of, 182–83

reproduction, 78, 193, 199, 232; and able-genderedness and able-bodiedness, 30; and curative intervention, 38, 44; curative violence and, 80; and deafness, 62; and degeneration, 55–56, 57; and disability as risk, 71; of disabled populations, 58, 67; and disabled women's activism, 22; disavowed, 200; and ethno-nation, 241n16; exploitation of surrogate, 69–70, 247n100; failure of, 90, 129; and family, 113; as genetically engineered, 74; and heredity drama, 51; illegitimate, 60; and labor, 101; of nondisability, 79; population control, 242n25; in premodern narrative, 29; prohibited, 76; quality of, 59; risk-free, 72; and state's control, 68; and transformation, 53, 54

Rhee, Syngman, 34

risk: of cure, 7, 13, 14; curing, 75; disability as, 72; and fetal disability, 245n79; or normalization, 201; and reproduction, 70, 72–74; speculative, 13, 138, 143, 232; of transmission, 193, 195

Robertson, Jennifer, 42–43, 240n2

Robinson, Michael, 45

"Rock" The (Kim Tong-ni), 40, 169, 180–83

Roh Moo Hyun, 1

Ruin, 247–48n102
R.U.R. (Rossum's Universal Robots) (Čapek),
  55–56, 57, 244n54
Ryu Mi-rye, 78

Sabangji (from Chosŏn dynasty), 28, 31
sacrifice: and cure, 83, 84, 95, 97, 99, 107,
  108; of family, 70, 119, 232, 233; of human
  life, 38, 39, 81, 82, 90–91, 94, 96, 118, 119;
  hyo, 87; and murder as, 136; and prejudice, 63; volunteering as, 209, 211
Saito Ayako, 155–56
Sase, Eriko, 195
Sejo (king), 28
Seo Dong-il, 198, 202–5. See also Pink Palace
Sergeant Kim's Return from Vietnam (Yi
  Sŏng-gu), 39, 87, 105–8, 109, 113
Sessions, The, 215
sex drive: of disabled men, 198, 202, 209;
  of disabled people, 200, 217, 220, 221;
  discourse of, 41, 199, 207, 219; representations of, 217
sex education, 45, 46
sex industry, 216; for disabled customers, 204; disabled people's experiences
  within, 221; police violence, 217; women
  in, 24, 109, 110, 202, 208, 209
sex surrogate, 198, 209
sex trade, 139, 200, 212, 214; Act on the Prevention of the Sex Trade and Protection
  of Its Victims, 205–6; anti–sex trade,
  207, 208, 215; disabled women in, 210;
  illegality of, 203; instrumentalization of,
  209; legalizing, 208; politics and, 221; and
  sexual oppression, 219; vs. specialized
  sexual services, 201–2
sex trafficking, 203
sexual assault, 52, 102, 122, 123, 127, 131, 219;
  and abortion, 64; abuse, 163
sexuality, 9, 16, 18, 75, 131, 137, 140, 203;
  anxiety about, 201; as awakened, 200;
  disabled, 112; and disabled women's
  movement, 22, 219; disciplining, 180;
  discrimination in, 215; as diversity, 216;
  essentialized, 205; and eugenics, 51, 55;
  hegemonic ideas about, 232; marginal-

ization by, 141; perceived hypersexuality,
  200; in premodern context, 26–31; privilege of, 212; as problems, 40, 198, 202,
  216, 217, 221; and rehabilitation, 78; representations of, 198, 217; repression of,
  204; as resource, 128; as sex drive, 220;
  and sex trade, 208, 209; social denial of,
  123, 197, 199, 218; and subjectivity, 202; as
  threat, 57, 66, 105; unruly, 109, 129. See
  also asexuality; heteronormativity
sexual liberalism, 201
sexual minorities, 22, 24, 220, 221, 222
sexual rights, of disabled people, 200, 202,
  208, 211, 213, 222
Sex Volunteer (Cho Kyeong-duk), 15, 41,
  198, 205, 211–17
Sex Volunteers (Kawai Kaori), 41, 198,
  209–11, 212
sex work, 111, 139–40
sex workers, 22, 198, 216, 217, 221; children
  of, 140; disabled, 109, 110, 210; and disabled men, 197–98, 203–5, 207, 212, 284;
  and disabled people, 214; and disabled
  women, 209; and foreign soldiers, 21,
  139; institutionalization of, 37; and Pink
  Palace, 208; sexual laborers, 222; vs. sex
  volunteers, 211; transgender, 209; violence against, 111
Sex Workers Day, 208
Shakespeare, Tom, 211
Shildrick, Margrit, 199, 201
Shin, Gi-wook, 45
Sim (on the Story of Sim Chŏng), 82, 84,
  89–91, 93–94, 97, 118, 249n7, 251n38
Sim Chŏng (Hwang Sok-yŏng), 92
Sim Chŏng (An Sŏk-yŏng, 1937), 39, 86,
  88–90, 89, 103; Hawai'i screening of,
  81, 88
Sim Chŏng: as exploited women, 93; film
  adaptions of, 251n42; in Kyŏngp'anbon,
  90; as metaphor, 92, 250n34; origins of,
  81–82; as proxy, 83, 117, 118; as religious
  offering, 91; Story of, 39, 81, 82, 87,
  101,103; in textbooks, 87–88, 96; translation of, 90. See also Dutiful Daughter
  Chŏng; Mother Star in Heaven

Sim Ch'ŏng (Yu Chong-mi), 250n30

Sim the Blind (Ch'ae Man-sik), 118

Sin Tong-il, 243n40

Sin Mi-hye, 218,

Sin Sang-ok, 39, 62, 92, 93, 251n42. See also
Dutiful Daughter Ch'ŏng; The Evening Bell

sinyŏsŏng (New Woman), 46, 135

Snyder, Sharon, 47, 109, 238n69

Sŏ Chŏng-ju: "The Leper," 174

So Hyŏn-suk, 242n25

Sŏ Kwang-je, 88

son preference, 59–60, 69–70, 76, 77, 90

Song of Songs, The (Yi Mun-yol), 40,
125–28, 129–32

Sŏngjong (king), 175

Sŏnjo (king), 175

Sorokto, 173, 176, 178–80, 183, 184–85,
187–88; Chahye Ŭiwŏn, 34, 50, 172;
Kaengsaengwŏn, 174; return to, 196

South Korea, 1, 9, 21, 50, 104, 105, 166, 167;
government of, 60; postcolonial, 4

sovereignty, 16, 29, 31, 92; compromised,
137; and eugenics, 47, 50, 61; health and,
19; loss of, 32; and segregation, 196; and
Sorokto, 188

Soviet Union, 187

spectacularized violence, 155

speculative risks, 13, 138, 143, 232

"Spinster's Song," A, 29, 30, 31, 51

Spring Fragrance, 88

Stein, Stanley, 167

sterilization, 74, 165; abuse, 219; disabled
people's resistance to, 67; and eugenics,
45, 48, 49, 192, 244n63; as eugenic surgery, 64; hysterectomy, 15; involuntary,
35, 58, 63, 65, 66–68, 70; obligatory, 217;
of people with Hansen's disease, 50, 69,
172, 176, 191, 263n90; of people with
mental illness, 33

Stevens, Bethany, 12

Stevenson, Lisa, 120, 236n30

stigma: courtesy stigma, 58, 63; and cultural
rehabilitation, 194; and cure, 169, 186;
of disability, 11, 78, 120, 123; of Hansen's
disease, 40, 166, 168, 169, 190, 193, 195,
196; history of, 225; of infertility, 59; and

Korean women in military camptown,
140; of mental illness, 159; moral, 202;
sexual, 221; of sex workers, 203, 210, 211,
216, 217

Stiker, Henri-Jacques, 238n70

"Story of Changhwa and Hongnyŏn," The,
51, 113–14

Story of Ongnye, The (Im Kwon-Taek), 39,
86, 98, 100–105

"Story of Sim Ch'ŏng," The ("Sim Ch'ŏng
chŏn"): 39, 81, 87, 101, 103, 118; plot of, 82

Suh, Ji-moon, 125

suicide, 55, 58, 60, 62, 80, 110, 111, 112,
114, 117; as form of curative violence,
38, 118–19, 120, 141, 159; implied, 118;
murder-suicide, 165; physician-assisted,
14; rate, 120, 253n77; and trauma, 116

Sujŏng (on Pansy and Ivy), 75–79

Sumi (on A Tale of Two Sisters), 114–18

Surong (on Adada), 133–34, 136

surrogate therapy, 209

Suyŏn (on A Tale of Two Sisters), 114–18

syphilis, 42, 175

T-4 euthanasia, 69

t'omangmin, 49

Taehan Empire, 31

Tale of Two Sisters, A (Kim Chi-un), 39, 87,
114–18

Tangp'yŏni (on The Song of Songs), 126–27

technology, 1, 2, 40, 185–86, 225; biomedical, 169; biotechnology, 5, 120; reproductive, 70, 72, 74, 233; and robots, 56,
244n54

Tell Them I'm a Mermaid, 237n36

"There a Petal Silently Falls" (Ch'oe Yun),
40, 125, 144, 147–55, 159; as representation of mental disability, 158

Thumbelina Wants to Be a Mother (Yu Hae-
jin), 12, 39, 70–74, 77, 79, 233; response
to, 73

time: as agent, 231; coevalness, 229; contracted, 2; crossing of, 10; curative, 8, 231;
folded, 1–2, 4, 9, 11, 41, 227, 229, 230, 231;
frozen, 231; in-between, 17; lived, 225; occupying, 26; panoptical, 2; sharing of, 24,